1979

1979
The Supreme Court Review

197
Th

"Judges as persons, or courts as institutions, are entitled to no greater immunity from criticism than other persons or institutions . . . [J]udges must be kept mindful of their limitations and of their ultimate public responsibility by a vigorous stream of criticism expressed with candor however blunt."
–Felix Frankfurter

". . . while it is proper that people should find fault when their judges fail, it is only reasonable that they should recognize the difficulties. . . . Let them be severely brought to book, when they go wrong, but by those who will take the trouble to understand them."
–Learned Hand

THE LAW SCHOOL
THE UNIVERSITY OF CHICAGO

upreme Court Review

EDITED BY
PHILIP B. KURLAND
AND GERHARD CASPER

THE UNIVERSITY OF CHICAGO PRESS
CHICAGO AND LONDON

INTERNATIONAL STANDARD BOOK NUMBER: 0-226-46432-6

LIBRARY OF CONGRESS CATALOG CARD NUMBER: 60-14353

THE UNIVERSITY OF CHICAGO PRESS, CHICAGO 60637

THE UNIVERSITY OF CHICAGO PRESS, LTD., LONDON

PRINTED IN THE UNITED STATES OF AMERICA

TO

ARTIE SCOTT

On the appearance of the
twentieth volume
in this series, because
she more than anyone
else has been responsible
for bringing these books
to successful publication.

CONTENTS

EDMUND W. KITCH

THE RETURN OF COLOR-CONSCIOUSNESS TO THE CONSTITUTION: WEBER, DAYTON, AND COLUMBUS

Twenty-five years after *Brown v. Board of Education*,[1] the Supreme Court has assured us that the answer to the "American dilemma" will not come through the first Mr. Justice Harlan's "color blindness"[2] but rather by acknowledging differences between blacks and whites as the basis for "affirmative action." That is the cumulative message of *Weber*,[3] *Columbus*,[4] and *Dayton*,[5] all handed down in the waning days of the 1978 term. Their remedies focus not on racial

---

Edmund W. Kitch is Professor of Law, The University of Chicago.

AUTHOR'S NOTE: I have benefited greatly from my discussions with my colleagues and particularly Douglas Laycock and Bernard D. Meltzer. I have also had the benefit of reading papers by Meltzer and Philip B. Kurland relating to aspects of the subject matter of this article which were in the process of publication when this was written. Meltzer, *The Weber Case: Double Talk and Double Standards*, 3 REGULATION No. 5, p. 34 (Sept./Oct. 1979), treats the reasoning of the *Weber* opinions and examines in detail their implication for affirmative action in private employment. Kurland, "*Brown v. Board of Education Was the Beginning*": *The School Desegregation Cases in the United States Supreme Court, 1954–79*, 1979 WASH. U. L. Q. 309 traces the history of school desegregation in the Supreme Court. I acknowledge with gratitude the research assistance of Roger Patterson and Ruth Hahn, members of the Class of 1981 at The University of Chicago Law School.

[1] 347 U.S. 483 (1954).

[2] Plessy v. Ferguson, 163 U.S. 537, 559 (1896) (dissenting).

[3] United Steelworkers of America v. Weber, 99 S. Ct. 2721 (1979).

[4] Columbus Board of Education v. Penick, 99 S. Ct. 2982 (1979).

[5] Dayton Board of Education v. Brinkman (II), 99 S. Ct. 2971 (1979).

discrimination but on redressing racial imbalance in the work force and the school population. They acknowledge that separate but unequal treatment under law is warranted by our history, because they deal with classes of persons and not with individuals.

I. United Steel Workers of America v. Weber

Weber was a white employee of a Kaiser plant located in the Deep South who sought, but was not eligible for, admission to the in-plant craft training program. Admission to the program is based on two seniority lists—one for minorities (blacks) and one for whites—with the selections for the program to be made alternately from each of them. Weber had less seniority than required for admission from the white list and more seniority than those on the black list. He brought a suit because several employees with less seniority than his were admitted to the program. The lower courts held that the racial quota involved violated the terms of the Civil Rights Act of 1964.[6] The Supreme Court reversed, holding that Kaiser's voluntary affirmative action program did not violate the statute. Both the Supreme Court and the lower courts reasoned from the premise that Kaiser had not itself previously engaged in racial discrimination in employment.[7]

Weber's argument was that the use of a racial classification to determine access to the training program was discrimination by race in violation of the statute. The Court rejected this argument on the ground that, although it was in accord with a "literal" construction of the statute, it was not in accord with the legislative "spirit" of the law. As Mr. Justice Rehnquist's persuasive dissent clearly demonstrates,[8] the spirit on which the Court relies was not that

---

[6] 563 F.2d 216 (5th Cir. 1977), aff'g 415 F. Supp. 761 (E.D. La. 1976). The minority category was open to all groups designated as minorities by the Office of Federal Contract Compliance including women. As the plan actually operated in the plant involved, only blacks benefited, and the courts treated the plan as an affirmative action plan for blacks.

[7] Thus the opinions did not address the question of the scope of remedies for illegal discrimination. After the holding in *Weber* that a nondiscriminating employer can grant quota preferences to blacks, it is difficult to believe that the Court will now hold that a discriminating employer cannot be ordered to do the same thing. Justices Brennan, Blackmun, Marshall, and White seem to agree. Mr. Justice Stewart thinks that that question is independent and unrelated because such an order would not result in a "voluntary" plan.

[8] 99 S. Ct. at 2736–53.

of the Congress but of a few sponsors of the legislation. The Court simply invalidated the political compromise that led to the Civil Rights Statutes of 1964—that the law was to enact not a special program of relief and assistance to blacks but a general principle of racial, sexual, religious, and ethnic neutrality.

The Court's opinion is brief; its reasoning enigmatic. It was joined by the four Justices who, in the previous Term, had written a separate opinion in *University of California Regents v. Bakke*[9] arguing that a medical school admissions preference quota was constitutional and legal under Title VI of the statute,[10] plus Mr. Justice Stewart, who in *Bakke* had joined an opinion that said that such a preference quota violated the statute.[11] The structure of the Court's argument in *Weber* is the same as that of the separate opinion in *Bakke*—reverse discrimination is justified by the need to remedy past discrimination. The distinction that seems to have moved Mr. Justice Stewart was that the Kaiser plan was private and voluntary. But the Court pointedly ignored the fact that the training program in *Weber* had been adopted by Kaiser and the Steelworkers Union under the threat of federal sanction.[12] The argument, most clearly spelled out in a footnote of the *Weber* opinion,[13] is that Congress, in formulating the standard applicable to private bodies in Title VII, had greater discretion than in formulating the standard applicable to public bodies under Title VI, which was the controlling law in *Bakke*.

The Court's textual basis for its tenuous distinction is section 703(j) of Title VII,[14] applicable to private employers, which has no analogue in Title VI, applicable to recipients of governmental funds. Section 703(j) had been added to the statute to allay fears that enforcement officials would use the threat of enforcement ac-

[9] 438 U.S. 265, 324 (1978).

[10] Title VI of the Civil Rights Act of 1964, as amended, 42 U.S.C. § 2000d *et seq.*

[11] 438 U.S. at 408.

[12] Kaiser, as a government contractor, was subject to Executive Order 11246, which imposes an affirmative action obligation. Inspectors from the Office of Federal Contract Compliance Programs had raised the question of Kaiser's compliance. 99 S. Ct. at 2731. The provisions of the plan were nationally negotiated for the aluminum industry and an identical plan was subsequently imposed on the steel industry by consent decree and approved by the Fifth Circuit. United States v. Allegheny-Ludlum Industries, Inc., 517 F.2d 826 (5th Cir. 1975).

[13] 99 S. Ct. at 2729 n.6.

[14] U.S.C. § 2000e–2(j).

tions to demand preferential employment practices. In relevant part, it reads: "Nothing contained in this subchapter shall be interpreted to require any employer . . . to grant preferential treatment to any individual . . . because of the race . . . of such individual . . . on account of an imbalance which may exist with respect to the total number . . . of persons of any race . . . employed by any employer . . . in comparison with the total number . . . of such race in any community . . . or in the available work force. . . ."[15] The Court argues that the absence of the phrase "require or permit" means that the statute does permit but not require. Mr. Justice Rehnquist points out the lack of force in this argument.[16] Since there was no reason to believe that the statute did not interdict such preferential treatment outside the context of a remedy to correct a statutory violation, there was no reason for the Congress to provide that it would not permit what it did not permit.

The most striking feature of the opinion in *Weber* is its relentless focus on a single ethnic minority—blacks—in its explanation of the meaning of the statute. The statute reads: "It shall be an unlawful employment practice for an employer . . . to discriminate against any individual . . . because of such individual's race, color, religion, sex, or national origin."[17] The discrimination at issue in *Weber* was discrimination in favor of blacks, so one might argue that no other statutory minorities were, in fact, involved in the case. But because the statute treats ethnic and other classifications as part of a parallel construction, one test that any construction of the statute should meet is whether it is workable in relation to all of the proscribed classifications. Indeed, the most powerful practical argument for a color-blind interpretation of the statute is that it is impossible to discriminate benevolently by means of a prohibited classification without injuring others by means of the same classification. But *Weber* held that one group—blacks—are entitled to be the beneficiaries of affirmative action. Are any other groups similarly entitled? If so, who are they? There are many candidates: *e.g.*, Jews, Catholics, Chicanos, American Indians, women, Irish, and so

[15] The section is set forth in 99 S. Ct. at 2728 n.5.

[16] 99 S. Ct. at 2748–49.

[17] Section 703(a) of the Civil Rights Act of 1964, 42 U.S.C. § 2000e–2(a). The section is set forth in 99 S. Ct. at 2726 n.2.

on, but the group of largest practical significance, because of its size, is women. If the size and position of blacks justifies a one-to-one ratio between blacks and whites, and the position of women would justify a similar preference ratio proportionate to their number in the workforce, either there will be little room left for young white males, or the relative advantage accorded to blacks will have to be significantly reduced. Do blacks have a special status under the statute or do they have to share this status with other significant groups? The Court must now be prepared to undertake that inquiry, group by group and classification by classification.

The opinion is Janus-faced. The legislative history marshalled in support of the Court's "legislative spirit" is black in its focus, and no similar legislative history exists for any other groups.[18] Congress' primary concern in enacting the prohibition against racial discrimination in Title VII of the Civil Rights Act of 1964 was with "the plight of the Negro in our economy," said the Court. That phrase is followed by a discussion of worsening black unemployment as of 1964 and the observation that:[19]

> Congress feared that the goals of the Civil Rights Act—the integration of blacks into the mainstream of American society—could not be achieved unless this trend were reversed. . . . Accordingly, it was clear to Congress that "the crux of the problem [was] to open employment opportunities for Negroes in occupations which have been traditionally closed to them," . . . and it was to this problem that Title VII's prohibition against racial discrimination in employment was primarily addressed.

There are nevertheless grounds to argue that the Court will, in due course, extend the special status recognized in *Weber* to many other groups. The Court leaves the question open by limiting its quotations from the legislative history to the "racial discrimination" prohibition. Because of their parallel position in the statute, there is an implication that each other prohibition has its own favored group (or groups)—Jews, Catholics (and Hindus?) for religion, women for sex, Latinos for national origin, and non-Negro, non-white races for color. The Court's reasoning from the structure of section 703(j) suggests that the "permit" logic applies to every

---

[18] 99 S. Ct. at 2727.

[19] *Id.* at 2727–28.

proscribed classification.[20] Indeed, one could imagine that under the Court's logic, the statute may be converted into a pervasive dispersion program. In any occupation where a group has been underrepresented, the statute would permit affirmative action to increase that group's representation. Thus affirmative action for men would be appropriate in the flight attendant, telephone operator, and elementary school teacher classifications, while affirmative action for women would be appropriate in the airlines maintenance, line repairman, and university teaching fields. Affirmative action for blacks would be appropriate in crafts, professional, and management fields, while affirmative action for whites would be appropriate for urban hotel services, urban bus drivers, parts of the postal service, and so on. But it would be difficult to reconcile such a sweeping program of social dispersion with the Court's emphasis in *Weber* on blacks as special beneficiaries of the statutory program.

II. Columbus and Dayton II

The opinions in these cases seem to hold only that the long and complex records support the determination of the courts below[21] that school officials had long engaged in intentional racial segregation of the schools. That innocuous appearance is deceptive. The Court endorses an approach to the "factual" question that makes proof of a neighborhood school policy into proof of racial discrimination. It then approves a remedy which, by implication, assumes that a neighborhood school policy, when combined with any significant residential segregation, is unconstitutional. It seems unlikely that the Court is so confused that it was unaware of what it was doing. The opinion was successful, however, in avoiding

[20] Section 703(j) itself repeats each of the proscribed classifications. Another reason that the special status is likely to be extended is the practical considerations emphasized by Mr. Justice Blackmun in his concurring opinion. He argued that employers must be able to settle charges of past discrimination by adopting affirmative action plans without fear that they will incur further liability. How an employer can escape liability for discrimination against some individuals in the past by undertaking to discriminate in favor of other individuals in the future is not clear. See Meltzer, *The Weber Case: Double Talk and Double Standards*, 3 Regulation No. 5, p. 34 at 38–39.

[21] *Columbus*, 583 F.2d 787 (6th Cir. 1978), aff'g 429 F. Supp. 229 (S. D. Ohio 1977); *Dayton II*, 583 F.2d 243 (6th Cir. 1978), reversing the unreported decision of the district court.

headlines such as "Supreme Court Holds All Northern Schools Unconstitutionally Segregated."

The *Dayton* decision has distinctive interest for two reasons. First, the Supreme Court had earlier in the same case held that a system-wide remedy was inappropriate on the state of the record and remanded for further hearings.[22] In *Dayton II*, with no new evidence worthy of mention by the Court, it affirms such a remedy. Second, the district judge, unlike the district judge in *Columbus*, had concluded on the basis of his review of the record that there was no constitutional violation with any continuing effect requiring a remedy. The Court of Appeals reversed and it is the "factual" determination of the Court of Appeals, not the District Court, that the Supreme Court affirms.

The approach to de facto school desegregation that the Supreme Court endorses, reflecting the approach worked out by the Sixth Circuit,[23] from which both cases came, has four elements: first, the existence of identifiably black schools in the school system in 1954. These are the schools in black neighborhoods. Their black character is confirmed by the fact that they were referred to at the time as the "negro schools" and by the fact that they had all black faculties and administration. The presence of significant black enrollment in other, "white," schools in the system is not relevant to this determination. "[T]he District Court found that the 'Columbus Public Schools were *officially* segregated by race in 1954.' "[24] Second, a legal determination that the existence of such schools in 1954 put the school system in precisely the same constitutional posture as the southern schools as of the same date: the school system had a continuing constitutional duty to eliminate identifiably black schools. "[T]he Board's duty to dismantle its dual system cannot be gainsaid."[25] Third, an intensive and detailed examination of school system actions since 1954 in order to determine whether the school

[22] Dayton Board of Education v. Brinkman, 433 U.S. 406 (1977).

[23] See Oliver v. Michigan State Bd. of Ed., 508 F.2d 178 (6th Cir. 1974); Bradley v. Milliken, 484 F.2d 215 (6th Cir. 1973); Davis v. School District of Pontiac, 443 F.2d 573 (6th Cir. 1971).

[24] 99 S. Ct. at 2946, quoting the district court, emphasis added by the Supreme Court.

[25] *Id.* at 2947.

system has taken all feasible actions to eliminate the identifiably black schools. The inevitable conclusion is that the school system has not,[26] as any student of northern school politics could have predicted. Fourth, the conclusion that the only way to eliminate the identifiably black character of some schools is to modify the neighborhood school policy through appropriate racial transfers (busing) so that no school has a distinctly black enrollment or faculty. "Petitioners also argue that the District Court erred in requiring that every school in the system be brought roughly within proportionate racial balance. We see no misuse of mathematical ratios . . . especially in light of the Board's failure to justify the continued existence of 'some schools that are all or predominantly of one race.' "[27]

In *Dayton*, the Court summed up as follows:[28]

> The basic ingredients of the Court of Appeals' judgment were that at the time of *Brown I*, the Dayton Board was operating a dual school system, that it was constitutionally required to disestablish that system and its effects, that it had failed to discharge this duty, and that the consequences of the dual system, together with the intentionally segregative impact of of various practices since 1954, were of systemwide import and an appropriate basis for a systemwide remedy.

The problem with this approach is that there is a simple explanation for many of the facts the Court considers so important, namely, a neighborhood school policy.[29] In standard equal protection analysis, a neighborhood school attendance policy would not be a suspect classification. Rather the Court would have to consider the reasonableness of the policy, and only if it found no legislative rationality for the classification might it declare it unconstitutional. There are substantial reasons for a neighborhood school attendance policy. They include: (1) minimizing travel costs, (2) the development of sustaining ties between a school and its surrounding community, and (3) the development of a partial market in school services through the tie between residential location and school

---

[26] *Id.* at 2948–49. [27] *Id.* at 2945 n.3. [28] 99 S. Ct. at 2977.

[29] The district court decision in *Columbus* which the court treats with a deference that will make it a model concluded that "Substantial adherence to the neighborhood school concept with full knowledge of the predictable effects of such adherence upon racial imbalance in a school system is one factor among many others which may be considered by a court in determining whether an inference of segregative intent should be drawn." 429 F. Supp. at 255.

attendance rights. Because the last point is infrequently made, it merits some elaboration. A stable neighborhood school attendance policy means that individuals can shop for school services through their selection of residential location. This attenuated property right generates the benefits that flow from market organization. On the supply side, it puts pressure on schools to provide services that are attractive to prospective residents or else face declining enrollment and budget. On the demand side, it enables many families to select the type of school service that fits their particular needs and preferences.

The constitutional argument against a neighborhood policy is weak. It is that the use of a neighborhood school policy, when combined with residential segregation, results in the educational segregation of blacks, and that the harm of such segregated education upon blacks outweighs the social considerations favoring a neighborhood school policy. The logic requires a rather unattractive premise, that blacks suffer from the singular disability that it is harmful to them to be educated in schools where the other students are of their own race. The California Supreme Court has not shrunk from saying so explicitly,[30] but more thoughful analysis shows that there is little to support such a premise.[31]

The constitutionality of a neighborhood school policy does not mean that a school system might not administer such a policy in an unconstitutional manner. A neighborhood school policy can, through racial gerrymandering, be used as a cover for a policy of racial separation indistinguishable from de jure segregation. Even stripped of the pervasive affirmative duty which the Court places on the school officials of Columbus and Dayton, some of their actions would have been unconstitutional under such a standard. But if a neighborhood school policy is constitutional, then the remedy should be confined to correcting the abuses of that policy. School boundaries can be redrawn. The school construction program can be closely monitored. Faculty assignment procedures can

[30] "Negro children suffer serious harm when their education takes place in public schools which are racially segregated, whatever the source of such segregation may be." Crawford v. Board of Education, 17 Cal.3d 280, 295 (1976), quoting U.S. Commission on Civil Rights, Racial Isolation in the Public Schools 193 (1967).

[31] Goodman, *De Facto School Segregation: A Constitutional and Empirical Analysis*, 60 Calif. L. Rev. 275, 307–310 (1972).

be revised. But the Court leaps from its system-wide violation to the conclusion that the only appropriate relief is system-wide racial balancing. That leap can be made only if it is assumed that a good-faith neighborhood school policy is an unconstitutional stopping point.

Brown I, which the Court repeatedly cites as a symbol for its 1954 desegregation decisions, was enigmatic.[32] The opinion of *Brown I* itself said the Court had found that separate education was inherently unequal.[33] This suggested that the Court had retained the separate but equal formulation of *Plessy v. Ferguson*[34] but had changed its mind about what was equal. The immediate extension of the doctrine without further explanation to a whole range of public facilities[35] put that proposition into doubt. And in *Brown's* companion case of *Bolling v. Sharpe*,[36] holding the federally segregated school system of the District of Columbia unconstitutional, the Court stressed the impermissibility of racial classification, appearing to follow the color-blind constitution of the first Harlan dissenting in *Plessy*.

The separate but equal formula of *Plessy* was supported by a theory of social welfare no longer acceptable. Separation of the races was then viewed as a reasonable social policy because blacks were said to be different:[37]

> Legislation is powerless to eradicate racial instincts or to abolish distinctions based upon physical differences, and the attempt to do so can only result in accentuating the difficulties of the present situation. If the civil and political rights of both races be equal one cannot be inferior to the other civilly or politically. If one race be inferior to the other socially, the Constitution of the United States cannot put them upon the same plane.

---

[32] Kurland, *Brown v. Board of Education Was the Beginning": The School Desegregation Cases in the United States Supreme Court, 1954–79*, 1979 Wash. U. L. Q. 309, shows that the Court has never developed a theory of what the constitutional violation is in the school desegregation cases but has gone forward to sweeping remedies for constitutional violations it has never explained.

[33] 347 U.S. at 495.

[34] 163 U.S. 537 (1896).

[35] Muir v. Louisville Park Theatricals Ass'n, 347 U.S. 971 (1954) (parks); Mayor of Baltimore v. Dawson, 350 U.S. 877 (1955) (beaches and bath houses); Holmes v. City of Atlanta, 350 U.S. 879 (1955) (golf courses); Gayle v. Browder, 352 U.S. 903 (1956) (public transportation).

[36] 347 U.S. 497 (1954).

[37] 163 U.S. at 551–52.

Under the Court's new theory, blacks must not be separated because they are, in fact, different, the differences being the consequence of social discrimination. This requires the arrangement of school and workplace so that blacks will associate with whites. The Court camouflages this theory with concepts of class liability and careful inattention to the critical and revealing question: How is the remedy related to the wrong? In *Weber*, young white workers must be accorded lower status because craft unions to which they never belonged, once, in a manner then thought legal, discriminated against blacks. In *Dayton* and *Weber* school children and their families must accept the burdens of busing because of long-ago and then legal actions of school boards. The methodology of the Court is to find unconstitutional but not necessarily malevolent acts on the part of a school official, a craft union, the society, and then order relief the adverse effects of which fall only on those—the young family, student, or worker—who have no demonstrable connection to the wrong being redressed. Meanwhile, the individuals responsible—the former school board officials, the former members of craft unions, the former members of the Court itself—remain unaffected, protected by the scope of their official immunities or the passage of time.

The Court has implemented its program in an evasive manner. *Weber*, the reader is told, simply reflects the "spirit" of a Congress of long ago. *Columbus* and *Dayton* only require the exercise of the chancellor's informed discretion to remedy proven constitutional violations. In the short run this is effective politics because it confuses the latent political opposition. In the long run, it is unwise. The advantage of covenants openly negotiated, openly arrived at, is that the very process of debate and consideration can educate the public and mobilize its support. An example is the debate over the Civil Rights Act of 1964, a debate that both exposed the divisiveness of a civil rights program based on a system of preferences and the broad base of support for the principle of nondiscrimination. It was the discovery and mobilization of that support that generated the growth and vigor of the enforcement program and the extent of voluntary compliance. The Court has now, deviously, fractured that compromise. That, in turn, will affect the politics of the program.

In the short run the Court's program may be modestly helpful to blacks. *Weber*, combined with the zeal of the enforcement agencies, should cause a substantial increase in the amount of pro-black affirmative action as management seeks what appears to be a safe harbor from the uncertainties of litigation. The competition of firms to fill their quotas will in turn, lead to an improvement in the market for employable blacks. The school cases seem less likely to have any effect, but it is conceivable that the number of blacks attending adequate schools might increase.

The kindest view one can take of the Court's program is that it is a system of covert reparations[38]—transferring wealth to blacks from nonblacks through the job market and school bureaucracies. When compared to a system of direct reparation—for instance a head tax upon all nonblacks, proceeds payable to blacks—its only advantage is its covert nature. The Court's program suffers from all the disadvantages of regulation-induced service transfers. First, the program reduces the efficiency of the institutions captured to administer the program. Business personnel decisions and school administration and planning are made complex and costly. Reporting requirements with their ministering personnel must mushroom. Second, the Court's path to its results assures substantial legal costs. Even though *Columbus* and *Dayton II* seem to command the outcome, every city remains entitled to a massive factual hearing about every feature of its school system from the founding of the public schools to the present. The amount of time that will be required to work out systems of affirmative action acceptable to the enforcement agencies, courts, employers, unions, and the affected protected groups staggers the imagination. Third, the services transferred are in-kind, and because the black recipients cannot sell to others their right to preference or to attend a particular school, the value of the service to the recipient will in many cases be less than its cost to those taxed. Most of the effect of the program will be on the cost, not the benefit side.

In the longer run, the Court is taking frightful risks. (1) Can the Court insist on such intrusive use of racial classification without teaching the country that policies based on racial classification are legitimate? (2) Will those who are asked to step aside for the bene-

---

[38] The case for an explicit program is discussed in BITTKER, THE CASE FOR BLACK REPARATIONS (1973). An explicit program does not appear to be politically viable, although some aspects of the war on poverty had characteristics of a service reparations program. The legislative programs, however, made use of less divisive classifications—classifications with relevancy to the legislative objectives—such as poor, urban, or disadvantaged.

fit of blacks not harbor ill will against them? Will this not be a particular problem for the young, who, having grown up on this side of the civil rights revolution, disassociate themselves from the racism of the old America, and may be surprised to learn that they are asked to pay for it? (3) Will the effect of pervasive affirmative action for blacks—combined with an equal pay principle—be to ensure that blacks are systematically promoted to the level just above their competence and cause affirmative action to become an engine of group defamation? (4) Is it possible to weaken the ability of families to select schools for their children through residential location without weakening support for public education? (5) What will the extent of white flight to private schools and suburban enclaves be, and what can the Court do about it? Will the school cases simply isolate blacks in decaying central cities? Will affirmative action create incentives for employers to locate jobs away from black labor? The logic of *Columbus* and *Dayton II* suggests that the Court will soon have little trouble finding the interdistrict violation necessary under the standard of *Milliken I*[39] to require interdistrict pupil transfer.[40] But as the federal courts reach across school district lines to achieve integration, the increased complexity and scope of the program will strain the resources of the courts and the symbolic hold of the rule of law.

Choices between short-run gains and long-run costs are easy to make if there is a strategy for enjoying the short-run gains and avoiding the costs. The Court, after all, can uninvent what it has invented. If the Court stresses that the burden of proof is on the plaintiff, that illegal discrimination requires proof not simply of effects but of intent, and limits remedies to correction of proved violations, the program quickly shrinks. In the school cases, that is the way the Court had began to talk in *Milliken I*, *Pasadena*,[41] and *Dayton I*,[42] although a close reader of the *Dayton I* opinion might notice that the Court left in effect the system-wide remedy it said

[39] Milliken v. Bradley, 418 U.S. 717 (1974), holding that an interdistrict remedy required proof of an interdistrict violation. The Sixth Circuit had had no difficulty upholding the remedy. Bradley v. Milliken, 484 F.2d 215 (6th Cir. 1973).

[40] The Third Circuit has already done so on the basis of reasoning similar to that of the Court in *Columbus* and *Dayton II*. Petitions for certiorari have been filed. Delaware State Board of Education v. Evans, No. 78–671; Alexis DuPont School Dist. v. Evans, No. 78–672.

[41] Pasadena City Board of Education v. Spangler, 427 U.S. 424 (1976).

[42] Dayton Bd. of Educ. v. Brinkman, 433 U.S. 406 (1977).

was unsupported by the evidence. In the employment area, *Washington v. Davis*[43] and the separate opinions of a majority of Justices in *Bakke*[44] pointed in the same direction. In light of *Weber*, *Columbus*, and *Dayton II*, some future historian will have to inquire whether those opinions really reflected doctrinal confusion or were instead a tactical feint, designed to delay and complicate the implementation of quotas and busing in the light of public opposition.

The Court's recent opinions suggest no theory as to how the program might end. In a footnote in *Weber* the Court cites the present disparity in white and black unemployment rates, observing that "[t]he problem that Congress addressed in 1964 remains with us."[45] The implication is that if that disparity disappeared, then the program might end.[46] In light of the federal minimum wage, the incentives created by the federal welfare system, and the impotence of the urban public schools, it seems unlikely that the disparity will disappear within the next several generations. *Weber*-sanctioned affirmative action will probably continue indefinitely unless Congress chooses to repudiate its newly discovered "spirit."

The emphasis in *Columbus* and *Dayton II* on the "contining constitutional duty" to desegregate, if taken literally, would mean that the school systems must be perpetually operated in a way that eliminates identifiable black schools each school year. In *Pasadena City Board of Education v. Spangler*,[47] the Court held such an order improper, but that case can be distinguished on the ground that the district court had not found that the school system operated a dual school system in 1954, and hence was not under what the Court calls the continuing constitutional duty to desegregate.

The future, however, is not entirely in the hands of the Court. The Court's program creates a set of expectancies and social dependencies that will not be easily set aside. Even now, the affirma-

---

[43] 426 U.S. 229 (1976).

[44] 438 U.S. 265 (1978).

[45] 99 S. Ct. at 2728 n.4.

[46] The Court described the affirmative action program in *Weber* as temporary, 99 S. Ct. at 2730, but did not explain how or when it would end. See *id.* at 2738 n.3. Pervasive affirmative action in employment will create odd racial age patterns in various subgroups of the work force which will have to be offset by future quotas if the target ratios are to be maintained. If, for instance, affirmative action causes heavy black hiring in particular jobs for the period 1979–85, there will be a heavy rate of black retirement when those workers reach retirement age as much as fifty years from now.

[47] 427 U.S. 424, 434–35 (1976).

tive action bureaucracies inside and outside of government would not lightly accept obsolescence of their function. The wall that the Court has built against public aid to church education means that church schools can gain from the erosion of support for public education. The dilemma for the Court in *Brown* was not that *Plessy* had outlived its time, but that reliance on the *Plessy* doctrine had generated a host of social expectations in the South that were not easily frustrated. How much more difficult will be the position of some future Court faced with the need to arrest a program so directly set in motion by the divided Court in *Weber* (5–2), *Columbus* (7–2), and *Dayton* (5–4).

BARBARA LERNER

EMPLOYMENT DISCRIMINATION: ADVERSE IMPACT, VALIDITY, AND EQUALITY

Nothing of him that doth fade
But doth suffer a sea-change
Into something rich and strange.
[SHAKESPEARE, *The Tempest*]

In the unstable world of the law of employment discrimination, *Griggs v. Duke Power*[1] has been temporarily eclipsed by two 1979 cases, *Steelworkers Union v. Weber*[2] and *Detroit Edison v. N.L.R.B.*[3] Overshadowed but unresolved, the issues in *Griggs* refuse to fade away. The problem is not with *Griggs* itself, a case rich in initial promise, but with its aftermath, a series of very different cases that were treated as if they were the same, making consistent application of the *Griggs* principle unworkable by fostering arbitrary ad hoc evasions and exceptions.

Barbara Lerner, the First Visiting Scholar in Measurement and Public Policy at the Educational Testing Service in Princeton, New Jersey, is a consultant in law and psychology.

AUTHOR'S NOTE: Professor Anne Anastasi was kind enough to read an earlier draft of this paper and to make helpful comments on it.

[1] 401 U.S. 424 (1971).

[2] 99 S. Ct. 2721 (1979).

[3] 99 S. Ct. 1123 (1979). This case and *Weber* are discussed in Section II.

I. Adverse Impact and Validation Requirements

Griggs was a particularly important decision interpreting Title VII[4] because in it, the Supreme Court first articulated the concept of "adverse impact" and its relation to the imposition of a validation requirement on employers. Validation is the scientific way of determining whether a selection device actually does what it is intended to do: to make reliable and meaningful distinctions between individuals on the basis of their ability to perform particular tasks with competence and/or to function successfully in particular jobs.[5]

All recognized scientific validation methods require the use of elaborate, formal procedures which are difficult, time-consuming, and costly.[6] As a result, no significant group of employers has routinely used any of these methods to ascertain the worth of all non-test selection devices, and only very large employers have shown a consistent tendency to use them for selection devices based on tests. What they have relied upon instead is what psychometricians call "face validity."

Face validity is not a scientific form of validation.[7] It is only

---

[4] 42 U.S.C. §§ 2000e *et seq.*

[5] See Anastasi, Psychological Testing (4th ed. 1976); see also American Psychological Association, American Educational Research Association, & National Council on Measurement in Education, Standards for Educational and Psychological Tests (1974); Division of Industrial-Organizational Psychology, Principles for the Validation and Use of Personnel Selection Procedures (1975); and Statement on the Uniform Guidelines on Employee Selection Procedures, prepared by the Committee on Psychological Tests and Assessments of the American Psychological Association, February 17, 1978.

[6] Accurate data on the money and time required for any of the three recognized validation strategies are not easy to obtain, as noted in the Comptroller General's Report, note 10 *infra.* William A. Gorham, former director of the Personnel Research and Development Center of the Civil Service Commission, in a speech to the Personnel Testing Council of Metropolitan Washington on November 27, 1978, estimated that adequate criterion validity studies tend to cost something between $100,000 and $400,000 and to take approximately two years. The old Equal Employment Opportunity Commission (EEOC) Guidelines required employers to use this approach wherever it was technically possible to do so. The new Uniform Guidelines allow somewhat greater scope for content validation, an approach which is often cheaper and less time consuming, but they are still quite restrictive in their treatment of construct validation.

[7] Face validity should not be a scientifically acceptable form of validity because in science, reasonable inferences—unsupported by empirical data collected, tested, and reported according to well-established scientific rules—are generally acceptable only as hypotheses. They are unacceptable when offered as a form of

a modern name for the basic, centuries-old standard of Anglo-American law—reasonableness—and business and factory managers are hardly the only ones who rely upon it in selecting people for jobs. Face validity or reasonableness is what courts, legislatures, and the professions also rely upon when they insist that a law degree is required for the practice of law, a psychology degree for the practice of psychology, or training in education for the practice of teaching. These requirements have never been validated. They probably could not be validated. Face validity has simply been accepted and enforced on the basis of its inherent plausibility for the jobs enumerated and for a myriad of other jobs for skilled workers, professional or nonprofessional, white collar or blue.

Endemic reliance on reasonableness notwithstanding, it was clear, after *Griggs*, that an employment selection device with "adverse impact" on members of particular groups could function as the trigger for a formal validation requirement. What was not clear then and is less clear now is the definition of adverse impact. Lack of a clear definition for so basic a term operates to turn the law in this area into a morass of confusion and uncertainty. To make a bad situation worse, there is also growing doubt about whether adverse impact—however defined—always triggers a validation requirement or does so only in certain types of cases. Worse still, there is also growing pressure to reject even the best validation evidence when adverse impact of one sort or another is deemed to exist.

The four federal agencies with major, overlapping responsibilities for the administration and enforcement of Title VII[8] have done much to foster the confusion and have taken no meaningful steps to reduce it. Working under a congressional mandate issued when Title VII was amended in 1972 to cover governmental as well as

---

proof. This stringent ideal is workable and useful in the realm of pure science in large part because decisions and conclusions in that realm can be postponed for as many years or centuries as may be required to establish or at least approximate a satisfactory empirical form of proof. It is neither workable nor useful as a standard for the business or legal world because in both it is necessary to decide whatever questions arise on the basis of the best evidence that can be obtained in a practical amount of time and at a feasible cost. Indefinite delay is simply not tolerable in everyday, practical contexts. See Lerner, *Washington v. Davis: Quantity, Quality and Equality in Employment Testing*, 1976 SUPREME COURT REVIEW 263, 303–04.

[8] The Department of Justice, the Department of Labor, the Civil Service Commission, and the Equal Employment Opportunity Commission.

private employers,[9] it took them six long years of bitter interagency struggle[10] to come up with a single set of uniform federal guidelines on employee selection procedures. The new uniform guidelines, finally issued in 1978,[11] replace a series of conflicting ones[12]

---

[9] Equal Employment Opportunity Act of 1972, 42 U.S.C. §§ 2000e *et seq.*

[10] See Gorham, *Political, Ethical and Emotional Aspects of Federal Guidelines on Employee Selection Procedure*, in SCHMIDT & HAMNER (eds.), CONTEMPORARY PROBLEMS IN PERSONNEL 159 (1977); *Problems with Federal Equal Employment Opportunity Guidelines on Employee Selection Procedures Need to Be Resolved.* Report to the Congress by the Comptroller General of the United States, February 2, 1978 (FPCD-77-54).

See also Henderson v. First National Bank, 360 F. Supp. 531, 545 (M.D. Ala. 1973), where the court "noted for the record and so finds that there is no pre-employment test, given and acted upon by any employer in the United States, or known to exist or yet devised, which has been determined by EEOC to meet the requirements contained in Regulation Paragraph 1607 [for test validation]." The reasons for this were aptly summarized in a memorandum submitted to Deputy Attorney General Tyler by David L. Rose, chief of the Employment Section of the Civil Rights Division of the Justice Department, and published in the Bureau of National Affairs Daily Labor Report on June 22, 1976. In explaining the need for the 1976 FEA Guidelines and the refusal of the EEOC to join with its sister agencies in endorsing them, Mr. Rose noted that: "An unstated or covertly stated reason may underlie the apparent EEOC refusal to modify its present guidelines. Under the present EEOC guidelines, few employers are able to show the validity of any of their selection procedures, and the risk of their being held unlawful is high. Since not only tests, but all other procedures must be validated, the thrust of the present guidelines is to place almost all test users in a posture of noncompliance; to give great discretion to enforcement personnel to determine who should be prosecuted; and to set aside objective procedures in favor of numerical hiring."

[11] 43 FED. REG. No. 166, 38290–38315, August 25, 1978. The new Uniform Guidelines represent, in effect, a compromise between the FEA Guidelines and the EEOC Guidelines which they replaced. As a result, it is no longer impossible to succeed in validating employment selection procedures under the Guidelines, but it is still very difficult. Thus, statements that most adverse-impact cases turn on the employers' success or failure in rebutting plaintiffs' prima facie case and not on the production of validation evidence that comports with federal guidelines are not likely to be rendered obsolete. See, *e.g.*, SCHLEI & GROSSMAN, EMPLOYMENT DISCRIMINATION LAW 1161 (1976). Note also that the single, clear validation victory thus far upheld by the Supreme Court was not achieved on the basis of any agency guidelines, but on the basis of the APA, AERA, NCME standards, note 5 *supra*. See United States v. South Carolina, 434 U.S. 1026 (1978).

[12] Prior to 1976, EEOC, the Office of Federal Contract Compliance of the Department of Labor, and the Civil Service Commission each issued separate guidelines in this area. See, EEOC, Guidelines on Employment Testing Procedures, 1966; EEOC, Guidelines on Employee Selection Procedures, 35 FED. REG. No. 149, 12333–12336, August 1, 1970; OFCC, Employment Tests by Contractors and Subcontractors Subject to the Provisions of Executive Order 11246, 33 FED. REG. No. 186, 14392–94, September 24, 1968; OFCC, Employee Testing and Other Selection Procedures, 36 FED. REG. No. 192, 19307–10, October 2, 1971; OFCC, Guidelines for Reporting Criterion Related and Content Validity, 39 FED. REG. No. 12, 2094–2096, 1974; United States Civil Service Commission, Examining Testing Standards and Employment Tests and Practices, 27 FED. REG. 127, 12984–90, June 30, 1972.

which previously tormented the many employers simultaneously subject to more than one of them. Alas, they do not even begin to answer the basic definitional question with which the Court first wrestled in 1971 in *Griggs*.

According to the 1978 guidelines, validation is only and always required when adverse impact exists. Adverse impact, they tell us, is "[T]he fundamental principle underlying the guidelines."[13] It is defined in § 16B as "[a] substantially different rate of selection in hiring, promotion, or other employment decision."[14] The obvious question here is, substantially different from what? Two answers are possible. One is that the guidelines do not really answer this fundamental question at all. The other is that they do, for example, in § 16R[15] which defines "selection rate," but in a way that wrongly suggests that the *Griggs* pool-of-applicants standard is the only relevant one. Neither interpretation provides a helpful answer; it matters little which is correct.

What does matter is the fact that a conscientious and intelligent employer could read and reread these guidelines without ever grasping the fact that the Supreme Court has defined and measured adverse impact—or disparate impact, as the Court prefers to call it—in at least three quite different ways. The Court used a pool-of-applicants standard in *Griggs*, general population figures in *Dothard*,[16] and data on the qualified labor force in the area of recruitment in *Furnco*.[17] Objections that *Furnco* was really a disparate treatment case like *McDonnell Douglas*[18] and not a disparate impact case like *Griggs* and *Dothard* do not hold up under scrutiny. On close examination, what may, initially, look like a nice legal distinction turns out to be a piece of arbitrary juggling, a sort of legal shell game. The plain truth is that if *Griggs* is still unqualifiedly good law, then dissenting Justices Marshall and Brennan were right:

On November 23, 1976, the Labor Department and the Civil Service Commission, joined by the Justice Department, issued the Federal Executive Agency Guidelines on Employee Selection Procedures, 41 FED. REG. 51744 (1976); EEOC, however, rejected the FEA Guidelines, republishing its own 1970 Guidelines instead. See EEOC Guidelines, 41 FED. REG. 51984 (1976).

[13] See Uniform Guidelines, note 11 *supra*, at 38290.

[14] *Id.* at 38307.

[15] *Id.* at 38308.

[16] Dothard v. Rawlinson, 433 U.S. 321 (1977).

[17] Furnco Constr. Corp. v. Waters, 438 U.S. 567 (1978).

[18] McDonnell Douglas Corp. v. Green, 411 U.S. 792 (1973).

plaintiffs in *Furnco* deserved a chance to show that the company's hiring practices did have adverse impact under the pool-of-applicants standard, even though there was none when the qualified labor force of the area of recruitment was used as the standard.[19]

Two inescapable questions are thus raised. Is *Griggs* still good law? Should it be? With regard to the first question, the unfortunate truth is that the Supreme Court has been no clearer than the guidelines. Witness Mr. Justice Blackmun, issuing a separate opinion in *General Electric v. Gilbert*[20] to tell us: "I do not join any inference or suggestion in the Court's opinion—if any such inference or suggestion is there—that effect may never be a controlling factor in a Title VII case, or that *Griggs* v. *Duke Power Co.* . . . is no longer good law."

The problem, it seems, is that the Court has been willing to accept the results of the *Griggs* standard in some cases but not in others. That is understandable because the results dictated by that standard are fair and reasonable when applied to some fact situations, unfair and unreasonable when applied to others. What is needed is a refinement of the *Griggs* standard plus a clear delineation of the sorts of factual situations to which it is applicable. To date, the Court has not succeeded in doing either of those things and, as a result, there is, as Mr. Justice Blackmun and others fear, danger that it will abandon *Griggs* or allow it to fade into insignificance.

Rejection rather than refinement of *Griggs* would be an example of throwing the baby out with the bathwater. The "baby" in *Griggs* is the principle that unjustified discriminatory impact is unlawful, even in the absence of disparate treatment and/or discriminatory intent. The *Griggs* case itself is a perfect example of the need for such a principle. There, a group of incumbent black employees were prevented from transferring from lower-paying jobs as laborers to higher-paying jobs as coal handlers because they did not possess high school diplomas and could not score at or above the national median, first on the Wonderlic Test, which purports to measure general intelligence, and later on the Bennett Test of Mechanical Comprehension. There was no disparate treatment in

[19] *Furnco*, 438 U.S. at 583.

[20] 429 U.S. 125, 146 (1976).

that case. The test and diploma requirements were applied to blacks and whites alike. There was no discriminatory intent: the company was willing to finance two-thirds of the cost of tuition for high school training for any of its employees, black or white. There was, however, clear disparate impact. The plant in question had a total of fourteen black employees, and thirteen of them had been prevented by these requirements from transferring from the job of laborer to that of coal handler. All of the coal handlers, with a single exception, were white. More importantly, this clear disparate impact was a result of requirements that were utterly lacking in justification.

Many lawyers, and some psychologists who should know better, have assumed that the challenged requirements in the *Griggs* case were unjustified simply because the company had never validated them. Such people are blithely indifferent to the fact that any blanket validation requirement would create general chaos and would work particularly great hardships on small employers who cannot afford the cost of validation. Costs be damned, they respond. No one should be permitted to use unvalidated selection procedures. Such responses seem seriously mistaken, because they presume that unvalidated selection devices are *ipso facto* invalid.

Some unvalidated procedures are invalid, others are not. That being the case, there is no scientific or legal basis for creating any presumption here, in the absence of solid evidence about the validity or invalidity of similar procedures in similar contexts. If there is no scientific basis for presuming the invalidity of all unvalidated selection procedures, then it would seem to follow that there is no compelling reason always to require employers to validate their selection procedures. And there are many strong policy reasons for not imposing such a blanket validation requirement on employers. Three are obvious and compelling.

First, as already noted, such a requirement would work an undue hardship on many small employers. Second, it would tend to have a chilling effect on all employers, big and small, discouraging badly needed experimentation and innovation in selection methods. Third, and most important, such a requirement would overstep the proper limits on government regulation in a free society, because it would impose a heavy legal burden on employers in the absence of any reason for believing that their procedures were harmful to the general public or unfair to any particular segment of it. The mere fact that a procedure is unvalidated is not sufficient to create a reasonable presumption of invalidity, nor is it enough to create a reasonable presumption of harm or unfairness either.

This does not imply that the rejected black applicant-plaintiffs in the *Griggs* case should have lost. No questionable presumption that unvalidated selection devices are per se invalid is required to reach the perfectly reasonable conclusions that the Court reached in *Griggs*. All that is necessary is recognition of the fact that there is no logical basis on which to assume that a high school degree or average verbal or mechanical comprehension skills bear any relationship to the strength, steadiness, and speed with which a person can shovel coal. In other words, these requirements are totally lacking in face validity in this unskilled job situation. And, because the rejected applicants in this case were incumbent employees, it was perfectly reasonable for the Court to hold, as it did, that the pool-of-applicants standard was a fair measure of adverse impact. Because the selection devices responsible for their rejection had no face validity, it was also perfectly reasonable for the Court to hold, as it did, that they could not stand without formal validation. Science sometimes proves common sense wrong, but in the absence of such proof, it remains the best guide we have. Intuitive conclusions from a purely rational base should give way to solid empirical disproof. They need not give way to assumptions unsupported by reason or empirical evidence.

Understood in this way, there is nothing wrong with the *Griggs* standard for adverse impact or with the *Griggs* validation requirement. Both are as reasonable as the broad principle in *Griggs*—that unjustified adverse impact is unlawful—only much more limited in their applicability. Unfortunately, the lower federal courts did not understand *Griggs* in this differentiated way and proceeded to apply its limited holdings in an unlimited fashion to very different fact situations, producing unfair and unacceptable results.

Washington v. Davis[21] is a classic example. There, the challenged selection device—in essence, a literacy requirement for would-be police officers—had compelling face validity and no adverse impact at all in terms of actual hiring: blacks were represented on the police force of the District of Columbia in large and growing numbers, and more were being hired all the time, in numbers equal to or ex-

---

[21] 426 U.S. 229 (1976).

ceeding their percentage of the qualified labor force of the area of recruitment.[22]

The defendants accused of unlawful discrimination in that case were Walter Washington, then mayor of the District of Columbia, and his police chief, Jerry V. Wilson. Their accusers were a group of external applicants who had been rejected for jobs as District police officers because they had failed a test of verbal ability that all successful applicants, black and white alike, had passed. Applying the *Griggs* pool-of-applicants standard, both the district and the appellate courts found adverse impact here, simply because a greater percentage of black than white external applicants failed the test.[23] This holding was unreasonable and certainly not required by *Griggs*.

The fact of applying for a job should not, without some additional evidence, be sufficient to create a presumption that one is qualified for it.[24] In disparate-treatment cases, it is not: plaintiffs must allege

---

[22] Aside from one national recruitment effort, the area of recruitment for the Washington, D.C. police force consisted primarily of an area with a fifty-mile radius from the center of the city. Blacks in the twenty- to twenty-nine-year-old age group eligible for employment as police officers constituted approximately 44 percent of the population of that area. From the time Chief Wilson took office in Agust 1969 and instituted an aggressive affirmative action recruitment program, 44 percent of all new officers hired were black. Davis v. Washington, 348 F. Supp. 15, 16 (D.D.C. 1972). By 1970, that figure had risen to 55 percent. Davis v. Washington, 512 F.2d 956, 961, n.32 (D.C. Cir. 1973).

[23] Between 1968 and 1971, 57 percent of black applicants from within the District failed the test as compared with a failure rate of 13 percent for white intra-District applicants. 512 F.2d at 958. For applicants from outside the District in 1970 and 1971, the failure rates were 47 percent for black applicants and 12 percent for white applicants. *Id.* at 959, n.10.

No generalizations about the relative abilities of black and whites, apart from these specific applicants, are warranted on the basis of these data. There is no reason to believe that either applicant group constitutes a representative sample of any larger group and no surprise in the fact that the two applicant groups are not comparable to each other either, since they differ markedly in manner of selection. Black applicants were widely and aggressively recruited; white ones were essentially self-selected. As a result, the two applicant groups also differ markedly in size. In 1970, for example, 72 percent of all applicants for the D.C. force were black and 56 percent of them passed the test, but only 52 percent of those who passed chose to report for duty. 512 F.2d at 961, n.32. In contrast, blacks and whites who did pass the test probably are comparable to each other, not only because both passed the same test but because both rejected the job, presumably in favor of other safer and/or more lucrative jobs, with about the same frequency: 51 percent of whites passing the test choose to report for duty.

[24] A person's willingness to take a job is a necessary but hardly a sufficient condition for employment. Application does not even constitute proof of willingness, especially when the applicants are external ones. Many unemployed make simul-

that they are qualified and offer some minimal evidence of that fact as part of their prima facie case.[25] In those disparate-impact cases where the applicants are incumbent employees, some minimal evidence already exists, justifying the presumption. Incumbent employees necessarily have already met whatever initial hiring standards their employers had. And they have already performed satisfactorily enough at what is usually a related job to have been retained by the very employers from whom they now seek promotion. External applicants are an unstable, shifting, ill-defined group of unknown persons who have selected themselves in unknown ways and for unknown reasons which bear no necessary relationship to their ability to perform the job in question. Unless there is something more than the mere fact of application to tie them together—some evidence of similar vocational experience, educational background, or current strength, skill, or ability—there is no reason to presume that any two external applicants or any two groups of external applicants are comparable to each other or fairly representative of any larger group defined by race, sex, religion, or ethnicity.

In contrast, incumbent employees with different racial or other extraneous characteristics constitute stable, clearly defined groups whose members are comparable to each other. For these reasons, it is fair to hold that significant discrepancies in the rate of promotion between incumbent applicants of one color, sex, or background and their workmates of a different color, sex, or background are sufficient to constitute at least a prima facie case of unjustified adverse impact. It is unreasonable to use that same standard for measuring adverse impact when the applicants in question are external ones and there is no basis, other than the common fact of their ap-

---

taneous applications to multiple employers, planning to accept a job only if they receive no offers for other jobs they consider more desirable. For evidence to that effect, see note 23 *supra*.

Still, in most instances, the percentage of applicants for any particular job who would take it, given the chance, seems high enough to justify a rebuttable presumption of willingness on the basis of application alone. And, because willingness is a necessary but not a sufficient condition, it is necessary to allow employers to use pool-of-applicant data to show that no qualified minority persons applied for the job in question as a way of rebutting a prima facie case of disparate impact. As indicated in note 26 *infra*, however, pool-of-applicant data are highly vulnerable to manipulation in such cases and it therefore becomes essential to give plaintiffs an opportunity to counter such a defense by showing that the employer's discriminatory actions unfairly discouraged qualified applicants by making them feel it would be futile to apply.

[25] *McDonnell*, 411 U.S. at 802.

plication, for presuming comparability. Such persons do not even approximate either a matched or a random sample. Instead, they constitute a sample which is biased in uncontrolled ways and highly vulnerable to manipulation,[26] negating any likelihood of meaningful generalizations about the abilities of members of different groups or about the reasonableness and fairness of employers and their selection methods.

Reasonableness and fairness, however, do not seem to be the issue for some advocates of the pool-of-applicants standard in external hiring situations. Rather, their primary effort seems to be directed toward maximizing the number of minority persons hired in order to encourage minority promotions and to reduce minority unemployment. Full employment for minority group members is certainly a worthy goal. But Title VII was never intended as a full-employment bill, either for minorities, for the poor, or for anyone else. Its purpose was and is to prevent discrimination in employment, and it is an abuse of function for the courts or the bureaucracy to distort that law in order to use it for different purposes, however worthy. For advocates of full employment, as for advocates of other desirable legislative goals, the legitimate and proper course is to secure new legislation specific to their purpose.

Genuine intellectual confusion also plays a significant role in the distortions and unclarities in the administration and enforcement of Title VII. But it is compounded by purposes foreign to the congressional intent underlying Title VII. Such a situation raises serious questions about encroachments on the powers of democratically elected representatives by agency officials, judges, and others not directly responsible to the electorate, Philip Kurland,[27] Raoul

---

[26] Manipulation can result from good motives or bad. It can operate to distort the composition of the pool of applicants by increasing or decreasing the percentage of minority applicants. In *Washington v. Davis*, for example, the police department's highly successful affirmative action recruitment program resulted in a pool of applicants that was 72 percent black, even though blacks constituted only about 44 percent of the population of the area of recruitment. On the other hand, as indicated in note 28 *infra*, an employer's discriminatory actions may serve artificially to decrease the percentage of qualified minority persons in his applicant pool. To ignore the substantial likelihood of effects such as these is to risk turning Title VII into an instrument for punishing those who seek to end discrimination and rewarding those who seek to perpetuate it.

[27] See KURLAND, WATERGATE AND THE CONSTITUTION 74 (1978): "[I]n continuing to expand its own role in the government of the United States, the third branch again proved that we have arrived at the stage described by Raoul Berger in his

Berger,[28] Alexander Bickel,[29] Louis Lusky,[30] and others have written persuasively about the growing danger of this sort of encroachment. Recently, they have been forcefully seconded by Mr. Justice Rehnquist, joined by Chief Justice Burger, dissenting in the *Weber* case. Suffice it to note here that when considering worthy purposes, the preservation of our democratic system of government is also such a purpose, and it is not fostered when those sworn to uphold the law persistently overstep the legitimate bounds of their authority.

Weber notwithstanding, Title VII was intended to assure equal treatment to equally qualified applicants, and no more. That is why the appropriate standard for a prima facie case of unjustified adverse impact in external hiring situations is a comparison between an employer's work force and the qualified labor force of the area of recruitment. The Supreme Court has, at long last, taken a few hesitant steps in that direction, as illustrated by its use of that standard in *Furnco* and in *Hazelwood*,[31] two recent external-hiring cases. But the Court has taken a long, circuitous route, strewing much debris along the path. As a result, there is considerable risk that meaningful legal distinctions will be lost. Clarification is what is needed; not just right results, but right reasons which provide a stable basis for predicting what should and will happen in future cases, and why.

In *Washington v. Davis*, the Supreme Court reached the right result, reversing the holding of the appellate court for the plaintiffs. Unfortunately, it did not do so by clarifying the limits on the pool-of-applicants standard or by clarifying the limits of the imposition of formal validation requirements. Instead, it did so by cutting

---

new book *Government by Judiciary*. Sooner or later, this country must directly face the question whether it is prepared to entrust the judiciary with the mantles of Plato's guardians. The answer to that question will also determine the future of American democracy and, perhaps, even of American liberty."

[28] See BERGER, GOVERNMENT BY JUDICIARY 314 (1977): "With Lincoln, I cling to faith in the ultimate good sense of the people; I cannot subscribe to the theory that America needs a savior, whether in the shape of a President or of nine–oftimes only five–Platonic Guardians."

[29] BICKEL, THE SUPREME COURT AND THE IDEA OF PROGRESS (1970).

[30] LUSKY, BY WHAT RIGHT? (1975).

[31] Hazelwood School District v. United States, 433 U.S. 299 (1977). See Sharf, *The Prima Facie Case: Keeping Title VII Honest*, in EQUAL EMPLOYMENT PRACTICE GUIDE 121 (October 1978).

back unnecessarily on the general principle in *Griggs,* that unjustified disparate impact is unlawful. In essence the Court said proof of such impact may be sufficient under Title VII but it is not enough in employment discrimination cases arising under the Constitution. There, proof of discriminatory intent is also required before an employment practice can be declared unlawful.

That holding should have been irrelevant to virtually all employment discrimination cases arising after 1972 when Title VII was amended. *Washington v. Davis* was decided in 1976 but it arose prior to 1972. Had it arisen a bit later, it would have been necessary to decide it under Title VII and there, under the general principle enunciated in *Griggs,* intent should not have been the critical factor. In fact, it has apparently become just that in most Title VII cases, because the Court has relied increasingly on the overworked old warhorse of intent, making it central, not only to Fifth and Fourteenth Amendment cases and to pattern and practice suits[32] brought by the government, but to ordinary Title VII cases brought by private plaintiffs as well.

The Court accomplished this by emphasizing the difference between disparate-impact cases like *Griggs* where discriminatory intent is not required and disparate-treatment cases like *McDonnell Douglas v. Green* and *McDonald v. Santa Fe Trail Co.*[33] where it is. The trouble with those categories is that few cases with multiple plaintiffs fit neatly or exclusively into one category or the other.[34] Most cases can be placed in either, and cases are now won or lost,

[32] Authorization for such suits is conferred by § 707(a) of Title VII, 42 U.S.C. § 2000e-(6)(a).

[33] 427 U.S. 273 (1976).

[34] The *McDonnell Douglas* case involved a single black plaintiff who charged that his former employer's refusal to rehire him was motivated by unlawful considerations of race. The *McDonald* case involved two white plaintiffs who alleged that their firing was motivated by unlawful considerations of race. In such cases, intent is not an additional element introduced by the Court as a *deus ex machina;* it is intrinsically and inevitably the issue, and the only one. In contrast, in class actions and other cases with numerous plaintiffs like *Griggs* and *Washington v. Davis,* subjective intent is not an inevitable issue. Such cases can be dealt with objectively, in terms of the statistical impact of selection practices and their business justification, or subjectively, by attempting to determine the motivation behind an employer's choice of selection practices. In other words, if a process produces fair and reasonable outcomes, it is not necessary to search for impurities in the hearts of its designers in order to damn it. Similarly, if a process produces unfair and unreasonable outcomes, purity of heart on the part of its designers need not save it.

depending upon the pigeonhole in which they are placed. The whole process begins to bear a disquieting resemblance to the bad old writ-of-action days when cleverness in juggling legal forms counted more heavily than the substance of cases. This unfortunate impression is reinforced by the fact that the Court itself has begun to juggle the categories in arbitrary ways in order to get results it wants in particular cases.

Furnco v. Waters is a good illustration of this. It is reasonably viewed as a disparate-impact case like *Griggs*, but its facts are more like those in *Washington v. Davis*, because Furnco's labor force fairly mirrored that of the qualified labor force of the area of recruitment and because their selection methods had considerable face validity. Defendants in that case, like those in *Washington v. Davis*, deserved to win but, under the *Griggs* standard, they would have lost and did at the appellate court level. The Supreme Court got out from under by treating *Furnco* as a disparate-treatment case requiring proof of discriminatory intent. It then used the appropriate standard—data on the qualified labor force in the area of recruitment—not to refute disparate impact but to disprove discriminatory intent.

Discriminatory intent is proved or disproved in exactly the way disparate impact ought to be in external hiring cases but is not. The Court has tended either to apply the pool-of-applicants standard or even more irrelevant general population figures, or to pretend that disparate impact is not the issue at all. As Mr. Justice Stevens warned, in a separate opinion in *Washington v. Davis*, "the line between discriminatory purpose and discriminatory impact is not nearly as bright, and perhaps not quite as critical, as the reader of the Court's opinion might assume."[35]

Category juggling aside, the Court has moved away from the pool-of-applicants standard in the last two years, utilizing general population figures in *Teamsters*[36] and in *Dothard*, and data on the qualified labor force of the area of recruitment in *Furnco* and in *Hazelwood*. Substitution of general population figures for pool-of-applicants data is an especially unfortunate development. Pool-of-applicants data are inappropriate for proving adverse impact in some

---

[35] 426 U.S. at 254.

[36] International Brotherhood of Teamsters v. United States, 431 U.S. 324 (1977).

employment discrimination cases, while general population figures are inappropriate in all of them.

In 1974, the Supreme Court itself gave a cogent explanation of why that is so, albeit in a different context. Speaking for the Court in *Mayor of Philadelphia v. Educational Equality League*, Mr. Justice Powell explained, "this is not a case in which it can be assumed that all citizens are fungible for purposes of determining whether members of a particular class have been unlawfuly excluded."[37] He then went on to distinguish between what he aptly termed "the relevant universe for comparison purposes" and "the population at large," chiding the appellate court for overlooking that distinction.[38]

Alas, the Supreme Court itself then proceeded to make the same egregious error only three years later, in *Teamsters* and again in *Dothard*. *Teamsters* and *Dothard* are both employment discrimination cases, the first involving truck drivers, the second prison guards. The Court, along with a number of law review commentators, considers general population figures to be appropriate in such cases apparently on the theory that anyone can drive a truck.[39] Similar attitudes lay behind the appellate court's rejection of a literacy re-

---

[37] 415 U.S. 605, 620 (1974).

[38] *Id.* at 620–21. See also Sharf, note 31 *supra*.

[39] See, *e.g.*, Shoben, *Probing the Discriminatory Effect of Employee Selection Procedures with Disparate Impact Analysis under Title VII*, 56 TEX. L. REV. 1, 13, 33 (1977). The author not only endorses Mr. Justice Stewart's contention that driving heavy trucks "requires skills commonly held or easily acquired by members of the general community," she also asserts, on the basis of no evidence whatsoever, that "Police, fire fighters, many factory workers, and bank tellers have jobs of this type," and therefore, "Plaintiffs should be able to establish a prima facie case with evidence that one or more of these requirements has the effect of excluding a disproportionate number of potential applicants from the general population on the basis of race, sex, or ethnicity." Earlier, on the same page, the author defined "these requirements" to include such selection devices as "height or weight standards, a physical agility test, a written test, a diploma requirement, or lack of an arrest record."

In other words, local government units should not be allowed to reject fire fighters who cannot read well enough to recognize words like "flammable" or "explosive" and who lack the agility to climb the ladders ubiquitous to their work without burdening taxpayers, black and white, with the cost of elaborate validation studies. Substituting logic for elitism, it would make more sense to insist on validation of the requirement that lawyers must possess J.D.'s. Fire fighting, like lawyering, is a highly skilled job, but the immediate negative consequences of incompetence are greater in the former case than in the latter. Few legal cases involve the risk of death; most fires do.

quirement for police officers in *Washington v. Davis:* anyone can be a cop.

Only cases like *Hazelwood*, according to this view, require a more differentiated standard, because that case involves teachers—middle-class professionals—and there the attitude is that special qualifications like university degrees are obviously needed and formal validation is, of course, unnecessary. In other words, people without advanced degrees are fungible, professionals are not. Such attitudes seem rife with unjustifiable depreciation of blue-collar workers with relatively little formal education who perform skilled jobs. They also seem dangerous in their implications, even for those with considerable formal education. By 1984, we may all be fungible.[40] In the meantime, it behooves us to fight for the presumption that none of us is. I have argued elsewhere about the nonfungibility of police officers, stressing the complexity and variety of the tasks they must perform.[41] Here, I focus on truck drivers, a seemingly harder case, because their job is considerably less complex and less varied.

Indeed, a major problem for long-distance drivers is boredom, a very serious problem because bored drivers are prone to fall asleep at the wheel with unpleasant consequences for themselves, their employers, and the general public. Some interesting selection devices could be developed to measure the capacity of potential drivers to entertain themselves, often with minimal external stimulation, by keeping their minds occupied rather than empty. It might then be discovered that it is useful for truck drivers to have brains as well as brawn, and that many truck drivers, black and white, do have both, even though few of them have college degrees. But no relevance need be assigned to such a premise. The inappropriateness of comparisons between the racial makeup of the general population and that of an employer's work force is evidenced by the obvious fact that general population figures count children equally with adults, and few children have the strength, skill, and attention span needed to drive heavy trucks. In more general terms, as long as we have child labor laws, general population figures will always produce gross overestimates of the labor force of any area. To dis-

---

[40] ORWELL, NINETEEN EIGHTY-FOUR (1949); see also ZAMYATIN, WE (1923).

[41] Lerner, note 7 *supra*.

miss this fact in making group comparisons as if the error were a constant one is simply wrong. We know that the ratio of children to adults differs markedly in different groups at different times and places, as does the ratio of older, retired people to active adults. As a result, the overestimation will often be significantly greater for some groups than for others.[42]

That many judges and law review commentators have nonetheless accepted or even espoused this general population standard is mystifying. One need not be a population expert to have at least a rough idea of the potential magnitude of these differences. Thus, in the Philadelphia case cited earlier, it was found that in 1971, 60 percent of the youngsters in the public schools in that city were black, but only 34 percent of the general population was black.[43] The odds seem very low that a discrepancy that large can be accounted for by differential rates of attendance at private schools by children of other races. Much smaller differences can make the difference between winning and losing in employment discrimination cases. Thus, in *United States v. City of Chicago*,[44] the evidence showed that in 1970, approximately one-third of the city's male population but only about one-fourth of its male labor force was black. Since differences like those are common, the likelihood is great that miscarriages of justice will result from continued confusion between general population figures and labor force figures. Perhaps some of those who persist in advocating the use of general population figures are simply confused, but most of them seem to have other axes to grind.

Whatever their merits, they are not legitimate under Title VII. Legitimate victims of discrimination can secure their rights as easily under fair standards for adverse impact as under unfair ones. In *Teamsters*, for example, plaintiffs clearly deserved to win out against their employer and would have done so under any of the standards discussed. Nothing would have been lost and much would have been gained if the Court had ignored general population figures

[42] See, *e.g.*, tables showing fertility rates or number of children in household by woman's education and family income for eight different American ethnic groups (American Indians, blacks, Chinese, Filipinos, Japanese, Jews, Puerto Ricans, and West Indians), in SOWELL (ed.), ESSAYS AND DATA ON AMERICA ETHNIC GROUPS (1978).

[43] 415 U.S. at 611.

[44] 411 F. Supp. 218, 233 (N.D. Ill. 1976), *aff'd* 549 F.2d 415 (7th Cir. 1977).

and focused on an appropriate standard. Ironically, because plaintiffs in that case were incumbent employees, most of whom were already performing jobs similar to the higher-paying ones to which they had been denied access,[45] the most appropriate standard in that case was the *Griggs* pool-of-applicants standard.

In contrast, in *Dothard v. Rawlinson*, the plaintiff was a single external applicant, claiming to represent the entire female population of the State of Alabama, and the Court allowed her to use national population figures on the height and weight of American women between the ages of eighteen and seventy-nine in order to prove that Alabama's statutory height and weight requirements for prison guards constituted unlawful sex discrimination. Alabama's size requirements were quite modest: they commanded that guards of either sex be at least five feet, two inches tall and weigh at least 120 pounds. Alabama also required external applicants to be between the age of twenty-and-a-half and forty-five. Neither the plaintiff nor the Court challenged that age requirement. They simply ignored it, including data on the height and weight of younger girls and older women[46]—two groups typically smaller than young and middle-aged adult women—to conclude that some 40 percent of all American women would be excluded by Alabama's size requirements.[47]

---

[45] Technically, because *Teamsters* was a pattern and practice suit, the plaintiff was the United States, but the employees on whose behalf the Attorney General sued worked for the defendant as local city drivers or servicemen. Hundreds of these men were black, met all qualifications for higher-paying long-distance driving jobs, and had applied for transfers to those jobs between July 2, 1965, the effective date of Title VII for private employers, and January 1, 1969. Hundreds of long-distance drivers were promoted from within or hired from outside during that period; none was black. 431 U.S. at 337, 341.

[46] Relatively few Americans, male or female, maintain the slenderness of their teens into their thirties and forties, and most Americans are ruefully aware of that fact through personal experience. It is less widely known but equally true that aged Americans tend to be shorter than young and middle-aged adults, in part because the percentage of foreign born is greater in the oldest segment of our population and most of these immigrants came from countries where nutritional and other environmental deficiencies limited physical growth. Between 1901 and 1920 alone, nearly 10 million Southern and Eastern Europeans migrated to the United States, the vast majority poor and hungry. See 2 MORISON & COMMAGER, THE GROWTH OF THE AMERICAN REPUBLIC 179 (1937); HANDLIN (ed.), IMMIGRATION AS A FACTOR IN AMERICAN HISTORY (1959); HANDLIN, THE UPROOTED (1951).

[47] The Court found that some 22 percent of American women between the ages of eighteen and seventy-nine would be excluded by the weight requirement and about 33 percent by the height requirement. It then concluded with this rather

The Court seemed impressed by the fact that while approximately 37 percent of Alabama's total labor force was female, only about 13 percent of its guards were. Apparently the Court assumed that but for the disparate impact of the height and weight requirements, equal percentages of males and females of all sizes would want to be prison guards. This assumption lacks face validity, and it was not supported by data of any kind to indicate how many diminutive women or men of any age wanted to be prison guards in Alabama. The point is particularly pressing in light of what a federal district court in *Pugh v. Locke*[48] described as the "rampant violence" and "jungle atmosphere" in those prisons which force guards to "spend all their time attempting to maintain control or to protect themselves."[49] The answer may well have been one: Ms. Rawlinson. Nonetheless, the Court, relying solely on these irrelevant general population figures, struck down the Alabama statute as unlawful under Title VII.

The Court in *Dothard*, however, was no more willing to live with the results of this standard than it was with the inappropriate application of the *Griggs* standard in *Washington v. Davis*. Accordingly, the Court held that although Alabama's long-standing height and weight requirements could not stand, its newly promulgated Regulation 204 was lawful. Regulation 204 made guard jobs in male maximum security prisons available to men only. Since some 75 percent of all prison guard jobs in the state are in such facilities, the result was a significant reduction in job opportunities for all Alabama women, even tall heavy ones with black belts in karate. The Court reached this unfortunate result by an extreme expansion of § 703(e) of Title VII. That section provides an exemption for jobs where sex is a bona fide occupational qualification, an exemption needed to cover jobs like those of wet nurses.

---

mysterious statement: "When the height and weight restrictions are combined, Alabama statutory standards would exclude 41.13% of the female population while excluding less than 1% of the male population.[12]" 433 U.S. at 329–30. Footnote 12 tells us that in combining male height and weight statistics, the Court proceeded by "adding the two together and allowing for some overlap." Presumably, the Court also allowed for "some overlap" between shortness and thinness in women, but no information is offered on how it determined the magnitude of "some" with sufficient precision to arrive at a total female exclusion figure of 41.13 percent.

[48] 406 F. Supp. 318, 325 (M.D. Ala. 1976).

[49] *Ibid.*

It should be noted that there were four separate opinions in *Dothard*, with a maximum of three votes for the reasoning in any one of them. Only Mr. Justice White saw that plaintiff had not really made out a prima facie case of sex discrimination with regard to Alabama's height and weight requirements.[50] All eight of the other Justices thought that she had, but there was a three-to-three split on what the defendant would have had to do to rebut that case.

Since the defendant, in effect, did nothing but rely on Regulation 204, the Justices' views on acceptable rebuttal evidence are dicta, not holdings. They are, nonetheless, extremely interesting. Mr. Justice Stewart, joined by Justices Powell and Stevens, thought that, absent Regulation 204, formal validation of Alabama's height and weight requirements would have been necessary.[51] Mr. Justice Rehnquist, joined by Justices Burger and Blackmun, took great care to emphasize his contrasting view that a reasonable argument would have sufficed here, such as an argument that the appearance of strength conveyed by a large or at least averaged-sized person of either sex was a reasonably job-related requirement for Alabama prison guards.[52]

Because formal validation should not be required for reasonable face-valid selection devices, this position was good news. There may, however, be bad news in another recent Rehnquist opinion. Speaking for seven of his brethren in *Furnco*, Mr. Justice Rehnquist, in attempting to explain why he chose to put that case in the disparate-treatment, rather than the disparate-impact, category, added a troubling footnote. He said, in relevant part, "[T]his case did not involve employment tests, which we dealt with in *Griggs* . . . and in *Albemarle* . . . or particularized requirements such as the height and weight specifications considered in *Dothard*."[53] Like Mr. Justice Blackmun,[54] I sometimes have trouble understanding exactly what Mr. Justice Rehnquist means. Nonetheless, his apparent distinction between adverse-impact cases which involve tests and adverse-impact cases which do not involve tests is disquieting. In the two adverse-impact test cases, Mr. Justice Rehnquist apparently assented to the notion that, given adverse impact, formal validation

---

[50] 433 U.S. at 348.

[51] *Id.* at 332.

[52] *Id.* at 339, 340.

[53] 438 U.S. at 575, n.7.

[54] See text *supra*, at note 20.

should be required.[55] In the adverse-impact nontest case, while he again found adverse impact to exist, he emphasized the view that a reasonable argument unsupported by formal validation would suffice.

Perhaps Mr. Justice Rehnquist simply changed his mind in the light of experience. (*Griggs* and *Albemarle* were decided prior to *Washington v. Davis*, *Dothard* afterward, in 1977.) If so, that would be an encouraging development. That, however, would not explain why he chose to make a distinction between test and nontest adverse-impact cases in his 1978 opinion in *Furnco*. Here, it may be useful to recall, the selection devices challenged in *Furnco* and upheld by the Court without formal validation were similar to those in *Dothard* insofar as neither involved tests.

All of this seems to raise at least the possibility that what Mr. Justice Rehnquist has in mind is not an across-the-board reasonableness standard for all selection devices but a double standard. Formal validation might always be required for tests with adverse impact, however defined, but not for nontest selection devices. Such a development would be unfortunate. Good tests, reasonably selected and applied to fit an employer's legitimate purposes, but not locally validated for those purposes, are not always better than what Mr. Justice Rehnquist called "particularized requirements" like those in *Dothard*, or subjective judgments, based on personal observation and recommendations, like those in *Furnco*. But there is no *a priori* reason to assume that they are worse. And properly standardized and administered tests do tend to have certain ad-

---

[55] *Griggs* was decided by a unanimous bench of eight which included Mr. Justice Rehnquist. In Albemarle Paper Co. v. Moody, 422 U.S. 405, 441–47 (1975), he issued a separate concurrence to discuss back pay and methods by which such awards might be determined. He expressed no disagreement and raised no questions about the treatment of the validation issue by the majority in that case. The treatment was Kafkaesque because the miniscule *n's* in many cells all but obliterated any realistic possibilities for the statistical significance demanded by the Court. Here it should be noted that the Court has required statistical significance only for validation efforts by the defendants, even when numerical limits made that impossible. It has not required statistical significance for proof of disparate impact, even in cases where the data readily lend themselves to such treatment, despite repeated suggestions to that effect in the literature. See, *e.g.*, Lerner, note 7 *supra;* Shoben, *Differential Pass-Fail Rates in Employment Testing: Statistical Proof under Title VII*, 91 Harv. L. Rev. 793 (1978). Recently, however, the Court has at least acknowledged the possible probative value of substituting statistical analysis for intuitive judgments in determining whether exclusionary impact exists. See Castaneda v. Partida, 430 U.S. 482 (1977), and *Hazelwood*, 433 U.S. 299 (1977).

vantages, with or without formal validation, such as objectivity, consistency of measurement, and comparability of results.[56]

Advantages notwithstanding, if employers find that the burden of validation can be lifted simply by switching from tests to other selection methods, many will switch. Some, of course, may continue to pursue the difficult and expensive course leading to one of the rare validation victories like that in *United States v. South Carolina*,[57] but they are likely to be a minority. Sadly, under such circumstances, the nontest methods adopted by the probable majority are not likely to offer better protection to potential victims of discrimination,[58] but they would be apt to result in quite significant decreases in the productivity and efficiency of government and private industry.[59] *Griggs* would survive, but in so strange and faded a form that it would only serve to defeat tests, not discrimination.

How great is the danger of such a double standard? I may have misunderstood Mr. Justice Rehnquist. And he may be a minority of one on this issue, despite the fact that he spoke for all but two members of the Court in *Furnco*. The idea of a double standard was not explicit in *Furnco* or in any other Supreme Court case to date. Yet the Court does seem more inclined to accept face-valid arguments—its own and those of others—in nontest cases than in test cases. And unless the Court finds a better way than it has thus far seized upon to resolve the growing tensions generated by *Griggs*, the double-standard idea may prove seductive to a weary and divided Court in search of fixed rules.

There is a way to rationalize the problems. I think the following propositions would do so:

1. General population figures are never an appropriate basis of comparison in disparate-impact cases. Adulthood is a minimum

---

[56] See generally ANASTASI, note 5 *supra*.

[57] 434 U.S. 1026 (1978), a per curiam opinion joined by five Justices. Justices Marshall and Blackmun took no part. Mr. Justice White dissented, joined by Mr. Justice Brennan.

[58] Lerner, note 7 *supra*.

[59] See Hunter & Schmidt, *Fitting People to Jobs: Implications of Personnel Selection for National Productivity*, in FLEISHMAN (ed.), HUMAN PERFORMANCE AND PRODUCTIVITY (in press); Schmidt, Hunter, McKenzie, & Muldrow, *The Impact of Valid Selection Procedures on Workforce Productivity*, J. APPLIED PSYCHOL. (in press).

qualification for virtually all jobs. Most jobs also require other qualifications not possessed by all adults. Truck drivers, for example, are usually required to have drivers licenses and reasonable driving records.

2. The pool-of-applicants standard is an acceptable basis for a prima facie case of disparate impact only in cases involving incumbent employees all of whom met the same initial hiring standards and are successfully performing related jobs.

3. In cases involving external applicants, the appropriate standard for a prima facie case of disparate impact is comparison between an employer's work force and the qualified labor force of the area of recruitment.

4. In the latter instance, pool-of-applicants data may be relevant in rebuttal, because willingness to take a job is a necessary, albeit not a sufficient, condition for hiring. In evaluating such data, the Court should take pains to avoid penalizing defendants for the consequences of affirmative action programs, their own or those of others in their area of recruitment.

5. Plaintiffs should be given an opportunity to counter such rebuttal evidence by showing that defendants' action distorted the data by convincing qualified applicants that it would be futile to apply.

6. When adverse impact under either of these standards is shown and not adequately rebutted, defendants should be given a chance to show that their selection devices—test or nontest—are justified in light of the nature of the job and its relation to the overall enterprise. Face validity, otherwise known as reasonableness, should suffice here.

7. If defendants' practices have significant adverse impact as defined herein and they are not justified by face validity, then they should be held unlawful unless defendant has formal validity evidence strong enough to prove that in this case, common sense is wrong.

II. Equality, Validity, and Empirical Reality

The standards listed above are offered as ways of resolving the existing confusion about the definition of adverse impact and about the circumstances under which it should trigger a formal validation requirement. Growing pressures exist, however, to reject even the best validation evidence when adverse impact exists. Much of the instability in discrimination law stems from the tension between proponents of equal opportunity for all individuals forever and proponents of equal results for particular groups now. Forces on the side of equal opportunity include a large majority of all Americans, black and white,[60] plus the clear expression of Congressional intent in Title VII.[61] Forces on the other side include most professional civil rights bureaucrats[62] and their allies, in and out of

[60] See Gallup, *80% Majority Favors Ability as Criteria for Admissions,* Washington Post, November 20, 1977; Bolce & Gray, *Blacks, Whites and "Race Politics,"* 54 PUBLIC INTEREST 61 (1979).

[61] As Mr. Justice Rehnquist noted in his detailed and irrefutable review of the legislative history of Title VII, "In most cases, '[l]egislative history . . . is more vague than the statute we are called upon to interpret' . . . Here, however, the legislative history of Title VII is as clear as the language of §§ 703(a) and (d), and it irrefutably demonstrates that Congress meant precisely what it said in § 703(a) and (d)—that no racial discrimination in employment is permissible under Title VII, not even preferential treatment of minorities to correct racial imbalance." See *Weber,* 99 S. Ct. at 4861.

[62] See, *e.g.,* comments made by Eleanor Holmes Norton, chairperson of the EEOC, at the Commission Meeting of December 22, 1977: "It is clear that the employers around the country are increasingly sophisticated in the validation of tests. Because employers make money and will learn to do what the government wants them to do. And the government says what we really want you to do is validate tests, that is what they are going to spend their money doing. And frankly, they have spent a great deal of money doing just that, and my hat is off to the psychologists. We do not see, however, comparable evidence that validated tests have in fact gotten black and brown bodies, or for that matter, females into places as result of the validation of those tests. In other words, we do not see the kind of causal relation that I think, when the great—and I regard it as a great—new enforcement tool was discovered some years ago, we do not see quite the causal relationship we had expected to see. Rather we are faced with the possible anomaly that tests could be validated and no effect or no appreciable effect flow to minorities and women, and in particular minorities, because of, perhaps, reasons more complicated than any of us understand, going at least to class and other background factors that militate against people who have come from such backgrounds taking tests as well as people who have not come from such backgrounds. So if the commission, in effect, says to employers, as long as you validate your tests we're really not concerned about you anymore, I believe, in effect, it is saying that the presence of real people who are not in the work force, is not as important as making sure that the tests have been validated. Therefore, I see some very positive advantages I must say in encouraging an employer to look at what the ultimate goal is. That is to say, did your work force have some minorities and females before the test was validated or does it have any appreciable number now that the test has been validated? And if you really don't want to go through that, but you are interested in getting excluded people in your work force, we would encourage you to do so." See also remarks of Senator Helms, *Bureaucratic Absurdities and Citizen Harassment,* 122 CONG. REC. 11782–84 (1976); and see sources cited and data provided in note 10 *supra.*

government,[63] along with their many friends in academia.[64]

People who are committed to equal results now tend to see adverse impact, justified or unjustified, as a *per se* violation of the law, and they tend to be hostile to tests in general and to valid tests in particular. The reasons for this are not hard to discern. In this country at this time, many clearly valid tests do have significant adverse impact, not on women or on nonwhites generally—Orientals as a group usually outscore whites as a group[65]—and not on blacks as individuals, but on blacks as a group.[66] This is distressing but not surprising in light of well-documented facts about how seriously inadequate a job American public schools, integrated or nonintegrated, have done in recent years, particularly in teaching poor children in general, and poor black children in particular, very basic things like literacy and numeracy.[67]

Literacy is especially important because it is essential for competent performance at almost any skilled job in today's economy, manual or nonmanual, and most valid employment tests for skilled jobs properly discriminate between literate and illiterate job applicants. Any test that does this is bound to have justified but ad-

---

[63] See e.g., Editorial, *Education Disgraced*, New York Times, June 6, 1979, p. A18; *Federal Contract Compliance Chief Discusses the Weber Decision and the Government's Next Steps*, New York Times, July 1, 1979, p. 6E; *Education Association Irked by Limit on Its Race Quotas*, New York Times, July 5, 1979; p. A12; and see Lerner, *Equal Protection and External Screening: Davis, DeFunis, and Bakke*, PROCEEDINGS OF THE 1977 ETS INVITATIONAL CONFERENCE (1978).

[64] Academics continue to insist that America is still a racist society. See Ladd & Lipset, *Academics: America's Most Politically Liberal Stratum*, 11 CHRONICLE HIGHER ED. (October 20, 1975); LIPSET, REBELLION IN THE UNIVERSITY (1976).

[65] See, *e.g.*, Schwartz, *The Culturally Advantaged: A Study of Japanese-American Pupils*, in EPPS (ed.), RACE RELATIONS 139 (1973); SOWELL, note 42 *supra*.

[66] See, *e.g.*, Humphreys, *Race and Sex Differences and Their Implications for Educational and Occupational Equality*, 26 EDUC. THEORY 135 (1976). For evidence showing that these differences cannot be explained on the theory that tests are valid for whites but not for blacks, see Hunter, Schmidt, & Hunter, *Differential Validity of Employment Tests by Race: A Comprehensive Review and Analysis*, PSYCHOL. BULL. (in press).

[67] See LERNER, MINIMUM COMPETENCE AND MAXIMUM CHOICE (in press) for a review of relevant research on this issue. See also COPPERMAN, THE LITERACY HOAX: THE DECLINE OF READING, WRITING AND LEARNING IN THE PUBLIC SCHOOLS AND WHAT CAN WE DO ABOUT IT (1978). And, for evidence that inner-city black parents are more dissatisfied with the inadequate job public schools are doing for their children than any other group in American society today, see GALLUP, A DECADE OF GALLUP POLLS OF ATTITUDES TOWARD EDUCATION, 1969–1978 (1978).

verse impact. Available data indicate that at least 41.6 percent of all blacks born in 1958 are functionally illiterate, as compared to "only" 8.2 percent of all whites born in that year.[68] Overall black-white differences in developed mathematical skills and other nonverbal abilities relevant to many jobs and sampled by many tests tend to be even greater than differences in verbal skills.[69] Thus, these tests, too, tend to have significant adverse impact, particularly when they are valid and job related.

To discuss these distressing facts as if the problem they reveal is one of test "bias" is to talk in what Orwell called "newspeak," a late twentieth-century language for rejecting truth by repudiating reality. The obvious and preferable alternative is to try to change the reality by changing the American educational system and our own cherished but erroneous attitudes and assumptions about it.[70] To begin to do that, it is necessary to recognize the ineffectiveness of previous attempts to deal with those problems on the basis of the empirically discredited hypothesis that integration, in and of itself, promotes achievement. That hypothesis had considerable face validity, but a large and impressive body of empirical data now exists which indicates that it was erroneous.[71] Busing may be a potent political symbol, but it is not a solution to educational problems and it often drains off resources and energies needed to create and implement new solutions that work.

Many who refuse to recognize these realities and to face up to these problems have concentrated power in government bureaucracies like the Equal Employment Opportunity Commission and the Office of Civil Rights, as well as in a number of highly organized and litigious lobbying groups like the NAACP and the National

---

[68] See NATIONAL ASSESSMENT OF EDUCATIONAL PROGRESS, FUNCTIONAL LITERACY, BASIC READING PERFORMANCE (1976). And see LERNER, note 67 *supra*, for an explanation of why the NAEP data underestimate the extent and severity of illiteracy among American young people of both races.

[69] See, *e.g.*, Maier, *Effects of General Ability, Education and Racial Group on Aptitude Test Performance*, Technical Research Note 228, U.S. Army Behavior and Systems Research Laboratory, 1971.

[70] My own suggestions on ways to change that reality for the better are contained in LERNER, note 67 *supra*.

[71] See especially ST. JOHN, SCHOOL DESEGREGATION: OUTCOMES FOR CHILDREN (1975); see also COLEMAN, ET AL., EQUALITY OF EDUCATIONAL OPPORTUNITY (1966); MOSTELLER & MOYNIHAN, ON EQUALITY OF EDUCATIONAL OPPORTUNITY (1972).

Education Association.[72] They and their allies on the high court itself must bear some of the responsibility for the tragic failure of the American educational system to equip so many children, black and white, with the competencies necessary to full participation in the modern world vocationally and in other ways.

At present, they show no signs of doing so.[73] Instead they have mounted an increasingly ferocious series of attacks on valid tests and the unpleasant truths they reveal.[74] They have succeeded in building into the 1978 guidelines[75] the myth of the alternative screening-method solution to the problem of adverse impact, forcing employers who use valid selection devices to spend time and money searching for other, equally valid devices with lesser adverse impact. In most cases, this is a chimera because there is no real alternative to the need for literacy, numeracy, and other job- and life-relevant skills that valid tests measure.

Antitesting forces have also mounted a propaganda campaign against tests and test producers[76] and have had some success in pass-

---

[72] See, *e.g.*, NAACP Resolution Calling for the Elimination of "Cultural Bias" from Testing, 1974; NEA Resolution Calling for the Elimination of All Standardized Intelligence, Aptitude and Achievement Testing, 1974. See also Jones, *Metropolitan Desegregation: Where Are the Courts Heading?* 10 URBAN REV. 128 (1978); and NAACP Legal Defense and Education Fund, *It's Not the Distance, "It's the Niggers,"* 1972; and see Statement by NEA Executive Director Terry Herndon, *The Standardized Testing Coverup*, released to the press on July 5, 1979.

[73] See note 72 *supra;* Columbus Board of Education v. Penick, 99 S. Ct. 294 (1979); Dayton Board of Education v. Brinkman, 99 S. Ct. 2971 (1979).

[74] See note 72 *supra.*

[75] 43 FED. REG. No. 166, at 38291 and § 6A at 38299 (August 25, 1978). And see additional comments made by Eleanor Holmes Norton, chairperson of the EEOC, at the Commission Meeting of December 22, 1977: "So that while I agree with both Commissioners on the importance of maintaining test validation, I suppose I disagree on the importance attached to it and in fact believe that test validation—that the employer community has now caught on to a nice new thing, and that if they continue to rely as heavily on validation, they could actually undercut the purpose of Title VII in erecting a barrier that would then be impenetrable. Namely, I have validated this test, you tell me I only got 2 percent blacks, well, go and do something about it. I believe that in very many instances, given the increasing sophistication of psychologists, that's exactly what is going to happen to us. And, frankly, I don't want to wait until that happens to try to fight my way out of that box. Thus, I think that by giving alternatives, we relieve especially minorities of the frustrations they find inevitably in taking validated tests."

[76] See, *e.g.*, Altman, *Citing New Law, Medical Schools to Bar Entry Tests in New York*, New York Times, July 18, 1979, p. A1; Meislin, *Carey Signs a Bill to Let Public See Tests for College*, New York Times, July 15, 1979, p. A1; and Nader, *Letter to the Editor of the New York Times*, August 3, 1979, p. A22.

ing senselessly harassing legislation like the LaValle bill enacted into law in New York in the summer of 1979.[77] The LaValle bill would force producers of admissions tests for colleges and professional schools to make their test questions and answers public shortly after their tests are administered. This mischievous requirement eviscerates existing copyright protections for all reputable test producers because such persons cannot in good conscience reuse any test item once it has been made public. As a result, they are forced either to withdraw from States with offensive statutes or to attempt to create an adequate number of new items for each test administration, a costly business that cannot be done quickly without sacrifice of quality.

The net effect on institutional consumers and the test-taking public is noxious. Inevitably, they must pay more for less, particularly since standardization and equating procedures designed to insure that the level of test difficulty remains constant from year to year can be rendered inoperative by blanket item disclosure requirements. Unfairness to test producers and consumers is not, however, the most serious hazard in blanket disclosure requirements. The erosion of standardization and equating procedures will make it difficult or impossible to collect comparable data on educational results in different times and places. Data of this sort show whether standards of achievement are being maintained or are being allowed to decline, as they did from 1963 to the present, as indicated by the marked decline in mean scores on the well-standardized exam that millions of college-bound students took throughout that period, the Scholastic Aptitude Test.[78]

Thus far, antitesting forces have not seemed to fare quite as well in court, as illustrated by the Supreme Court's five-to-four affirmance, in *National Education Association v. South Carolina*,[79] of the judgment of a three-judge district court panel in *United States v. State of South Carolina*.[80] There the use of a content-valid test for would-be teachers which satisfied professional standards was upheld, despite the fact that it had marked adverse impact. That case was particularly reassuring to psychometricians and

---

[77] N.Y. Laws 1979.

[78] See Wirtz (chairman), *Report of the Advisory Panel on the SAT Score Decline*, College Board (1977).

[79] 434 U.S. 1026 (1978).

[80] 445 F. Supp. 1094 (D.S.C. 1978).

other concerned scientists because in it the Court said: "To the extent that the EEOC Guidelines conflict with well-grounded expert opinion and accepted professional standards, they need not be controlling."[81] Reassurance was badly needed because earlier court decisions had raised the Lysenkoist specter of a judiciary arrogating to itself the power to decide essentially scientific questions by fiat, relying on politicized agency guidelines and ignoring professional standards that make scientific fidelity their sole touchstone.[82]

Two 1979 decisions, *Weber* and *Detroit Edison*, have, however, been less reassuring. The *Weber* case did not deal with tests at all, but it is an important employment discrimination case because it represents the most significant high-Court victory by those pressing for equal results by any means now, no matter the cost. In *Weber*, a five-man majority twisted the clear equal opportunity language of Title VII, pretending that it was intended to insure proportional representation for all black workers now and that it could be construed to condone discrimination against white workers for that purpose. This, despite the fact that only three years earlier, the same Court had held that Title VII forbids discrimination against whites as well as against nonwhites in an opinion written for a unanimous bench by Mr. Justice Marshall in *McDonald v. Santa Fe Trail Co.*,[83] another case involving allegedly voluntary discrimination against white workers by a private employer.[84] The *Weber* decision is a gross and blatant refusal by the Court to enforce the legislative will. Its usurpation of legislative power easily justifies Mr. Justice Rehnquist's use of Orwellian terms.[85]

The potential for disaster may, however, be even greater in the Court's initial response, in the *Detroit Edison* case, to a new line of attack on valid tests in education and employment. Frank special preferences for members of particular racial or ethnic groups violate the Congressional intent expressed in Title VII. The new

---

[81] *Id.* at 1113, n.20.

[82] See Lerner, *The Supreme Court and the APA, AERA, NCME Test Standards*, 33 Am. Psychol. 915 (1978).

[83] 427 U.S. 273 (1976).

[84] If the definition of voluntary action used in these cases were applied to criminal confessions, it would be possible to condone torture.

[85] 99 S. Ct. at 2736.

line of attack involves efforts to reject clear and compelling empirical demonstrations of the validity of particular tests in particular situations by attacking the face validity of those tests on an item-by-item basis.

Such attacks are utterly unjustified. Arguments about the face validity of test items are relevant only when test use has been justified on the basis of face validity. When test use has been justified by the much more stringent standards for any of the three types of formal validity currently recognized by the American Psychological Association and its sister organizations,[86] attacks on face validity are, in effect, attempts to refute empirical data about reality with suppositions or opinions about what reality ought to be. Such attacks have occurred with increasing frequency in recent years,[87] but not in court, because to mount such an attack in court, it would be necessary first to gain access to all of the actual test items used in the particular administration of the test under attack, and, until 1979, there was no legal way to do that with secure tests in current use. Obtaining sample items from prior administrations of major tests was rarely a problem. Reputable producers of widely used, nonclinical selection tests routinely release such information to give all potential test takers an equal opportunity to familiarize themselves with the types of questions involved. But the secrecy of current items on secure tests has been closely and effectively guarded by organizations and individuals producing those tests and by all psychometric experts bound by the Code of Ethics of the American Psychological Association.[88] Professionals did this themselves, without need of legal compulsion, in order to prevent the kinds of unfairness and invalidity that would result if some test takers had advance information about "live" test items while others did not. Copyright laws buttressed these voluntary professional efforts to safeguard test security by enabling test developers to sue anyone who obtained illegitimate access to actual test items and made illegal

---

[86] The three types are content validity, criterion validity, and construct validity. See note 5 *supra;* Lerner, note 7 *supra*, at 297–300, for an analysis of the most common misconceptions about the validation process and the relationship between different types of validity.

[87] See notes 72 and 77 *supra;* see also HOFFMAN, THE TYRANNY OF TESTING (1964); and HOUTS (ed.), THE MYTH OF MEASURABILITY (1977).

[88] See Principle 8, AMERICAN PSYCHOLOGICAL ASSOCIATION, ETHICAL STANDARDS FOR PSYCHOLOGISTS (1977 revision).

use of them. As indicated, legislation enacted in New York has changed this situation for the worse, and the legislation currently being proposed in Congress[89] could do even greater damage.

In *Detroit Edison*, decided on March 5, 1979, the Supreme Court dealt with questions of test security and subject confidentiality for the first time. Its holding, while vindicating those interests, did so on too narrow and precarious a basis to reassure any member of the scientific community. The original plaintiff in the *Detroit Edison* case was a union representing ten disgruntled workers who had been denied promotion to the job of instrument person B at the company's Monroe, Michigan, plant because they had failed to achieve passing scores on a test used to assess the competence of applicants for that skilled job. The union challenged the company's use of the test, demanding and receiving extensive data on the rationale for relying upon it to screen applicants for the job in question. The data that the company released established three facts beyond dispute: (1) The test at issue was a formally validated test. (2) The method used to validate it was the criterion validity method. (3) The criterion utilized was clearly job related. In other words, the company had chosen to eschew the easy path of face validity altogether. It had spent considerable amounts of time, money, and effort to meet the much more stringent scientific standards laid down by relevant professional groups, and it had succeded. It had solid empirical evidence showing that workers who failed the test were not, in fact, competent to perform the job of instrument person B, and it was willing to share that evidence with the union without judicial compulsion.

Union officials, backed by the NLRB[90] and by a divided Sixth Circuit Court of Appeals,[91] responded by demanding that the company also give union representatives all of the actual test questions and answers and that it release lists pairing the names of test takers with their score, without permission of those tested. Because actual test questions and answers were relevant only to an attack on the face validity of the test, release of these data to union officials could have served no legitimate union purpose and it would have had major adverse effects on the company and its psychologists. Had

[89] See, *e.g.*, H.R. 4949, 96th Cong., 2d Sess. (1978).

[90] 218 N.L.R.B. 1024 (1975).

[91] N.L.R.B. v. Detroit Edison Co., 560 F.2d 722 (1977).

the company agreed to breach test security, it would have destroyed the test's fairness and validity, making its continued legitimate use impossible. Further, it would have put its own psychologists in the position of having either to refuse and resign or to violate the Code of Ethics of the APA which forbids breaches of test security and of subject confidentiality.[92]

The company refused to do that and, ultimately, the Supreme Court upheld its right to refuse in a five-to-four decision. But the Court explicitly refused to do so by holding that the union had no legitimate right to the data it sought, substantial or insubstantial. Instead, the Court chose to reach its decision by weighing and balancing the interests at stake and deciding that the company's interest in test security and subject confidentiality outweighed the union's interest in obtaining these data in this particular case and that the NLRB had therefore exceeded its remedial discretion in ordering disclosure.

In other words, the Court reached its decision by weighing legitimate and illegitimate interests on the same subjective scale and, while it reached the right results in this particular case, it refused to do so on the basis of a legal principle or rule that would prohibit similar attacks on similar tests in future situations. The rule the Court should have adopted is the obvious and fair one: arguments about the face validity of test items are relevant only when test use has been justified on that basis; data relevant to such an attack must be released only in those situations.

Such a rule would provide a neutral, principled basis for consistent judicial decision making in future cases. It could not be used as a basis for capricious and arbitrary decisions for or against future plaintiffs or defendants because it would establish a precedent presumably binding on the Court that issued it and on all lower courts and agencies governed by its rulings. The Court in the *Detroit Edison* case rejected this principled course, choosing instead to leave the judiciary with the sort of unlimited illicit discretion Mr. Justice Frankfurter warned against when he said "We do not sit like a Kadi under a tree dispensing justice."[93]

The unfortunate truth is that the Justices of our current Court do something very much like that in a distressingly high proportion of their cases, making the law itself more and more unstable, un-

---

[92] See Principle 5, note 88 *supra*.

[93] Terminiello v. Chicago, 337 U.S. 1, 11 (1949).

predictable, and chaotic and increasing the already alarming tension between this Court's ideas about law and those of prior Courts and of the country as a whole.[94] The next decade is likely to be an extremely difficult one, nowhere more so than in the area of employment discrimination law.

In that key area, the Court concluded its 1979 term by putting its seal of approval on open, special preferences for members of some groups at the expense of others, and by leaving the door wide open to illegitimate attacks on the use of valid tests of competence for members of any group. New coalitions devoted to equal results for the competent and incompetent of both races are currently organizing themselves to march through that door, claiming to speak for black Americans though public opinion poll data have repeatedly and consistently shown that most black Americans, like most white Americans, are realistic enough to value competence and objective, even-handed appraisals of it, rejecting special preferences and lower standards for members of any group.[95]

Popular values notwithstanding, empirical data already make it unmistakably clear that standards have declined markedly over the last decade and a half, in academic performance and, increasingly, in economic productivity, as well as in a number of other significant areas.[96] And there is growing evidence indicating that the relationship between the proper use of valid employment screening devices and economic productivity is an unusually strong and close one.[97] All in all, it seems reasonable to suggest that the Court's efforts will shrink the great American pie at an even faster rate in the coming decade, leaving little to distribute to anyone, competent or incompent, black or white.

---

[94] Currently, the Supreme Court ranks low in popular esteem, down more than fifty points since 1949, when it won the approval of 83.4 percent of the population. In 1975, only 32.6 percent of the population approved of the job the Court was doing (according to Harris survey results for the same year, only 28 percent). See JANOWITZ, THE LAST HALF-CENTURY: SOCIAL CHANGE AND POLITICS IN AMERICA (1978).

[95] See note 60 *supra*.

[96] See Lerner, *Tests and Standards Today: Attacks, Counterattacks and Responses*, in LENNON (ed.), IMPACT OF SOCIAL CHANGE ON TESTING (in press); Wirtz, note 78 *supra;* Wynne, *Behind the Discipline Problem: Youth Suicide as a Measure of Alienation*, 59 PHI DELTA KAPPAN 307 (1978); see also Gross, *How to Kill a College*, SATURDAY REV. 13 (February 1978); HANDLIN & HANDLIN, FACING LIFE: YOUTH AND THE FAMILY IN AMERICAN HISTORY 258–89 (1971); RIESMAN, GUSFIELD, & GAMSON, ACADEMIC VALUES AND MASS EDUCATION ix–x (1975).

[97] See note 59 *supra*.

WALTER HELLERSTEIN

HUGHES v. OKLAHOMA: THE COURT, THE COMMERCE CLAUSE, AND STATE CONTROL OF NATURAL RESOURCES

The Supreme Court's recent Commerce Clause opinions reflect an apparent effort to rationalize and modernize the analytical framework for delineating the implied restraints that the Clause imposes on state legislation. In the state tax field, the Court has articulated a coherent set of criteria controlling the validity of state taxes on interstate commerce[1] and has discarded doctrine inconsistent with these standards.[2] In the state regulatory context, the Court has likewise enunciated meaningful decisional principles governing the con-

---

Walter Hellerstein is Associate Professor of Law at the University of Georgia.

Author's Note: The author would like to thank Gregory S. Alexander, Jerome R. Hellerstein, Paul M. Kurtz, D. Robert Lohn, and Michael Wells for their helpful comments on an earlier draft of this article.

[1] Japan Line, Ltd. v. County of Los Angeles, 99 S. Ct. 1813, 1819–20 (1979); Department of Revenue v. Association of Washington Stevedoring Cos., 435 U.S. 734, 750 (1978); Complete Auto Transit, Inc. v. Brady, 430 U.S. 274, 279, 287 (1977); Colonial Pipeline Co. v. Traigle, 421 U.S. 100, 108 (1975). See also note 30 *infra*.

[2] Department of Revenue v. Association of Washington Stevedoring Cos., 435 U.S. 734 (1978), *overruling* Joseph v. Carter & Weekes Stevedoring Co., 330 U.S. 422 (1947), and Puget Sound Stevedoring Co. v. State Tax Commission, 302 U.S. 90 (1937); Complete Auto Transit, Inc. v. Brady, 430 U.S. 274 (1977), *overruling* Spector Motor Service, Inc. v. O'Connor, 340 U.S. 602 (1951).

stitutionality of state regulations affecting interstate commerce[3] and has applied them without substantial concern for their impact on its precedents of an earlier era.[4] To be sure, not all of the Court's contemporary Commerce Clause opinions fit easily into the suggested pattern,[5] and what appears as a clear pattern may be only a haphazard arrangement. *Hughes v. Oklahoma*[6] emerges, however, as yet another piece in the developing mosaic of the Court's Commerce Clause jurisprudence.

I. The Hughes Decision

A. THE FACTS AND PROCEEDINGS BELOW

The essential facts in the case were simple and undisputed. Through its Wildlife Conservation Code,[7] Oklahoma had established a statutory scheme governing the acquisition, transportation, and sale of minnows in the State. The Code provided for the licensing of persons seeking to seine, transport, or sell minnows in the State for commercial purposes.[8] It imposed no restriction on the number of minnows a person so licensed was permitted to take from state waters. The Code stipulated, however, that "[n]o person may transport or ship minnows for sale outside the state which were seined or procured within the waters of this state."[9] The prohibition was inapplicable to persons "leaving the state possessing three (3) dozen or less minnows" or to the "sale and shipment of minnows raised in a regularly licensed commercial minnow hatchery."[10] In substance, then, the statute forbade the transportation for out-of-state

---

[3] City of Philadelphia v. New Jersey, 437 U.S. 617, 624 (1978); Raymond Motor Transportation, Inc. v. Rice, 434 U.S. 429, 441–42 (1978); Hunt v. Washington Apple Advertising Commission, 432 U.S. 333, 352–54 (1977); Great Atlantic & Pacific Tea Co. v. Cottrell, 424 U.S. 366, 371–72 (1976); Pike v. Bruce Church, Inc., 397 U.S. 137, 142 (1970).

[4] City of Philadelphia v. New Jersey, 437 U.S. 617, 621–23 (1978); Raymond Motor Transportation Co. v. Rice, 434 U.S. 429, 442–43 (1978).

[5] See, e.g., Moorman Manufacturing Co. v. Blair, 437 U.S. 267 (1978) (taxation); Exxon Corp. v. Governor of Maryland, 437 U.S. 117 (1978) (regulation).

[6] 99 S. Ct. 1727 (1979).

[7] Okla. Stat. Ann. tit. 29 (West 1974).

[8] *Id.* at § 4–116. Persons acquiring and transporting minnows for their own use and children under sixteen selling minnows in the counties of their residence were exempt from these licensing requirements under specified conditions, as were retailers selling lawfully acquired minnows. *Ibid.*

[9] *Id.* at § 4–115(B).

[10] *Id.* at § 4–115(B)(1), (2).

sale of large quantities of "natural" (as distinguished from hatchery-bred) minnows procured from Oklahoma waters. It did not impose any limitation on the disposition of hatchery-bred minnows, or on the procurement or sale of natural minnows within Oklahoma, or on the out-of-state transportation of natural minnows for purposes other than sale. Anyone convicted of violating these provisions was subject to a fine ranging from $100 to $200.[11]

William Hughes, a licensed minnow dealer of thirty years' standing under the laws of Texas, carried on a regular commercial minnow business near Wichita Falls, Texas, not far from the Oklahoma border. In the spring of 1976, Hughes purchased for $350 a load of natural minnows from an Oklahoma minnow dealer licensed as such under Oklahoma's Wildlife Conservation Code. On his way back to Wichita Falls with the load of minnows in his vehicle, Hughes was arrested by an Oklahoma Game Ranger. He was charged with "Unlawfully Transporting for Sale Outside of the State of Oklahoma Minnows Which Were Seined or Procured within the Waters of Oklahoma"[12] in violation of the Conservation Code. The parties submitted the evidence to the trial court upon stipulated facts; the court found Hughes guilty as charged and fined him $200.

On appeal, Hughes's sole assignment of error was that Oklahoma's ban on the exportation of minnows violated the Commerce Clause. He relied on the Supreme Court's decision in *Foster-Fountain Packing Co. v. Haydel*,[13] which struck down a Louisiana statute forbidding the shipment beyond the State of shrimp taken in Louisiana waters until the heads and shells had been removed. Because the statute permitted the out-of-state exportation of shrimp after their heads and shells had been removed (as well as the exportation of the heads and shells themselves), the Court in *Foster-Fountain* determined that the statute's "purpose is not to retain the shrimp for the use of the people of Louisiana; it is to favor the canning of the meat and the manufacture of bran in Louisiana."[14] It concluded that the law's effect was "directly," *i.e.*, impermissibly, "to obstruct and burden interstate commerce."[15] In so holding, the Court had

[11] *Id.* at §§ 4–115(D); 4–116(E).

[12] Hughes v. State, 572 P.2d 573, 574 (Okla. Crim. App. 1977).

[13] 278 U.S. 1 (1928). [14] *Id.* at 13. [15] *Ibid.*

to distinguish its earlier decision in *Geer v. Connecticut*,[16] which sustained over Commerce Clause objections a Connecticut statute forbidding the transportation outside the State of game birds lawfully killed within the State. The ground of distinction was that Connecticut had prevented the game from becoming an article of interstate commerce by requiring it to be retained for consumption or use in the State, whereas Louisiana allowed "its shrimp to be taken and all the products thereof to be shipped and sold in interstate commerce," thereby "releas[ing] its hold" on the shrimp and putting "an end to the trust upon which the State is deemed to own or control the shrimp for the benefit of its people."[17]

In *Hughes*, the Oklahoma Court of Criminal Appeals found *Geer* and its progeny rather than *Foster-Fountain* controlling. It reasoned:[18]

> The United States Supreme Court has held on numerous occasions that the wild animals and fish within a state's borders are, so far as capable of ownership, owned by the state in its sovereign capacity for the common benefit of all its people. Because of such ownership, and in the exercise of its police power, the state may regulate and control the taking, subsequent use and property rights that may be acquired therein. . . . Oklahoma law does not prohibit commercial minnow hatcheries within her borders from selling stock minnows to anyone, resident or nonresident, and minnows purchased therefrom may be freely exported. However, the law served to protect against the depletion of minnows in Oklahoma's natural streams through commercial exportation. No person is allowed to export natural minnows for sale outside of Oklahoma. Such a prohibition is not repugnant to the commerce clause.

B. THE SUPREME COURT'S OPINION

The Supreme Court reversed and held that the Oklahoma law violated the Commerce Clause.[19] Repudiating its decision in *Geer v. Connecticut*, the Court determined that Oklahoma's statutory scheme must be evaluated under the same criteria governing the validity of state regulation of other natural resources, and that, under these criteria, Oklahoma's law could not withstand constitutional scrutiny. Oklahoma never suggested and the Court never

---

[16] 161 U.S. 519 (1896).

[17] 278 U.S. at 13.

[18] 572 P.2d at 575.

[19] 99 S. Ct. 1727 (1979).

considered that Congress had, in fact, consented to the statute by making it unlawful for any person knowingly "to transport . . . in interstate or foreign commerce, any black bass and other fish, if such . . . transportation is contrary to the law of the State . . . from which such black bass or other fish is transported."[20] Indeed, a similar provision may be read as granting congressional consent to the result in *Geer* as well.[21] Thus, *Hughes* may well have been wrongly decided in light of Congress' broad power to consent to state laws that would, in the absence of such consent, impose an impermissible burden on interstate commerce.[22] In any event, *Hughes* retains its significance for purposes of the present inquiry as the most recent expression of the Court's views regarding the negative implications of the Commerce Clause.

1. *The overruling of Geer v. Connecticut.* The state court's reliance on *Geer* as a basis for sustaining Oklahoma's ban on the transportation of natural minnows for out-of-state sale was fully understandable. *Geer* had, after all, upheld over Commerce Clause objections a prohibition against the transportation beyond the State of game birds lawfully killed within it. Once the Supreme Court agreed to hear Hughes's appeal, however, it was apparent that a defense predicated on *Geer* would face rough going.

The Court's analysis in *Geer* was rooted in its understanding of "the earliest traditions [of] the right to reduce animals *ferae naturae* to possession,"[23] which it gleaned from a reading of Athenian,[24] Roman,[25] Salic,[26] feudal,[27] and English common law.[28] The Court had reasoned that wild game within a State, until reduced to possession, belonged to the people, who "owned" the game collectively for the common benefit of all;[29] that the State, as representative of its citizens, was invested with the authority to exercise the power

---

[20] 16 U.S.C. § 852 (1976); *cf.* United States v. Howard, 352 U.S. 212 (1957). I am indebted to Professor William Cohen of the Stanford Law School for bringing this point to my attention.

[21] See 18 U.S.C. § 43 (1976).

[22] Prudential Insurance Co. v. Benjamin, 328 U.S. 408, 434–36 (1946); In re Rahrer, 140 U.S. 545 (1891); see Southern Pacific Co. v. Arizona, 325 U.S. 761, 769 (1945).

[23] 161 U.S. at 522.

[24] *Ibid.*

[25] *Id.* at 522–23.

[26] *Id.* at 523–25.

[27] *Ibid.*

[28] *Id.* at 526–28.

[29] *Id.* at 529.

that was derived from this "common ownership" "as a trust for the benefit of the people";[30] that this power could be exercised not only to control the taking of game within the State but also to determine the nature of the property rights acquired in any game so taken;[31] that the power therefore could be employed "to keep the property, if the sovereign so chooses, always within its jurisdiction for every purpose";[32] and, that:[33]

> The power of the State to control the killing of and ownership in game being admitted, the commerce in game, which the state law permitted, was necessarily only internal commerce, since the restriction that it should not become the subject of external commerce went along with the grant and was part of it.

The Court in *Geer* proffered a second ground for its determination that Connecticut's embargo on the exportation of game did not offend the Commerce Clause. The statute represented an appropriate exercise of the State's police power derived from "the duty of the State to preserve for its people a valuable food supply."[34] The Court declared that the existence of this power was "equally conclusive"[35] of the outcome of the case as was the existence of state authority "derived from the common ownership of game and the trust for the benefit of its people which the State exercises in relation thereto."[36] From this one might conclude that the "police power" rationale was independent of the "common ownership" rationale. Yet in the next breath the Court inextricably linked the two theories in observing that the State's police power to protect its people against adulteration of food carried with it "the existence of a like power to preserve a food supply which belongs in common to all the people of the State which can only become the subject of ownership in a qualified way, and which can never be the object of commerce except with the consent of the State and subject to the conditions which it may deem best to impose for the public good."[37]

Whether *Geer* was predicated on one or two theories, its rationale (in either configuration) had been discredited by subsequent Su-

---

[30] *Ibid.*

[31] *Id.* at 530.

[32] *Ibid.*

[33] *Id.* at 532.

[34] *Id.* at 534.

[35] *Ibid.*

[36] *Ibid.*

[37] *Id.* at 535.

preme Court cases. The proposition that the State "owned" wild game within its borders for the common benefit of its citizens had been undermined by a series of decisions explicitly or implicitly rejecting such a contention. The Court had sustained the exercise of the federal treaty-making power over migratory birds in the face of a State's claim that this interfered with the State's ownership and control of wild animals within its boundaries, and it had remarked in passing that "[t]o put the claim of the State upon title is to lean upon a slender reed."[38] It had invalidated a prohibition on the exportation of shrimp taken within state waters until their heads and shells had been removed, dismissing arguments advanced by the State on the basis of its alleged ownership of the shrimp.[39] It had struck down a state tax and regulatory scheme that discriminated against out-of-state commercial shrimp fishermen, disparaging the "ownership theory" as a legal fiction that stood as a proxy for other values the State might legitimately pursue, but not by discriminatory means.[40] And, most recently, the Court had repudiated *Geer's* reasoning by making short shrift of the argument that a State's purported ownership of fish swimming in its territorial waters empowered it to forbid nonresident federal licensees from fishing there:[41]

> A State does not stand in the same position as the owner of a private game preserve and it is pure fantasy to talk of "owning" wild fish, birds, or animals. Neither the States nor the Federal Government, any more than a hopeful fisherman or hunter, has title to these creatures until they are reduced to possession by skillful capture. . . . The "ownership" language of cases such as those cited by appellant must be understood as no more than a 19th-century legal fiction expressing "the importance to its people that a State have power to preserve and regulate the exploitation of an important resource." . . . Under modern analysis, the question is simply whether the State has exercised its police power in conformity with the federal laws and Constitution.

Indeed, under the weight of these precedents, the State in *Hughes*

[38] Missouri v. Holland, 252 U.S. 416, 434 (1920).

[39] Foster-Fountain Packing Co. v. Haydel, 278 U.S. 1, 11–13 (1928). See text *supra*, at notes 13–17.

[40] Toomer v. Witsell, 334 U.S. 385, 339–406 (1948).

[41] Douglas v. Seacoast Products, Inc., 431 U.S. 265, 284–85 (1977) (citations omitted).

was forced to concede that "State 'ownership' may no longer be acceptable as a descriptive term of valid state interests in wildlife."[42]

Nor had the proposition that the States possessed the power (and, indeed, the duty) to conserve for their own citizens a valuable local food supply weathered the ravages of subsequent case law. The Court had held that States lacked the power to prohibit or limit the exportation of natural gas in the face of claims advanced by the States that they possessed "[t]he right to conserve, or . . . reserve, the resources of the State for the use of the inhabitants of the State, present and future."[43] The Court reasoned in these cases that whatever police power the States might have to conserve natural resources located within their borders, this power could not be exercised to limit the shipment or sale of privately owned resources in interstate commerce merely because they were needed by in-state consumers.[44] *Geer* and its progeny were distinguished on the ground that they involved resources deemed to be owned by the State[45]—a proposition whose erosion was continuing apace with the dismantling of the broadly conceived conservation rationale. Moreover, as if events were conspiring to augur the impending demise of *Geer*, the Court had recently been provided with an opportunity to match its unkind remarks about *Geer's* ownership rationale with similarly critical comments about its conservation rationale. In holding that a State lacked power under the Commerce Clause to forbid the transportation of waste from other States into privately owned landfills within the State, the Court cited favorably its "decisions holding that a State may not accord its own inhabitants a preferred right of access over consumers in other States to natural resources located within its borders."[46]

In *Hughes*, the Court was faced with the first case "in modern times to present facts essentially on all fours with *Geer*."[47] Having traced the deterioration of *Geer's* analytical underpinnings, the Court had no qualms about administering the coup de grâce: "We

[42] Brief for Appellee, p. 6.

[43] West v. Kansas Natural Gas Co., 221 U.S. 229, 250 (1911); Pennsylvania v. West Virginia, 262 U.S. 553, 598–99 (1923).

[44] *West*, 221 U.S. at 255; *Pennsylvania*, 262 U.S. at 599.

[45] *West*, 221 U.S. at 253–54. The majority opinion in *Pennsylvania*, 262 U.S. 553, did not allude to *Geer*, although Justice Holmes relied upon it in dissent. *Id.* at 601.

[46] City of Philadelphia v. New Jersey, 437 U.S. 617, 627 (1978).

[47] 99 S. Ct. at 1736.

now conclude that challenges under the Commerce Clause to state regulations of wild animals should be considered according to the same general rule applied to state regulations of other natural resources, and therefore expressly overrule *Geer*."[48]

2. *The Court's opinion on the merits.* Once it had discarded the "common ownership" and local conservation rationales underlying *Geer*, the Court was compelled to draw upon other principles of adjudication to resolve the controversy before it. Here the Court turned to a formulation of the criteria governing the constitutionality of state regulations affecting interstate commerce that has become familiar reading to students of the Court's recent Commerce Clause opinions:[49]

> Where the statute regulates evenhandedly to effectuate a legitimate local public interest, and its effects on interstate commerce are only incidental, it will be upheld unless the burden imposed on such commerce is clearly excessive in relation to the putative local benefits. . . . If a legitimate local purpose is found, then the question becomes one of degree. And the extent of the burden that will be tolerated will of course depend on the nature of the local interest involved, and on whether it could be promoted as well with a lesser impact on interstate activities.

Under these standards, the Court easily concluded that Oklahoma's statutory scheme failed to pass constitutional muster. Rather than regulating "evenhandedly," the law discriminated on its face against interstate commerce by blocking the flow of such commerce in natural minnows at the State's borders.[50] After suggesting that discrimination of this nature might give rise to "a virtually *per se* rule of invalidity,"[51] the Court nevertheless proceeded to

---

[48] *Ibid.*

[49] Pike v. Bruce Church, Inc., 397 U.S. 137, 142 (1970) (citations omitted), quoted in *Hughes*, 99 S. Ct. at 1734.

[50] See text *supra*, at notes 7–11. The flow was not blocked entirely; a trickle—three dozen or less natural minnows—could be exported from the State with impunity. *Ibid.*

[51] *Hughes*, 99 S. Ct. at 1737. The Court did not actually use the quoted phrase in *Hughes*, but it had employed the phrase in practically the identical context in City of Philadelphia v. New Jersey, 437 U.S. 617, 624 (1978): "where simple economic protectionism is effected by state legislation a virtually *per se* rule of invalidity has been erected. . . . The clearest example of such legislation is a law that overtly blocks the flow of interstate commerce at a State's borders." The Court in *Hughes* explicitly referred to this passage from *City of Philadelphia*. 99 S. Ct. at 1737.

evaluate the justification offered by the State for the discrimination but only under "the strictest scrutiny of any purported legitimate local purpose and of the absence of nondiscriminatory alternatives."[52]

The "legitimate local purpose" advanced by Oklahoma in defense of the statute was its function as a "conservation measure."[53] The Court acknowledged that the State's interest in preserving the ecological balance in its waters by restricting the removal of large numbers of minnows might well qualify as a legitimate local purpose.[54] Indeed, the Court was willing to characterize such interests as "similar to the States' interests in protecting the health and safety of their citizens,"[55] interests to which it has traditionally accorded considerable deference.[56] But the question under the rubric articulated by the Court was one of degree, and whether the burden imposed by the State on interstate commerce was constitutionally tolerable would turn not only on the local interest involved but also on the availability of less burdensome means for achieving the same ends. The Court was firm in its conviction that the Oklahoma law failed on this score. The State had "chosen to 'conserve' its minnows in the way that most overtly discriminates against interstate commerce . . . even though nondiscriminatory alternatives would seem likely to fulfill the State's purported legitimate local purpose more effectively."[57] Thus Oklahoma had, with a commercially insignificant exception, flatly proscribed the exportation of natural minnows for out-of-state sale, even though it might have pursued its objectives as well by restricting the number of minnows licensed dealers could take from state waters or by limiting the way in which such minnows might be disposed of in the State.[58] While the Commerce Clause does not require the States to fine tune their legislation to minimize any conceivable impact it might have on interstate commerce, Oklahoma's effort to conserve its minnows reflected, at best, an unjustifiable indifference to such impact.

The State attempted to defend the means by which it had chosen

---

[52] 99 S. Ct. at 1737.

[53] Brief for Appellee, p. 2.

[54] 99 S. Ct. at 1737.

[55] *Ibid.*

[56] Pike v. Bruce Church, Inc., 397 U.S. 137, 143 (1970).

[57] 99 S. Ct. at 1737.

[58] *Ibid;* see text *supra,* at notes 7–11.

to implement its legislative ends by contending that the statutory scheme embodied a closer fit between means and ends than might appear at first blush. Oklahoma argued that the ban on commercial exportation was the most effective means to maintain the desired ecological balance. The prohibition on transportation for out-of-state sale, it was claimed, would assure that minnows seined and sold in Oklahoma would be "returned to Oklahoma waters in the form of bait," a procedure that served to "accommodate the recreational fisherman, while preserving the habitat and balance of aquatic wildlife provided by nature."[59] The Court dismissed this suggestion in a footnote.[60] It observed that this theory, which the State was advancing for the first time on appeal, was predicated on factual assumptions that were unsupported by the record, and it characterized the argument as a "*post-hoc* rationalization."[61] The State's "bare assertion"[62] was wholly inadequate to overcome the presumptive invalidity of a facially discriminatory statute.

Mr. Justice Rehnquist dissented from the Court's decision in an opinion joined by the Chief Justice. Mr. Justice Rehnquist had no quarrel with the Court's abandonment of the "common ownership" doctrine of *Geer*. He would, however, have sustained the Oklahoma statute relying on the principles underlying *Geer's* "alternative basis"—"that a State, in the exercise of its police power, could act to preserve for its people a valuable food supply, even though interstate commerce was remotely and indirectly affected."[63] Apart from the technical dispute over the independent significance of the *Geer* Court's alternative rationale,[64] the crux of the disagreement between the majority and dissenting opinions was the weight each

---

[59] Brief for Appellee, p. 3.

[60] 99 S. Ct. at 1737 n.20.

[61] *Ibid.*

[62] *Ibid.*

[63] *Id.* at 1738 n.3.

[64] Mr. Justice Rehnquist was of the view that the *Geer* Court's "police power" rationale was independent of its "common ownership" rationale. In light of his views regarding the scope of this police power, see 99 S. Ct. at 1739–40 and text *infra*, at note 65, he saw no reason to overrule *Geer*. The majority, on the other hand, relying on the *Geer* Court's failure to distinguish clearly between the premises underlying the two rationales, see text *supra*, at note 37, believed that the "police power" rationale was simply a corollary of the "common ownership" rationale. 99 S. Ct. at 1732 n.6. The majority also believed, however, that the "alternative basis" of *Geer* (as quoted *supra*, in the text above and at note 34), even if viewed independently, had failed to survive subsequent Supreme Court decisions. See 99 S. Ct. at 1732 n.6 and text *supra*, at notes 43–46.

gave the State's interest in conservation and the view each held of what constitutes discrimination against interstate commerce. Mr. Justice Rehnquist, unlike the majority, would have permitted the State's "special interest" in preserving wildlife to prevail over Commerce Clause objections unless it represented "a naked attempt to discriminate against out-of-state enterprises in favor of in-state business unrelated to any purpose of conservation."[65] Consistent with this view, he found no discrimination in the Oklahoma scheme because the proscription on exportation applied to residents and nonresidents alike, did not protect residents from out-of-state competition, and was not employed as a means of inducing nonresident minnow exporters to shift their business operations into the regulating State. For the majority, by contrast, the fact that the state regulation substantially obstructed the flow of interstate commerce was in itself sufficient to condemn the regulation– or at least render it highly suspect–regardless of whether the obstruction had a differential economic impact on in-state and out-of-state interests.

Mr. Justice Rehnquist carried his dispute with the majority one step further by asserting, in light of the fact that hatchery-bred minnows were freely available for exportation, that the record did not support a determination that interstate commerce in minnows had been blocked by the Oklahoma legislation. In substance, Mr. Justice Rehnquist was willing to sustain the statute failing proof by Hughes that the purchase of hatchery-bred rather than natural minnows would have been less desirable, more costly, or otherwise burdensome to his business operations. Mr. Justice Rehnquist would thus have stood the majority's analysis on its head: while the Court, having found discrimination on the face of a statute, would impose upon the State the burden of demonstrating the absence of less discriminatory means for accomplishing the same ends, he would impose upon a person subject to a discriminatory statute the burden of demonstrating the absence of equally efficient alternatives to avoid its impact.

Viewing the Court's decision in *Hughes* in isolation, one would

---

[65] 99 S. Ct. at 1740. The "Commerce Clause objections" referred to in the text are those based on the negative implications of the Clause unimplemented by congressional legislation. Mr. Justice Rehnquist recognized that state regulations for the protection of wildlife would have to yield under other standards, to conflicting federal statutes and treaties as well as to the strictures of the Fourteenth Amendment. *Ibid.*

be hard pressed to conclude that it represented a case of much significance. It merely abandoned some quaint and antiquated doctrine about state "ownership" of wild animals to bring the law governing state regulation of such creatures into conformity with modern thinking about the constraints imposed by the Commerce Clause on state regulation of other matters. There are, however, at least two aspects of the *Hughes* decision that warrant further consideration. First, *Hughes* is the most recent of a series of Supreme Court opinions dealing with the limitations that the Commerce Clause imposes on state regulation, and its import may be more fully appreciated when viewed against the background of the Court's contemporary doctrine in this area. Second, *Hughes* is a case about state control over natural resources, a subject whose importance needs no emphasis in an era preoccupied with energy and the environment.

II. Commerce Clause Restraints on State Regulation: General Principles

It is a commonplace of modern Commerce Clause analysis that the Court, in delineating the implied limitations that the Clause imposes on state legislation, is engaged in a delicate balancing of state and national interests.[66] The critical analytical problem, therefore, is to determine how the accommodation between competing demands of national economic unity and legitimate state policy is reached. The Court's recent Commerce Clause opinions—of which *Hughes* is the latest—suggest that the balancing process is being undertaken in a more consistent fashion than in the past.

It was in 1970 that the Court first articulated the formulation of Commerce Clause principles to which it has returned with remarkable regularity ever since. In *Pike v. Bruce Church, Inc.*,[67] an Arizona official had issued an order prohibiting a company from transporting Arizona-grown cantaloupes to California because they had not been packed according to the requirements of an Arizona statute. The company had been conducting its packing operations in Cali-

[66] This contemporary understanding has been shaped not only by scholarly commentary, see Dowling, *Interstate Commerce and State Power*, 27 Va. L. Rev. 1, 21–28 (1940); Dowling, *Interstate Commerce and State Power—Revised Version*, 47 Colum. L. Rev. 547, 550–552 (1947); Freund, *Umpiring the Federal System*, 54 Colum. L. Rev. 561 (1954); but by judicial opinions as well. See, *e.g.*, Southern Pacific Co. v. Arizona, 325 U.S. 761, 770–71 (1945).

[67] 397 U.S. 137 (1970).

fornia, and it was stipulated that "the practical effect of the [state official's] order would be to compel the company to build packing facilities in . . . Arizona."[68] Recognizing that the order "affected" and "burdened" interstate commerce, and that the critical question was whether it did so unconstitutionally, the Court unanimously declared:[69]

> Although the criteria for determining validity of state statutes affecting interstate commerce have been variously stated, the general rule that emerges can be phrased as follows: Where the statute regulates evenhandedly to effectuate a legitimate local public interest, and its effects on interstate commerce are only incidental, it will be upheld unless the burden imposed on such commerce is clearly excessive in relation to the putative local benefits. If a legitimate local purpose is found, then the question becomes one of degree. And the extent of the burden that will be tolerated will of course depend on the nature of the local interest involved, and on whether it could be promoted as well with a lesser impact on interstate activities. Occasionally the Court has candidly undertaken a balancing approach in resolving these issues, but more frequently it has spoken in terms of "direct" and "indirect" effects and burdens.

Under these standards, the Arizona statute at issue failed to survive constitutional scrutiny. The State's interest in "promot[ing] and preserv[ing] the reputation of Arizona growers by prohibiting deceptive packaging"[70] carried insufficient weight to offset the nation's interest in unfettered interstate commerce.

As Professor Kurland has observed, *Pike* was just "[a]n old-fashioned Commerce Clause case" whose outcome was predictable, and the fact that it even elicited an opinion from the Court may well have been "testimony to the advocate's skills of appellant's counsel and little more."[71] Nevertheless, the doctrinal formulation enunciated in *Pike* was repeated in *Great Atlantic & Pacific Tea Co. v. Cottrell*,[72] which invalidated a Mississippi regulation banning

---

[68] *Id.* at 140.

[69] *Id.* at 142. (Citations omitted.)

[70] *Id.* at 143.

[71] Kurland, *Enter the Burger Court: The Constitutional Business of the Supreme Court, O.T. 1969*, 1970 SUPREME COURT REVIEW 1, 79–80 (1970). The editors of the *Harvard Law Review* did not deem the case worthy of comment in their Supreme Court Note for that year. Note, *The Supreme Court, 1969 Term,* 84 HARV. L. REV. 32 (1970).

[72] 424 U.S. 366, 371–72 (1976).

the sale in Mississippi of milk from other States unless such other States accepted Mississippi milk on a reciprocal basis. The *Pike* formulation was cited in *Hunt v. Washington State Apple Advertising Commission*,[73] which struck down a North Carolina statute requiring that apples marketed within the State in closed containers be graded only according to the applicable United States standard. It was quoted in *Raymond Motor Transportation, Inc. v. Rice*,[74] holding unconstitutional Wisconsin regulations governing the length and configuration of trucks permitted to travel on highways in the State. It was reiterated in *City of Philadelphia v. New Jersey*,[75] disapproving a New Jersey law prohibiting the importation into the State of most solid or liquid waste collected outside its territorial limits. And finally, it was set forth in *Hughes v. Oklahoma*, where it was characterized as "[t]oday's principle."[76] Indeed, with one exception,[77] this catalogue embraces every significant[78] opinion handed down by the Court over the last decade in which it has applied the substantive standards[79] derived from the negative implications of the Commerce Clause to state regulation of interstate commerce.[80]

---

[73] 432 U.S. 333, 350, 353 (1977).

[74] 434 U.S. 429, 441–42 (1978).

[75] 437 U.S. 617, 624 (1978).

[76] 99 S. Ct. at 1734.

[77] Exxon Corp. v. Governor of Maryland, 437 U.S. 117 (1978) (upholding over Commerce Clause objections a state statute forbidding producers or refiners of petroleum products from owning or operating retail gasoline stations in the state).

[78] I do not regard either Ray v. Atlantic Richfield Co., 435 U.S. 151 (1978), or Allenberg Cotton Co. v. Pittman, 419 U.S. 20 (1974), as "significant." *Ray* was a case dealing primarily with federal preemption of state law, see note 80 *infra*, and its treatment of the Commerce Clause claim was cursory. See 435 U.S. at 179–80. *Allenberg Cotton* involved the question whether a foreign corporation could be denied the right to sue in the State's courts because it had not qualified to do business there. The essential question was whether the corporation had sufficient contacts with the State to justify the qualification requirement, and the Court concluded that it did not. 419 U.S. at 33. Hence the refusal by the State to honor and enforce the contracts of an exclusively interstate business was deemed to violate the Commerce Clause. *Id.* at 34.

[79] In Hughes v. Alexandria Scrap Corp., 426 U.S. 794 (1976), the Court upheld a Maryland statutory scheme involving the payment to scrap processors by the States of cash bounties that favored in-state processors in alleged violation of the Commerce Clause. The Court held that the negative implications of the Commerce Clause were not applicable to the scheme at issue, although the Court did advert to the *Pike* formulation in passing. *Id.* at 804–05. The case is discussed in text *infra*, at notes 144–49.

[80] The generalization in the text is not directed to two categories of cases which sometimes share common doctrinal themes with, but are in significant respects distinct from, the cases that are the subject of this article. First, the Court's opinions

Before we consider what this development may signify, it may be useful as a preliminary matter to establish what it does not signify. First, it does not signify any substantive departure from the standards the Court has employed in the past in adjudicating Commerce Clause attacks on state regulation. Indeed, every one of the elements of the *Pike* test can be found explicitly or implicitly in many of the Court's prior opinions.[81] Nor does adoption of the *Pike* test—if adoption it be—promise greater precision in judgment or predictability of outcomes than in the past. The Commerce Clause balance will continue to be struck substantially as it has always been struck

---

addressing Commerce Clause limitations on state taxation may refer to the regulatory cases and the principles underlying them. See, *e.g.*, Boston Stock Exchange v. State Tax Commission, 429 U.S. 318, 328–29, 335–36 (1977). Nevertheless, the controversies in this area frequently involve issues that are unique to the exercise of state tax power, see generally HELLERSTEIN & HELLERSTEIN, STATE AND LOCAL TAXATION, CASES AND MATERIALS 237–335, 391–454, 662–92 (4th ed. 1978), and generally cannot be fruitfully assimilated with the regulatory cases for purposes of analysis. It might be noted, however, that the Court has enunciated and reiterated a set of decisional principles governing the validity of state taxes on interstate commerce, a development that may loosely be seen as parallel to the development in the regulatory context. See *id.* at 249, 287; notes 1 & 2 *supra;* Blumstein, *Some Intersections of the Negative Commerce Clause and the New Federalism: The Case of Discriminatory State Income Tax Treatment of Out-of-State Tax-exempt Bonds,* 31 VAND. L. REV. 473 (1978); Hellerstein, *State Taxation and the Supreme Court: Toward a More Unified Approach to Constitutional Adjudication?*, 75 MICH. L. REV. 1426, 1441–52 (1977).

Second, the Court's opinions confronting questions of federal preemption of state law may draw on principles one ordinarily associates with the negative implications of the Commerce Clause, especially in cases in which those implications might have provided an alternative ground of decision. See Douglas v. Seacost Products, Inc., 431 U.S. 265, 285–87 (1977); Morrison, *The Right to Fish for Seacoast Products: Gibbons v. Odgen Resurrected,* 1977 SUPREME COURT REVIEW 239, 246–50 (1977); Note, *Pre-emption as a Preferential Ground: A New Canon of Construction,* 12 STAN. L. REV. 208, 219–21 (1959). Nevertheless, federal preemption cases usually involve considerations quite different from those derived solely from the negative implications of the Commerce Clause, and the discrete analytical framework within which preemption cases are adjudicated reflects these differences. Jones v. Rath Packing Co., 430 U.S. 519, 525–26 (1977). To be sure, if a preemption claim is rejected, the Court must in many instances squarely confront a claim based entirely on the implied restraints of the Commerce Clause. See, *e.g.*, City of Philadelphia v. New Jersey, 437 U.S. 617, 620–21 n.4 (1978). But if the Commerce Clause claim has in substance been disposed of through the resolution of the preemption question, it is likely to be given short shrift. See, *e.g.*, Ray v. Atlantic Richfield Co., 435 U.S. 151, 179–80 (1978).

[81] See, *e.g.*, Huron Portland Cement Co. v. City of Detroit, 362 U.S. 440, 443 (1960). ("Evenhanded local regulation to effectuate a legitimate local interest is valid unless . . . unduly burdensome on . . . interstate commerce"); Dean Milk Co. v. City of Madison, 340 U.S. 349, 354 (1951) (State cannot exercise "its unquestioned power to protect the health and safety of its people" in a discriminatory fashion "if reasonable nondiscriminatory alternatives, adequate to conserve legitimate local interests, are available").

by conscientious judges, by a careful weighing of the competing state and national interests in light of all the facts and circumstances of the case.[82] Whether a consumer protection law limiting the grading of apples marketed in the State to "U.S. grades" satisfies the standards of *Pike*[83] can scarcely tell us whether a highway safety law forbidding the operation in the State of trucks longer than fifty-five feet will do so.[84] At most, the fluid criteria of *Pike* provide a framework for Commerce Clause analysis; they provide no litmus test of constitutionality.[85]

Still, it would be wrong to dismiss the Court's repeated invocation of the *Pike* formulation as merely an accident of opinion drafting or a prefunctory nod to doctrinal consistency. The Court's recent Commerce Clause opinions stress common themes that are reflected in the *Pike* formulation and the patterns of emphasis are worthy of note. First, the Court has been more forthright than in the past in accepting its own role of making the "delicate adjustment of the conflicting state and federal claims"[86] required by the Commerce Clause. The open acknowledgment that it is balancing interests[87] and the explicit weighing of the competing considerations[88] tend to illuminate the Commerce Clause calculus. As a result,

---

[82] FRANKFURTER, THE COMMERCE CLAUSE UNDER MARSHALL, TANEY AND WAITE 21–22, 33–34 (1964 ed.).

[83] *Hunt*, 432 U.S. 333.

[84] *Raymond Motor*, 434 U.S. 429.

[85] Indeed, a textual analysis of the *Pike* formulation raises many more questions than it answers. Thus the formulation does not tell us when a statute regulates "evenhandedly," see note 102 *infra* and accompanying text, nor what constitutes a "legitimate local public interest," nor what kinds of effects on interstate commerce are "incidental." It does not tell us whether a statute's failure to meet any one of these tests necessarily means that it is unconstitutional, or whether one must continue to balance state and national interests, but with altered presumptions. See text *infra*, at notes 103–06. And it does not tell us what respect is to be accorded to various local interests nor how to determine whether an alternative scheme might promote such interests "as well." See text *infra*, at notes 89–93 and 107–10. This is not meant to suggest, however, that the *Pike* formulation was designed to answer any of these questions. See generally Blasi, *Constitutional Limitations on the Power of States to Regulate the Movement of Goods in Interstate Commerce* 18–21, paper presented at the Conference on the Judicial Role in Economic Integration, Bellagio, Italy, July 17–21, 1979 (to be published).

[86] H.P. Hood & Sons, Inc. v. DuMond, 336 U.S. 525, 553 (1949) (Black, J., dissenting), quoted in *Cottrell*, 424 U.S. at 371, and *Raymond Motor*, 434 U.S. at 440.

[87] *Pike*, 397 U.S. at 142; *Cottrell*, 424 U.S. at 371–72; *Hunt*, 432 U.S. at 350, 353; *Raymond Motor*, 434 U.S. at 441–43; *City of Philadelphia*, 437 U.S. at 624; *Hughes*, 99 S. Ct. at 1734, 1736.

[88] *Pike*, 397 U.S. at 145–46; *Cottrell*, 424 U.S. at 375–76; *Hunt*, 432 U.S. at 351–54; *Raymond Motor*, 434 U.S. at 444–46; *Hughes*, 99 S. Ct. at 1737–78.

we may speak with more confidence about the narrow principle for which a particular case stands as well as the Court's view of the relative importance of various state interests. For example, it seems fair to conclude from *Pike* itself that a State's legitimate interest in preserving the reputation of a local industry is less substantial than the nation's interest in permitting business operations to be performed at their most efficient locations.[89] Moreover, we know that the State's interest asserted in *Pike* is less substantial in the Court's eyes than the State's interest in the safety, health, or employment of its citizens.[90] We have also been told in recent opinions that the State's interest in safety ranks high in the Court's constellation of values,[91] that highway safety may enjoy an especially exalted status,[92] and that the State's interests in conservation and protection of wild animals are "similar" to its interest in health and safety.[93]

Second, the Court's apparent conviction that the *Pike* formulation embodies the controlling criteria for adjudicating contemporary Commerce Clause controversies is evidenced by its willingness to repudiate doctrine and precedent inconsistent with the *Pike* standards. In *Raymond Motor*, the Court emphatically rejected Wisconsin's contention, based on earlier cases,[94] that "the general rule of *Pike* is not applicable to a State's regulation of motor vehicles in the promotion of safety"[95] and that "the inquiry under the Commerce Clause is ended without a weighing of the asserted safety purpose against the degree of interference with interstate commerce."[96] In *City of Philadelphia*, the Court rejected New Jersey's contention, based on earlier cases,[97] that innately harmful articles such as wastes were "not legitimate subjects of trade and commerce"[98] and therefore fall outside the pale of Commerce Clause

---

[89] *Pike*, 397 U.S. at 143, 145–46.

[90] *Id.* at 143, 146.

[91] *Raymond Motor*, 434 U.S. at 443.

[92] *Ibid.*

[93] *Hughes*, 99 S. Ct. at 1737.

[94] *E.g.*, South Carolina State Highway Department v. Barnwell Bros., 303 U.S. 177 (1938).

[95] *Raymond Motor*, 434 U.S. at 442.

[96] *Id.* at 443. This was not the first time the Court had rejected such a claim. See Bibb v. Navajo Freight Lines, 359 U.S. 520, 528–29 (1959). As to the application of "the general rule of *Pike*" in the highway safety context, see note 118 *infra*.

[97] *E.g.*, Bowman v. Chicago & Northwestern R. Co., 125 U.S. 465 (1888).

[98] *Id.* at 489, quoted in *City of Philadelphia*, 437 U.S. at 622.

protection and the general principles set forth in *Pike*. "All objects of interstate trade merit Commerce Clause protection; none is excluded by definition at the outset."[99] And in *Hughes*, the Court overruled *Geer* and thus brought Commerce Clause challenges to state regulation of wild animals under "the same general rule applied to state regulatio[n] of other natural resources,"[100] namely, the rule of *Pike*.[101]

Third, the Court has focused considerable attention on two substantive aspects of the *Pike* formulation in resolving the disputes before it. The first is one that has always been a critical factor in Commerce Clause analysis: whether the state law, on its face or in effect, regulates "evenhandedly." Although there is nothing in its opinions to suggest that the Court is drawing brighter lines than in the past between "evenhanded" and discriminatory legislation,[102] the Court has made it clear that when, in its judgment, a state law fails to accord "evenhanded" treatment to interests protected by the Commerce Clause, the consequences are pratically inevitable. Thus when a state law "overtly blocks the flow of interstate commerce at a State's borders,"[103] "a virtually *per se* rule of invalidity has been erected."[104] At the very least, once a determination is made that a state law discriminates against interstate commerce, the State is under a heavy burden to demonstrate that the local interest allegedly justifying the discrimination could not be effectuated by less discriminatory means.[105] If, on the other hand, the Court determines that a statute regulates "evenhandedly," its chances of surviving constitutional scrutiny are greatly enhanced.[106]

The other substantive aspect of the *Pike* formulation which has played a key role in recent Commerce Clause cases is the Court's searching evaluation of the alternatives available to the State to achieve its purported objectives when the means the State has actu-

---

[99] *City of Philadelphia*, 437 U.S. at 622.

[100] *Hughes*, 99 S. Ct. at 1736.

[101] *Id.* at 1734.

[102] *Compare* Exxon Corp. v. Governor of Maryland, 437 U.S. 117 (1978), *with Hunt*, 432 U.S. 333; see note 77 *supra;* Blumstein, note 80 *supra*, at 501–08; Note, *The Supreme Court, 1977 Term*, 92 Harv. L. Rev. 57, 66–75 (1978).

[103] *City of Philadelphia*, 437 U.S. at 624.

[104] *Ibid;* see also *Hughes*, 99 S. Ct. at 1737.

[105] *Hunt*, 432 U.S. at 353; *Hughes*, 99 S. Ct. at 1736.

[106] See text *supra*, at note 70.

ally chosen are found to be burdensome or discriminatory. The Court noted in *Cottrell* that Mississippi had "the obvious alternative of applying its own standards of inspection to shipments of milk from a nonreciprocating State,"[107] instead of completely barring such shipments. It noted in *Hunt* that North Carolina could effectuate its goal of protecting consumers from fraud or confusion "by permitting out-of-state growers to utilize state grades only if they also marked their shipments with the applicable U.S.D.A. label,"[108] instead of insisting on the exclusive use of the latter. And it indicated in *Hughes* that Oklahoma might have achieved its conservation objectives by limiting the numbers of minnows that could be taken from state waters by licensed dealers rather than through its choice of a method "that most overtly discriminates against interstate commerce."[109] Although the consideration of less burdensome alternatives is not novel Commerce Clause jurisprudence,[110] the Court seems to be weighing this factor in the balance with greater care and consistency than before.[111]

There are yet further indicia not directly identifiable with the *Pike* formulation which also suggest that the Court's reiteration of a single test embodying its approach to Commerce Clause questions is not mere happenstance. Four of the six decisions invoking the *Pike* standard were unanimous;[112] in the other two, only the Chief Justice and Mr. Justice Rehnquist dissented.[113] Moreover, the Court's opinions were written by four Justices who span the Court's ideological spectrum.[114] One may reasonably conclude that whatever is going on is going on with a substantial degree of consensus.

As I indicated earlier, it is important to resist the temptation to

---

[107] *Cottrell*, 424 U.S. at 377.

[108] *Hunt*, 432 U.S. at 354.

[109] *Hughes*, 99 S. Ct. at 1737.

[110] See note 81 *supra*.

[111] See Note, *State Environmental Protection Legislation and the Commerce Clause*, 87 HARV. L. REV. 1762, 1781 (1974).

[112] *Pike*, 397 U.S. 137; *Cottrell*, 424 U.S. 366 (Stevens, J., did not participate); *Hunt*, 432 U.S. 333 (Rehnquist, J., did not participate); *Raymond Motor*, 434 U.S. 429 (Blackmun, J., joined in the opinion of the Court, but wrote a concurring opinion joined by the Chief Justice and Justices Brennan and Rehnquist, see note 118 *infra;* Stevens, J., did not participate).

[113] *City of Philadelphia*, 437 U.S. 617, *Hughes*, 99 S. Ct. 1727.

[114] Chief Justice Burger (*Hunt*); Mr. Justice Stewart (*Pike* and *City of Philadelphia*); Mr. Justice Brennan (*Cottrell* and *Hughes*), and Mr. Justice Powell (*Raymond Motor*).

see more in the Court's opinions than is actually there. We must not forget that the Court has written Commerce Clause opinions in recent years that do not conform precisely to the suggested pattern;[115] that, in any event, the pattern embodies little that is new from a doctrinal standpoint;[116] and, more generally, that the Court in deciding Commerce Clause cases today is not doing anything fundamentally different from what it has always done in resolving these controversies.[117] Furthermore, even assuming that the *Pike* formulation embraces the criteria the Court has presently adopted for adjudicating Commerce Clause cases, the formulation is sufficiently imprecise that the result of its application to particular disputes remains highly uncertain.[118] Nevertheless, while there may be less in these opinions than meets the eye, they do attest to the Court's achievement of an increased measure of doctrinal consistency in an important area of constitutional law.

III. Commerce Clause Restraints on State Control of Natural Resources

If a new war is going to be fought over the control and exploitation of the nation's natural resources,[119] the Supreme Court will surely be an important battleground. Although such conflicts are nothing new to the nation or the Court,[120] they have acquired special significance in an age of anxiety over shortages of energy and other natural resources. The problem, of course, is not limited to controversies in which the States themselves are the face-to-face

[115] See notes 77–79 *supra*.

[116] See note 81 *supra*.

[117] See text *supra*, at notes 66 and 82.

[118] Indeed, Mr. Justice Blackmun's concurring opinion in *Raymond Motor*, 434 U.S. at 448–51, which three other Justices joined, supports the view that the Court's reliance on the *Pike* standard in different contexts does not mean that the Court is striking a similar balance in each case. Mr. Justice Blackmun opined that "if safety justifications are not illusory, the Court will not second-guess legislative judgment about their importance in comparison with related burdens on interstate commerce." *Id.* at 449. Of course, the general point seems implicit in the *Pike* formulation itself.

[119] See, *e.g.*, "The Second War between the States," Business Week 92–114 (May 17, 1976); but see Pack, *Frostbelt and Sunbelt: Convergence over Time*, 4 Intergovernmental Perspective 8–15 (Fall 1978).

[120] See, *e.g.*, Pennsylvania v. West Virginia, 262 U.S. 553 (1923); Kansas v. Colorado, 206 U.S. 76 (1907).

combatants, although we have recently witnessed our share of these.[121] More frequently the conflict arises, as in *Hughes v. Oklahoma*, in the form of a dispute between a private party seeking to use a resource and a State that has imposed limitations on its use.

Whatever questions there may once have been about the nature of the restraints that the Commerce Clause imposes on state control of natural resources, *Hughes* and other Supreme Court decisions of recent vintage[122] have enunciated a number of propositions that, for the moment at least, can be regarded as settled. Some of these propositions represent a simple application of the *Pike* formulation to natural resource regulation; others relate to specific issues arising in the natural resource context. The apparent harmony among members of the Court regarding the proper approach to many problems it has confronted in connection with natural resource regulation has not, however, led to a resolution of all of them.

A. STATE CONTROL OF PRIVATELY OWNED NATURAL RESOURCES

The implied restraints imposed by the Commerce Clause on state control of privately owned natural resources are in principle identical to the Commerce Clause restraints imposed on other aspects of state regulation. A statute regulating privately owned natural resources must do so "evenhandedly." It may not discriminate against interstate commerce by preventing the shipment of the resource outside the State,[123] by restricting access to the resource from outside the State,[124] or by providing that in-state demands for the resource be accorded preference over out-of-state demands.[125] The needs of local consumers for privately owned natural resources located within a State, even if they constitute legitimate local public interests, do not justify discriminatory legislation.[126] Although the Court could conceivably be persuaded to sustain such legislation in

---

[121] Maryland v. Louisiana, No. 83 Orig., Motion for leave to file bill of complaint granted, 99 S. Ct. 2876 (1979); City of Philadelphia v. New Jersey, 437 U.S. 617 (1978).

[122] *City of Philadelphia*, 437 U.S. 617; Hicklin v. Orbeck, 437 U.S. 518 (1978); Baldwin v. Fish & Game Commission, 436 U.S. 371 (1978); Douglas v. Seacoast Products, Inc., 431 U.S. 265 (1977).

[123] West v. Kansas Natural Gas Co., 221 U.S. 229 (1911).

[124] *City of Philadelphia*, 437 U.S. 617.

[125] Pennsylvania v. West Virginia, 262 U.S. 553 (1923).

[126] Foster-Fountain Packing Co. v. Haydel, 278 U.S. 1, 10 (1928).

the absence of nondiscriminatory alternatives capable of achieving the same objective, the burden of persuasion on the State in this context seems well nigh insuperable.[127]

Evenhanded regulation of privately owned natural resources, on the other hand, is quite likely to withstand Commerce Clause scrutiny. The States have a legitimate local interest in conserving natural resources located within their borders,[128] and it is an interest that ranks high in the Court's hierarchy of legitimate local purposes.[129] Since the burden that evenhanded regulation imposes on interstate commerce will be tolerated unless it is "clearly excessive in relation to the putative local benefits,"[130] such regulation of natural resources will generally be sustained even if its effect is to increase the price[131] or decrease the supply[132] of the resource.[133] The possibility that the regulation may be economically inefficient ordinarily gives rise to no substantial constitutional objection.[134] The Constitution did not enact Adam Smith's *Wealth of Nations* any more than it enacted Herbert Spencer's *Social Statics*.[135]

B. STATE CONTROL OF STATE-OWNED NATURAL RESOURCES

When the focus shifts from privately owned natural resources to those that are owned by the State, the Commerce Clause analysis becomes considerably more problematic. Indeed, in holding in *City*

---

[127] *Hughes*, 99 S. Ct. at 1736–38; *City of Philadelphia*, 437 U.S. at 626–27; see text *supra* at notes 103–05.

[128] Cities Service Gas Co. v. Peerless Oil & Gas Co., 340 U.S. 179 (1950).

[129] *Hughes*, 99 S. Ct. at 1737.

[130] *Pike*, 397 U.S. at 142.

[131] *Cities Service Gas Co.*, 340 U.S. 179.

[132] Parker v. Brown, 317 U.S. 341, 367 (1943).

[133] The results of a number of earlier cases are consistent with the statement in the text, although the reasoning underlying them does not reflect modern Commerce Clause analysis. For example, Commerce Clause objections to state statutes regulating the production of natural gas were routinely dismissed on the ground that production was a local activity distinct from interstate commerce. See, *e.g.*, Champlin Refining Co. v. Corporation Commission, 286 U.S. 210, 235 (1932). In these cases, the Court gave more serious attention to the claim that the statutes violated the resource owners' economic due process rights, but these claims too were generally rejected. See, *e.g.*, *ibid;* see also Summers, *The Modern Theory and Practical Application of Statutes for the Conservation of Oil and Gas*, 13 TULANE L. REV. 1 (1938); Note, *The Constitution and State Control of Natural Resources*, 64 HARV. L. REV. 642, 644 (1951).

[134] Exxon Corp. v. Governor of Maryland, 437 U.S. 117, 124–29 (1978); see TRIBE, AMERICAN CONSTITUTIONAL LAW, 25 (1979 Supp.).

[135] Lochner v. New York, 198 U.S. 45, 75 (1905) (Holmes, J., dissenting).

of Philadelphia that New Jersey could not bar the importation of out-of-state waste into privately owned landfills in the State, the Court explicitly declined to express any "opinion about New Jersey's power, consistent with the Commerce Clause, to restrict to state residents access to state-owned resources."[136] There is little direct guidance from the Court regarding the limitations that the Clause imposes on state control of such resources, and, as indicated below, what guidance there is does not all point in the same direction.

It must be stressed from the outset that the references to the State's ownership interest in a natural resource as an organizational principle should not be taken to suggest that the State's ownership interest is necessarily a critical or, in some instances, even a helpful concept for purposes of analyzing the limitations that the Commerce Clause imposes on state control of natural resources. As will be seen, the nature of the State's ownership interest in a natural resource is generally only one of several factors to be considered in the Commerce Clause calculus. Still, it does seem useful, at least as a starting point of analysis, to distinguish between two types of situations involving state control of natural resources that are not privately owned. First, there are cases in which the State possesses interests in natural resources which, if they were held by a private person, would be regarded as amounting to substantial ownership, as, for example, a State's interest in trees growing on state lands. Second, there are cases in which the State's interest, even if characterized in terms associated with ownership, would ordinarily be regarded as significantly more limited, as, for example, a State's interest in water running in intrastate streams.

If a State enjoys conventional ownership rights in a natural resource, two (sometimes overlapping) considerations emerge that seem to limit the application of the Commerce Clause principles established with regard to state control of privately owned natural resources. First, there is the notion that the Commerce Clause does not require a State to spend state funds, provide state services, or otherwise distribute its resources—whether natural or man-made—to in-state residents and businesses and out-of-state residents and businesses on a nondiscriminatory basis.[137] Second, when a State

[136] 437 U.S. at 627 n.6.

[137] See text *infra*, at notes 139–43.

is acting as a purchaser or seller in—as distinguished from a regulator of—the market, there is authority to suggest that it is not restrained by the negative implications of the Commerce Clause.[138] Both of these considerations and their impact on the Commerce Clause require further elaboration.

The proposition that the State may, at least in some circumstances, favor resident individuals and businesses in the distribution of state resources without violating the Constitution would seem to be a logical corollary of the basic assumptions underlying our federal system. "If," to take an example from *McCready v. Virginia*,[139] "Virginia had by law provided for the sale of its once vast public domain, and a division of the proceeds among its own people, no one, we venture to say, would contend that the citizens of other States had a constitutional right to the enjoyment of this privilege of Virginia citizenship."[140] Nor, it may be suggested, would anyone venture to say that such action would be proscribed by the negative implications of the Commerce Clause. Whatever limitations the Constitution in general and the Commerce Clause in particular impose on the ability of the States to discriminate in favor of local interests and to prevent nonresidents from becoming residents,[141] it is difficult to imagine these limitations extending so far as to bar the States from making any distinctions between in-state and out-of-state interests in distributing state resources without destroying the essential fabric of our constitutional plan. Although the principle that a State may favor its own in the distribution of state resources without running afoul of the Commerce Clause has arguably been accorded implicit sanction in the few cases that have presented the issue,[142] the Court has formally maintained a posture of neutrality regarding a State's "power, consistent with the Commerce Clause . . . to spend state funds solely on behalf of state residents and businesses."[143]

---

[138] See text *infra*, at notes 144–49.

[139] 94 U.S. 391 (1876).

[140] *Id.* at 395–96.

[141] And these are substantial. See text *infra*, at notes 159–76.

[142] Hughes v. Alexandria Scrap Corp., 426 U.S. 794 (1976), discussed in text *infra*, at notes 144–49; American Yearbook Co. v. Askew, 409 U.S. 904, *aff'g*, 339 F. Supp. 719 (M.D. Fla. 1972) (sustaining over Commerce Clause objections statute requiring that all public printing be done in the State).

[143] *City of Philadelphia*, 437 U.S. at 627 n.6.

The Court has been explicit, however, in approving the doctrine that the Commerce Clause imposes no restraints on the State when it enters the marketplace as a purchaser, and the State is therefore free under the Clause to favor in-state residents and businesses when spending state funds in that capacity. In *Hughes v. Alexandria Scrap Corp.*,[144] the Court upheld a Maryland statute designed to encourage the disposal of abandoned automobiles through payments of cash bounties to scrap processors. The Court found that the statute did not violate the Commerce Clause, even though the distribtuion of the bounties favored in-state interests.[145] The Court recognized that it was confronted with a "situation . . . without precedent in this Court."[146] It distinguished previous cases in which a State had sought to "interfer[e] with the natural functioning of the interstate market either through prohibition or through burdensome regulation"[147] from the case before it in which the State had simply "entered into the market itself" "as a purchaser, in effect, of a potential article of interstate commerce."[148] And it concluded that "[n]othing in the purposes animating the Commerce Clause prohibits a State . . . from participating in the market and exercising the right to favor its own citizens over others."[149]

Whatever may be the limits of these two related but analytically distinct principles,[150] their logic suggests that the Commerce Clause

---

[144] 426 U.S. 794 (1976).

[145] To be eligible for the bounty, scrap processors were required in some instances to provide documentation of title to the junk automobiles. The documentation requirements for out-of-state processors were more burdensome than those imposed on processors with plants in Maryland.

[146] 426 U.S. at 807.

[147] *Id.* at 806.

[148] *Id.* at 806, 808.

[149] *Id.* at 810. Most other courts that have considered Commerce Clause challenges to resident preferences in state purchasing or contracting have likewise rejected them, sometimes resting their conclusions on the perceived distinction between a State's governmental functions, which were thought to be subject to the negative strictures of the Commerce Clause, and its proprietary functions, which were not. See, *e.g.*, American Yearbook Co. v. Askew, 339 F. Supp. 719, 725 (M.D. Fla. 1971), *aff'd*, 409 U.S. 904 (1972); Schrey v. Allison Steel Manufacturing Co., 75 Ariz. 282 (1953); Tribune Printing & Binding Co. v. Barnes, 7 N.D. 591, 597 (1898); but see Garden State Dairies, Inc. v. Sills, 46 N.J. 349 (1966), noted in 80 Harv. L. Rev. 1357 (1967); see generally Comment, *In-State Preferences in Public Contracting: States' Rights Versus Economic Sectionalism*, 49 U. Colo. L. Rev. 205, 216–22 (1978). In other cases, the fact that the benefits were financed largely by the resident's own tax dollars was thought to be important. See, *e.g.*, Reeves, Inc. v. Kelley, 586 F.2d 1230, 1233 (8th Cir. 1978), discussed *infra*, at notes 177–86.

[150] And there are definite limits to them. In addition to those discussed below,

would not prevent a State from distributing or selling state-owned natural resources to in-state residents or businesses on a preferential basis. And this is a sound conclusion. While one may be troubled by some of its implications[151] and dissatisfied with the analysis by which some courts have reached it,[152] the opposite conclusion would be even more disturbing. To preclude the States from preferring in-state interests in the distribution of state natural resources would deprive the States of an important attribute of their separate existence as independent political units in the federal system.[153] The denial to the States of the power to provide for their residents as such would undermine the relationship between the States and their residents. Moreover, forbidding the States from preferring their own in the distribution of their resources would introduce into the federal system an unsettling asymmetry between the respective obligations the resident and nonresident owe to the State and the benefits they enjoy there.[154] Whether it would be good national policy to deny the States the power to favor in-state interests in this context and whether Congress in pursuit of such policy

---

see text *infra*, at notes 159–75, it is worth noting that the Court has dismissed arguments that the States may discriminate against interstate commerce in their regulation of state highways because of the State's ownership interests in the roads. Buck v. Kuykendall, 267 U.S. 307 (1925); see also South Carolina State Highway Department v. Barnwell Bros., 303 U.S. 177, 187–89 (1938); *cf.* West v. Kansas Natural Gas Co., 221 U.S. 229, 261–62 (1911); see generally Linde *Constitutional Rights in the Public Sector: Justice Douglas on Liberty in the Welfare State*, 40 WASH L. REV. 10, 49–67 (1965). Although the State is plainly acting as a regulator in this context, if there were no limits to the theory that the State could favor in-state interests in distributing state-owned resources, one might contend that the State is simply providing a state-owned resource, a highway, to in-state interests on a preferential basis. The Court's unwillingness to brook State discrimination against instrumentalities of interstate commerce regardless of any asserted ownership interest by the State in their highways simply underscores the point made earlier in the text that state ownership, standing by itself, is no talisman of Commerce Clause analysis.

[151] See, *e.g.*, Hughes v. Alexandria Scrap Corp., 426 U.S. 795, 817–18, 828–29 (1976) (Brennan, J., dissenting); Linde, note 150 *supra;* Note, *State Purchasing Activity Excluded from Commerce Clause Review*, 18 B.C. IND. & COM. L. REV. 893 (1977).

[152] The governmental-proprietary distinction, see note 149 *supra*, has been a darling of academic criticism. See, *e.g.*, DAVIS, ADMINISTRATIVE LAW TREATISE § 25.07 (1958); PROSSER, HANDBOOK OF THE LAW OF TORTS § 131, at 979, 982 (4th ed. 1971); see generally Wells & Hellerstein, *The Governmental-Proprietary Distinction in Constitutional Law*, 66 VA. L. REV. (April 1980).

[153] *Cf.* National League of Cities v. Usery, 426 U.S. 833 (1976).

[154] See Hellerstein, *Some Reflections on the State Taxation of a Nonresident's Personal Income*, 72 MICH. L. REV. 1309, 1318–19 (1974).

could legislate to that end[155] are, of course, different questions. The only question here is whether the Commerce Clause by its own force withdraws this power from the States. While the Commerce Clause may have been designed to create a national common market, it would take more than a "great silence"[156] to sever the special relationship between a State and its in-state residents and businesses.[157]

It is important to recognize, however, that the suggested conclusion, even if correct, is a narrow one. It does not tell us whether the disposition of state-owned natural resources on a preferential basis to in-state residents and businesses would pass muster under other contitutional provisions, although it seems likely that it would.[158] Nor does it indicate the force of two limiting principles, whose impact is substantial. First, whatever distinctions the State may make between in-state and out-of-state interests with regard to the allocation of the State's natural resources, it is plain that it has only minimal powers to deny anyone the right to become a resident of the State or to accord him less than the full panoply of privileges it accords its long-time residents.[159] If a New Yorker

---

[155] *See National League of Cities*, 426 U.S. 833.

[156] H.P. Hood & Sons v. DuMond, 336 U.S. 525, 535 (1949).

[157] *Cf.* Toomer v. Witsell, 334 U.S. 385, 408 (1948) (Frankfurter, J., concurring).

[158] *Alexandria Scrap Corp.*, 426 U.S. 794 (in-state preference in distribution of cash subsidies no violation of Equal Protection Clause); Starns v. Malkerson, 401 U.S. 985 (1971), *aff'g*, 326 F. Supp. 234 (D. Minn. 1970), and Sturgis v. Washington, 414 U.S. 1057, *aff'g*, 368 F. Supp. 38 (W.D. Wash. 1973) (resident preference in tuition rates at state universities no violation of "right to travel" or Equal Protection Clause); see also Vlandis v. Kline, 412 U.S. 441, 452–53 (1973); *cf.* Heim v. McCall, 239 U.S. 175 (1915), and Crane v. New York, 239 U.S. 195 (1915) (resident preference in public employment no violation of Equal Protection or Due Process Clauses). Although the Court has expressed some doubt about the continuing vitality of *Heim* and *Crane*, see Hicklin v. Orbeck, 437 U.S. 518, 531 n.15 (1978), it would appear that they are still good authority for the proposition that a State may favor its own residents over nonresidents with regard to state employment, even if the State may not favor those of its own residents who are American citizens over aliens, whether resident or nonresident. Sugarman v. Dougall, 413 U.S. 634 (1973); C.D.R. Enterprises, Ltd. v. Board of Educ., 412 F. Supp. 1164 (E.D.N.Y. 1976), *aff'd sub nom.* Lefkowitz v. C.D.R. Enterprises, Ltd., 429 U.S. 1031 (1977); see Note, *The Supreme Court, 1977 Term*, 92 Harv. L. Rev. 57, 83 n.47 (1978). But *cf.* Ambach v. Norwick, 99 S. Ct. 1589 (1979); Foley v. Connelie, 435 U.S. 291 (1978). See generally Rosberg, *Protecting the Right of Free Movement of Persons in the United States*, 87–93, 100–02, paper presented at the Conference on the Judicial Role in Economic Integration, Bellagio, Italy, July 17–21, 1979 (to be published).

[159] See Memorial Hospital v. Maricopa County, 415 U.S. 250 (1974); Dunn v. Blumstein, 405 U.S. 330 (1972); Shapiro v. Thompson, 394 U.S. 618 (1969); but see Sosna v. Iowa, 419 U.S. 393 (1975); see generally Rosberg, note 158 *supra*, at 50–68.

wants to enjoy the benefits Alaska may be bestowing upon its residents as a result of its ownership of vast amounts of oil, there is little more than the price of transportation to prevent him from doing so. Second, the power the States may have to discriminate in favor of their in-state residents and businesses in the distribution of state-owned natural resources does not permit the States to attach conditions to the use or disposition of the resource that might independently burden interstate commerce or some other constitutionally protected interest. While Alaska may be able to sell its oil to residents at a preferred price, it may not, as the Court recently informed us in *Hicklin v. Orbeck*,[160] compel "all businesses that benefit in some way from the economic ripple effect of Alaska's decision to develop its oil and gas resources to bias their employment practices in favor of the State's residents."[161]

In *Hicklin*, the Supreme Court struck down under the Privileges and Immunities Clause an Alaska statute requiring that residents be preferred over nonresidents with regard to "all employment which is a result of oil and gas leases, easements, leases or right-of-way permits for oil or gas pipeline purposes . . . to which the state is a party."[162] One of the grounds on which Alaska sought to defend the statute was that it owned all of the oil and gas with respect to which the employment preferences were required, and that the Privileges and Immunities Clause was inapplicable to "decisions by the states as to how they would permit, if at all, the use and distribution of the natural resources which they own."[163] The Court responded:[164]

> We do not agree that the fact that a State owns a resource, of itself, completely removes a law concerning that resource from the prohibitions of the Clause. . . . Rather than placing a statute completely beyond the Clause, a State's ownership of the property with which the statute is concerned is a factor —although often the crucial factor—to be considered in evaluating whether the statute's discrimination against noncitizens violates the Clause.

The State's ownership was not enough to justify the discrimination in *Hicklin* because Alaska had "little or no proprietary interest in

[160] 437 U.S. 518 (1978).

[161] *Id.* at 531.

[162] Alaska Stat. § 38.40.050(a) (1977), quoted at 437 U.S. 529.

[163] Brief for Appellee, p. 20 n.14, quoted at 437 U.S. 528.

[164] 437 U.S. at 528–29.

much of the activity swept within the ambit of [the statute]"[165] and "the connection of the State's oil and gas with much of the covered activity [was] sufficiently attenuated so that it cannot justifiably be the basis for requiring private employers to discriminate against nonresidents."[166]

Hicklin was decided under the Privileges and Immunities Clause, which in some instances provides an alternative to the Commerce Clause as a basis for constitutional adjudication.[167] The analytical route by which a decision is reached under the two Clauses, however, is ordinarily quite different.[168] Even so, the Court in *Hicklin* specifically relied on "the mutually reinforcing relationship"[169] between the Privileges and Immunities and Commerce Clauses in an extensive dictum invoking precedents under the latter to bolster its conclusion under the former. The Court referred to its decisions establishing that the Commerce Clause forbade the States from attempting to preserve for their own residents the benefits of privately owned natural resources located within their borders.[170] It went on to observe that in *Foster-Fountain Packing Co. v. Haydel*,[171] involving Louisiana's prohibition on the out-of-state shipment of shrimp prior to local processing, the Court had limited the implications of the still vital doctrine of *Geer*—that Louisiana's purported ownership of the shrimp justified the State's discrimination in favor of in-state interests. The Court in *Foster-Fountain* had found that

---

[165] *Id.* at 529.

[166] *Ibid.*

[167] *Cf.* Ward v. Maryland, 12 Wall. 418 (1870). Notwithstanding the occasional overlap, there are considerable differences in the scope of the two Clauses. The Privileges and Immunities Clause affords no protection to corporations, Paul v. Virginia, 8 Wall. 168 (1868), and thereby has no application to many enterprises engaged in interstate commerce. Moreover, even though a state law does not discriminate against nonresidents, so that no objection to it could plausibly be raised under the Privileges and Immunities Clause, it might still be offensive to the Commerce Clause. *Cf.* Bibb v. Navajo Freight Lines, Inc., 359 U.S. 520 (1959) (nondiscriminatory highway-safety regulation).

[168] *Compare, e.g., Pike*, 397 U.S. 137, *with Hicklin*, 437 U.S. 518. In contrast to the Court's internal agreement over the governing decisional principles in the Commerce Clause context, there is continuing disagreement among members of the Court regarding the proper approach to Privileges and Immunities questions. *Compare Hicklin*, 437 U.S. 518, *with* Baldwin v. Fish and Game Commission, 436 U.S. 371 (1978); see TRIBE, *supra* note 134, at 34–40.

[169] 437 U.S. at 531.

[170] *Id.* at 532, discussing *West*, 221 U.S. 229, and *Pennsylvania*, 262 U.S. 553; see text *supra*, at notes 43–46 and 123–25.

[171] 278 U.S. 1 (1928). See text *supra*, at notes 13–17.

"by permitting its shrimp to be taken and all the products thereof to be shipped and sold in interstate commerce, the State necessarily releases its hold and, as to the shrimp so taken definitely terminates its control."[172] Based on its reading of all these cases, the Court concluded that:[173]

> the Commerce Clause circumscribes a State's ability to prefer its own citizens in the utilization of natural resources found within its borders, but destined for interstate commerce. Like Louisiana's shrimp in *Foster Packing*, Alaska's oil and gas here are bound for out-of-state consumption . . . Although the fact that a state-owned resource is destined for interstate commerce does not, of itself, disable the State from preferring its own citizens in the utilization of the resource, it does inform analysis under the Privileges and Immunities Clause as to the permissibility of the discrimination the State visits upon nonresidents based on its ownership of the resource. . . . [T]he breadth of the discrimination mandated by [the statute] goes far beyond the degree of resident bias Alaska's ownership of the oil and gas can justifiably support.

Although the Court in *Hicklin* was only incidentally concerned with the Commerce Clause, several inferences regarding its view of the restraints the Clause imposes on state control of state-owned natural resources may fairly be drawn from its remarks. The Court is apparently of the view that the Commerce Clause imposes some limits on a State's ability to prefer in-state residents and businesses in the utilization of state-owned natural resources destined for interstate commerce. *Foster-Fountain*, which the Court treated in the same breath as the "private ownership" cases, might have been dismissed as a case involving the "fiction" of state ownership in which the Court had enunciated a rule that was consistent with the reality of private control. But in *Hicklin* it was clear that Alaska owned the oil and gas as much as it is capable of owning anything.[174] Yet the analogy the Court drew between *Foster-Fountain* and *Hicklin* leaves little doubt that it would strike down on Commerce Clause grounds restrictions on state-owned natural resources of the type Louisiana sought to impose on the commercial exploitation of its shrimp. Thus any ban or conditions on the private sale, use, or exportation of a state-owned natural resource favoring in-state in-

[172] 278 U.S. at 13, quoted at 437 U.S. at 533.

[173] 437 U.S. at 533.

[174] *Id.* at 528 n.11.

terests would very likely be invalidated. On the other hand, the Court did allow that "the fact that a state-owned resource is destined for interstate commerce does not, of itself, disable the State from preferring its own citizens in the utilization of that resource."[175] The Court thereby reinforced the central conclusion advanced above, namely, that the Commerce Clause does not forbid the States, at least under some conditions, from favoring in-state residents and businesses in the allocation of state-owned natural resources.

Finally, and perhaps as a useful reminder of the unsettled state of the law in this area, the most recent word from the Court bearing on these issues injects a distinct element of uncertainty with regard to its views. In *Reeves, Inc. v. Kelley*,[176] the South Dakota Cement Commission, created by the state legislature to carry out the manufacture, distribution, and sale of cement as "works of public necessity and importance,"[177] refused to sell cement to out-of-state customers in accordance with its policy of supplying all South Dakota customers first. The United States Court of Appeals for the Eighth Circuit, reversing the decision of the district court, held that the Commission's action did not violate the Commerce Clause. Relying principally on the Supreme Court's decision in *Hughes v. Alexandria Scrap Corp.*, the court observed that:[178]

> South Dakota has not attempted to pass any regulation or prohibition on any private industry functioning in commerce. It has simply acted in a proprietary capacity as a seller of cement within the interstate cement market.

The court refused to attribute any significance to the fact that Maryland was a purchaser in *Alexandria Scrap*, whereas South Dakota was a seller in the case before it, on the reasonable premise that the holding in *Alexandria Scrap* was rooted in the distinction between the State's participation in and its regulation of the market, not in the distinction between inward- and outward-moving commerce.[179] And it concluded:[180]

> While a state is similar to private business when it participates in the market in a purely proprietary capacity, it is also some-

[175] 437 U.S. at 533.

[176] 586 F.2d 1230 (8th Cir. 1978).

[177] *Id.* at 1231.

[178] *Id.* at 1232.

[179] *Id.* at 1233 n.4.

[180] *Id.* at 1233 (citations omitted).

> what different. As a government providing a public service and utilizing the money and resources of its residents, it has a right and perhaps even an obligation to consider their common good and conserve their resources so long as it does not do so by attempting to regulate or control commerce among the states. . . . The factual background in these cases does not indicate that South Dakota has attempted to control channels of interstate commerce. Accordingly, we hold the commerce clause does not prohibit the State of South Dakota "from participating in the market and exercising the right to favor its own citizens over others." *Hughes* v. *Alexandria Scrap Corp. Cf. American Yearbook Co.* v. *Askew.*

The unsuccessful purchaser petitioned the Supreme Court for certiorari and, three weeks after its decision in *Hughes v. Oklahoma*, the Court issued the following order::

> Petition for writ of certiorari granted, judgment vacated and case remanded to the Court of Appeals for further consideration in light of *Hughes* v. *Oklahoma*. . . .[181]

The Court's reference to *Hughes v. Oklahoma* is puzzling. From a doctrinal standpoint, *Hughes* did little more than extinguish what little life was left in the fiction of state ownership of wildlife located within its borders and thus brought the framework for adjudicating state regulation of such wildlife into line with the general principles of *Pike* and the privately owned natural resource cases. But South Dakota's ownership of the cement at issue in *Reeves* was not based on any fiction. It was like Alaska's gas and oil in *Hicklin*. Perhaps, as *Hicklin* suggests, there are Commerce Clause limits on what South Dakota may do with its cement. But unless *Hughes v. Oklahoma* in some mysterious way undermined *Hughes v. Alexandria Scrap*, it is difficult to see the precise bearing that a case dealing with a State's regulation of wildlife owned by nobody has on a case dealing with a State's sale of cement owned by the State.

There are, however, other plausible explanations of the Court's cryptic remand. First, the Court may not have been concerned about the precise bearing of *Hughes v. Oklahoma* on *Reeves, Inc. v. Kelley*. It might have been trying to make the more general point to the Court of Appeals that a State's alleged ownership of a resource—fictional or actual—is but one of many factors to be taken

[181] 99 S. Ct. 2155 (1979).

into account in the Commerce Clause balance and that the court had accorded too much weight to the fact of state ownership. If this is what the Court is saying, however, it would seem on the facts presented to signal a retreat from the implications of *Hughes v. Alexandria Scrap Corp.* Second, it is possible that the Court really perceives no constitutional distinction between the "private" and "public" ownership cases. One would, however, expect the Court to be more explicit in articulating its position on this matter, especially in light of its specific discussion of the issue in earlier cases.[182] Third, it is possible that the Court viewed the South Dakota Cement Commission as more of a regulator of than a participant in the market, although the record below does not provide much support for this position. Finally, it is possible that the Court viewed the case as presenting difficult issues that were likely to arise only in rare instances. By remanding the case, the Court might have hoped to receive further illumination about the problem or, alternatively and perhaps preferably, to have it disappear. On remand, the Court of Appeals adhered to its earlier holding.[183]

C. STATE CONTROL OF NATURAL RESOURCES IN WHICH OWNERSHIP INTERESTS ARE NOT CLEARLY ESTABLISHED

The discussion in the preceding two subsections was addressed to cases of state control of natural resources in which ownership of the resource, whether private or public, was clearly established under conventional property-law concepts. There is, however, a third category of cases involving state control of natural resources such as wildlife, water, and air in which ownership interests, if they exist at all, are often not well established.

In *Hughes v. Oklahoma* the Court was dealing with wildlife, a natural resource that in its view was owned by no one. "[I]t is pure fantasy to talk of 'owning' wild fish, birds, or animals. Neither the

---

[182] See text *supra*, at notes 136 and 162–73.

[183] Reeves, Inc. v. Kelley, 603 F.2d 736 (8th Cir. 1979). The court found *Hughes v. Oklahoma* distinguishable because South Dakota had not prevented privately owned articles of trade from being shipped in interstate commerce. "We conclude that [South Dakota's] action is more similar to Maryland's preference for its residents in its entry into the automobile scrap processing market, upheld in *Hughes* v. *Alexandria Scrap Corp.*, than conduct at which the prohibitions of the Commerce Clause have historically been directed." Reeves sought Supreme Court review of the Court of Appeals' decision on remand, 48 L.W. 3310 (Nov. 6, 1979), and, at this writing, its petition for certiorari was awaiting Supreme Court action.

States nor the Federal Government, any more than a hopeful fisherman or hunter, has title to these creatures until they are reduced to possession by skillful capture."[184] In thus repudiating the "19th-century legal fiction" of state ownership,[185] the Court concluded that "challenges under the Commerce Clause to state regulations of wild animals should be considered according to the same general rule applied to state regulations of other natural resources."[186] What the Court meant, of course, was the same general rule it had applied to state regulation of privately owned natural resources. Although one might have argued as an original proposition that the State should be accorded greater leeway in controlling unowned than privately owned natural resources, the *Hughes* opinion contains little evidence that a distinction between the two types of cases may properly be drawn.[187] If, therefore, a determination is made that a claim of state ownership to a resource is a "fiction," it seems fair to infer from *Hughes* that state regulation of the resource must satisfy the criteria of *Pike*, and no special weight will be attributed to the absence of private ownership. Hence game birds,[188] natural minnows,[189] shrimp,[190] and other free-roaming[191] and free-swimming[192] creatures, whose peculiar constitutional status has long

---

[184] 99 S. Ct. at 1735–36, quoting *Douglas*, 431 U.S. at 284.

[185] 99 S. Ct. at 1736.

[186] *Ibid.*

[187] Mr. Justice Rehnquist expressed the "hope" that some of the principles he thought were controlling may have survived the overruling of *Geer*, 99 S. Ct. at 1379 (see text *supra*, at notes 63–65), but his references to those statements in the Court's opinion acknowledging the power and interest of the States to protect and conserve wildlife within their borders provide scant basis for such optimism. The State's power to conserve natural resources located within their borders through evenhanded measures has been a consistent theme in the Court's opinions dealing with privately owned natural resources. See text *supra*, at notes 123–33. While the Court declared that the States' interests in conserving wildlife were "similar" to their interests in protecting the health and safety of their citizens, 99 S. Ct. 1737, it might well reach the same conclusion regarding the States' interests in conserving privately owned natural resources. See text *supra*, at notes 123–33.

[188] *Geer*, 161 U.S. 519; *cf.* Missouri v. Holland, 252 U.S. 416 (1920).

[189] *Hughes*, 99 S. Ct. 1727.

[190] Toomer v. Witsell, 334 U.S. 385 (1948); *Foster-Fountain Packing*, 278 U.S. 1.

[191] *Cf.* Baldwin v. Fish & Game Commission, 436 U.S. 371 (1978); Kleppe v. New Mexico, 426 U.S. 529 (1976); Lacoste v. Louisiana Department of Conservation, 263 U.S. 545 (1924); Patsone v. Pennsylvania, 232 U.S. 138 (1914).

[192] Bayside Fish Flour Co. v. Gentry, 297 U.S. 722 (1936); Manchester v. Massachusetts, 139 U.S. 240 (1891); *cf.* Douglas v. Seacost Products, Inc., 431 U.S. 265 (1977); Takahashi v. Fish & Game Commission, 334 U.S. 410 (1948); Lawton v. Steele, 152 U.S. 133 (1894); see generally Morrison, note 80 *supra*, at 250–55.

commanded the Court's attention, are now apparently to be treated substantially the same as privately owned natural resources for purposes of Commerce Clause adjudication.[193]

Once one leaves the area of wildlife, however, the terrain becomes less certain. Two cases handed down by the Court in the heyday of nineteenth-century legal fictions suggest some of the difficulties likely to be encountered in this context under contemporary Commerce Clause analysis. In *McCready v. Virginia*,[194] a Maryland resident, who had planted oysters in Virginia's inland tidewaters, was convicted of violating a statute forbidding nonresidents from planting oysters in Virginia waters. Over McCready's objections that the prohibition violated the Privileges and Immunities and Commerce Clauses, the Court sustained the conviction. Dismissing the latter claim on the ground that production is not commerce,[195] the Court devoted its principal attention to the former.

It began with the "settled" doctrine that "each State owns the beds of all tide-waters within its jurisdiction . . . [and] the tidewaters themselves."[196] "For this purpose," the Court continued, "the State represents its people, and the ownership is that of the people in their united sovereignty."[197] The Court therefore reasoned that the State:[198]

> has the right to appropriate its tide-waters and their beds to be used by its people as a common for taking and cultivating fish. . . . Such an appropriation is in effect nothing more than a regulation of the use by the people of their common property.

---

[193] This is not to suggest, however, that every state law that would pass constitutional muster as an evenhanded regulation of wildlife would likewise survive constitutional scrutiny as a regulation of privately owned resources. A law forbidding any hunting of certain animals might well be sustained as an evenhanded conservation measure; a law forbidding any production of oil from privately owned wells would raise more difficult constitutional issues. This may simply be another way of saying that the Court's decision in *Hughes* has not divested the States of their traditional role as managers of wildlife located within their borders, so long as such management is undertaken on a nondiscriminatory basis.

[194] 94 U.S. 391 (1876).

[195] *Id.* at 396–97. McCready also argued that the statute was preempted by federal laws "relating to the coast trade," *id.* at 394, but the Court did not explicitly address this contention. The Court's decision in *Douglas*, 431 U.S. 265 (1977), may be read as casting some doubt on the continuing validity of the Court's disposition of this issue in *McCready*. See Lewis & Strand, Douglas v. Seacoast Products, Inc.: *The Legal and Economic Consequences for the Maryland Oystery*, 38 Md. L. Rev. 1, 8 (1978); see also note 80 *supra*.

[196] 94 U.S. at 394.

[197] *Ibid.*

[198] *Id.* at 395.

In light of these principles, and the premise that the Privileges and Immunities Clause "extended only to such privileges and immunities as are 'in their nature fundamental; which belong of right to the citizens of all free governments,' "[199] the Court had no hesitation in concluding that Virginia had not denied a Maryland resident a "privilege" or "immunity" of citizenship by confining the use of Virginia's oyster beds to its own residents. "We think we may safely hold that the citizens of one State are not invested by this clause of the Constitution with any interest in the common property of the citizens of another State."[200]

From a doctrinal standpoint, *McCready* has unquestionably been eroded. Production may not be commerce, but its regulation by the State will be limited by the negative implications of the Commerce Clause if such production substantially affects commerce among the States.[201] It may be that only "fundamental" rights are protected by the Privileges and Immunities Clause,[202] but the Court today might strike down the Virginia statute under that Clause as an impermissibly pervasive discrimination against nonresidents to achieve whatever goals it may permissibly pursue as a consequence of its ownership of the resource.[203] Moreover, the Court has repeatedly asserted that "[t]he whole ownership theory, in fact, is now generally regarded as but a fiction expressive in legal shorthand of the importance to its people that a State have power to preserve and regulate the exploitation of an important resource."[204] For some or all of these reasons, most observers have routinely concluded that *McCready* is "anachronistic,"[205] subject to "significant doubts,"[206] and "a derelict on the sea of legal history."[207]

---

[199] *Ibid.*, quoting Corfield v. Coryell, 6 Fed. Cas. 546 (Case No. 3,230) (C.C.E.D. Pa. 1825).

[200] 94 U.S. at 395.

[201] Parker v. Brown, 317 U.S. 341, 359–68 (1943); *cf.* United States v. Darby, 312 U.S. 100 (1941); Philadelphia v. New Jersey, 437 U.S. 617, 621–23 (1978).

[202] See Baldwin v. Fish & Game Commission, 436 U.S. 371 (1978).

[203] *Hicklin*, 437 U.S. 518.

[204] Toomer v. Witsell, 334 U. S. 385, 402 (1948).

[205] Note, *Domicile Preferences in Employment: The Case of Alaska Hire*, 1978 Duke L.J. 1069, 1076 (1978).

[206] Nowak, Rotunda, & Young, Handbook on Constitutional Law 278 (1978).

[207] Morrison, note 80 *supra*, at 252. Professor Morrison was referring generally to the "*Corfield* category of special interests," *ibid.*, which was embodied in the holding of *McCready*. *Id.* at 252 n.72.

Perhaps so. But *McCready* may not be ready for last rites. The Commerce Clause[208] would today impose some limits on the restrictions Virginia might place on the use of its tidelands. The central question, however, is whether those limits are the same as the restraints imposed on its control of wildlife or whether they are more akin to the limits imposed on its control of state-owned natural resources, which contemplate the possibility of some in-state preferences, without regard to the availability of nondiscriminatory alternatives. The discrediting of the "common ownership" doctrine does not necessarily resolve the issue. That doctrine has been maligned largely in cases involving the State's claim to ownership of wildlife which, as a practical matter, nobody owned.[209] But tidelands are arguably analytically distinct from fish and birds. The States have an interest in their tidelands which, while distinguishable from A's fee interest in Blackacre, may nevertheless be characterized as a substantial one.[210] Hence, even if the "common ownership" theory on which the State's claims were originally predicated has no place in contemporary Commerce Clause analysis—whether wildlife or tidelands are at issue—it does not necessarily follow that the consequences in each instance are the same. Exposure of the fiction of "common ownership" of game may lead to the conclusion that in reality it is owned by no one and that the Commerce Clause criteria governing privately owned natural resources should therefore apply.[211] But exposing the fiction of "common ownership" of tidelands may reveal that in reality the State's ownership

---

[208] With regard to the Privileges and Immunities Clause, it is quite possible that the Court would reach a different conclusion in *McCready* today for the reason suggested above. See text *supra*, at note 203. Some support for the continuing vitality of the holding of *McCready*, however, may be found in Baldwin v. Fish & Game Commission, 436 U.S. 371, 383, 386 (1978) (sustaining Montana's elk-hunting license scheme which discriminated against nonresidents) and in parts of the following discussion.

[209] *Hughes*, 99 S. Ct. 1727, 1735–36 (minnows); *Baldwin*, 436 U.S. 371, at 385–86 (elk); *Douglas*, 431 U.S. 265, at 284 (fish); *Toomer*, 334 U.S. 385, at 401–02 (shrimp); Missouri v. Holland, 252 U.S. 416, 434 (birds); *cf*. Manchester v. Massachusetts, 139 U.S. 240, at 265 (1891) (fish).

[210] See Note, *The Public Trust in Tidal Areas: A Sometime Submerged Traditional Doctrine*, 79 YALE L.J. 762 (1970); the Submerged Lands Act, 43 U.S.C. §§ 1301–15 (1976) (conveying to the States "title," "ownership," and "the right and power to manage, administer, lease, develop and use" the lands beneath the oceans and natural resources within state territorial jurisdiction); and *Douglas*, 431 U.S. at 284–85.

[211] See text *supra*, at notes 184–93.

interest is significant, and that the appropriate analogy for Commerce Clause purposes would be to state mineral holdings or state forests rather than wildlife. There is considerable learning and controversy concerning the States' interest in the tidelands,[212] and no claim to expertise is being made here. The point is only that tidelands may be different from wildlife with regard to the reality of state ownership and its recognition for Commerce Clause purposes.[213]

A second factor that might bear on the determination whether Virginia's oyster beds should be treated differently from unowned resources under the Commerce Clause is the extent to which the State itself had acted as a proprietor of the resource. If the States had expended large sums of money to develop, manage, and cultivate oyster beds located in state waters, one might regard the entire enterprise as a "statewide oyster 'farm' "[214] subsidized by the State, to which access might reasonably be limited to in-state residents and businesses under the principle discussed in the preceding subsection.

While these factors could breathe some new life into *McCready*, there are countervailing considerations that should not be ignored. The general drift of Supreme Court doctrine in this area has been toward greater freedom in the interstate market,[215] and, when the case is close, "free trade" interests are likely to prevail over the States' interests in providing for their own, which are easily portrayed as forces of "economic Balkanization."[216] Moreover, in dealing with the tidelands, the Court may feel it is dealing with a resource that is impressed with a national interest,[217] and it thus might be particularly vigilant in protecting the resource from local economic prejudice. Finally, even if some concession to the States'

---

[212] See, *e.g.*, United States v. California, 332 U.S. 19 (1947), and sources cited therein; see also note 210 *supra*.

[213] Whatever the impact the States' "ownership" of their tidelands under 43 U.S.C. §§ 1301–15 (see note 210 *supra*) on the negative implications of the Commerce Clause, the Court made it clear in *Douglas* that such "ownership" did not permit them to limit the rights of federal licensees, who are nonresidents of the State, to fish in their waters. It has been suggested, however, that the statutory preemption in *Douglas* was "only the old negative implications of the Commerce Clause in a new guise." Morrison, note 80 *supra*, at 250; see note 195 *supra*.

[214] Lewis & Strand, note 195 *supra*, at 13–14.

[215] See text *supra*, at notes 70–80.

[216] *Hughes*, 99 S. Ct. at 1731.

[217] See notes 210 and 212 *supra*.

ownership interest in their tidelands is made, it must be kept in mind that the States are confined in their ability to translate this ownership interest in a resource into restrictions that would independently burden the Commerce Clause.[218] Indeed, in *Johnson v. Haydel*,[219] a companion case to *Foster-Fountain*, the Court invalidated Louisiana's attempt to impose, with respect to oysters it claimed to own, restrictions similar to those it had sought to impose on the interstate shipment of shrimp. Whatever limits Virginia may still be able to impose on access to its oyster beds under a refurbished version of *McCready*, it surely may not impose any limitations on the disposition of oysters taken from those beds, beyond those limitations that are permissible as applied to a privately owned resource.

Like their interest in oyster beds located within their jurisdictions, the States' interest in water situated within their borders may be strong enough to raise questions regarding their power over the resource that cannot be disposed of merely by reference to cases involving wildlife. In *Hudson County Water Co. v. McCarter*,[220] the Court upheld a New Jersey statute making it unlawful for anyone to export "the waters of any fresh water lake, pond, brook, creek, river or stream of this State into any other State, for use therein."[221] Over objections predicated on the Contract, Commerce, Due Process, Equal Protection, and Privileges and Immunities Clauses, the Court sustained an injunction against a water company under contract with the City of New York to prevent the company from carrying waters of a New Jersey river outside the State. Without deciding whether the State could prohibit the acquisition of large quantities of water from state streams in its capacity as "owner" of the bed of the stream and of all rights in the water not belonging to riparian proprietors,[222] the Court preferred to rest its decision "upon a broader ground . . . [that] is independent of the more or less attenuated residuum of title that the State may be said to possess."[223] In substance, the Court held that the State's "police power . . . to protect the atmosphere, the water and the forests within its territory,"[224] authorized it "to maintain

[218] See text *supra*, at notes 160–75.

[219] 278 U.S. 16 (1928).

[220] 209 U.S. 349 (1908).

[221] *Id.* at 353.

[222] *Id.* at 354.

[223] *Id.* at 355.

[224] *Ibid.*

the rivers that are wholly within it substantially undiminished, except by such drafts upon them as the guardian of the public welfare may permit."[225] The Court relied in part on *Geer's* "preservation" rationale,[226] as well as on *Geer's* holding that a State might qualify the property interest one receives in a resource to prevent it from becoming an object of interstate commerce.[227]

Like *McCready*, *Hudson County* has suffered serious erosion from a doctrinal point of view. The general proposition that a State may "preserve" natural resources located within its borders by forbidding their exportation or by qualifying the property interest that private parties acquire in such resources was finally laid to rest with the overruling of *Geer*. While the State's alleged "ownership" of the water might have provided an independent ground for such a holding, the Supreme Court, as noted, explicitly refused to rest its decision on that ground.[228] By its own terms, then, *Hudson County* represents a precedent of doubtful validity.

But what about its outcome? If the New Jersey statute were defended today on the ground that New Jersey's ownership interest in the water was sufficient to remove it from the rules of the privately owned resource cases, which it clearly could not survive, would the statute nevertheless withstand Commerce Clause scrutiny? I should think not. Even if a State enjoyed conventional ownership rights in a natural resource, thus implicating the rules applicable to state control of state-owned resources, it seems highly unlikely for reasons suggested above[229] that an absolute bar on the exportation of the resource is the type of preference for in-state interests that might be tolerated on the basis of state ownership. But *Hudson County* is an easy case.[230]

---

[225] *Id.* at 356.

[226] *Ibid.* See text *supra*, at notes 34–37.

[227] 209 U.S. at 357. See text *supra*, at notes 23–33. Notwithstanding the Court's disclaimer of relying on state ownership of the resource as the basis of its decision, see text *supra*, at notes 222–23, its reliance on this aspect of *Geer* suggests that "common ownership" principles were nevertheless informing the Court's thinking.

[228] The New Jersey courts, however, had done so. McCarter v. Hudson County Water Co., 70 N.J.Eq. 525 (1905), *aff'd*, 70 N.J.Eq. 695 (1906).

[229] See text *supra*, at notes 160–75.

[230] Indeed, in Carr v. City of Altus, 385 U.S. 35, *aff'g*, 255 F. Supp. 828 (W.D. Tex. 1966), the Court cast doubt on the holding of *Hudson County* by summarily affirming the decision of a three-judge federal district court which held unconstitutional a Texas statute forbidding the shipment outside the State of water

Suppose New Jersey limited to in-state residents and businesses access to all waters in the State, subject to preexisting private rights in such waters. Would this pass constitutional muster? The issue could only be resolved by analysis of the complex and confusing problems associated with state "ownership" of water[231] to determine whether the appropriate analogy for purposes of Commerce Clause analysis is to wildlife or to state lands or to something else. Again, no claim is made here to any expertise in the field of water rights. The point to be made is a narrow one that state control of water, like control of oyster beds, raises questions under the Commerce Clause that have not been answered by *Hughes v. Oklahoma*. Moreover, these questions, while arising in cases that can be viewed as curious relics from the distant past, may surface in the future in connection with existing state legislation that embodies their holdings.[232]

IV. Conclusion

The Court's decision in *Hughes v. Oklahoma* reflects and reinforces its general approach to Commerce Clause limitations on state regulation. The interment of the artificial exception to this approach that had been associated with the notion that a State "owns" its wildlife is a sound development,[233] although the result in *Hughes* may be questioned in light of congressional legislation

---

withdrawn from underground sources within the State. The district court, "[c]onsidering the statute in question only with regard to whether it regulates the transportation and use of water after it has been withdrawn from a well and becomes personal property" concluded that such water was like any other privately owned property and that the natural gas cases, see notes 123 and 125 *supra*, were controlling. *Id.* at 839. But see West v. Kansas Natural Gas Co., 221 U.S. 229, 258–60 (1911) (distinguishing *Hudson County*); see generally Comment, *"It's Our Water!"—Can Wyoming Constitutionally Prohibit the Exportation of State Waters?*, 1975 Land & Water Rev. 119.

[231] See Trelease, *Government Ownership and Trusteeship of Water*, 45 Calif. L. Rev. 638 (1957).

[232] See, *e.g.*, Md. Nat. Res. Code Ann. §§ 4–1003, 1004(b), considered in Lewis & Strand, note 195 *supra*, at 2 nn. 3 and 4; Wyo. Stat. § 41–10.5, considered in Comment, note 230 *supra*.

[233] The common-trust doctrine has application far beyond the negative implications of the Commerce Clause, for example, as a basis for state standing to assert the common interests of its citizens in environmental and other litigation. See, *e.g.*, Commonwealth v. S.S. Zoe Colocotroni, 456 F. Supp. 1327, 1336–37 (D.P.R. 1978). There is nothing in *Hughes* to suggest that these applications of the common-trust doctrine are affected by the Court's decision.

arguably consenting to laws like Oklahoma's.[234] The confidence with which the Court disposed of the controversy in *Hughes*, moreover, cannot obscure the significance of the underlying conflict between the nation's interest in unfettered commerce among the States and the States' interest in controlling the disposition of their natural resources, a conflict that extends far beyond the question of whether Oklahoma may keep natural minnows within its borders. Lurking behind the "fictions" of State ownership, which the Court found so easy to abandon in *Hughes*, are realities of state ownership that present much harder cases.

---

[234] See text *supra*, at notes 20–22.

BERNARD SCHWARTZ

OLD WINE IN OLD BOTTLES? THE RENAISSANCE OF THE CONTRACT CLAUSE

In *United States Trust Co. v. New Jersey*,[1] the Supreme Court struck down a state law as violative of the Contract Clause. A year later, in *Allied Structural Steel Co. v. Spannaus*,[2] a second state law was invalidated on the same ground. These were the first cases in some forty years in which the Court used the Contract Clause to invalidate state legislation.[3] What are the implications of the Court's revival of the Contract Clause? Will it restore that constitutional provision to its place as a primary protection for economic interests? Will it have even broader consequences, as a forerunner of judicial activism in the area of property rights comparable with that which the Court has displayed, in recent years, in protecting personal right and liberties?

The two decisions under discussion show how risky it is to assume that constitutional doctrine has become settled. Not too long ago, constitutional commentators took it for granted that the Contract Clause had become moribund. Like the report of Mark Twain's death, however, the anticipated demise had been grossly exag-

---

Bernard Schwartz is the Edwin D. Webb Professor of Law at New York University.

[1] 431 U.S. 1 (1977). [2] 438 U.S. 234 (1978).

[3] See Brennan, J., dissenting, in *United States Trust Co.*, 431 U.S. at 60.

gerated.[4] Too many of us had forgotten that, despite its disuse, "the Contract Clause remains part of the Constitution. It is not a dead letter."[5] Desuetude does not deprive a statutory, much less a constitutional, provision of its potential. The Contract Clause, in repose for four decades, can be given new life whenever enough Justices see fit to revive it.

I. General Background

Charles A. Beard told us that the economic history of the States between the Revolution and the adoption of the Constitution is compressed in the Contract Clause.[6] During the pre-Constitution period the States had exercised authority to interfere with contracts:[7]

> to such an excess . . . as to break in upon the ordinary intercourse of society, and destroy all confidence between man and man. The mischief had become so great, so alarming, as not only to impair commercial intercourse, and threaten the existence of credit, but to sap the morals of the people, and destroy the sanctity of private faith.

To guard against the continuance of the evil,[8] the Framers inserted the Contract Clause—that "added this constitutional bulwark in favor of personal security and private rights"[9]—into the organic charter which they wrote.

There can be no doubt about the importance of the Contract Clause to the Framers. Webster went so far as to declare, in his argument in a Contract Clause case:[10]

> The constitution was intended to accomplish a great political object. Its design was not so much to prevent injustice or injury in one case, or in successive single cases, as it was to make

---

[4] *Cf.* Freund, *Review and Federalism*, in Supreme Court and Supreme Law 91 (Cahn ed. 1954).

[5] *Allied Structural Steel Co.*, 438 U.S. at 241.

[6] Beard, An Economic Interpretation of the Constitution of the United States 179 (1935).

[7] Marshall, C.J., dissenting, in Ogden v. Saunders, 12 Wheat. 213, 355 (1827).

[8] *Ibid.*

[9] The Federalist, No. 44, 282 (Mentor ed. 1961).

[10] Ogden v. Saunders, 12 Wheat. 213, 237 (1827).

> general salutary provisions, which, in their operation, should give security to all contracts.

Constitutional commentators during the first century of the Republic all concurred on the crucial importance of the Contract Clause.[11] According to Sir Henry Maine, indeed, "in point of fact there is no more important provision in the whole Constitution."[12] Writing in 1885, Maine characterized the Contract Clause as "the basis of the credit of many of the great American Railway Incorporations."[13] It is, he went on, its principle "which has in reality secured full play to the economical forces by which the achievement of cultivating the soil of the North American Continent has been performed."[14] At a time when no other constitutional provision would serve the purpose, corporate property rights were brought under the fostering guardianship of the Contract Clause. Those who were called upon to pool their wealth and talents in the vast corporate enterprises needed for the nation's development were thus ensured that their contributions would not remain at the mercy of what Justice Story termed "the passions or the popular doctrines of the day."[15] Before the decisions of the Marshall Court giving effect to the Contract Clause, there were relatively few manufacturing corporations in the country. Under the confidence created by those decisions, such corporations proliferated to such an extent that they soon transformed the face of the nation.[16]

The Maine statement on the importance of the Contract Clause could scarcely be made today. As the Supreme Court explained in 1978, "Although it was perhaps the strongest single constitutional check on state legislation during our early years as a Nation, the Contract Clause receded into comparative desuetude with the adoption of the Fourteenth Amendment, and particularly with the development of the large body of jurisprudence under the Due Process Clause of that Amendment in modern constitutional history."[17]

---

[11] See, *e.g.*, Story, Commentaries on the Constitution of the United States § 1369 (1833); Cooley, Constitutional Limitations 273 (1868); Miller, Lectures on the Constitution of the United States 529 (1893).

[12] Maine, Popular Government 247 (1886).

[13] *Id.* at 248.

[14] *Ibid.*

[15] Quoted in 4 Beveridge, Life of John Marshall 278 (1919).

[16] See Dodd, American Business Corporations until 1860 (1954).

[17] *Allied Structural Steel Co.*, 438 U.S. at 241.

In this sense, the history of the Contract Clause has well exemplified Cardozo's famous remark that the law has "its epochs of ebb and flow."[18] The first century of the Republic witnessed the Contract Clause's flood season. Its doctrinal foundations were laid in Marshall's day.

The post-Civil War period saw the high point of Contract Clause jurisprudence.[19] The principles developed under Marshall were applied to the new factual situations presented by the accelerated industrial expansion that characterized the latter part of the century. During the period, the Contract Clause was by far the most important organic provision applied in cases involving the validity of state legislation. In the Chase and Waite Courts, there were forty-nine cases in which state laws were ruled unconstitutional because they impaired the obligation of contracts.[20] The Contract Clause itself was invoked successfully in almost half the cases in which state legislation was struck down by the highest tribunal.[21]

If, as just indicated, the Contract Clause jurisprudence reached its flood during 1865–88, in the years that followed an ebb flow set in. From 1890 on, the Contract Clause became of steadily diminishing significance in our constitutional law.

Nor is the date of the beginning of the decline of the Contract Clause a matter of mere conjecture. For it was in 1890 that the first Supreme Court decision, in which the Due Process Clause furnished the basis for holding a state regulatory law invalid, was rendered.[22] After 1890, the Supreme Court steadily broadened the scope of due process as a substantive check upon legislative power. The Contract Clause became of diminishing importance as the Supreme Court came to give to the Due Process Clause a breadth that made it an even more inclusive sanctuary for economic interests than the Contract Clause itself had ever been.[23] In the Court's 1978 explanation of the decline of the Contract Clause, particular weight was given

---

[18] Cardozo, *A Ministry of Justice*, 35 HARV. L. REV. 113, 126 (1921), reprinted in CARDOZO, LAW AND LITERATURE 41, 69 (1931).

[19] See CORWIN, THE CONSTITUTION OF THE UNITED STATES OF AMERICA: ANALYSIS AND INTERPRETATION 361 (1953).

[20] See WRIGHT, THE CONTRACT CLAUSE OF THE CONSTITUTION 93–4 (1938).

[21] *Id.* at 95.

[22] Chicago, etc. Railway Co. v. Minnesota, 134 U.S. 418 (1890).

[23] *Cf.* WRIGHT, note 20 *supra*, at 95.

to "the large body of jurisprudence under the Due Process Clause of [the Fourteenth] Amendment."[24]

II. Basic Limitations

The post-1890 decline of the Contract Clause may be traced not only to the rise and expansion of substantive due process but also to four basic limitations imposed by the Supreme Court before 1890 on the operation of the Clause:

1. The rule limiting the Clause's application to cases involving laws with retrospective, not prospective, effect.[25]
2. The rule that public contracts are to be strictly construed in favor of the State.[26]
3. The rule that the States may not contract away certain basic, inalienable governmental powers, and that state attempts to do so are void and hence do not create contractual obligations within the meaning of the Contract Clause.[27]
4. The rule that public contracts, particularly corporate charters, may be subjected to the reserved power of the State to amend and repeal.[28]

These principles have been developed to protect the public against the consequences of improvident legislative action that might otherwise be rendered invulnerable under the Contract Clause. "The Framers fully recognized that nothing would so jeopardize the legitimacy of a system of government that relies upon the ebbs and flows of politics to 'clean out the rascals' than the possibility that those same rascals might perpetuate their policies simply by locking them into binding contracts."[29]

The most important of the four limitations and the one most pertinent to this article is the third—namely, the rule that there are certain basic governmental powers that may not be contracted away. The Contract Clause does not require a State to adhere to a contract that surrenders an essential attribute of its sovereign

---

[24] *Allied Structural Steel Co.*, 438 U.S. at 241.

[25] Ogden v. Saunders, 12 Wheat. 213 (1827).

[26] Charles River Bridge v. Warren Bridge, 11 Pet. 420 (1837).

[27] West River Bridge Co. v. Dix, 6 How. 507 (1848).

[28] Miller v. The State, 15 Wall. 478 (1873).

[29] *United States Trust Co.*, 431 U.S. at 45 (Brennan, J., dissenting).

powers.[30] The leading case is *Stone v. Mississippi*.[31] The state legislature had given a company a franchise to conduct a lottery for twenty-five years. Three years later, it enacted a statute making it unlawful to conduct lotteries. The law was upheld against the contention that it violated the Contract Clause. A franchise to conduct a lottery is but a contract at will. Despite its contractual basis, such a franchise is always subject to the overriding governmental authority to suppress a form of gambling that is deemed to have an adverse effect upon public morals.

Stone v. Mississippi turns upon the proposition that the Contract Clause does not require a State to adhere to a contract that surrenders an essential governmental power. "Decisions of this Court for at least a century have construed the Contract Clause largely to be powerless in binding a State to contracts limiting the authority of successor legislatures to enact laws in furtherance of the health, safety, and similar collective interests of the polity."[32] The States cannot bargain away their police power.[33] Hence, as the Court recently put it, "it is to be accepted as a commonplace that the Contract Clause does not operate to obliterate the police power of the States."[34] Legislators cannot contract away their continuing duty to safeguard public health, safety, morals, and welfare. On the contrary, all contracts are made subject to the paramount governmental duty.[35] Lawful exercises of the police power stand paramount to rights held under contract.[36] In this sense, the police power itself becomes an implied condition of every contract and, as such, as much "part of the contract as though it were written into it."[37] "As Mr. Justice Holmes succinctly put the matter . . . , 'One whose rights, such as they are, are subject to state restriction, cannot remove them from the power of the State by making a contract about them. The contract will carry with it the infirmity of the subject matter.' "[38]

---

[30] *Id.* at 23.

[31] 101 U.S. 814 (1880).

[32] *United States Trust Co.*, 431 U.S. at 33 (Brennan, J., dissenting).

[33] *Stone*, 101 U.S. at 817.

[34] *Allied Structural Steel Co.*, 438 U.S. at 241.

[35] Veix v. Sixth Ward Building & Loan Ass'n, 310 U.S. 32, 38 (1940).

[36] *United States Trust Co.*, 431 U.S. at 33 (Brennan, J., dissenting).

[37] East New York Savings Bank v. Hahn, 326 U.S. 230, 232 (1945).

[38] *Allied Structural Steel Co.*, 438 U.S. at 241–42, quoting from Hudson Water Co. v. McCarter, 209 U.S. 349, 357 (1908).

The obligation of contracts, like the freedom of contract guaranteed by due process, must give way before the ever-broadening reach of the police power,[39] particularly in the economic sphere. It is the normal thing for a law enacted to accomplish economic objectives to have an effect upon provisions of contracts already in existence. This is true whether the law affects utility rate contracts[40] or contractual agreements between landlords and tenants,[41] or provides for liquidation of a scheme for guaranteeing bank deposits.[42] Private rights, even if acquired through contract, are subordinate to reasonable exercises of state regulatory power.[43] Where state power is exercised in a manner otherwise appropriate in regulation of the economy, it is no objection that the performance of existing contracts may be frustrated by the regulatory prohibitions.[44] Otherwise, one would be able to obtain immunity from state regulation by making private contractual arrangements.[45]

Perhaps the most striking case involving the principle under discussion is *Home Building & Loan Ass'n v. Blaisdell*,[46] "the leading case in the modern era of Contract Clause interpretation,"[47] which upheld state power to enact moratorium laws for the relief of debtors during the Great Depression. The economic emergency furnished legitimate occasion for exercise of the police power to protect both debtors and the community against the collapse of values that had occurred. The ruling that the moratorium law was a proper exertion of the police power readily enabled the Court to dispose of the claim that it violated the Contract Clause. The basic principle, it reiterated, is that reservation of the police power is read into all contracts, and there is no reason not to apply this principle to the mortgages covered by the moratorium law.

---

[39] *United States Trust Co.*, 431 U.S. at 48 (Brennan, J., dissenting).

[40] See, *e.g.*, Union Dry Goods Co. v. Georgia Pub. Serv. Corp., 248 U.S. 372 (1919); Midland Realty Co. v. Kansas City Power Co., 300 U.S. 109 (1937).

[41] Marcus Brown Holding Co. v. Feldman, 256 U.S. 170 (1921).

[42] Abie State Bank v. Bryan, 282 U.S. 765 (1931).

[43] *United States Trust Co.*, 431 U.S. at 50 (Brennan, J., dissenting).

[44] Home Building & Loan Ass'n v. Blaisdell, 290 U.S. 398, 438 (1934).

[45] *United States Trust Co.*, 431 U.S. at 22.

[46] 290 U.S. 398 (1934).

[47] *United States Trust Co.*, 431 U.S. at 15.

III. United States Trust Co. v. New Jersey

The rule that the Contract Clause is not violated by any law that constitutes a valid exercise of the police power means that the Clause itself is not a substantial bar against governmental action. Hence it was that, after 1890, the Contract Clause receded into relative desuetude[48] in Supreme Court jurisprudence, to be replaced by the less rigid demands of the Due Process Clause. For over forty years no state law had failed to run the Contract Clause gauntlet. Though several cases involving the Clause arose during the Great Depression, "this emergence of the clause into prominence was a flash in the pan. During the last decade hardly a case involving the clause has reached the Court."[49] This comment by Corwin, published in 1953, could have been made with equal accuracy two decades later. All this has now been changed with the decisions in the *United States Trust* and *Allied Structural Steel* cases. There the Court "dust[ed] off"[50] the Contract Clause and restored it to its place as a primary protection for property rights.

United States Trust Co. v. New Jersey arose out of legislative action by New Jersey and New York repealing a statutory covenant affecting the Port Authority of New York and New Jersey. The Port Authority was established under a 1921 bistate compact to improve transportation facilities in the port of New York area. The toll bridges and tunnels it built and operated produced substantial revenues which were pledged to secure the payments of bonds issued to private investors. In 1962, responding to increasing concern over mass transit facilities in the area, the New Jersey and New York legislatures authorized the Authority to acquire and operate the Hudson & Manhattan Railroad, a bankrupt commuter line. Responding to bondholder anxiety over the Authority's entry into the unprofitable mass transit field, the two legislatures enacted a 1962 statutory covenant in which they covenanted and agreed with each other and with the holders of Authority bonds that none of the revenues pledged to secure Authority bonds would be applied to railroad purposes, except in specified limited cases. In effect, the covenant ensured that the Authority would not venture further

---

[48] *Allied Structural Steel Co.*, 438 U.S. at 241.

[49] Corwin, note 19 *supra*, at 362.

[50] *United States Trust Co.*, 431 U.S. at 44 (Brennan, J., dissenting).

in the mass transit field, since it severely limited the Authority's ability to subsidize rail-passenger transportation from revenues and reserves from its other profitable operations. In 1974, however, the two legislatures retroactively repealed the 1962 covenant. Appellant, as a trustee for and a holder of Port Authority bonds, brought suit for declaratory relief, claiming that the 1974 repealing statute impaired the obligation of the States' contract with the bondholders in violation of the Contract Clause. The state courts held that the statutory repeal was a reasonable exercise of the police power and, as such, not prohibited by the Contract Clause. The Supreme Court, by a bare plurality, reversed.

The Court concluded that the statutory repeal impaired the obligation of the States' contract, since it totally eliminated an important security provision for the bondholders. The holding that the obligation of contract was "impaired" did not, however, end the matter. The Court recognized that, under the principles heretofore discussed, the prohibition against impairment is not an absolute one to be read with the literal exactness of a mathematical formula.[51] The crucial question was whether the impairment at issue was valid. In answering it, the Court indicated that the standard of judicial review would depend upon whether the contract was private or public.

When state impairment of the obligation of private contracts is alleged, the theme of judicial deference (which has increasingly dominated Contract Clause jurisprudence) is appropriate. "As is customary in reviewing economic and social regulation courts properly defer to legislative judgment as to the necessity and reasonableness of a particular measure."[52] The same is not true when the alleged impairment involved public contracts. "The Court indicated that impairments of a State's own contracts would face more stringent examination under the Contract Clause than would laws regulating contractual relationships between private parties."[53] Modification of a contract to which the State itself is a party must be evaluated "with particular scrutiny."[54] In such a case, "complete

[51] *Cf. Home Building & Loan Ass'n*, 290 U.S. at 428.

[52] *United States Trust Co.*, 431 U.S. at 22–23.

[53] *Allied Structural Steel Co.*, 438 U.S. at 244 n.15.

[54] *Id.* at 244.

deference to a legislative assessment of reasonableness and necessity is not appropriate because the State's self-interest is at stake."[55]

What then of the principle already discussed under which the States cannot bargain away their essential governmental powers—particularly the police power? New Jersey had argued that the repealing statute was a valid exercise of the State's police power; hence, it overrode the inconsistent provisions of the 1962 covenant. The Court rejected the argument. It did so because, in its view, the 1962 covenant involved only a financial obligation and, as such, did not fall within the governmental powers that could not be contracted away. The undertaking that revenues and reserves securing the bonds would not be depleted by the operation of deficit-producing passenger railroads did not contract away the police power. "Such a promise is purely financial and thus not necessarily a compromise of the State's reserved powers."[56]

The Court refused to engage in a balancing approach under which the harm to bondholders caused by repeal of the covenant would be weighed against the goals of mass transportation, energy conservation, and environmental protection which motivated the repeal. "We do not accept this invitation to engage in a utilitarian comparison of public benefit and private loss."[57] The State could not refuse to meet financial obligations simply because it preferred to spend the money to promote the public good rather than the private welfare of creditors.

On the other hand, the Court did state that the covenant repeal could be upheld "if that impairment was both reasonable and necessary to serve the admittedly important purposes claimed by the State."[58] The Court was, in effect, reading a fifth limitation into the Contract Clause, in addition to the four already considered: an impairment of contract can be upheld if it is both reasonable and necessary to serve an important public purpose. In the instant case, however, the Court held that the impairment was neither necessary to achieve the States' plan to encourage private automobile users to shift to public transportation nor reasonable in light of the circumstances. Total repeal of the covenant was not essential, since

[55] *United States Trust Co.*, 431 U.S. at 26.

[56] *Id.* at 25.

[57] *Id.* at 29.

[58] *Ibid.*

the States' plan could have been implemented with a less drastic modification of the covenant. In addition, without modifying the covenant at all, the States could have adopted alternative means to achieve their twin goals of discouraging automobile use and improving mass transit. The Contract Clause takes away state freedom to impose a drastic impairment when a more moderate course would serve its purpose equally well.

Nor can the repeal be held reasonable on the basis of the need for mass transportation, energy conservation, and environmental protection, since the 1962 covenant was adopted with full knowledge of those concerns. "Indeed, the covenant was specifically intended to protect the pledged revenues and reserves against the possibility that such concerns would lead the Port Authority into greater involvement in deficit mass transit."[59] It is true that, during the years between adoption of the covenant and its repeal, public perception of the importance of mass transit grew because of increased concern with environmental protection and energy conservation. But these were only changes of degree, not of kind, and did not make the repeal reasonable in the light of changed circumstances.

IV. Dual Standard of Review

The *United States Trust* decision was rendered by a bare plurality of the Court. Mr. Justice Brennan, who spoke for the dissenters, accused the Court of "dust[ing] off the Contract Clause and thereby undermin[ing] the bipartisan policies of two States that manifestly seek to further the legitimate needs of their citizens."[60] *United States Trust*, he asserted, rejected the accepted understanding of the Contract Clause and remolded it "into a potent instrument for overseeing important policy determinations of the state legislature."[61]

The Brennan attack stressed what he termed the Court's "novel standard"[62] for reviewing a State's attempt to relieve itself of its own contractual obligations. Mr. Justice Brennan asserted that the Court's stricter standard of judicial review under the Contract

---

[59] *Id.* at 32.

[60] *Id.* at 44–45.

[61] *Id.* at 33.

[62] *Id.* at 53.

Clause when public contracts were at issue was backed by no case and found no support in the legislative history of the Clause.[63]

It is certainly true that the Court's dual standard of review finds no support in the Contract Clause's historical background and rationale. But that is because the issue of the proper standard of review in cases involving public contracts was never thought of, much less discussed, by the men of 1787. Since they did not expressly consider whether the Contract Clause was a protection for those who entered into public contracts, it is scarcely surprising that they did not deal with the proper standard of review in cases where obligations involving the State were impaired. It was only after public contracts were ruled within the reach of the Contract Clause that the question of proper review standard became pertinent.

It is also true that there is no Contract Clause case supporting the Court's dual standard of review. But there is the suggestive analogy of the *Gold Clause Cases*. The first of them was *Norman v. Baltimore & O.R. Co.*[64] It arose out of Congressional and executive action reducing the gold content of the dollar. Under the devaluation program, gold payments by the Treasury were suspended and all persons were required to deliver to the Treasury all gold and gold certificates owned by them in exchange for other currency. In addition, a Joint Resolution abrogated so-called gold clauses (which purported to give obligees a right to require payment of obligations to them only in gold) in all private contracts and government bonds. Under the Resolution, all such contracts and bonds must be "discharged upon payment, dollar for dollar, in any coin or currency which at the time of payment is legal tender."

In the *Norman* case, the holder of a railroad bond bearing an interest coupon payable in gold, with a face value of $22.50, which had been issued before the gold content of the dollar had been lowered, brought suit for payment in gold or for $38.10, the equivalent of gold in devalued dollars. The Court denied his claim, holding that he was required to accept the face value of his interest coupon in the devalued dollars. It is, said the Court, for Congress to determine what constitutes valid money and to fix its value. Congressional power in this respect cannot be frustrated by private contracts such as the gold clauses: "Contracts, however express, cannot

[63] *Id.* at 53 n.16.

[64] 294 U.S. 240 (1935).

fetter the constitutional authority of the Congress."[65] To make devaluation effective and to secure a uniform currency, Congress may invalidate private contracts that interfere with the purposes of devaluation. Abrogation of the gold clauses might reasonably be deemed by Congress to be an appropriate means of carrying out its devaluation policy. "Can we say that this determination is so destitute of basis that the interdiction of the gold clauses must be deemed to be without any reasonable relation to the monetary policy adopted by the Congress?"[66]

A more difficult question was presented in *Perry v. United States*,[67] where gold clauses in the Government's own bonds were at issue. The *Perry* plaintiff sued as owner of a Liberty Loan bond, issued in 1918, which provided that the principal and interest would be paid "in United States gold coin of the present standard of value." The Court held that the Joint Resolution, insofar as it abrogated gold clauses in government as well as private contracts, went too far. When the United States borrows money, it creates a binding obligation to pay the debt as stipulated and cannot thereafter vary its agreement. The power to coin money and regulate the value thereof may not be so exercised as to impair the terms of the obligations which the Government has issued. "Having this power to authorize the issue of definite obligations for the payment of money borrowed, the Congress has not been vested with authority to alter or destroy those obligations."[68]

The *Gold Clause Cases* turn upon application of a dual standard of review of legislation abrogating contractual gold clauses. "There is a clear distinction between the power of the Congress to control or interdict the contracts of private parties when they interfere with the exercise of its constitutional authority, and the power of the Congress to alter or repudiate the substance of its own engagements when it has borrowed money under the authority which the Constitution confers."[69]

The same can well be said of state acts which impair the obligation of contracts. There is a similar distinction between state interferences with obligations arising from private contracts and state acts which alter or repudiate the substance of its own engagements.

---

[65] *Id.* at 307.

[66] *Id.* at 313.

[67] 294 U.S. 330 (1935).

[68] *Id.* at 353.

[69] *Id.* at 350–51. See MASON, HARLAN FISKE STONE 388–92 (1956).

In the latter instance, the State's own self-interest is at stake. In a case such as *United States Trust*, the Contract Clause would provide no protection if the States could reduce their financial obligations whenever they wanted to spend the funds covered by the covenant for what they regarded as another important public purpose.

Mr. Justice Brennan also asserts that the *United States Trust* decision is contrary to the basic principle that the Contract Clause is qualified by the police power. The Court answers this assertion by holding that the covenant which had been impaired involved only a financial obligation and did not contract away the police power. The State may enter into binding financial obligations which may not be abrogated by future exercises of public power.

The Court does indicate that the Contract Clause is not an absolute bar to subsequent modification of a State's own financial obligations. It notes that an impairment of the State's financial obligations "may be constitutional if it is reasonable and necessary to serve an important public purpose."[70] The principle thus stated brings us to the nub of the *United States Trust* decision. The dual standard of review upon which it turns permits the Court to subject the impairment of the State's own obligations to the strictest scrutiny. Only if the impairment was "both reasonable and necessary"[71] to serve the purposes of mass transportation, energy conservation, and environmental protection claimed by the States can it be upheld. The scope of review permitted under this standard is far broader than under the deferential standard that had previously governed in Contract Clause decisions. The Court itself speaks of the "complete deference to a legislative assessment of reasonableness and necessity"[72] appropriate in other cases. In them, the dominant question for the courts was that of "reasonableness" rather than that of "necessity." In *United States Trust*, on the other hand, the Court decided, on its own independent judgment, that the covenant repeal was not necessary to accomplish the State's transportation, energy, and environmental goals.

In terms of other cases involving economic legislation, the States' action in *United States Trust* bore, at the least, a rational relationship to the goals in question. Under the "careful scrutiny"[73] re-

[70] 431 U.S. at 25.

[71] *Id*. at 29.

[72] *Id*. at 26.

[73] *Id*. at 29 n.27.

quired in *United States Trust,* however, that was not enough. The Court determined not whether the covenant repeal was reasonable but whether it was necessary to attain the legislative goals. It answered that question in the negative. The reasons it gave for doing so demonstrate the extent of judicial scrutiny in such a case. According to the Court, repeal of the covenant was not necessary, first of all, because a less drastic modification would have sufficed to attain the States' goals of discouraging auto use and improving mass transit. Second, without modifying the covenant, the States could have adopted alternative means to achieve their goals. The deference normally given to legislative discretion in choosing among alternatives was not appropriate; a State is not free to consider impairing the obligations of its own contracts on a par with other policy alternatives.

United States Trust states that a contract impairment may be constitutional if it is reasonable and necessary to serve an important public purpose. The Court notes that this is also the rule that governs impairments of private contract obligations. Under *United States Trust,* however, there is now a substantial difference in application of the rule in cases involving public, as compared with those involving private, contracts. In the latter cases, the emphasis on review is on the adjective "reasonable": as in other cases dealing with economic rights, the theme is that of deference to legislative determinations which are rationally related to legitimate legislative goals. In public contract cases, the emphasis is on the adjective "necessary":[74] as in *United States Trust* itself, the reviewing court must determine, on its own judgment, whether the impairing act is essential to attainment of the justifying public purposes. In making that determination, the court must apply the test of the least restrictive alternative that has been developed as a fundamental element of strict-scrutiny review in other areas of constitutional law.[75] The drastic impairment in *United States Trust* is not permitted when the Court concludes that "an evident and more moderate course would serve [the States'] purposes equally well."[76]

[74] Of course, the opposing views here parallel those in the famous Hamilton-Jefferson debate over the Necessary and Proper Clause, which was resolved by McCulloch v. Maryland, 4 Wheat. 316 (1819).

[75] See Massachusetts Board of Retirement v. Murgia, 427 U.S. 307 (1976).

[76] *United States Trust Co.,* 431 U.S. at 31.

V. Allied Structural Steel Co. v. Spannaus

The decision in the *United States Trust* case was based upon the principle that impairments of a State's own contracts would face stricter scrutiny under the Contract Clause than impairments of contracts between private parties. The same was not true of the decision in *Allied Structural Steel Co. v. Spannaus*, since the state law at issue there affected only private contractual obligations. But the result was the same.

Appellant in *Allied Structural Steel* had a pension plan for its employees, including those in its Minnesota office. Under the plan, employees who quit or were discharged before age sixty-five who had not acquired vested pension rights were not entitled to any pensions. The case arose out of enactment of the Minnesota Private Pension Benefits Protection Act. It provided that an employer who had established an employee pension plan was subject to a "pension-funding charge" if he either terminated the plan or closed a Minnesota office. The charge was to be assessed if the pension funds were not sufficient to cover full pensions for all employees who had worked at least ten years. Soon after enactment of the law, appellant closed its Minnesota office and discharged eleven of its Minnesota employees. Nine of them did not have any vested pension rights but had worked for the company for more than ten years. The State notified appellant that it owed a pension-funding charge of $185,000 under the provisions of the Private Pension Benefits Protection Act. Appellant then brought suit in a federal district court asking for injunctive and declaratory relief. It claimed that the Act unconstitutionally impaired its contractual obligations to its employees under its pension plan.

The Supreme Court agreed with appellant's claim, holding that Minnesota's imposition of the new obligation on the employer violated the Contract Clause. There was no doubt, said the Court, that the Minnesota law did operate as a substantial impairment of a contractual relationship: the impact of the law upon appellant's contractual obligations was both substantial and severe. It retroactively modified the compensation that appellant had agreed to pay its employees, and it did so by changing appellant's obligations in an area where the element of reliance was vital—funding of the pension plan. Moreover, the vesting requirement was imposed only on employers who terminated their pension plans or who, like appellant, closed their Minnesota offices. This forced the employer to make all the retroactive changes in its contractual obligations at one time. "Thus, the statute in question here nullifies express terms of the company's contractual obligations and imposes a completely unexpected liability in potentially disabling amounts."[77]

It is true that, unlike the law at issue in *United States Trust*, the Minnesota statute plainly involved an exercise of the State's police power. That did not, however, require the law to be upheld. Even police power legislation, according to the Court, may prove unable to run the Contract Clause gauntlet. "If the Contract Clause is to retain any meaning at all, however, it must be understood to impose *some* limits upon the power of a State to abridge existing contractual relationships, even in the exercise of its otherwise legitimate police power."[78]

The limits which the Contract Clause imposes even upon the police power were drawn by the Court from prior cases, particularly the *Blaisdell* case,[79] where the Minnesota mortgage moratorium law had been upheld. Most commentaries on *Blaisdell* have focused on the economic emergency which called forth the moratorium law. The *Allied Structural* opinion stressed that the *Blaisdell* law was also "enacted to protect a basic societal interest, not a favored group,"[80] that its relief was appropriately designed for the need it was enacted to meet, that the imposed conditions were reasonable, and that it was limited to the duration of the emergency.

In the case of the pension benefits law, on the other hand, there was no showing "that this severe disruption of contractual expectations was necessary to meet an important general social problem."[81] The pension law was found not to possess the attributes of the *Blaisdell* law that had enabled the latter to survive challenge under the Contract Clause. It did not effect a temporary alteration of contractual relationships but worked a severe, permanent, and immediate change in those relationships. Its aim was leveled not at every employer, or even at every employer who left the State, but only at those who had in the past established pension plans for their employees. Unlike the *Blaisdell* law, this law can hardly be charac-

[77] 438 U.S. at 247.

[78] *Id.* at 242.

[79] 290 U.S. 398 (1934).

[80] 438 U.S. at 242.

[81] *Id.* at 247.

terized as one enacted to protect a broad societal interest rather than a narrow class. The pension law was not even purportedly enacted to deal with a broad, generalized economic or social problem; it has an extremely narrow focus and enters an area never before subject to regulation by the State: "if the Contract Clause means anything at all, it means that Minnesota could not constitutionally do what it tried to do to the company in this case."[82]

VI. Enlarging Contract Obligations

Mr. Justice Brennan, who had dissented from what he called the Court's "dust[ing] off" of the Contract Clause in the *United States Trust* case, also delivered a strong dissent in *Allied Structural Steel.* He asserted that until then the Court had interpreted the Contract Clause only as prohibiting state acts which effectively diminished or nullified the obligation due a party under the terms of a contract: "The Clause was . . . intended by the Framers to be applicable only to laws which altered the obligations of contracts by effectively relieving one party of the obligation to perform a contract duty."[83] The Minnesota Pension Act did not abrogate or dilute any obligation due a party to a contract; instead, the law imposed new, additional obligations. In this case, the Court had converted the Contract Clause into a limitation on state power to enact laws that impose duties additional to obligations assumed under private contracts.

According to Mr. Justice Brennan, the Contract Clause's term "impairing" cannot be interpreted as including laws which create new duties. Such an interpretation, however, takes too narrow a view of the Contract Clause's language and history. It is true that the word "impair" does mean to diminish. But that is not its only meaning. Taken literally, the word means to make worse or less valuable. It follows that another accepted meaning is to damage or injure.[84] Under this meaning, the Minnesota pension law can be said to impair appellant's contractual obligations; imposing the additional obligations upon it did injure its contractual position.

Mr. Justice Brennan asserts categorically that the Framers never contemplated the application of the Contract Clause to a case like

[82] *Id.* at 250–51.

[83] *Id.* at 257.

[84] See 6 Oxford English Dictionary 72.

Allied Structural Steel. Yet, he concedes, "the debates in the Constitutional Convention and the subsequent public discussion of the Constitution are not particularly enlightening in determining the scope of the Clause."[85] He goes on to say that "the sole evil at which the Contract Clause was directed"[86] was the theretofore rampant debtors' relief legislation, interfering with the ability of creditors to secure payment from the security provided by the contract. His interpretation may be the correct one. With all respect, however, it must be said that the legislative history equally supports the opposite view.

A motion to add a Contract Clause to the Constitution was made on August 28, 1787, by Rufus King, who "moved to add, in the words used in the Ordinance of Cong[ress] establishing new States, a prohibition on the States to interfere in private contracts."[87] The motion failed to pass. The short debate on King's motion was notable for its absence of any reference to debtors' relief legislation,[88] and the same was true of other references to the Contract Clause in the Framers' Convention—which scarcely supports the Brennan view on "the sole evil at which the Contract Clause was aimed."

The wording of the Contract Clause was arrived at in the Committee on Style, which added to the prohibition against bills of attainder and ex post facto laws a prohibition against "altering or impairing the obligation of contracts."[89] Two days later, in a further refinement, the committee dropped the word "altering."[90] We know nothing of the discussion in the committee, and since the committee's draft clause was accepted without debate, we can only guess at the reasons for the changes. Since King was a member of the Committee on Style, we can assume that he tried to retain at least the substance of his original proposal. He may well have considered the prohibition against "altering" as a stylistic refinement, since "impairing" might be deemed to include alterations which substantially changed contract obligations.

This is, of course, all speculation, since, as stated, there is no indi-

---

85 438 U.S. at 257.

86 *Ibid.*

87 2 Farrand, Records of the Federal Convention of 1787 439 (1911).

88 *Id.* at 439–41.

89 See Wright, note 20 *supra,* at 9.

90 2 Farrand, note 87 *supra,* at 597.

cation as to why the Committee on Style made its changes[91] or why Rufus King went along with them.[92] There is, however, an interesting indication of the Framers' intent in the Convention discussion of the ex post facto aspect of the Contract Clause. After King made his motion on August 28, George Mason objected that the proposed clause went "too far," since statutes limiting the period for bringing actions might be necessary. James Wilson then said that the answer to Mason's objection was "that *retrospective* interferences only are to be prohibited."[93] At which point Madison asked, "Is not that already done by the prohibition of *ex post facto* laws?"[94]

The next day John Dickinson cited Blackstone to show that the ex post facto prohibition applied only to criminal cases.[95] Dickinson's demonstration indicated that, without the Contract Clause, there would be no bar to retrospective civil legislation.[96] From this point of view, the Contract Clause was intended to fill the gap as an ex post facto clause on the civil side, at least so far as contractual obligations were concerned.

If that is true, it supports the interpretation of the Contract Clause as a reenactment of the Northwest Ordinance's prohibition against interferences with contracts, in light of Wilson's caution that only retrospective interferences were to be prohibited. This was the view indicated in the *Federalist*,[97] and it accorded with the notion of inviolable natural rights which prevailed at the time.[98] Even Thomas Paine could assert, not long before the Framers' Convention, that "a lawful contract or agreement . . . cannot be affected by any act made afterwards."[99]

If Mr. Justice Brennan's interpretation of the Contract Clause as not applicable to imposition of additional contract obligations is

---

[91] WRIGHT, note 20 *supra*, at 9.

[92] If, indeed, King did. We do not know that he did since, as stated, the debates and votes in the committee were not made public. The tradition is that James Wilson wrote the Contract Clause for the committee. See SHIRLEY, THE DARTMOUTH COLLEGE CAUSES AND THE SUPREME COURT OF THE UNITED STATES 216 (1879). But it is hard to believe King did not play a part, since he made the original motion for a Contract Clause.

[93] 2 FARRAND, note 87 *supra*, at 440.

[94] *Ibid.*

[95] *Id.* at 448–49.

[96] See WRIGHT, note 20 *supra*, at 10.

[97] Note 9 *supra*, at Nos. 7, 44, pp. 65, 282–83.

[98] See WRIGHT, note 20 *supra*, at 18.

[99] COMPLETE WRITINGS OF THOMAS PAINE 380 (Foner ed. 1945).

not borne out by the legislative history, neither is it borne out by the judicial interpretation of the Clause. According to *Allied Structural Steel*, "The novel construction of the Contract Clause expressed in the dissenting opinion is wholly contrary to the decisions of this Court."[100] It is true that early cases support the Brennan view—notably *Satterlee v. Matthewson*,[101] where the Court upheld a statute that gave validity to a contract which the highest state court had held invalid at common law. A law which gave validity to a void contract was ruled not one which impaired the obligation of that contract: "it surely cannot be contended, that to create a contract, and to destroy or impair one, mean the same thing."[102]

The *Allied Structural Steel* majority recognizes that *Satterlee* arguably supports the Brennan view that the Contract Clause forbids only state laws that diminish the duties of a contractual obligor and not laws that increase them. Yet, as it notes, that "narrow view . . . has since been expressly repudiated."[103] Since 1833, when *Satterlee* was cited as authority for sustaining a law reviving a contract which was voidable for usury,[104] the Court has followed the rule first stated by way of *obiter* in a 1907 case: "any attempt to increase the obligation beyond that incurred by the stockholder would fall within the prohibition of the Constitution."[105] This dictum was acted upon in *Detroit United Ry. v. Michigan*[106] and *Georgia Ry. & Power Co. v. Decatur*.[107] In those cases the Court struck down statutes which extended the obligation of a street railway to charge the fare fixed in its contract with the city (franchise) in new territory annexed to the city. The Court held that such a statute "does substantially impair the obligation of the contract by adding to its burdens."[108]

According to Mr. Justice Brennan, referring to the *Detroit United* and *Georgia Ry.* cases, "These opinions reflect the then-prevailing philosophy of economic due process which has since been repudi-

---

100 438 U.S. at 244 n.16.

101 2 Pet. 380 (1829).

102 *Id.* at 413.

103 438 U.S. at 244 n.16.

104 Ewell v. Daggs, 108 U.S. 143, 151 (1883).

105 Bernheimer v. Converse, 206 U.S. 516, 530 (1907). Interestingly enough, the first statement of this principle was by Justice Washington, who had also delivered the *Satterlee* opinion. Green v. Biddle, 8 Wheat. 1, 84 (1823).

106 242 U.S. 238 (1916).

107 262 U.S. 432 (1923).

108 *Id.* at 439.

ated."[109] It is difficult to see how this pejorative due process characterization is pertinent, however, since the cases in question were decided under the narrow prohibition in the Contract Clause, not the broad contours of the Due Process Clause. Mr. Justice Brennan goes on to make the bare assertion, "In my view, the reasoning of *Georgia Ry.* and *Detroit United Ry.* is simply wrong."[110]

This assertion is not supported by any reasoning other than the arguments based upon the language and intent of the Contract Clause. It ignores the fact that the *Detroit United–Georgia Ry.* approach has never been overruled. In particular, *Detroit United* was specifically followed in *Columbia Ry., Gas & Electric Co. v. South Carolina*,[111] decide shortly before *Georgia Ry.* itself. The facts in *Columbia Ry.*, more than those in any other reported case, show why the Brennan conception of the Contract Clause is too narrow. The company in *Columbia Ry.* had acquired a canal from public trustees and agreed to extend it, as soon as practicable, to a certain point. A later statute provided that, because the canal had not been completed to that point, the company's title was forfeited and transferred from the company to the State. This statute was ruled violative of the Contract Clause, with the Court declaring expressly that "[t]he impairment of a contract may consist in increasing its burdens as well as in diminishing its efficiency."[112]

It is difficult to believe that Mr. Justice Brennan and his fellow dissenters in *Allied Structural Steel* would uphold the statute at issue in *Columbia Ry.* Yet the Brennan dissent does not even cite the *Columbia Ry.* decision, despite the fact that it is the strongest support for the rule that a statute which increases contractual burdens may violate the Contract Clause.

The *Columbia Ry.* case demonstrates the logical fallacy of the view that the Contract Clause reaches only state acts which diminish, but not those which increase, obligations due under a contract. The *Allied Structural Steel* opinion points out that "in any bilateral contract the diminution of duties on one side effectively increases the duties on the other."[113] The converse is also true: increasing the

---

[109] 438 U.S. at 259 n.7.

[110] *Ibid.*

[111] 261 U.S. 236 (1923).

[112] *Id.* at 251.

[113] 438 U.S. at 245, n.16.

burdens of one party to a contract normally has the effect of diminishing the obligation of the other.[114]

This is illustrated clearly by the *Columbia Ry.* case. As already noted, the Court there struck down the state statute, which provided that the company forfeit its title to the State because of its failure to complete the canal, as one which greatly increased the burdens of the company's contractual obligation. But the statute in question not only increased the burdens of the company; it also had the effect of weakening an obligation of the State. The grant of the canal to the company by the public trustees as agent of the State implied a contractual obligation by the State not to reassert a claim to the canal. This obligation of the State was plainly diminished by the later statute.[115]

The same can be said of the statute at issue in the *Allied Structural Steel* case. Before the Minnesota pension law, an employee had a vested right to a pension only if he met the strict requirements of the employer's pension plan. After the law, which on its face merely increased the employer's obligations, an employee acquired full pension rights, fulfilling the obligations by working only ten years.

VII. Personal to Property Rights

In his *United States Trust* dissent, Mr. Justice Brennan noted "that this is the first case in some 40 years in which this Court has seen fit to invalidate purely economic and social legislation on the strength of the Contract Clause."[116] But more, he asserted, was at stake than the Court's resurrection of the Contract Clause from constitutional limbo. In earlier days "this Court treated 'the liberty of contract' under the Due Process Clause as virtually indistinguishable from the Contract Clause."[117] More recently, however, the Court "wisely" has come to embrace a unified deferential approach to legislative action attacked under constitutional provisions protecting property rights.[118] To Mr. Justice Brennan, the *United States Trust* decision has more disturbing implications than revival of the

[114] *Cf.* Hale, *The Supreme Court and the Contract Clause*, 57 Harv. L. Rev. 512, 516, n.24 (1944).

[115] *Ibid.*

[116] 431 U.S. at 60.

[117] *Id.* at 61.

[118] *Ibid.*

Contract Clause alone: "today's case signals a return to substantive constitutional review of States' policies, and a new resolve to protect property owners whose interest or circumstances may happen to appeal to Members of this Court."[119]

United States Trust does provide for strict scrutiny under the Contract Clause in cases involving contracts of the State itself. In doing so, it extends, for the first time, the broader review role which the Court has adopted in cases involving personal rights to cases in which economic rights are restricted. In this sense, *United States Trust* substantially alters modern constitutional jurisprudence governing regulation of private economic interests.[120]

Allied Structural Steel carries the protection of rights under the Contract Clause still further, for it applies to purely private contracts in which the State's self-interest is not at stake. The *Allied Structural Steel* decision virtually imposes upon state laws which impair the obligations of private contracts the need to meet the conditions which called forth the mortgage moratorium legislation sustained in the *Blaisdell* case,[121] except perhaps for the requirement of the existence of an emergency. The Court stressed that the *Blaisdell* law was "enacted to protect a basic societal interest";[122] its terms were reasonable and limited in duration. The *Allied Structural Steel* pension law was, in the Court's view, not similar. It was aimed only at employers who closed their Minnesota offices after having established pension plans; it worked a severe and permanent change in contractual relationships under those plans. Unlike the *Blaisdell* law, it had an extremely narrow focus and in an area never before subjected to regulation by the State.

Under *Allied Structural Steel*, the validity of a state law impinging on private contracts will turn on whether it is aimed at a generalized social problem, whether its duties apply to a broad class of persons, whether it is temporary or permanent, and whether it deals with an area previously subject to regulation. "The necessary consequence of the extreme malleability of these rather vague criteria is to vest judges with broad subjective discretion to protect property interests that happen to appeal to them."[123]

---

[119] *Ibid.*

[120] *Cf. id.* at 33.

[121] See text *supra*, at notes 46–47.

[122] 438 U.S. at 242.

[123] *Spannaus*, 438 U.S. at 261 (Brennan, J., dissenting).

From what has been said, *United States Trust* and *Allied Structural Steel* seem out of line with the thrust of modern Supreme Court jurisprudence in cases involving property rights. These recent Contract Clause decisions appear to apply the stricter scrutiny which the Court has come to deem appropriate in cases in which personal rights are at issue. Do they, as such, presage an extension of judicial activism in reviewing state acts which impinge upon economic interests? Will broader review of impairments of contract obligations lead to broader review of infringements of the "liberty of contract" guaranteed by the Due Process Clause?

If future decisions answer these questions in the affirmative, it will support the position of critics of the Court's double standard of review, which allows strict scrutiny in cases involving personal rights and requires deference to the legislator in cases involving regulation of property rights. In these recent Contract Clause cases, the Court has, for the first time in four decades, subjected legislative acts infringing upon private economic interests to the standard of strict scrutiny. Such an extension of strict scrutiny beyond the area of personal rights indicates that those who supposed that judicial activism could be confined to the area of personal rights were unrealistic in their assumption.

It is true that, from the *Carolene Products* case[124] in 1938 to the *United States Trust* case in 1977, the protection of personal rights was the area that found judicial favor. But *United States Trust* and *Allied Structural Steel* show that it was unwarranted to assume that the Court would continue to intervene actively only in cases involving personal rights. As Justice Frankfurter once put it:[125]

> Yesterday the active area in this field was concerned with "property." Today it is "civil liberties." Tomorrow it may again be "property." Who can say that in a society with a mixed economy, like ours, these two areas are sharply separated, and that certain freedoms in relation to property may not again be deemed, as they were in the past, aspects of individual freedom?

Unrestrained judicial activism, today, on matters of personal right inevitably opens the door to similar activism, tomorrow, on matters of economic interest. That is true for two reasons. In the

---

[124] United States v. Carolene Products Co., 304 U.S. 144 (1938).

[125] FRANKFURTER, OF LAW AND MEN 19 (1956).

first place, as Justice Holmes declared in a celebrated passage, "The great ordinances of the Constitution do not establish and divide fields of black and white."[126] Nor does the organic instrument differentiate qualitatively between the different provisions that make up its text. As no constitutional guaranty enjoys preference, the Justices are not justified in engaging in mutilating selection of the Constitution, giving full effect only to those parts which for the moment find personal favor with individual Justices.[127]

Second, as Judge Learned Hand once put it, "Just why property itself was not a 'personal right' nobody took the time to explain."[128] More recently the Supreme Court itself has recognized that "the dichotomy between personal liberties and property rights is a false one. . . . In fact, a fundamental interdependence exists between the personal right to liberty and the personal right in property. Neither could have meaning without the other."[129]

The interdependence referred to was all but self-evident to those who drew up the organic structure. If anything is clear from the words and actions of the Framers, it is that, to them, property was an important as liberty. "The preservation of property . . . " declared a member of the first Supreme Court who had been one of the men of 1787, "is a primary object of the social compact."[130] Without property rights, the Framers well knew, the rights of the person himself would be devoid of practical content. "Property must be secured," affirmed John Adams, "or liberty cannot exist."[131]

More recently, such emphasis on protection of property has come to seem misplaced. In today's hierarchy of values, the rights of property tend to be relegated to a lesser level. For we have forgotten what, to the Framers, was the self-evident truth, that both person and property must be placed upon a plane of protection, since both are equally essential to freedom. The ultimate social interest in our system may be that in the individual life. But the fulfillment of that

---

[126] Springer v. Philippine Islands, 277 U.S. 189, 209 (1928) (dissenting).

[127] *Cf.* Ullmann v. United States, 350 U.S. 422, 429 (1956).

[128] Hand, *Chief Justice Stone's Conception of the Judicial Function*, 46 Col. L. Rev. 696, 698 (1946), reprinted in Hand, The Spirit of Liberty 201, 206 (Phoenix ed. 1975).

[129] Lynch v. Household Finance Corp., 405 U.S. 538, 552 (1972).

[130] Paterson, J., in Vanhorne's Lessee v. Dorrance, 2 Dall. 304, 310 (C.C. Pa. 1795).

[131] 6 Works of John Adams 280 (C. F. Adams ed. 1851).

social interest is impossible without the institution of property.[132] The very maintenance of individuality is closely entwined with the property rights of the individual: "you take my life, / When you do take the means whereby I live."[133]

It is consequently not accurate to think of the personal rights–property rights dichotomy as involving only a conflict between individual and social interests. If balance we must, should we not place on the individual's side the importance of the institution of property in the free society? The vindication of property rights themselves may, in other words, be stated in terms of social interests. The society which has a clear interest in furthering the general progress and the individual life also has an interest in securing property rights insofar as they contribute to the advance of those interests.

From this point of view, the recent Contract Clause cases represent a first swing in the judicial pendulum away from the jurisprudence which had, since 1937, placed property rights virtually beyond the pale of constitutional protection. If this is true, Mr. Justice Brennan's apprehension that they may foreshadow a wider swing, which will extend the Court's activist posture beyond the area of personal rights, may be soundly based. As Mr. Justice Brennan points out, there is a close relationship between contract rights and other property rights.[134] Other constitutional protections are akin to the Contract Clause in protecting property, and the liberty of contract protected by due process was once treated by the Court as all but indistinguishable from the Contract Clause.[135] The historical tendency for the Contract Clause and the Due Process Clause to coalesce[136] may be repeated in our own day.

---

[132] CHAFEE, HOW HUMAN RIGHTS GOT INTO THE CONSTITUTION 2 (1952).

[133] MERCHANT OF VENICE, 4. 1. 77–78.

[134] *United States Trust Co.*, 431 U.S. at 60 (dissenting).

[135] *Id.* at 60–61.

[136] Hale, *The Supreme Court and the Contract Clause: III*, 57 HARV. L. REV. 852, 890 (1944).

SANFORD LEVINSON

"THE CONSTITUTION" IN AMERICAN CIVIL RELIGION

In his classic article *Constitution and Court as Symbols*,[1] Max Lerner pointed to the role of the United States Constitution in what later analysts would term America's civil religion.[2] "Every tribe," said Lerner "clings to something which it believes to possess supernatural powers, as an instrument for controlling unknown forces in a hostile universe."[3] The American tribe is no different. "In fact the very habits of mind begotten by an authoritarian Bible and a religion of submission to a higher power have been carried over to an authoritarian Constitution and a philosophy of submission to a 'higher law'; and a country like America, in which its early tradition had prohibited a state church, ends by getting a state church after all, although in a secular form."[4] And, of course, as indicated by Lerner's title, the United States Supreme Court plays an es-

Sanford Levinson is Professor of Law, University of Texas.

AUTHOR'S NOTE: I am grateful to Paul Brest, Amy Gutmann, Stanley N. Katz, Walter Murphy, and Richard Rabinowitz for their comments on an earlier draft of this article.

[1] Lerner, *Constitution and Court as Symbols*, 46 YALE L.J. 1290 (1937).

[2] See, *e.g.*, RICHEY & JONES, EDS., AMERICAN CIVIL RELIGION (1974). This excellent volume contains, among others, the influential 1967 essay by Robert Ballah, *Civil Religion in America*, which sparked much of the revived interest in the notion.

[3] Lerner, note 1 *supra*, at 1294–95. [4] *Id*. at 1294.

sential role in the religion. It is, so to speak, the institutional church that incarnates the sacred document. As Professor Alpheus T. Mason once wrote: "In our tripartite constitutional system, it is the Holy of Holies."[5] There is more than one theorist who views the Supreme Court as the "rock" upon which the Constitution stands and the Court's pronouncements therefore as "the keys to the kingdom" of the heavenly status of a country ruled "by law" instead of by people.[6]

Religious language is a natural part of America's political vocabulary. In a remarkable 1838 address on "The Perpetuation of Our Political Institutions," Abraham Lincoln called for self-conscious adherence to the "political religion of the nation"—"reverence for the laws."[7] Representative Barbara Jordan was simply affirming this call when she articulated her own creed, just prior to voting for the impeachment of Richard Nixon: "My faith in the Constitution is whole, it is complete, it is total, and I am not going to sit here and be an idle spectator to the diminution, the subversion of the Constitution."[8]

Those historians and sociologists who have revived interest in the study of civil religion usually emphasize its integrative function. Thus, Robin Williams refers to the fact that certain "symbols can supply an overarching sense of unity even in a society otherwise riddled with conflict."[9] What is remarkable about this emphasis of unity provided by civil religion is the way it overlooks the fact that religion, especially over the past 500 years, has served much more as a source of deep cleavage than of unity. Indeed, the most fundamental schism in Western religious history came precisely from disputes over the interpretation to be given the pas-

[5] Mason, *The Supreme Court: Temple and Forum*, 48 YALE REV. 524, 526 (1959).

[6] "And I say this to you: You are Peter, the Rock; and on this rock I will build my church, and the forces of death shall never overpower it. I will give you the keys of the kingdom of Heaven; what you forbid on earth shall be forbidden in heaven, and what you allow on earth shall be allowed in heaven." *Matthew* 16:18–19.

[7] Lincoln, *The Perpetuation of Our Political Institutions*, in THE POLITICAL THOUGHT OF ABRAHAM LINCOLN 16–17 (1961 ed.).

[8] Quoted in Levinson, *The Specious Morality of the Law*, HARPER'S 35 (May 1977).

[9] WILLIAMS, AMERICAN SOCIETY: A SOCIOLOGICAL INTERPRETATION (1951), quoted in Herberg, *America's Civil Religion: What It Is and Whence It Comes*, in RICHEY & JONES, note 2 *supra*, at 76.

sage from Matthew alluded to earlier about "the rock" upon which Christianity was to be built,[10] for the claim of the Roman Catholic Church, and more particularly of papal supremacy within the Church, rests in significant measure on this passage. A key element of the protestant Reformation, of course, was the rejection of the Church's authority, and even in this "post-Christian" age, we have not yet left behind the implications of Luther's momentous revolt.

There is, then, a double message contained within the analogy of the Constitution to a sacred text or the Supreme Court to a holy institution. The first, emphasizing unity and integration, is the one with which we are most familiar. I propose here, however, to examine the alternative message, which is the potential of a written constitution to serve as a source of disintegration. Indeed, many classic constitutional controversies have their parallels within the religious disputes of the sixteenth and seventeenth centuries. The object of this analysis is not only to present a somewhat different perspective from which to look at the Constitution, but also to attack by implication any confidence that having "the Constitution" as a common symbol guarantees meaningful national political unity.

Two aspects of the Protestant Reformation are of central import: The first is the argument as to the source of Christian doctrine. The second concerns the institutional nature of Christianity, even assuming agreement on its doctrinal basis. The two are, of course, interrelated, but can be analytically separated.

It is a commonplace that the Protestant reformers, especially the followers of Martin Luther, emphasized the centrality of Scripture to Christianity.[11] *Sola scriptura* were the great watchwords; an authentic Christianity must be based on the Scriptures alone. "The BIBLE, I say, the BIBLE only, is the religion of Protestants."[12] Not the least important program of the reformers was their insistence on translation of the Bible into vernacular languages, so that the divine word could be known directly even to readers untrained in Latin.[13]

---

[10] See note 6 *supra*.

[11] See 3 CAMBRIDGE HISTORY OF THE BIBLE: THE WEST FROM THE REFORMATION TO THE PRESENT DAY 1–6 (Greenslade ed.) (1963).

[12] *Id.* at 175, quoting CHILLINGWORTH, THE RELIGION OF PROTESTANTS: A SAFE WAY TO SALVATION (1638).

[13] CAMBRIDGE HISTORY, note 11 *supra*, at 94–174.

The Catholic Church did not, of course, reject Scripture. Indeed, one of the principal bases of its institutional authority was the passage from Matthew. Yet it supplemented reliance on Scripture with the independent authority of oral tradition. As declared at the Council of Trent—the 1546 counterattack against Protestant heresies—unwritten traditions were coequal in stature to Scripture, and these traditions were stated to be those "which were received by the apostles from the lips of Christ himself, or by the same apostles at the dictation of the Holy Spirit and were handed down and have come down to us."[14] The key to the authoritativeness of tradition was its preservation "by unbroken succession in the Church."[15] According to one commentator, "the Council could fairly claim that Bible and Tradition were to be received *pari affectu*, with an equal reverence from believers."[16]

Frank Kermode points out, moreover, that it had been seriously proposed by some members of the Council that tradition be accorded supremacy: "[F]or since scripture was always subject to the superior traditional knowledge of the Church, it could be called redundant and, in the hands of ignorant outsiders, a source of error."[17] Even if the "inutility" of Scripture was rejected, its linkage to tradition remained central. As Cardinal Bellarmine argued in his treatise *The Word of God*, Lutherans were mistaken in asserting that "everything necessary for faith and behavior is contained in the scriptures," for "as well as the written word of God we require the unwritten word, that is, the divine and apostolic traditions."[18] Because Scripture is often "ambigous and perplexing," says Bellarmine, there are "many places in which we shall be unable to reach certainty" unless the text is supplemented "by accepting the traditions of the Church."[19]

The traditional Catholic emphasis on the capacity of human reason to supply the teachings of natural law should also be mentioned, because this source provided yet another means by which

---

[14] *Id.* at 193–94.

[15] *Id.* at 193–94.

[16] *Id.* at 201.

[17] Kermode, *Institutional Control of Interpretation*, 43 SALMAGUNDI 72, 78 (Winter 1979).

[18] Quoted in 2 SKINNER, THE FOUNDATIONS OF MODERN POLITICAL THOUGHT: THE AGE OF REFORMATION 146 (1978).

[19] *Id.* at 146.

the necessity of reliance on the written text could be limited.[20] Early Protestants, on the other hand, by returning to a much more Augustinian emphasis on human depravity, rejected right reason as well as the Church's institutional traditions.[21]

One vital difference then between the initial reformers—particularly Luther—and the Church concerned the exclusivity of Scripture as the basis of Christian doctrine and behavior. Yet, we are reminded that this disagreement is not sufficient to explain the schism between these two segments of Christianity:[22]

> The reformers dethroned the pope and enthroned the Bible. This is the common assertion; but when so stated it is not valid, because a book cannot replace a man. A book has to be interpreted. This was the main reason why authority had come to be ascribed to the pope in faith and morals.

As the quotation from Cardinal Bellarmine indicates, one cannot understand the historical reality of the schism without recognizing the importance of the connection between an emphasis on tradition and the need for an institutional authority to articulate this unwritten body of knowledge. And to this day defense of the authority of the Church emphasizes the relative subordinance of "Scripture and the subsequent documents of the tradition" to "a living magisterium that articulates universal Christian meanings."[23] The problem of institutional authority, however, presents itself even if one agrees that Scripture alone is the proper guide. It is possible to proclaim the authority of Scripture while assigning the duty of interpretation to a particular institution whose decisions as to disputed passages are to be accepted as final by all members of the denomination.

Martin Luther's attack on the Church was not confined simply to its use of unwritten tradition as a supplement to Scripture. He attacked its authority as an institution. In his 1520 *Open Letter to the Christian Nobility of the German Nation*, Luther denounced what he termed the "second wall" of the Church's defense of its own authority: "[W]hen the attempt is made to reprove them out

---

[20] See *id.* at 148–66. [21] *Id.* at 3–6.

[22] 3 Cambridge History, note 11 *supra*, at 1.

[23] Chirico, Infallibility: The Crossroads of Doctrine 219–20 (1977). Part of Father Chirico's argument emphasizes the historicity of all documents.

of the Scriptures, they raise the objection that the interpretation of the Scriptures belongs to no one except the pope."[24]

Luther begins his attack on papal authority by asking, "And if it were true, where would be the need or use of the Holy Scriptures?" He goes on, after quoting from Scripture, to make an argument concerning the ability of any true Christian to offer a "true understanding" of the text: "[A]n ordinary man may have true understanding; why then should we not follow him? Has not the pope erred many times? Who would help Christendom when the pope errs, if we were not to believe another, who had the Scriptures on his side, more than the pope?"[25] As to the passage from Matthew about the keys of the kingdom, Luther's response is that "it is plain enough that the keys were not given to Peter alone, but to the whole community."[26] Again he points to the dilemma of fitting in papal infallibility with traditional Christian doctrine: "[I]t is not the pope alone who is always in the right if the article of the Creed is correct: 'I believe one holy Christian church,' otherwise the prayer must run: 'I believe in the pope at Rome,' and so reduce the Christian Church to one man—which would be nothing else than a devilish error."[27] He then concludes his argument by evoking the powerful image of the priesthood of all believers:[28]

> Since we are all priests and all have one faith, one gospel, and one sacrament, why then should we not have the authority to test and determine what is right in the faith? Abraham had to listen to Sarah who was more subject than we are to anyone on earth, and Balaam's ass was wiser than the prophet himself. If then God could speak through an ass against a prophet, when can he not speak through a godly man against the pope?
>
> . . . Therefore it behooves every Christian to espouse the cause of the faith, to understand and defend it, and to rebuke all errors.

This argument can easily enough be read as rejecting the institutional competence of any organized church to proclaim its sole authority over interpretation of Scripture.[29] Protestantism has

---

[24] LUTHER, THREE TREATISES 13 (1974 ed.).

[25] *Id.* at 21.

[26] *Id.* at 22.

[27] *Id.* at 23.

[28] *Ibid.*

[29] See SKINNER, note 18 *supra*, at 10–15. "The true Church becomes nothing more than an invisible *congregatio fidelium*, a congregation of the faithful gathered together in God's name. . . . While introducing . . . later concessions [in regard to

had, of course, an extremely complex historical reality, including organization into institutional churches, and a complete understanding of even radical Protestants like the Baptists requires recognition of the ways by which religious communities are formed and exercise authority over their members.[30] Nonetheless, if one focuses on the logic of certain Protestant arguments, there is a strong push to a radically deinstitutionalized relationship between the individual believer and the God revealed in Scripture.

It cannot be stressed too much, moreover, that rejection of institutional authority is not at all the equivalent of antinomianism, which is rejection of the binding authority of the Word (or Law) itself. Instead it is up to each believer to decide what the Word actually requires. This version of the Protestant tradition was explicated in America by Roger Williams. "In vain have English Parliaments permitted English Bibles in the poorest English houses, and the simplest man and woman to search the Scriptures, if yet against their souls' persuasion from the Scripture, they should be forced (as if they lived in Spain or Rome itself without the sight of a Bible) to believe as the Church believes."[31] This emphasis on individual competence served as an essential underpinning of Williams's theory of qualified religious toleration, though the intra-Protestant struggles of the seventeenth and eighteenth centuries should serve as reminders that toleration was the historical exception rather than the rule.

The deinstitutionalization of authority could also have volatile implications for political structure, especially when that structure

---

visible embodiment of the Church], however, Luther continued to insist that the true Church has no real existence except in the heart of its faithful members. His central conviction was always that the Church can simply be equated with *Gottes Volk*, 'the people of God living from the word of God.'" *Id.* at 10–11.

[30] I am indebted to Richard Rabinowitz for making me recognize that the Protestant experience has often been communitarian. The Catholic theologian, Hans Küng, even while attacking—often like a latter-day Luther—claims of papal infallibility, nevertheless quotes an Evangelical theologian for the proposition that the "Reformers themselves were by no means inclined to let the Church become a debating hall for all possible types of belief." For Küng, "All this, seen in its brutal reality, forms for the Catholic theologian the historical evidence for the fact that the alternative to the authoritarian Roman doctrinal system, certainly cannot be Protestantism which protests against all authority in the Church (it scarcely exists in Protestantism anyway)." Küng, Infallible? An Inquiry 142 (1971), quoting Steck, *Die Autorität der Offenbarung. Das Erste Vatikanum im Urteil evangelischer Theologie*, Publik (Jan. 16, 1970).

[31] 3 Cambridge History, note 11 *supra*, at 186.

was viewed as under obligation to follow divine law. As one of the most radical Puritan theorists, Christopher Goodman, argued, God's law was "not geven onely to the Rulers and Governors (thoghe I confesse it chieflie apperteyneth to their office to see it executed, for which cause they are made Rulers) but also is common to all the people, who are likewise bownde to the observation of the same."[32] This meant that "if the Magistrates would whollye despice and betraye the justice and Lawes of God, you which are subjects with them shall be condemned except you mayntayne and defend the same Lawes agaynst them."[33] A conscientious Protestant under Goodman's formulation may therefore have a religious duty to commit civil disobedience rather than acquiesce in the magistrate's misapplication of God's law.

It is obviously true that there are many rooms within the vast house of Protestantism, and no description of Protestantism per se captures the subtleties of specific denominations. Nor is Catholicism the simple monolith sometimes caricatured by its opponents. The analysis sketched above, however, captures two fundamental differences between Protestantism and Roman Catholicism. To summarize, then, "protestantism" herein refers either (1) to an emphasis on the exclusivity of Scripture as the basis of doctrine, or (2) to the legitimacy of individual interpretation as against the claims of a specific institution. "Catholicism" herein refers either (1) to the legitimacy of unwritten tradition in addition to Scripture, or (2) to the authority of a particular institution to give binding interpretations of disputed aspects of relevant materials.

* * *

This brief *excursus* into religious history has ended. I return to my principal subject: the implications of religious analogies for understanding the róle of the Constitution within American civil religion. I propose to take seriously an epithet once hurled at Langdell by Oliver Wendell Holmes—that he was "the greatest living

---

[32] Goodman, *How Superior Powers Ought to Be Obeyd of Their Subjects: And Wherein They May Lawfully by Gods Worde Be Disobeyed and Resisted. Wherein Also Is Declared the Cause of All This Present Miserie in England, and the Onely Way to Remedy the Same* (Geneva, 1558), in MORGAN, ED., PURITAN POLITICAL IDEAS 10 (1965). See also SKINNER, note 18 *supra*, at 235–38, for a discussion of Goodman's radicalism.

[33] MORGAN, note 32 *supra*, at 9.

legal theologian."[34] What could be a more appropriate vocation than that of theologian in any culture organized around sacred texts or traditions? Indeed, if sociologists and anthropologists are correct, we cannot escape membership in some civil faith even if we wished to, for the alternative to organizing belief is chaos. Least of all are adepts in the law as skeptical and irreligious as they sometimes profess to be, for faith in "the rule of law" continues to be articulated as an operative ideal.[35] Legal disputation continues unabated, however, and the disputes go to the heart of American politics.

Any discussion of methods of constitutional interpretation carries with it a threat of political instability. A method inevitably suggests a way of differentiating correct from incorrect interpretations. To talk about "correct" or "valid" decisions requires coming to terms with those decisions which are "incorrect" or "invalid." The great merit of constitutionalism is that it provides a way of holding even government officials to standards of judgment. The potential danger for these same officials and their supporters is that ordinary citizens may justify disobedience of the law on the basis of the Constitution. As Louis Hartz pointed out, "consensus" on the Constitution as the basis of authority did not guarantee stability to the United States, for the South could make cogent recourse to the same Constitution as Lincoln during the crisis of 1860–61.[36] The very ambiguity of the written Constitution helped to legitimize civil war.[37]

It is therefore in the interests of the State—presumably only the "creature" of the Constitution—to meld with its creator and become the interpreter of the Constitution. The Supreme Court plays this role admirably. For all the talk of its status as an "umpire," the Court is, as Madison recognized in the Virginia Resolution of 1798, an

---

[34] Quoted in 2 Howe, Justice Oliver Wendell Holmes: The Proving Years 156 (1963).

[35] See Levinson, *The Specious Morality of the Law*, Harper's 35–43, 99 (May 1977); Levinson, *Taking Law Seriously: Reflections on "Thinking Like a Lawyer,"* 30 Stan. L. Rev. 1071 (1978).

[36] Hartz, The Liberal Tradition in America (1955).

[37] This is not to say that constitutional ambiguity alone accounts for potential instability. It is more than possible that the State could violate even the clearest provision of the Constitution, or that enforcement of a clear provision, like the fugitive slave provision, would encourage some citizens to revolt. It is obvious, though, that most serious constitutional disputes involve less than crystal-clear clauses of the Constitution.

intimate part of the structure of the State—more particularly, the national government. As such, a significant role of the Court throughout our history has been to legitimize dubious activity of that government by trying to assure the populace that such activity was indeed constitutional.[38]

There are, however, conflicting concepts of constitutionalism, paralleling the varied concepts of Christianity found in Catholicism and Protestantism. One must first decide what "the Constitution" is even prior to deciding what it means. Does "the Constitution," correctly understood, refer only to the specific text of the document written in 1787 and amended infrequently thereafter, or does it include as well an unwritten component derived from implicit assumptions of American political traditions?[39] Second, we must confront the separate question of institutional authority to interpret the Constitution. Is the Constitution institutionalized ("incarnated") in the specific judicial structure—and its human members—of this country?

Thus, there are two separate variables for each of what I have labeled the "catholic" and "protestant" positions. As to source of doctrine, the protestant position is that it is the constitutional text alone (A), while the catholic position is that the source of doctrine is the text of the Constitution plus unwritten tradition (B). As to the ultimate authority to interpret the source of doctrine, the protestant position is based on the legitimacy of individualized interpretation (C), while the catholic position is that the Supreme Court is the dispenser of ultimate interpretation (D). It is not necessary that one be "protestant" or "catholic" along both dimensions. There is no logical connection between Constitution-identity and who is to be the authorized interpreter of the Constitution. It is therefore

---

[38] See BLACK, THE PEOPLE AND THE COURT: JUDICIAL REVIEW IN A DEMOCRACY 56–86 (1960). Professor Black built in part on the earlier work of Robert Dahl, *Decision-Making in a Democracy: The Supreme Court as a National Policy-Maker*, 6 J. PUB. L. 279 (1957). See also Adamany, *Legitimacy, Realigning Elections, and the Supreme Court*, 1973 WIS. L. REV. 790; Funston, *The Supreme Court and Critical Elections*, 69 AM. POL. SCI. REV. 795 (1975); Casper, *The Supreme Court and National Policymaking*, 70 AM. POL. SCI. REV. 50 (1976). Professor Black is, by and large, a defender of the activist judicial position. But see BLACK & ECKHARDT, TIDES OF POWER 2 (1976).

[39] Munzer & Nickel, *Does the Constitution Mean What It Always Meant?*, 77 COLUM. L. REV. 1029, 1033–37 (1977); Grey, *Do We Have an Unwritten Constitution?*, 27 STAN. L. REV. 703 (1975).

possible to generate four intellectually plausible positions: (1) "protestant-protestant" (A + C), (2) "protestant-catholic" (A + D), (3) "catholic-protestant" (B + C), and (4) "catholic-catholic" (B + D). It is my central argument that a significant number of constitutional theories can be organized under one or another of these four categories.[40] It is to the explication of these elements that I now turn.

A

I begin with the problem of the source of American constitutional law. What is "the Constitution" whose authority binds us together in a common polity? Consider, for example, the analysis of Justice Hugo Black.[41] "It is of paramount importance to me that our country has a written constitution."[42] Black was famous for carrying around a copy of the Constitution in his coat pocket. Like a Biblical fundamentalist, he wanted the sacred text instantly available so as to be able to resolve disputes by pointing to the text. Eric Sevareid once asked Black about this habit, saying "Mr. Justice, I would think you'd know the Constitution by heart at this time. Why do you always carry that little book of the Constitution?" Black responded, "Because I don't know it by heart. I can't—my memory is not that good. When I say something about it, I want

---

[40] These variables do not, of course, explain all constitutional theories, in part because they do not account for differences in methods of textual interpretation, *e.g.*, "literalism" as distinguished from "historical," "purposive," or other methods. See BREST, PROCESSES OF CONSTITUTIONAL DECISIONMAKING (1975). Christian disputation is, of course, replete with arguments relevant to those problems. See, *e.g.*, the individual contributions of Grant, McNeill, and Terrien to the general article *History of the Interpretation of the Bible,* in 1 THE INTERPRETER'S BIBLE 106–41 (1952); see also KERMODE, THE GENESIS OF SECRECY: ON THE INTERPRETATION OF NARRATIVE (1979). But there are no distinctly "Protestant" or "Catholic" approaches to texts comparable to the (admittedly oversimplified) differences regarding the source of doctrine and the role of the institutional mediator between the source and the individual believer.

[41] Black was raised as a member of the Clay County, Alabama, Primitive Baptist Church. Although he left the substantive religious beliefs of his childhood behind as he grew older, it is possible that the methods of religious interpretation that he learned as a child influenced his constitutional methodology as a Justice. See BLACK, MY FATHER: A REMEMBRANCE 10–14 (1975). This suggestion should not be read as evidence of a necessary homology. However intriguing such a hypothesis may be, I have not done the necessary work to test it and nothing in this article depends on the existence of such a homology.

[42] BLACK, A CONSTITUTIONAL FAITH 1 (1968).

to quote it precisely."[43] It is this faith that precise quotation of constitutional text is dispositive that identifies Black as a legal protestant. For Black the Constitution meant the relatively easily understood text, and nothing else.[44] Another example of his protestantism is his admission to Sevareid that he saw no reason why a nonlawyer could not serve on the Supreme Court. Better the contribution of a conscientious fellow citizen who shared what Black so aptly termed his "constitutional faith" than the sophistic interpretations—so often departing from the text—of allegedly well-trained lawyers like his great adversary Justice Felix Frankfurter.

Justice Black's textualism manifested itself, for example, in regard to the constitutional basis for a so-called right to "privacy." He rejected the existence of such a right:[45]

> I refuse to go farther than a specific provision can be taken under the Necessary and Proper Clause. Thus, as I made clear recently in my dissent in *Griswold* v. *Connecticut*, 381 U.S. 479, 507 (1965), I can find in the Constitution no language which either specifically or implicitly grants to all individuals a constitutional "right of privacy." There are, of course, guarantees in certain specific constitutional provisions which are written in part so that they protect privacy at certain times and places with respect to certain activities. But, even though I like my privacy as well as the next person, I am nevertheless compelled to admit that the states have a right to invade it unless prohibited by some specific constitutional provision.

Like others of this orthodox persuasion, Black was unwilling to

---

[43] Quoted in Bobbitt, A Theory of the Constitution 50–51 (unpublished manuscript).

[44] There is a pronounced tendency in fundamentalist Protestantism to be suspicious of the very notion of interpretation. See, *e.g.*, the comments of Gerrard Winstanley, one of the radical "Diggers" in seventeenth-century England: "And so though the Laws be good, yet if they be left to the will of a Judge to interpret, the Execution hath many times proved bad. And truly as the Laws and people of Nations have been abused by suffering men Judges to alter the sense by their Interpretation: So likewise hath the scriptures of *Moses*, the Prophets, Christ, and his Apostles, been darkened and confounded by suffering Ministers to put their Inferences and Interpretations upon them. And surely both the Judges for the Law, and the Ministers for God's word, have been both unfaithful servants to man and to God, by taking upon them to expound and interpret that Rule which they are bound to yield obedience to, without adding to, or diminishing from." WINSTANLEY, THE LAW OF FREEDOM IN A PLATFORM OR, TRUE MAGISTRACY RESTORED 49 (1652) (Schocken ed. 1973); see HAYES, WINSTANLEY THE DIGGER: A LITERARY ANALYSIS OF RADICAL IDEAS IN THE ENGLISH REVOLUTION (1979).

[45] BLACK, note 42 *supra*, at 9.

recognize the shifting needs of society as a warrant for supplementing or overriding the bare bones of a sacred text.[46]

If Justice Black was the quintessential "protestant" in the sense of emphasizing the written text, then the great exemplar of "catholicism" was his colleague John Marshall Harlan. In his dissent in *Poe v. Ullman*,[47] one of the great opinions in American judicial history, Harlan's "catholicism" emerges with great clarity. In that opinion he firmly rejected the argument that the meaning of the Due Process Clause of the Fourteenth Amendment was restricted to those rights which can be read from the words of the constitutional document. Instead, Harlan posited the existence of tradition as a source of valid constitutional doctrine. Here was an analogue to the Council of Trent, for Harlan did not reject the text so much as he supplemented its teachings with an equally valid, albeit unwritten, constitutional tradition:[48]

> Due process has not been reduced to any formula; its content cannot be determined by reference to any code. The best that can be said is that through the course of this Court's decisions it has represented the balance which our Nation, built upon postulates of respect for the liberty of the individual, has struck between that liberty and the demands of organized society. . . . The balance of which I speak is the balance struck by this country, having regard to what history teaches are the traditions from which it developed as well as the traditions from which it broke. That tradition is a living thing.

Only a "protestant" could confuse Harlan's argument with an assertion of a right of judges to "roam at will in the limitless area of their own beliefs as to reasonableness."[49] But, just as much to the point, only a "catholic" would accept without cavil Harlan's assurances that, "If the supplying of content to this Constitutional concept has of necessity been a rational process, it certainly has not

---

[46] Although this article concentrates on divisions within Christianity, other religions are obviously not free from the same strains. Indeed, a central tenet of this article is that these strains are structurally generated by the focus on a document that is thought to be normatively binding for a group. For a fascinating essay on dilemmas facing the Conservative movement within Judaism, see Dorff, *Towards a Legal Theory of the Conservative Movement*, 27 CONSERVATIVE JUDAISM 65–77 (Spring 1973).

[47] 367 U.S. 497, 522 (1961) (Harlan, J., dissenting).

[48] *Id.* at 542.

[49] BLACK, note 42 *supra*, at 36.

been one where judges have felt free to roam where unguided speculation might take them."[50]

Although Ronald Dworkin is properly classified as an institutional "protestant," the adjudicative approach he has outlined is within this "catholic" tradition. Most of his discussion concerns common-law cases which, by definition, precludes reliance on written texts. But even his theory of American constitutionalism partakes of "catholicism." He invites adjudicators engaging in constitutional interpretation to reflect on the changing moral structure of society, including its background unwritten "principles," rather than rely on written text. He is especially critical of that branch of textualism, akin to religious fundamentalism, which gives to the text the meaning allegedly desired by its drafters.[51]

The debate now raging between those who define "the Constitution" as the text of a specific document and those who add an "unwritten Constitution"[52] is significantly similar to that which took place four centuries ago. And not the least of the similarities is the tone of frustration and, sometimes, anger which pervades the debate. This comparison between religious and legal disputation illuminates this bitter tone. Constitutionalism, like religion, represents an attempt to render an otherwise chaotic order coherent, to supply a set of beliefs capable of channeling our conduct. However much traditional religion may have lost its power to structure reality for Western intellectuals, analogues present themselves in the guise of various civil religions. Yet recourse to "the Constitution" as a source of guidance within our own polity simply begs the question of what counts as "the Constitution," not to mention what interpretive guidelines must be followed.

---

[50] 367 U.S. at 542. This is the sentence omitted by the ellipsis in the text at note 48 *supra*.

[51] See DWORKIN, TAKING RIGHTS SERIOUSLY (1978), especially *Constitutional Cases*, at 131–49. The most prolific advocate of "intentionalism" is surely Raoul Berger. See, especially, BERGER, GOVERNMENT BY JUDICIARY: THE TRANSFORMATION OF THE FOURTEENTH AMENDMENT (1977). See also Cover, *Book Review*, THE NEW REPUBLIC 26–28 (Jan. 14, 1978), and reply by Berger, *id.* at 7 (Feb. 1, 1978).

[52] See, *e.g.*, Ely, *Constitutional Interpretivism*, 53 IND. L. J. 399 (1978); Grey, *Origins of the Unwritten Constitution: Fundamental Law in American Revolutionary Thought*, 30 STAN. L. REV. 843 (1978); Grey, *Do We Have an Unwritten Constitution?*, 27 STAN. L. REV. 703 (1975). Although Ely rejects the possibility of pure textualism, his article contains an excellent summary of that position.

Since questions of Constitution-identity are metatheoretical, moreover, all suggested answers inevitably appear circular. There is simply no way of referring *to* "the Constitution" for a criterion as to *what* "the Constitution" is. Whatever the process by which understandings of concepts like "the Constitution" emerge, it is doubtful that logical argumentation plays a crucial role. But shared experiential understandings are obviously contingent social events, and if history can be said to "teach" anything, it is the fragility of such shared notions.

B

The possibility of radical indeterminancy in regard to God's law or to the Constitution is one of the sources, of course, of a search for some visible institution which will provide firm answers to those questions which might otherwise tear us apart. The primary Roman Catholic position has emphasized papal supremacy, including, under some circumstances, infallibility.[53] Similarly, the United States Supreme Court has been happy, especially over the past two decades, to reward itself with the title of "ultimate interpreter of the Constitution."[54] To know what "the Constitution" means, therefore, it is enough to know what a specific institution—the Supreme Court—has said about it. Even more to the point, of course, is the linked injunction to obey the Court's judgment. One might not have to agree with the Court's decision, but one must do what the Court says, or so it is argued by judicial "catholics."[55] The argument in its purest form is found in a letter by Professor Leo Pfeffer, de-

[53] See CHIRICO, note 23 *supra;* KÜNG, note 30 *supra*, for a defense and attack respectively regarding papal infallibility.

[54] See, *e.g.*, Cooper v. Aaron, 358 U.S. 1, 18 (1958); Powell v. McCormack, 395 U.S. 486, 521 (1969); United States v. Nixon, 418 U.S. 683, 704 (1974).

[55] It should be pointed out that one distinguished strain of Roman Catholic thought strongly attacked any argument that the Pope was absolutely sovereign and unchallengeable. As Skinner points out, an important source of constitutionalist argument is the conciliarist tradition within the Catholic Church. See SKINNER, note 18 *supra*, at 36–47. If it is grossly inaccurate to summarize Catholicism as emphasizing strictly papal authority, it is nevertheless true that even the conciliarist tradition is institutionalist, representing a way for the organized Church to correct the errors of a renegade Pope. See GAIL, THE THREE POPES (1969); MURPHY, THE VICAR OF CHRIST 596–605 (1979). The analogy asserted in this article does not require a resolution of the dispute between papalists and conciliarists, since both are distinguished by their institutionalism from the radical ideas of Luther.

nouncing a bill which would give tax credit to families with children in private (including parochial) schools:[56]

> Under our system the ultimate responsibility for interpreting the Constitution rests with the Supreme Court. Those who disagree with a particular decision can resort to constitutional amendment to overrule it, and that has been done more than once in our history. What they may not do is to disregard the judgments of the Court and proceed as if they had never been handed down or, indeed, as if the Court had reversed itself. When such a path is followed by Congress, it is particularly unfortunate, for each of its members does take an oath to support the Constitution as interpreted by the Supreme Court. If Congress does not follow the Constitution, how can we expect the people to respect and obey it?

This may be Professor Pfeffer's understanding of "our system." It may be a widely shared one. It is certainly not the only understanding available to a good-faith citizen of the American polity, for there is a "protestant" response that can be made.

William Nelson has pointed out that colonial juries often exercised authority to make their own determinations of "the law" as well as to decide "factual" disputes.[57] Indeed, he notes that there are instances in which juries were charged by more than one judge—who gave conflicting instructions. And John Adams entered into his diary the observation that it was "not only . . . [every juror's] right but his Duty . . . to find the Verdict according to his own best Understanding, Judgment and Conscience, tho in Direct opposition to the Direction of the Court."[58] It is true that the nineteenth century saw a systematic effort to minimize discretionary authority of juries by enhancing judicial power.[59] But we are not thereby confined to antiquarian, pre-Constitutional sources for "protestant" argumentation. Both Andrew Jackson and his protagonist, John Calhoun, rejected judicial supremacy insofar as that meant judicial

[56] N.Y. Times, p. A22, Feb. 16, 1978. Pfeffer, as special counsel to the American Jewish Congress, has prevailed in a number of Supreme Court cases striking down legislation aiding parochial schools.

[57] Nelson, *The Eighteenth-Century Background of John Marshall's Constitutional Jurisprudence*, 76 Mich. L. Rev. 893, 911–13 (1978).

[58] *Id.* at 916, quoting 1 Legal Papers of John Adams 230 (Wroth & Zobel eds. 1965).

[59] See Horowitz, The Transformation of American Law 228 (1977).

authority to give binding interpretations of the Constitution.[60] And a Justice of the Wisconsin Supreme Court, in *Ableman v. Booth*,[61] explicitly denied that it was obligated to follow the precedent of *Prigg v. Pennsylvania*,[62] stating that "duty and obligation require a departure from such precedent and authority, in obedience to a paramount law—the *fundamental law*, to which each and all are usually bound."[63] Even today the question of "lawful departures" from rules enunciated by courts continues to exercise legal philosophers.[64]

It is no surprise that few endorsements of "protestantism" can be found in the writings of judges, who, after all, gain their own legitimacy from the institutions of which they are a part. However much Justice Black might have been a "protestant" along the dimension of sources of constitutionalism, he certainly never exhibited sympathy with those who deviated from judicial mandates.[65] But philosophers are more imaginative, and Ronald Dworkin's work provides an example of current argumentation favoring the individualized interpretation characteristic of protestantism.

Much discussion of Dworkin's work has emphasized his methodology of approaching the legal problems that are to be analyzed. This aspect of his argument can be assimilated to "catholicism." But there has been relatively less attention to his argument concerning the relationship between the Constitution and specific institutions.

---

[60] The classic arguments of both Jackson and Calhoun, as well as Webster's vigorous defenses of judicial supremacy, are reprinted in REMINI, ED., THE AGE OF JACKSON (1972).

[61] In the Matter of Booth, 3 Wis. 1, 8, *rev'd*, 21 How. 506 (1859); on remand, 11 Wis. 517 (1859). I owe this reference to Professor Philip Bobbitt, of the University of Texas Law School.

[62] 16 Pet. 359 (1842).

[63] 3 Wis. at 91.

[64] KADISH & KADISH, DISCRETION TO DISOBEY: A STUDY OF LAWFUL DEPARTURES FROM LEGAL RULES (1973).

[65] Justice Black was one of the five necessary votes to the decision in Walker v. City of Birmingham, 388 U.S. 307 (1967), holding that there was no right to disobey a presumptively unconstitutional injunction. On the other hand, it is difficult to fit precedent into the suggested framework. Justice Black arguably illustrated his "protestantism" by being relatively quick to overrule any past decisions he thought mistaken. Concomitantly, Frankfurter and Harlan, though not strict precedentialists in the English sense, gave much greater legitimacy to past decisions as examples of the tradition which lay aside the raw text. Perhaps the discussion should be viewed in terms of attitudes toward institutional continuity, with Frankfurter's and Harlan's greater concern about continuity being exemplary of their own "catholicism." In any event, this essay does not focus on the role of precedent.

Dworkin refers to his ideal adjudicator Hercules as if he were necessarily a judge, but the question of method is logically independent of institutional role, and Hercules could be an ordinary citizen just as easily as a Justice of the United States Supreme Court.[66]

One of Hercules' functions is to discover when courts can be said to have made mistakes or errors in interpretation. The true Constitution is not necessarily to be found in judicial opinions. "We cannot assume . . . that the Constitution is always what the Supreme Court says it is."[67] Although he would give judicial decisions respectful consideration,[68] he argues that the American version of constitutionalism "does not make the decision of any court conclusive. Sometimes, even after a contrary Supreme Court decision, an individual may still reasonably believe that the law is on his side."[69] Like Justice Frankfurter, Dworkin might agree that, although "[j]udicial exegesis is unavoidable . . . the ultimate touchstone of constitutionality is the Constitution itself and not what we have said about it."[70] Under this formulation judicial decisions, far from being ultimate interpretations, are simply suggested interpretations of the sacred document (or document plus tradition), interpretations which can be rejected if thought unacceptable.

Indeed, echoing the argument of Christopher Goodman, the conscientious citizen within a constitutional order may have a duty to resist magisterial deviations from the constitutional command. It is important to note that this formulation of the problem is not at all the same as positing the validity of morals or conscience against the demands of law, for that way of stating the problem begs a central question: Who gets to determine what counts as "law"? One achievement of Dworkin's formulation is that it en-

---

[66] See Levinson, note 35 *supra*, 30 STAN. L. REV. at 1090.

[67] DWORKIN, note 51 *supra*, at 211.

[68] Because Dworkin has often been in the position of defending judicial decisions against accusations of improper activism and concomitant lack of deference to majority rule, his overall position has sometimes been misinterpreted as strongly projudicial. See, *e.g.*, Walzer, *Book Review*, THE NEW REPUBLIC 28–30 (June 25, 1977). But this view misses the point that Dworkin never presents any argument for judicial supremacy. Instead, he attacks the view that some other institution, such as the legislature, is sufficiently supreme as to require judicial deference. But then he turns around and, in his essays on civil disobedience, shows why the individual need not automatically defer to judicial decision.

[69] DWORKIN, note 51 *supra*, at 214–15.

[70] Graves v. New York, 306 U.S. 466, 491–92 (1939) (Frankfurter, J., concurring).

ables a person to speak of law independently of the statements found in judicial decisions. One need not assert the rejection of law in the name of a "higher" morality. Thus it may be the institutional official who has made the legal mistake. In this view, it is the disobedient citizen who is being faithful to the law. To reject the ultimate authority of the Supreme Court is not in the least to reject the binding authority of the Constitution, but only to argue that the Court is to be judged by the Constitution itself rather than the other way around.[71]

As Dworkin argues: "A citizen's allegiance is to the law, not to any person's view of what the law is, and he does not behave unfairly so long as he proceeds on his own considered and reasonable view of what the law requires."[72] As if frightened by the implication of his comment, Dworkin immediately goes on to insist "that this is not the same as saying that an individual may disregard what the courts have said,"[73] a reservation that can mean no more than that an individual must at least consider the merits of a judicial interpretation rather than flinging it unread into the trash. In any case, after this slight bow toward judicial authority, Dworkin returns to his central theme: "But if the issue is one touching fundamental personal or political rights, and it is arguable that the Supreme Court has made a mistake, a man is within his social rights in refusing to accept that decision as conclusive."[74] The only thing this sentence can mean is that it is the conscientious individual, and not the Supreme Court, who is the ultimate interpreter of the Constitution. It is the province and duty of the citizen to declare what the law is. A "protestant" Constitution is a deinstitutionalized Constitution.

Acceptance of a deinstitutionalized Constitution raises interesting questions about the obligations of particular citizens called

---

[71] Nothing in this article should be read as presupposing that "the Constitution" is necessarily moral or that following its commands, assuming that they can be known, may not require the conscientious legalist to engage in iniquitous acts. Indeed, one reason for my dubiety about the merits of "constitutional faith" is precisely that the Constitution, correctly interpreted, may be grossly immoral. See note 35 *supra*. Nonetheless, the potential conflict between law and morality is wholly independent of my central point, the difficulty of understanding what it means for a Constitution to stand above the social order as a source of judgment, regardless of whether we agree with the judgment.

[72] Dworkin, note 51 *supra*, at 214–15.

[73] *Ibid.*

[74] *Ibid.*

lawyers (or law teachers). To put the matter most starkly, Is a lawyer's primary obligation to "the law" or to judges who make claims to incarnate the law? We often refer to lawyers as "officers of the court," but this notion depends for its power on the identification of courts with the law and Constitution that lawyers are sworn to uphold. But if a lawyer accepts the notion of a deinstitutionalized Constitution, then it becomes altogether possible that conflicts will arise between the lawyer's duty to the court and the duty to maintain the Constitution. At the very least, a lawyer would be bound to present a more pluralistic notion of "the law" than a prediction of judicial behavior.[75]

Consider the following possibility. A client wishes to know whether or not he can refuse induction into the armed forces on grounds of selective conscientious objection. The client informs his lawyer that he has considered many of the classic arguments concerning the relationship between law and personal morality and has concluded that, in case of conflict, law ought to prevail. That is, he has concluded that Socrates was correct not to escape and that Captain Vere behaved correctly in putting Billy Budd to death. What the client wants from his lawyer is a considered judgment as to the possibility of both resisting induction and yet remaining the legalist he wishes to be.[76]

If the lawyer accepts the Supreme Court as ultimate interpreter, then the client should be advised that, as a result of the *Gillette* decision,[77] there is no constitutional right to selective conscientious objection. But consider a "protestant" lawyer's answer to that question.

---

[75] But *cf.* HOLMES, COLLECTED LEGAL PAPERS 172–73 (1920): "Take the fundamental question, What constitutes the law? You will find some text writers telling you that it is something different from what is decided by the courts of Massachusetts or England, that it is a system of reason, that it is a deduction from principles of ethics or admitted axioms or what not, which may or may not coincide with the decisions. But if we take the view of our friend the bad man we shall find that he does not care two straws for the axioms or deductions, but that he does want to know what the Massachusetts or English courts are likely to do in fact. I am much of his mind. The prophecies of what the courts will do in fact, and nothing more pretentious, are what I mean by the law."

[76] It is obvious that the client rejects a radical "price-theory" of law, which holds that law is without obligatory force but merely sets out a set of socially determined prices for the privilege of engaging in given behavior. See note 75 *supra.*

[77] Gillette v. United States, 401 U.S. 437 (1971). See Greenawalt, *All or Nothing at All: The Defeat of Selective Conscientious Objection*, 1971 SUPREME COURT REVIEW 31.

Instead of taking down the relevant volume of the *United States Reports* and pointing to the dispositive decision, the lawyer might wish to note that some commentators criticize the decision as a "mistake." The lawyer surely is ethically bound to point out that the client might well go to jail for refusing induction, but this is not the equivalent of "breaking the law." For the only person who can truly determine whether or not the law is being broken is the person conscientiously reflecting on his or her own activity. If the client is persuaded that the Supreme Court was correct in *Gillette*, then, given his legalism, he must accept induction. If, on the other hand, he believes that the Court erred, then he becomes licensed, even within the terms of his own legalism, to reject the decision and to refuse induction. That is, *Gillette* becomes legal dross when placed next to "the touchstone" of the Constitution itself.[78]

The final decision is then the client's and not the lawyer's. A protestant constitutionalism that is true to itself would not substitute a priesthood of lawyers for a pontifical Court. And Dworkin, though recognizing the role of the legal community in assessing decisions, specifically rejects the view that only the legally trained can criticize courts. The reason he gives relates to his methodological argument that the law is intertwined with ordinary positive morality.[79]

One more example might further elaborate the point as to the implications of rejecting the Court as ultimate interpreter. Consider James St. Clair's duty on the afternoon that the "tapes case"[80] was decided. Did he have a duty to encourage President Nixon to comply with the decision? Traditional analysis surely says yes. The Court–insisting on its role as ultimate interpreter–had spoken loudly and clearly on the principal issue. But what if St. Clair and/ or Nixon were genuinely convinced that the Court had made a

---

[78] See text *supra*, at note 71. The similarity between Frankfurter's formulation and the oft-derided statement of Mr. Justice Roberts in United States v. Butler, 297 U.S. 1, 62 (1936), that the task of the judge is "to lay the article of the Constitution which is invoked beside the statute which is challenged and to decide whether the latter squares with the former" is patent. I offer this comparison not to denigrate Frankfurter, but rather to suggest that Robert's statement, however maladroit it was, captures a profound truth about what it means to take a constitution seriously.

[79] DWORKIN, note 51 *supra*, at 215. As to the crucial distinction between positive and critical morality, see Griffiths, *Book Review*, 53 N.Y.U. L. REV. 1124 (1978).

[80] United States v. Nixon, 418 U.S. 683 (1974).

grievous mistake, so that the message that afternoon, instead of one of compliance, stated something like the following:

> We have read the decision extremely carefully and are convinced that the Court has erred on an issue of "fundamental personal [and] political rights." We are therefore refusing to comply with the decision. We ask only the following, that when the House Impeachment Committee (and the American people) considers this conduct, they will ask the right question. That question is not, "Did the President disobey a court order," but rather, "Is the President engaged in a conscientious effort to effectuate his oath to support the Constitution?" And, even if the Committee wrongly rejects that as the correct question, they must then proceed to decide who is correct as between the President and the Court concerning the substantive issue of constitutional interpretation involved. Under no circumstance can the Committee simply assume that the Court's view is correct, for that would be to violate their own oath, which is, after all, to the Constitution, rather than "the Constitution as interpreted by the Supreme Court."

There is, I submit, no clear rejoinder to this argument if one rejects the "catholic" status of the Supreme Court as authoritative mediating institution between "the Constitution" and the individual citizen. Justice Jackson once made his own play on the notion of a "papal" Court: "We are not final because we are infallible, but we are infallible only because we are final."[81] But the question of finality is more open than Jackson recognized, at least if one accepts the basic structure of "protestant" constitutionalism, including its Dworkinian version.

To be sure, Dworkin does not defend promiscuous disobedience of judicial decisions. He requires not only that they be considered in coming to one's own decision, but also that disobedience be contemplated only in certain situations—where fundamental moral or political rights are at stake—and in certain ways, *i.e.*, without personal injury to others or destruction of their property.[82] To return once more to the doctrines of sixteenth- and seventeenth-century disputation, he seems closer to advocacy of passive resistance than of active opposition to a State's command, at least insofar as active

---

[81] Brown v. Allen, 344 U.S. 443, 540 (1953) (Jackson, J., concurring).

[82] DWORKIN, note 51 *supra*, at 202.

opposition is anything more than counseling others not to obey the mistaken decisions. Although sympathetic to the claims of draft resisters, Dworkin would probably not be so solicitous of the rights of those who sought actively to impede the operation of the military during the Vietnam War.

These examples concern the rights of individual citizens. Even more complex questions are raised, though, when considering individuals filling certain roles. As the Nixon example suggests, it is not at all clear that a conscientious executive or legislator must be bound by judicial decisions.[83] Indeed, the introduction of institutionally defined, though not judicial, officials suggests a more complex notion of "protestantism" (as opposed to "papalism") than the individualist one I have been emphasizing. The most radical version of constitutional protestantism approaches anarchy: The priesthood of all believers becomes the lawyerhood of all citizens. Yet, just as there are more moderate institutional versions of religious Protestantism, one can point to more restrained versions of the legal analogue. Professor Laurence Tribe seems to adopt such a moderate version in his endorsement of the equal legitimacy of different institutions' interpretations of the Constitution.[84] His argument, however more moderate than Dworkin's, is nonetheless "protestant" insofar as it rejects the Supreme Court as the "ultimate interpreter" of the Constitution and endorses instead a pluralized set of interpretations. Once again Justice Harlan is useful as an example of more "catholic" argumentation, insofar as his dissents in *Katzenbach v. Morgan*[85] and *Oregon v. Mitchell*[86] are at least partly based on his rejection of the capacity of Congress to engage in its own acts of binding constitutional interpretation of the Fourteenth Amendment.

The authority of the Catholic Church is not founded on Hobbes's arguments for an absolute sovereign in order to prevent chaos or on Dostoevskian analysis of the incapacity of people to bear

---

[83] See, *e.g.*, Andrew Jackson's veto of the second Bank of the United States, in REMINI, note 60 *supra*, at 79; see also MORGAN, CONGRESS AND THE CONSTITUTION (1966).

[84] See TRIBE, AMERICAN CONSTITUTIONAL LAW 27–33 (1978), discussion of Oregon v. Haas, 420 U.S. 714 (1975); Katzenbach v. Morgan, 384 U.S. 641 (1966).

[85] 384 U.S. 641, 659 (1966) (Harlan, J., dissenting).

[86] 400 U.S. 112, 152 (1970) (Harlan, J., dissenting).

the uncertainties of freedom. Instead, it is based on a reading of Scripture, however controversial that reading may be. It is a notorious embarrassment for those who would defend a "catholic" Supreme Court, though, that it is impossible to point to any piece of constitutional text which supports judicial supremacy. It is not difficult, of course, to defend judicial review insofar as it refers to the duty of judges to support the supremacy of the Constitution as against ordinary legislation or official acts, but such arguments apply as easily to "executive review," "congressional review," and ultimately "citizen review"—*i.e.*, the "protestant" structure—of ordinary acts of all branches of government, including courts.

Perhaps the strongest argument for judicial oversight should be labeled "judicial view" rather than "judicial review," for as Charles Black has pointed out, in many situations courts are examining activity where no one has engaged in thoughtful contemplation of constitutional requirements prior to acting.[87] That is, it is surely a prerequisite of constitutionalism that officials in fact take due regard of the constraints upon them before acting. In the absence of such regard, judicial oversight provides the only guarantee that "the Constitution" will be considered at all.

The critical problem, of course, arises when other individuals or institutions do purport to have considered what the Constitution requires of them. "If Chief Doe," argues Black, "did not in good faith consider the federal constitutional problem, his judgment on it is nonexistent. If he did consider it, his judgment, I think it is not too unkind to say, is worthless. When the accused person appeals to the Court on the federal constitutional ground, he is appealing to the very first official authorized or competent—or, for that matter, likely—to consider his claim."[88] One may well be wary of Chief Doe's capacities in all too many given instances, but Black slides much too quickly over the problem of comparative competence. The very notion of competence suggests the presence of privileged techniques of interpretation that can be recognized and transmitted

---

[87] Black, Structure and Relationship in Constitutional Law 88–89 (1969).

[88] *Ibid.*; see also Black, note 38 *supra*, at 14–23. "We entrusted the task of constitutional interpretation to the courts because we conceived of the Constitution as law, and because it is the business of courts to resolve interpretative problems arising in law. A law which is applied by a court, but is not to be interpreted by a court, is a solecism simply unknown to our conceptions of legality and the legal process." *Id.* at 15.

and, moreover, that these techniques are peculiarly usable by members of a particular institution, the judiciary. But this suggestion begs the central question, and it is an enduring contribution of Protestantism to Western democratic theory to emphasize the ability of ordinary men and women, assuming their conscientious commitment to a shared faith, to engage in their own reflection about the implications of sacred texts.

Because courts can view or review only a very small portion of official acts, it is crucial to the maintenance of a constitutional order that individuals believe themselves obligated to be conscientious adjudicators even in the absence of coercive constraints provided by courts.[89] Indeed, without a modicum of belief in the actuality of conscientious activity by officials, the notion of "presumption of constitutionality" of official acts makes no sense whatsoever, since the presumption presupposes that the officials in question have in fact contemplated constitutional requirements.[90]

Insofar as one is wary of Chief Doe, the United States Congress, or the President, the reasons for that wariness may apply as well to courts, since they are ultimately the creatures of the local, state, and national political structures that generate legislative and executive officials. So "citizen review" is a vital necessity of any polity that purports to call itself constitutional, as opposed to those regimes that, as Lerner suggests, simply use "the Constitution" as a symbol to legitimate their own exercises of power.

This discussion of institutional authority is important only be-

---

[89] See Brest, *The Conscientious Legislator's Guide to Constitutional Interpretation*, 27 STAN. L. REV. 585 (1975).

[90] If we are to continue taking constitutionalism seriously as a source of official behavior, for example, we must learn to be more condemnatory than we are about such behavior as revealed in an anecdote about Senator Moynihan: "One day last fall, a delegation of women visited to insure his support for an approaching key vote on the equal rights amendment. Moynihan was reassuring, for his supporters heavily favored the amendment. But after the delegation left, he began to question his position. Actually, he and his staff had grave misgivings about the E.R.A., based on their interpretation of the law. His intellectual guilt oozing, Moynihan complained to an aide, 'Isn't there any residuum of self-respect around here? Not much in my case, I know, but we're dealing with *constitutional procedures*.' When the vote comes Moynihan votes with the women; but an aide painstakingly notes that the issue will ultimately be settled in the courts." Rattner, *Upstart in the Senate*, NEW YORK TIMES MAGAZINE 10, 12 (Jan. 7, 1979). There is surely no argument for applying the tenets of so-called judicial restraint in reviewing a law passed by legislators as casual of their constitutional duty as Senator Moynihan was here.

cause of the fact that there is disagreement about what constitutes correct interpretation of "the Constitution." But "the Constitution" is no different, of course, from other pieces of writing (to which "tradition" may or may not be attached), and much recent discussion of literary interpretation has focused on the problem of validity. Interestingly enough, some critics counterpose the plurality of literary interpretations with a presumably different situation in the law. Thus E. D. Hirsch notes that "in legal questions, changed interpretations can be institutionalized by a pronouncement from the highest court. . . . No one, for example, would hold that a law means 'what the judges say a law means' if there were not a supreme tribunal to decide what, after all, the judges say. There could never be such arbitrary tribunals in the domain of knowledge and scholarship."[91] Elsewhere, Hirsch has referred to two "institutions that control interpretation"—"the Supreme Court of the United States and the *Instituto Biblico* of Rome—both of which have 'controlling force.' "[92]

What is most interesting about Hirsch's formulation, of course, is the implicit denial that legal analysis constitutes "knowledge." His perception of the Court, that is, is quite Hobbesian insofar as he emphasizes its essentially "arbitrary" stance relative to the material it is interpreting.[93] Even though Hirsch resolutely opposes those who deny the possibility of any valid interpretation,[94] he seems to exhibit great skepticism as to the use of such language in regard to judicial interpretation. Thus one ultimately cannot speak of the validity of a particular act of constitutional interpretation by the Supreme Court, but can only describe what the Court said on a given day or predict what it will say tomorrow.

---

[91] HIRSCH, VALIDITY IN INTERPRETATION 123 n.53 (1967). On critical pluralism, see BOOTH, CRITICAL UNDERSTANDING: THE POWERS AND LIMITS OF PLURALISM (1979).

[92] Hirsch, *Book Review*, N.Y. REV. OF BOOKS 20 (June 14, 1979). My former colleague, Professor Walter Murphy, informs me that Hirsch is incorrect. The institution he presumably means to refer to is the Congregation for the Sacred Doctrine of the Faith, but even it operates under the authority of the Pope and does not share the Pope's undelegable power as ultimate authority. In practice, though, the Congregation apparently can be said to have the last word.

[93] See WOLIN, POLITICS AND VISION 265 (1960).

[94] See HIRSCH, THE AIMS OF INTERPRETATION 1–13 (1976). Hirsch is particularly antagonistic toward claims of radical indeterminacy of meaning, such as may be found in GADAMER, TRUTH AND METHOD (1975). See HIRSCH, note 91 *supra*, App. II, at 245–64.

C

I have reached the end of the elaboration of the parallels between Protestant and Catholic approaches to Christian doctrine and "protestant" and "catholic" modes of approaching the United States Constitution. It may be helpful by way of summary to try very briefly to fill in the categories set out above. Justices Black and Harlan easily fit, respectively, into the designations of "protestant-catholic" and "catholic-catholic." Neither challenged judicial supremacy, but they disagreed fundamentally about what constituted "the Constitution," with Harlan rejecting the emphasis on "writtenness" that characterized Black's approach.

Ronald Dworkin, as we have seen, is quintessentially "catholic-protestant." Like Harlan he is willing to go well beyond the text in order to derive constitutional understandings. Unlike most judges, however, he radically rejects the notion that Supreme Court decisions are necessarily final in the sense of requiring obedience by conscientious citizens.

I confess that I have been unable to think of a "protestant-protestant." In part this is because most proponents of civil disobedience throughout our history have juxtaposed distinctly moral claims against those made by what they often conceded was "the law."[95] Robert Cover has pointed out, for example, that several of the most radical abolitionists in fact adopted a highly positivistic theory of law and never doubted that "the Constitution" protected slavery.[96] More recently, most resisters subordinated claims about the illegality of the war to arguments as to its immorality. Few dissenters have ever presented themselves in the posture of the hypothetical draft resister described earlier, who placed nonjudicially supported legal claims against judicially asserted ones. One could imagine a "protestant-protestant" easily enough, though, by assuming that my hypothetical resister justified his resistance on the grounds that the constitutional text clearly places authority in Congress to declare war and that the failure of Congress to do so freed the citizenry from the duty to obey the Selective Service Act.

---

[95] See, *e.g.*, the materials collected in VEYSEY, ED., LAW AND RESISTANCE: AMERICAN ATTITUDES TOWARD AUTHORITY (1970); LYND, ED., NONVIOLENCE IN AMERICA: A DOCUMENTARY HISTORY (1965).

[96] COVER, JUSTICE ACCUSED: ANTISLAVERY AND THE JUDICIAL PROCESS 153 (1975).

It is obvious that one need not be a "legalist," either because one thought "the law" was immoral or, more radically, because one doubted the very ability to make meaningful reference to an impersonal "law."[97] One is as free to renounce constitutional faith as to reject in toto the validity of Christianity. But so long as one finds it meaningful to speak of being bound by "the Constitution" and by the "rule of law," it is necessary to confront the questions discussed herein.

It is clear that the ability of "the Constitution" to provide the unity so desperately sought as a preventive against disorder depends on resolving the same issues that split Christianity. "With a numinous document like the Constitution or the Bible, the principles and methods of correct interpretation are as important as they are problematical."[98] Only if there is widespread agreement on "principles and methods of correct interpretation" can a written Constitution be said to be a source of stability. Or, in the alternative, only if an institution is accorded absolute supremacy in the interpretation of the creed will disorder be prevented. But sophisticated legal theorists agree on none of these premises. We are not sure what "the Constitution" consists of or how it is to be interpreted or who is to be the authoritative interpreter.

It is unlikely, moreover, that any of the participants in the debates about constitutional theory are going to have their minds changed by reading a polemic by a person of another sect, any more than Baptist theologians are likely to convert to Catholicism or vice versa when presented with a "refutation" of the other's position. The religious wars of the sixteenth and seventeenth centuries came to an end only when religion became sufficiently privatized so as not to remain an essential element of public order. New conceptions of the nation-state, and of constitutionalism, were called upon to provide order.[99]

Part of the apparatus of the new nation-states was a "civil religion" to replace as an anchoring structure the divisive sectarian religions. There were presumably millions of people who could join Felix Frankfurter in his reflection that, "[a]s one who has no ties with any formal religion, perhaps the feelings that underlie religious

---

[97] See SHKLAR, LEGALISM (1964).

[98] HIRSCH, note 94 *supra*, at 20.

[99] This is one of the themes developed by Skinner in his magisterial study, note 18 *supra*, especially at 348–59.

forms for me run into intensification of my feelings about American citizenship."[100] It is appropriate that he was moved to this exercise in self-reflection by a case arising during World War II that forced the Court to examine the nature of commitment to the Constitution that was required in order to become an American citizen.[101]

It is ironic that a culture which has experienced a centuries-long "melancholy, long-withdrawing roar" from religious faith can believe so blithely in the continuing reality of a collectivity of citizens organized around a constitutional faith. The "death of constitutionalism" may be the central event of our time just as the "death of God" was that of the past century (and for much the same reason).

---

[100] Statement at conference, Dec. 5, 1942, Frankfurter Papers, Library of Congress, quoted in BAKER, FELIX FRANKFURTER 290 (1969); see also Levinson, *The Democratic Faith of Felix Frankfurter*, 25 STAN. L. REV. 30 (1973).

[101] Schneiderman v. United States, 320 U.S. 118 (1943). The case involved the question whether a Communist could be attached to the principles of the Constitution. In order to answer that question, it would, of course, be necessary to decide what the "Constitution" is.

GARY L. McDOWELL

JOSEPH STORY'S "SCIENCE" OF EQUITY

I

The sea of national politics into which Joseph Story was launched in 1811 by his appointment to the United States Supreme Court was rough and choppy. Jefferson had relinquished the presidency to James Madison in 1809, preserving the Republican ascendance there. The leadership of the Federalists, which had passed from Hamilton to Marshall in 1804, continued to rest securely in the nation's highest Court. When Associate Justice William Cushing died in 1810, Jefferson rejoiced at the prospect of the Republicans gaining a hold on the Court as well as on the presidency. He warned that it was necessary to proceed with great caution in choosing the right replacement for Cushing. To find a man with "firmness enough to preserve his independence on the same Bench with Marshall"[1] was no mean task. Jefferson was convinced Joseph

Gary L. McDowell is Assistant Professor of Political Science, Dickinson College.

AUTHOR'S NOTE: I am indebted to Professors Henry J. Abraham, Ralph A. Rossum, and Robert A. Rutland, and to my wife, Karla, for generously reading and commenting on earlier drafts of this paper.

[1] Jefferson to Gallatin, Sept. 27, 1810, in 12 WRITINGS OF THOMAS JEFFERSON 429 (Library ed. 1903).

Story was a poor choice as a Republican nominee. He thought him "too young," and worse, he believed him to be "unquestionably a tory."[2] Madison, following Jefferson's advice, looked elsewhere, but without success. His first choice, Levi Lincoln, was confirmed but refused to serve for reasons of poor health; his second choice, Alexander Walcott, was rejected by the Senate; and his third choice, John Quincy Adams (an admitted foe of Blackstonian jurisprudence) was also confirmed by the Senate but refused the appointment in order to continue in his diplomatic post. Madison, in desperation, appointed the thirty-two-year-old Story, a lawyer from Salem, Massachusetts, the youngest man ever to serve on the Supreme Court.[3]

From Jefferson's point of view, Story proved to be even more disappointing than he had imagined. Not only was Story a student of Mansfield and Blackstone, both of whom Jefferson held in utter contempt as "Tories," but he became Marshall's right hand on the Court. As has been observed, it seems "Marshall himself could not have appointed a more congenial ally."[4] For Joseph Story soon proved himself to be a strong nationalist with marked Federalist sympathies.

Beyond his close personal and professional ties to Marshall and his fondness for Blackstone and Mansfield, Story's ardent nationalism was fired by another and more subtle force. Story believed that the growing force of the democratic social and intellectual undercurrents in America was beginning to erode the foundation on which the Constitution and its regime rested. He feared that "the spirit of the age [had] broken loose from the strong ties, which [had] hitherto bound society together by the mutual cohesions and attractions of habits, manners, institutions, morals, and literature."[5] Story found his country in the grip of "a general skepticism —a restless spirit of innovation and change—a fretful desire to provoke discussions of all sorts, under the pretext of free inquiry, or of comprehensive liberalism."[6] This spiritual disease did not simply

[2] Jefferson to Madison, Oct. 15, 1810, in 9 FORD, ED., WRITINGS OF THOMAS JEFFERSON 282 (1899).

[3] See MCCLELLAN, JOSEPH STORY AND THE AMERICAN CONSTITUTION 39–45 (1971); DUNNE, JUSTICE JOSEPH STORY AND THE RISE OF THE SUPREME COURT 77–82 (1970).

[4] MCCLELLAN, note 3 *supra*, at 43.

[5] STORY, MISCELLANEOUS WRITINGS 747 (W. W. Story ed. 1852) (hereinafter MISCELLANEOUS WRITINGS).

[6] *Ibid.*

reject the treatment of old things as "a matter of reverence or affection," but it was worse: It encouraged a "gross overvaluation and inordinate exaggeration of the peculiar advantages and excellencies" of the present over all other ages.[7] Story was not against progress—indeed, he firmly embraced the notion of the constant evolution of society—but he agreed with Edmund Burke that "to innovate is not to reform."[8] The skepticism of the age, Story thought, threatened to abandon the fundamental truths that mankind had come to know through the course of its history in favor of blind and often mindless change.

This spirit of skepticism and innovation gradually crept to the surface and began to infect the political thinking of the time. By 1832, Story found the political situation in America "truly alarming," and this situation was made worse by the fact that it was accompanied by "no correspondent feeling of . . . danger."[9] He expressed his concern vividly to Richard Peters: "We have been and are too prosperous to be able to rouse ourselves; I fear we shall be ruined like all other Republics, and by the same means; an overwhelming conceit and confidence in our wisdom, and a surrender of our principles at the call of corrupt demagogues."[10]

Story was certain that the "old constitutional doctrines" were "fast fading away" and were being replaced by new principles forged by the new and dangerous public opinion.[11] From this new public mind, Story could "augur little good."[12] The infection of this mindless spirit of democracy gnawed at the soul of his beloved republic. The people, on whom the republic rested and in whom Story had never had much faith, had become "stupified . . . by the arts of demagogues and the corrupted influences of party."[13] As a result, the nation had been dragged down into a "state of unexampled distress and suffering" from which it was unlikely to escape.[14]

In 1829, the democratic seeds planted by the Jeffersonian Republicans sprang into full bloom in the form of the hillbilly demo-

---

[7] *Ibid.* [8] *Id.* at 359.

[9] Story to Peters, Dec. 27, 1832, in 2 LIFE AND LETTERS OF JOSEPH STORY 112 (W. W. Story ed. 1851) (hereinafter LIFE AND LETTERS).

[10] *Ibid.*

[11] Story to McLean, May 10, 1837, *id.* at 272.

[12] *Ibid.* [13] *Id.* at 273. [14] *Ibid.*

cracy of Andrew Jackson. The nationalism of Story was never compatible with the nationalism of the Jacksonians, and one of the most glaring points of difference arose over the efforts to codify the Common Law. The codification movement which began in the early 1820s reached maturity in the 1830s. It was a natural corollary to the Jacksonian creed as it had been to the Jeffersonian. Both strains of democracy looked with fear on the judicial power and especially on judicial discretion; both found comfort in clearly promulgated laws passed by the legislature pursuant to a strictly construed Constitution. The Common Law was anathema to such political thought. Not only was it a body of "foreign jurisprudence," but it was seen as nothing more than the arbitrary opinions of judges which could only undermine constitutional republicanism.[15] It was the codification movement more than anything else which prompted Story to undertake the arduous task of providing exhaustive commentaries on nearly every aspect of American law.

Equity was one aspect of the inherited English law which epitomized all that the proponents of codification found obnoxious. "In respect to equity jurisprudence," Story wrote in 1820, "where so much is necessarily left to discretion (. . . judicial, not to arbitrary discretion), it is of infinite moment that it be administered upon determinate principles."[16] But in America there had been considerable deviations from the established principles of Equity. Indeed, a "more broad and undefined discretion has been assumed, and a less stringent obedience to the dictates of authority. Much is left to the habits of thinking of the particular judge, and more to that undefined notion of right and wrong, of hardship and inconvenience, which popular opinions alternately create and justify."[17]

The problem was not that Equity lacked exact principles and settled rules, but rather that Equity had not yet been cultivated as a science. The confusion over Equity led to a "spectral dread of it" as "a transcendental power, acting above the law, and superseding and annulling its operations" at the whim of any judge.[18] To the contrary, Story insisted that Equity was, more than any other single department of the law, "completely fenced in by principle."[19] If

---

[15] Story to Brazer, Nov. 10, 1836, *id.* at 240.

[16] MISCELLANEOUS WRITINGS, at 167.

[17] *Id.* at 223. [18] *Id.* at 540. [19] *Ibid.*

the Common Law were to be preserved, it was necessary to cultivate Equity as a "science," for at bottom Equity was the heart of the Common Law,[20] in that it "addressed to the consciences of men, the most beneficient and wholesome principles of justice."[21] Story wrote,[22]

> The principles of equity jurisprudence are of a very enlarged and elevated nature. They are essentially rational, and moulded into a degree of moral perfection which the law has rarely aspired to. . . . The great branches of jurisprudence mutually illustrate and support each other. The principles of one may often be employed with the most captivating felicity in the aid of another; and in proportion as the common law becomes familiar with the lights of equity, its own code will become more useful and more enlightened.

Story established his reputation as *the* defender of the Common Law in his *Commentaries on Bailments* in 1832, his magnificient *Commentaries on the Constitution of the United States* in 1833, and his *Commentaries on the Conflict of Laws* in 1834. Story then focused his attention on producing a systematic treatment of Equity. The result was the internationally acclaimed *Commentaries on Equity Jurisprudence* in 1836, followed two years later by an "appropriate sequel," *Commentaries on Equity Pleadings*. It is in these works that Story's notions of equity jurisprudence were comprehensively expressed.

II

Story wrote the commentaries on both equity jurisprudence and equity pleadings with an eye toward educating the students of American law "in the great doctrines of Equity, a subject of almost infinite complexity and variety."[23] He saw the great tradition of Equity jurisprudence from Aristotle to Blackstone as having fallen on hard times within America's legal profession. Equity was no longer carefully studied and had never been cultivated as a science. As a result, Equity had come to be viewed positively by lawyers and negatively by the codifiers as a source of nearly unbounded judicial discretion. Story's effort was directed toward a regeneration of the original understanding of Equity which had begun with Aristotle: a source of judicial power whereby in particular cases in

---

[20] *Ibid.* [21] *Id.* at 202. [22] *Id.* at 233–34. [23] *Id.* at 167.

which justice would be lost by too close an adherence to the letter of the law, the positive law could be bent and softened as necessary.

Story did not view his efforts on behalf of Equity as entirely original. His was merely the American extension of that which Lord Bacon and Lord Hardwicke had begun in England many years before. Bacon's "Ordinances in Chancery" had set the business of chancery on a regular course and, in Story's view, thereby accomplished for the "practical administration of equity" what his *Novum Organum* had achieved for "the study of physics and experimental philosophy."[24] With procedure in England's chancery thus organized by Bacon, it was left to Lord Hardwicke "to combine the scattered fragments into a scientific system; to define with a broader line the boundaries between the departments of the common law and chancery; and to give certainty and rigor to the principles, as well as the jurisdiction, of the latter."[25] Story intended to offer no less to his American brethren. He viewed Equity as a system of "curious moral machinery," whose principles were at once "enlarged and elevated" yet practical.[26] Equity was that field of the law where the precepts of natural justice were most directly brought down to touch the affairs of men.[27]

Story's Equity jurisprudence combined the earlier perspectives of Bacon and Hardwicke on the procedural and substantive aspects of Equity and thus can be understood as the last powerful modern articulation of the original Aristotelian concept of juridical equity. Story understood that the efficacy of Equity would be better preserved if it came to be viewed as being bound, no less than the Common Law, to procedure and precedent, the two great principles of the idea of the rule of law. Even though the principles of Equity were founded in natural justice or natural law, the jurisdiction of its administration could never be "so wide and extensive as that which arises from the principles of natural justice."[28] In any civilized country—even in Rome—it is necessary to leave "many matters of natural justice wholly unprovided for; from the difficulty of framing any general rules to meet them, and from the doubtful nature

[24] *Id.* at 203. [25] *Id.* at 204–05. [26] *Id.* at 233–34.

[27] 1 STORY, COMMENTARIES ON EQUITY JURISPRUDENCE 1–2 (14th ed. 1918) (hereinafter EQUITY JURISPRUDENCE).

[28] *Id.* at 2.

of the policy of attempting to give a legal sanction to duties of imperfect obligation, such as charity, gratitude, and kindness."[29] There is, then, a necessary distinction between *natural* Equity and *civil* Equity.

Civil Equity, in the more limited sense of the word, is that element of civil law which is used in contradistinction to strict law. Story accepted (and quoted as his authority) Aristotle's definition of "equity" as the "correction of the law" whenever the strict law is defective by reason of its universality.[30]

In this sense, as the correction of the strict law, Story understood Equity as being necessarily applied to the "interpretation and limitation of the words of positive or written laws; by construing them, not according to the letter but according to the reason and spirit of them."[31] In this method of equitable interpretation, the primary rule was the same as it was for Common Law interpretations:[32]

> The fundamental maxim . . . in the interpretation of statutes, or positive laws, is, that the intention of the legislature is to be followed. This intention is to be gathered from the words, the context, the subject matter, the effects and consequences, and the spirit or reason of the laws. But the spirit and reason are to be ascertained, not from vague conjecture, but from the motives and language apparent on the face of the law.

This procedure of interpreting the law by its Equity is necessary in "every rational system of jurisprudence, if not in name, at least in substance."[33] This is the case because "Every system of laws must necessarily be defective" and cannot possibly furnish rules applicable to the infinite variety of human affairs.[34] Under any system of positive laws (or "any code, however minute and particular"), "cases must occur to which the antecedent rules cannot be applied without injustice, or to which they cannot be applied at all. It is the office therefore of a judge to consider whether the antecedent rule does apply, or ought, according to the intention of the lawgiver, to apply to a given case."[35]

---

[29] *Ibid.* [30] *Id.* at 30. [31] *Id.* at 7.

[32] Story, *Law, Legislation, and Codes*, 7 ENCYC. AMERICANA 576 (1st ed., Lieber ed., 1831). The rareness of these volumes suggests that the reprinting in MCCLELLAN, note 3 *supra*, is a better source of reference, and will be used hereinafter. The quotation in the text may be found in MCCLELLAN at 360.

[33] 1 EQUITY JURISPRUDENCE, at 7.

[34] *Id* at 9. [35] *Ibid.*

This emphasis on equitable interpretation, Story remarked, had led to many mistaken notions concerning the powers of courts of Equity. And Story believed it necessary to clear the air of these erroneous impressions. First, he insisted, the "proposition . . . that equity will relieve against a general rule of law, is . . . . neither sanctioned by principle nor by authority."[36] Story accepted Sir Joseph Jekyll's dictum:[37]

> . . . discretion is a science, not to act arbitrarily, according to men's wills and private affections; so that discretion which is executed . . . is to be governed by the rules of law and equity, which are not to oppose, but each in its turn to be subservient to the other. This discretion in some cases follows the law implicitly; in others assists it, and advances the remedy; in others again it relieves against the abuse, or allays the rigor of it. But in no case does it contradict or overturn the grounds or principles thereof. . . .

Second, Story dismissed as "equally untenable" the proposition that every matter which is inconsistent with the intention of the legislator or is contrary to the principles of natural justice should find relief in Equity.[38] Story observed that[39]

> so far from a Court of Equity supplying universally the defects of positive legislation, or peculiarly carrying into effect the intent as contradistinguished from the text of the Legislature, it is governed by the same rules of interpretation as a Court of Law, and is often compelled to stop where the letter of the law stops. It is the duty of every court of justice, whether of law or of equity, to consult the intention of the Legislature. And in the discharge of this duty, a Court of Equity is not invested with a larger or a more liberal discretion than a Court of Law.

Third, Story insisted, contrary to some prevalent opinions, that courts of Equity are surely bound by precedent. Nothing could be more absurd or more dangerous than the assumption that every case in Equity "is to be decided upon circumstances, according to the arbitration or discretion of the judge, acting according to his own notions *ex aequo et bono*."[40] Story chose rather to embrace the

---

[36] *Id.* at 13.

[37] *Id.* at 15–16. See Cowper v. Cowper, 2 P. Wms. 720, 24 Eng. Rep. 930 (1734).

[38] 1 Equity Jurisprudence, at 15.

[39] *Ibid.*

[40] *Id.* at 18.

opinion of Blackstone, who had held courts of Equity to be "a labored connected system, governed by established rules, and bound down by precedents, from which they do not depart."[41] To this trilogy of errors about the powers of courts of Equity, Story offered an emphatic refutation:[42]

> If . . . a Court of Equity . . . did possess the unbounded jurisdiction which has been thus generally ascribed to it, of correcting, controlling, moderating, and even superseding the law, and of enforcing all the rights, as well as the charities, arising from natural law and justice, and of freeing itself from all regard to former rules and precedents, it would be the most gigantic in its sway, and the most formidable instrument of arbitrary power, that could well be devised. It would literally place the whole rights and property of the community under the arbitrary will of the judge, acting, if you please, *arbitrio boni judicis*, and it may be *ex aequo et bono*, according to his own notions and conscience; but still acting with a despotic and sovereign authority.

In Story's view the most important maxim of Equity jurisprudence was *Aequitas Sequitur Legem:* Equity Follows the Law. The jurisdiction of Equity, he believed, must be of a permanent and fixed character no less than ordinary legal jurisdiction. Equity, like the law, had a definite body of fixed principles on which courts of Equity were to act. And perhaps most important, Equity was a part of the law; it was not some philosophic scheme divorced from the law itself. After he had attempted to dismiss the inaccurate or inadequate notions of Equity which had poisoned public opinion toward Equity jurisprudence, Story then attempted to give some positive statement of Equity.

"Equity Jurisprudence" Story defined as "that portion of remedial justice which is exclusively administered by a Court of Equity as contradistinguished from that portion of remedial justice which is exclusively administered by a Court of Common Law."[43] In light of the fundamental maxim that "Equity follows the law," the jurisdiction of courts of Equity extends only to the relief a court of law would grant if it could. Whenever a "*complete*, *certain*, and *adequate* remedy exists at law, Courts of Equity have generally no jurisdiction."[44]

---

[41] *Ibid.* [42] *Id.* at 21. [43] *Id.* at 26.

[44] Dunne, *Joseph Story's First Writing on Equity*, 14 AM. J. LEGAL HIST. 79, 79–80 (1970).

In the courts of law "there are certain prescribed forms of action to which the party must resort to furnish him a remedy; and, if there be no prescribed form to reach such a case, he is remediless" in the law courts.[45] And it is in cases such as these that Equity serves as an "auxiliary to the law."[46] Story elaborated by noting that[47]

> . . . there are many cases in which a simple judgment for either party, without qualifications or conditions or peculiar arrangements, will not do entire justice *ex aequo et bono* to either party. Some modifications of the rights of both parties may be required; some restraints on one side, or on the other, or perhaps on both sides; some adjustments involving reciprocal obligations or duties; some compensatory or preliminary or concurrent proceedings to fix, control, or equalize rights; some qualifications or conditions, present or future, temporary or permanent, to be annexed to the exercise of rights or the redress of injuries.

In such cases where ordinary courts of law are incapable "from their very character and organization" of giving relief, courts of Equity are not so restrained.[48] "Although they have prescribed forms of proceedings, the latter are flexible, and may be suited to the different postures of cases. They may adjust their decrees so as to meet most if not all of these exigencies; and they may vary, qualify, restrain, and model the remedy so as to suit it to mutual and adverse claims, controlling equities, and the real and substantial rights of all the parties."[49]

The great object of Equity in its role as auxiliary to the Common Law is justice; and justice often demands more than ordinary courts of law can provide. Quoting Blackstone's ruminations, Story outlined the more important powers and duties of Courts of Equity. Such courts are established[50]

> to detect latent frauds and concealments which the process of Courts of Law is not adapted to reach; to enforce the execution of such matters of trust and confidence as are binding in conscience, though not cognizable in a Court of Law; to deliver from such dangers as are owing to misfortune and oversight; and to give a more specific relief, and more adapted

---

[45] 1 EQUITY JURISPRUDENCE, at 23.

[46] Dunne, note 44 *supra*, at 79.

[47] 1 EQUITY JURISPRUDENCE, at 27.

[48] *Ibid.*

[49] *Ibid.*

[50] *Id.* at 28; see 1 BLACKSTONE, COMMENTARIES ON THE LAWS OF ENGLAND 92.

> to the circumstances of the case, than can always be obtained by the generality of the rules of the positive or common law.

Thus, it is of greatest importance that remedies at law be plain, adequate, and complete. If they are not, Equity will very likely assert jurisdiction. In order to effect a plain, adequate, and complete remedy in all cases, the jurisdiction of Equity courts sometimes is concurrent with the jurisdiction of law courts; sometimes it is exclusive of it; and sometimes it is auxiliary to it.[51] But it is never superior to it in any abstract theoretical sense.

Story did embrace, however, the idea that Equity extended to all cases where natural justice gave a right but the Common Law had provided no means of enforcing it. It was not his position, though, that Equity in contradistinction to the Common Law had a direct reference to natural law. In his view, Equity was a part of the broader Common Law which itself was a reflection of the natural law and a system of rights and obligations dictated by natural justice. Story understood the Common Law—and thereby the spirit of that Common Law, Equity—as a "system having its foundations in natural reason; but at the same time, built up and perfected by artificial doctrines, adapted and moulded by the artificial structure of society."[52] Equity, like the broader Common Law, was founded on the law of nature. It was a system of rules which had existed "antecedently" to man and which, through history, had been given concrete expression in statutes, treatises, and especially in judicial opinions. But it in no way was dependent on these literary devices for its existence. The law of nature, to Story, was "nothing more than those rules which human reason deduces from the various relations of man, to form his character, and regulate his conduct."[53] Many of those rules of human conduct found themselves clearly promulgated in the strict law, while others were left to the realm of Equity jurisprudence by their very nature and character. And, therefore, Equity jurisprudence had a particular and specific jurisdiction based on the objects left to its cognizance.

Story found the "peculiar province" of Equity courts to be administering the defects of the strict law "in cases of *frauds*, *acci-*

---

[51] 1 Equity Jurisprudence, at 32–33.

[52] Miscellaneous Writings, at 524.

[53] *Id.* at 535, 506.

dents, mistakes, or *trusts*."[54] In cases of fraud, Equity would interfere and would compel complete restitution; in cases of accident or mistake, Equity would interfere to administer proper and effectual relief by commanding specific performance; in cases of trusts, Equity would apply the principles of conscience and enforce the expressed or implied trusts according to good faith. Basically, Story understood Equity as had Hamilton in *The Federalist:* a means of offering relief from "hard bargains."[55] Story further elaborated his understanding of Equity:[56]

> Sometimes, by fraud or accident, a party has an advantage in proceeding in a court of ordinary jurisdiction, which must necessarily make that court an instrument of injustice, if the suit be suffered; and equity, to prevent such a manifest wrong, will interpose, and restrain the party from using his unfair advantage. Sometimes, one party holds completely at his mercy the rights of another, because there is no witness to the transaction, or it lies in the privity of an adverse interest; equity in such cases will compel a discovery of the facts, and measure substantial justice to all. Sometimes, the administration of justice is obstructed by certain impediments to a fair decision of the case in a court of law; equity, in such cases, as auxiliary to the law, removes the impediments. Sometimes, property is in danger of being lost or injured, pending a litigation; equity there interposes to preserve it. Sometimes oppressive and vexatious suits are wantonly pursued and repeated by litigious parties; for the preservation of peace and of justice, equity imposes in such cases an injunction of forbearance.

It was of grave importance to Story that students of the law be able to distinguish between what we have called the substantive and the procedural aspects of Equity jurisprudence. On the one hand, there was the general sense of Equity "which is equivalent to universal or natural justice, *ex aequo et bono*" and, on the other, there was the technical sense "which is descriptive of the exercise of jurisdiction over peculiar rights and remedies."[57] Those who confused the two aspects often concluded—incorrectly—that "Courts of Law can never administer justice with reference to principles of universal or natural justice, but are confined to rigid, severe, and uncompromising rules, which admit of no equitable considera-

---

[54] THE FEDERALIST, No. 80, 379 (Cooke ed. 1961).

[55] Dunne, note 44 *supra*, at 79.

[56] *Ibid.*

[57] 1 EQUITY JURISPRUDENCE, at 8.

tions."[58] On the contrary, the decisions in courts of law are often "guided by the most liberal equity."[59] For courts of law to be rigidly bound by the mere letter of the law would be as inefficacious and dangerous as if courts of Equity were completely unbound by the letter of the law. Considerations of law and considerations of Equity were so closely knitted together that even the question of whether all remedial justice should be in one class of courts or split into two was more often debated than answered. Story concluded that this question could "never . . . be susceptible of any universal solution applicable to all times and all nations and all changes in jurisprudence."[60] It would always depend on the "mixed question of public policy and private convenience."[61] Although he was unwilling to make universal proclamations on the question of jurisdictions, Story did have a particular personal view of the matter.

Story believed that "the administration of equity should be by a distinct court, having no connection with, or dependence upon, any court of common law."[62] Should both law and Equity be administered in the same court, it would be a dangerous judicial arrangement for two reasons. First, the equity of a case might transfer itself to the law of the case and thus give an unwholesome liberality to the decision of the court. Second, the questions of law in a particular case might tend to "narrow down the comprehensive liberality of equity."[63] Either circumstance could, and probably would, occur if Equity and law were mixed in the same jurisdiction. Such a mixture, "whenever it takes place," Story asserted, "is decidedly bad in flavor and in quality."[64]

Story viewed separate jurisdictions as beneficial for several other reasons. Using a division-of-labor argument, Story suggested that a steady devotion to one pursuit (either Equity or law) would give the jurist greater accuracy and acuteness: "[T]he subdivision of labor gives greater perfection to the whole machinery" of justice.[65] There was also the problem that much of the business of a court of Equity was in granting injunctions against judgments obtained at law, so that a conflict of interest was quite probable. But

[58] *Id.* at 38–39.

[59] *Id.* at 39.

[60] *Id.* at 40.

[61] *Ibid.*

[62] Miscellaneous Writings, at 169.

[63] *Ibid.*

[64] *Ibid.*

[65] *Id.* at 169.

the most important reason he found was that separate jurisdictions of law and Equity would "act as checks and balances to each other."[66] This rather novel view of a divided judicial authority saw that a rigid separation would "have the most salutary influence upon all judicial proceedings,"[67] by keeping the courts sufficiently independent so as to "prevent any undue ascendency by either."[68]

Story recognized the inherent danger of lodging law and Equity in the same hands, as had the Anti-Federalists Robert Yates as "Brutus" and Richard Henry Lee as the "Federal Farmer," during the struggle for the ratification of the Constitution.[69] But Story's view was broader. Not only was Equity a danger to law, but law was also a danger to Equity. Courts of both law and Equity were necessary to the administration of justice, and justice was more likely to be realized where Equity could not easily slip over and liberalize the strictness of law and where the law, in turn, could not restrict the more liberal principles of Equity. Story realized that in those States where such jurisdictional questions were being asked, those favoring a union of law and Equity in the same jurisdiction would have recourse to the federal analogy. To him, however, the federal analogy was inappropriate. It was at the State level where the "great mass of equity suits" would take place. The federal courts exercised only a limited jurisdiction in Equity cases. They could only by the qualified nature of their authority take cognizance of suits in Equity "where the United States or aliens, or citizens of other states are parties."[70] Given the fact that the Constitution created a judicial power rather than an intricately eleborate judicial system, there was an "inherent difficulty in separating the supreme jurisdiction at law from that in equity."[71] Thus, Story had no dif-

---

66 *Id.* at 172. 67 *Ibid.* 68 *Ibid.*

69 "Brutus" contended that the judicial power, by extending to Equity, would naturally empower the courts to "explain the constitution according to the reasoning spirit of it, without being confined to the words or letter." In the course of such equitable interpretations, he warned, the judges would feel no necessity to confine themselves to "any fixed or established rules, but will determine, according to what appears to them, the reason and the spirit of the constitution." Letter of Brutus, Jan. 31, 1788, in KENYON, ED. THE ANTI-FEDERALISTS 338 (1966). "The Federal Farmer" was equally wary of the Equity power: "It is a very dangerous thing to vest in the same judge power to decide on law, and also general powers in equity; for if the law restrain him, he is only to step into the shoes of equity, and give what judgment his reason or opinion may dictate." Letter of the Federal Farmer, Oct. 10, 1787, *id.* at 232.

70 MISCELLANEOUS WRITINGS, at 170–71.

71 *Id.* at 171.

ficulty in accepting as legitimate the rigid procedural distinction between law and Equity that Congress had imposed on the inferior federal courts in the Judiciary and Process Acts of the First Congress.

Story recognized that there was a close connection between substantive Equity and procedural Equity, between the idea itself, *ex aequo et bono*, and the administration of that idea. In particular, Story found that the lack of knowledge of special Equity pleadings had contributed in no small way to the loss of respect for Equity jurisprudence generally. Toward remedying this sorry state of affairs, he turned his attention from the principles of Equity to the forms of Equity. In this sense, Story's *Commentaries on Equity Jurisprudence* and his *Commentaries on Equity Pleadings* form a comprehensive whole.

Joseph Story considered his *Commentaries on Equity Pleadings* an "appropriate sequel" to his earlier work on Equity jurisprudence. In the later work on pleadings, his intention was to connect the principles of Equity he had developed in his work on Equity jurisprudence with "the forms of the proceedings, by which rights are vindicated, and wrongs are redressed, in Courts of Equity."[72] In American law, Story saw a "looseness and inartificial structure" in its pleadings.[73] This betrayed "an imperfect knowledge both of the principles and forms" which in turn not only deprived the pleadings in the American legal process of "elegance and symmetry" but also subjected them "to the coarser imputation of slovenliness."[74] But a lack of elegance and polish was not the only problem. The lack of emphasis on special pleadings generally had resulted in a superficiality in American legal education.

"The forms of pleading," argued Story, "are not, as some may rashly suppose, mere trivial forms; they not unfrequently involve the essence of the defence; and the discipline, which is acquired by a minute attention to their structure, is so far from being lost labor, that it probably more than all other employments, leads the student to . . . close and symmetrical logic."[75] Special pleading, in Story's opinion, contained the "quintessence of the law."[76] This attention to detail helped to develop a "scrutinizing logic" which would counteract any tendency to "undue speculation." By encour-

[72] STORY, COMMENTARIES ON EQUITY PLEADINGS xiii (5th ed. 1852).

[73] MISCELLANEOUS WRITINGS, at 232.

[74] *Ibid.* [75] *Ibid.* [76] *Id.* at 233.

aging an uncompromising attention to the forms of the ancient law, Equity pleadings led the way to a deeper understanding of the substance of Equity by submerging the student into the deep currents of the Common Law itself.

It was not only necessary that the principles of Equity be scientifically cultivated to insure its uniformity and certainty, but it was also essential that there should be some prescribed forms established for its administration. This was of special significance in the federal court where procedure alone separated law from Equity. In a very fundamental sense, the preservation of the substantive principles of Equity was dependent on the procedural forms of Equity pleadings. For only by reducing both form and substance to clearly exposited principles and rules could Equity be presented as safe and thus be secured against the growing democratic wave of the codification movement.

Story's purpose in writing his massive commentaries on many parts of the Common Law, including his *Commentaries on Equity Jurisprudence* and *Commentaries on Equity Pleadings*, was to commend and recommend the Common Law "upon true, old, and elevated principles"[77] and, while adamantly denying the methodology of the codification movement, to introduce uniform principles and rules of law and Equity throughout the nation, at both the State and the federal level. Story firmly believed that it was necessary to have "sufficient knowledge of the old law" and yet not be "a slave to its forms."[78] Equity, like the Common Law generally, was not a static entity but a dynamic system of jurisprudence made up of "artificial doctrines" which rested firmly on the foundation of the law of nature. It was natural and totally acceptable to Story that as society progressed from its rude beginnings, both law and Equity should be invigorated "with new principles, not from the desire of innovation, but the love of improvement."[79] It was the growing popularity of radical innovation that he feared the most. Against this ominous threat, Story attempted to rally the thoughtful men of his profession. "I would speak," he said,[80]

> to the consciences of honorable men, and ask how they can venture, without any knowledge of existing laws, to recom-

---

[77] Story to Kent, Oct. 27, 1832, 2 LIFE AND LETTERS, at 109.

[78] *Id.* at 75.

[79] *Ibid.*

[80] MISCELLANEOUS WRITINGS, at 515.

> mend changes which may cut deep into the quick of remedial justice, or bring into peril all that is valuable in jurisprudence by its certainty, its policy, or its antiquity. Surely they need not be told, how slow every good system of laws must be in consolidating; and how easily the rashness of an hour may destroy what ages have scarcely cemented in a solid form. The oak, which requires centuries to rear its trunk, and stretch its branches, and strengthen its fibres, and fix its roots, may yet be levelled in an hour. It may breast the tempest of a hundred years, and survive the scathing of the lightning. It may even acquire vigor from its struggles with the elements, and strike its roots deeper and wider as it rises in its majesty; and yet a child, in the very wantonness of folly, may in an instant destroy it by removing a girdle of its bark.

III

Story sought a cure for the distemper of his age in the Common Law. It was not that he opposed any codification (he even thought the Common Law could be strengthened by some codification),[81] but rather, that he opposed the immoderation of most of the codifiers. His view of man was less confident than theirs. To suppose that man is capable of framing a comprehensive legal code, he argued, "is to suppose that he is omniscient, all-wise, and all-powerful; that he is perfect, or that he can attain perfection; and that he can see all the future in the past; and that the past is present to him in all its relations."[82] Such an assumption struck Story as preposterous: "The statement of such a proposition carries with it its own refutation. While man remains as he is, his powers, and capacities, and acts, must forever be imperfect."[83]

Story understood law to be something broader and deeper than mere positive decrees of the public will. "Laws," he insisted, "are the very soul of a people; not merely those which are contained in the letter of their ordinances and statute books, but still more those which have grown up of themselves from their manners, and religion, and history."[84] Law, to Story, was "founded, not upon any will, but on the discovery of a right already existing, which is to be drawn either from the internal legislation of human reason, or the

---

[81] McCLELLAN, note 3 *supra*, at 369.

[82] *Id.* at 365.

[83] *Ibid.* See also MISCELLANEOUS WRITINGS, at 70.

[84] McCLELLAN, note 3 *supra*, at 350.

historical development of the nation."[85] Hence, mere popular consent was not, for Story, the true law. The Common Law was the true law. The Common Law drew its authority not from the transient decrees of a legislative body but from both philosophy and history; it was the point where theory and practice in human affairs touched. And the relationship between law and society was symbiotic. Not only was law formed by the manners, morals, and habits of a people, but it in turn operated forcibly and silently to help form people's manners, morals, and habits.

The main thrust of the codification movement was aimed at reducing the uncertainty of the Common Law which they saw as its great flaw. Their intention was to replace it with clear and objective codes which would not need judicial discretion to be interpreted and administered. But the uncertainty attributed to the Common Law by "the vulgar," Story argued, was not the result of judicial discretion but, rather, was the natural result of the "endless complexity and variety of human actions."[86] These immeasurable uncertainties could not be resolved by any legal code. They could only be resolved by human judgment which took into account not only the particular circumstances of each case but also the ancient laws which had been "fashioned, from age to age, by wise and learned judges."[87] This ancient Common Law was comprised of general principles which were accepted not simply because they were old but because they contained certain truths to which man could look for distinction and guidance. To Story, the abandonment of the Common Law in favor of "comprehensive" codes would only introduce more uncertainty in the form of judicial discretion into the legal process.[88]

Another advantage which Story saw in the Common Law was its tendency to be less static than statute law. Although the Common Law was a system of "general juridical truths," it was still capable of "continually expanding with the progress of society."[89] In this regard the Common Law "resembles the natural sciences, where new discoveries continually lead the way to new, and sometimes astonishing results."[90] Indeed, the Common Law itself was a science. There is no science, Story wrote,[91]

---

[85] *Id.* at 354–55.

[86] MISCELLANEOUS WRITINGS, at 70.

[87] *Id.* at 66.

[88] *Id.* at 166–67.

[89] *Id.* at 702.

[90] *Id.* at 526.

[91] *Id.* at 504.

> so vast, so intricate, and so comprehensive, as that of jurisprudence. In its widest extent it may be said almost to compass every human action; and in its minute details, to measure every human duty. If we contemplate it in the highest order of subjects which it embraces, it can scarcely be surpassed in dignity. It searches into and expounds the elements of morals and ethics, and the eternal law of nature, illustrated and supported by the eternal law of revelation.

Story accepted as his obligation the "scientific" exposition of the Common Law in order to brace it against the passionate gusts of the codifiers. His "science," however, following in the tradition of Blackstone and Kent, was an attempt to distinguish and clarify parts of the Common Law by offering a "clear exposition of principles and authorities" which were scattered throughout a huge number of reports and treatises.[92] His "science" was an attempt to organize and methodize the grand principles of the Common Law and thereby reduce the obscurity and strengthen the tradition of the Common Law in America. True to the tradition to which he subscribed, he adopted the mode of writing commentaries on the law, whereby he braided together legal treatises, political philosophy, and judicial opinions into a cord with which he could tie the past to the present in order better to prepare for the future.

Story's major premise was always that the Common Law offered a safer course for republican government than did the utopian solutions of the codifiers. Although the Common Law was mutable and flexible, it was not arbitrary. Judicial discretion was not the same as "arbitrary" discretion.[93] The Common Law, Story insisted, "controls the arbitrary discretion of judges, and puts the case beyond the reach of temporary feelings and prejudicies, as well as beyond the peculiar opinions and complexional reasoning of a particular judge; for he is hemmed around by authority on every side."[94] Of no slight weight in moderating judicial opinions was the "consciousness . . . that the decision will form a permanent precedent, affecting all future cases."[95] This knowledge would necessarily introduce "great caution and deliberation" in giving an opinion.[96] Story saw Common Law interpretations as pointing "to one great object—certainty and uniformity of interpretation."[97] And to preserve that certainty and uniformity in the administration of justice

---

92 *Id.* at 76.

93 *Id.* at 167.

94 McClellan, note 3 *supra*, at 359.

95 *Ibid.*

96 *Ibid.*

97 *Id.* at 363.

it was necessary to preserve the Common Law. Story's equity jurisprudence, like his Common Law jurisprudence generally, was intended as an effort to preserve as much of the older natural law tradition as possible in the face of growing professional and popular distrust of that tradition and the growing trust in legal positivism.

Story was, in sum, the last major defender of the original understanding of Equity as it had been transmitted from Aristotle to Blackstone. He saw Equity not as a mere set of procedural remedies but as a system of jurisprudence, an auxiliary to the strict law, which aimed at an understanding of justice which transcended the fluctuating decrees of popular consent. Story, more than any other man of his time, sought the recovery and preservation of the ethical and moral basis of the law. He attempted this recovery and preservation through the "scientific" elaboration of the vast tradition of the Common Law of which Equity was a part.

Story's series of commentaries offered a viable alternative to drastic codification. Through his herculean efforts, his beloved Common Law was given greater uniformity and clarity. The legal commentary combined with limited codification, in his view, could serve "to bring the law into a state approximating the exactness of Science."[98] By his voluminous outpouring, he was able to undermine the movement of the most zealous Benthamites toward a complete codification of the Common Law. But even though he was able to slow and even to weaken the codification movement, he was unable to stop its march for very long.

Through his *Commentaries on Equity Jurisprudence* and his *Commentaries on Equity Pleadings*, Joseph Story made a valiant effort to teach both his profession and the public a lesson in the law: Equity is a substantive body of law necessary to the administration of justice which can either be abused or destroyed by a disregard for its procedure. This lesson either fell on deaf ears or was misunderstood. In 1848, only three years after Story's death, the codification movement won its first major victory in New York with the adoption of the Field Code of Civil Procedure.[99] With this victory began the transformation of the substantive idea of Equity through the reform of its procedure.

---

[98] Story to Grimké, as cited in McClellan, note 3 *supra,* at 94.

[99] See Reppy, ed., David Dudley Field Centenary Essays: Celebrating One Hundred Years of Legal Reform (1949).

RICHARD A. POSNER

THE UNCERTAIN PROTECTION OF PRIVACY BY THE SUPREME COURT

The Constitution of the United States contains no reference to privacy. But notions of privacy have long played an important role in constitutional adjudication as values either protected by specific constitutional provisions or that must be weighed in the interpretation of other provisions which protect competing values. Moreover, since 1965, privacy has become the basis of a constitutional right not anchored in any specific provision of the Constitution. My purpose here is to examine the Supreme Court's constitutional judgments dealing with privacy. Any novelty in my approach lies in the emphasis on careful explication of the meaning of the ambiguous word "privacy."

I. What Does "Privacy" Mean?

I begin by examining the evolution of the concept outside the courtroom.[1] Etymologically, the word "privacy" is related to

Richard A. Posner is the Lee and Brena Freeman Professor of Law, The University of Chicago.

Author's Note: I wish to thank Frank Easterbrook, Anthony Kronman, John Langbein, Bernard Meltzer, George Stigler, Geoffrey Stone, and James White for their helpful comments on an earlier draft of this article.

[1] The discussion in this part of the paper draws heavily on Posner, *Privacy, Secrecy, and Reputation*, 28 Buff. L. Rev. 1, 3–7 (1979); see also Gross, *The Concept of Privacy*, 42 N.Y.U.L. Rev. 34 (1967).

"privation" and "deprivation"; originally, to be private meant to be deprived. The unfavorable connotation of the word reflected a world in which solitude was dangerous—was in fact an effective method of punishment—because of the prevailing insecurity in the countryside surrounding the small villages or bands in which people lived.

As the countryside became more secure, people discovered the advantages of occasional solitude, and privacy began to lose its unfavorable connotation. Two kinds of advantage of privacy should be distinguished. One is the opportunity that it affords to think, plan, and reflect without frequent interruption. This advantage became increasingly important as the mental component in both work and leisure came to predominate over the physical. It explains why people engaged in mental work generally have their own offices and those engaged in purely physical work generally do not. The other advantage of solitude is the opportunity it affords a person to conceal selected aspects of his thought and activity in order to enhance his reputation. Much of this concealment is harmless and some of it socially beneficial—as when inventors conceal their inventions in order to be able to obtain a profit from inventing. Secrecy here is socially beneficial because it provides incentives to invent. Some concealment of personal information, however, is akin to the concealment by sellers of defects in their products. An example would be the concealment by an applicant to the police force of a history of serious mental illness.

I have thus far been speaking of privacy as a purely physical concept, as living or working out of sight or hearing of (all or most) other people. This was the original meaning. But what was initially just a by-product of physical privacy—the ability to conceal information about oneself—has in the last century blossomed into an independent meaning of privacy. Take the case of wiretapping. Even if the tap is installed on the premises of the person whose line is being tapped, there is no invasion of his physical privacy—no interruption in his mental activity, no increase in the noise level, in short, no disruption of peace and quiet. This is true, by definition, of all unobtrusive surveillance, in contrast to the activity of the photographer Gallela who, in his efforts to photograph Mrs. Onassis, physically impeded her movements until judicially enjoined from doing so.[2] The same is true of hunting down records of a

[2] See Gallela v. Onassis, 487 F.2d 986 (2d Cir. 1973). The "seclusion" one enjoys

person's health or employment or credit or arrests. In all these instances there is an invasion of privacy in the sense of secrecy, but not in the sense of seclusion—what I call physical privacy.

To be sure, a loss of secrecy may interfere with one's tranquillity and repose just as much as a loud knock on the door in the middle of the night. The difference is that often, although not always,[3] the source of distress in the loss-of-secrecy case is that the individual has been concealing material adverse information about himself in order to manipulate and mislead other people. Because this is such a common motive for keeping information private, privacy as secrecy has in my opinion a weaker claim to the protection of society than the interest in being free from intrusions that disrupt private activities without unmasking—that is, without producing information that may have social value.

Sometimes the same act will invade both seclusion and secrecy. An example is a search of a man's home (particularly when he is at home; but even when he is not, the search will invade his seclusion if it creates a mess) to uncover incriminating documents. Even a subpoena *duces tecum* is an invasion of physical as well as informational privacy, because the person subpoenaed must interrupt his normal activities to respond to the subpoena. But it is important to keep the two interests, seclusion and secrecy, distinct in thinking about the right of privacy. Although there are good reasons for limiting even unobtrusive surveillance and thus for protecting some forms of privacy in the sense of secrecy, in general the case for protecting privacy in the sense of seclusion, physical privacy, is stronger, or at least clearer. An individual's claim to be allowed to conceal information about himself—a criminal record, a history of bankruptcy, poor grades in college, a dishonorable discharge from the army, or whatever—is frequently nothing more than a claim to be allowed to manipulate other people's opinion of him and induce them to enter into transactions that they would refuse to enter into if they knew the truth.

The element of fraud in the concealment of personal information undermines claims for legislative or judicial protection against dis-

while walking on public streets is, of course, limited, but such as it is, it is invaded by a person who impedes one's movements, as Gallela did Mrs. Onassis's.

[3] The traditional but declining reticence about nudity is an example of concealment that does not appear to be primarily motivated by a desire to manipulate other people's impressions.

closure of pertinent information to creditors, employers, and other potential transacting partners.[4] Where, however, the information is sought not by members of the public, acting as it were in self-protection, but by the government, the claim of privacy as secrecy is stronger. The government is not subject to the discipline of the marketplace which will punish a private firm or individual who demands information beyond the point where the value of the information equals the price of obtaining it.[5] In the absence of market discipline, there is no presumption that the government will strike an appropriate balance between disclosure and confidentiality.[6] And the enormous power of government makes the potential consequences of its snooping into people's private lives far more ominous than those of snooping by a private individual or firm.

II. Privacy Law to Griswold

Until the publication in 1890 of Warren and Brandeis's seminal article on the right of privacy,[7] privacy had received little attention as a legal category. As Warren and Brandeis noted, however, it had received legal protection in several contexts. The common law of trespass and (as against federal officers) the Fourth Amendment provided legal protection for physical privacy. So did the Third Amendment which forbade the quartering of troops in private homes in peacetime without the owner's consent. The law of trade secrets and common-law copyright protected the secrecy of new inventions and unpublished works of literature or art. And the *Boyd* case had recently applied the Fourth and Fifth Amendments to an order to produce a document.[8]

---

[4] This position is argued in Posner, *The Right of Privacy*, 12 Ga. L. Rev. 393 (1978). Professor Kronman mentions the recent case of "a school bus driver indicted for the abuse and rape of two retarded children; he had previously been convicted of sodomy, child abuse, assault and battery and contributing to the delinquency of a minor, but because of . . . the Massachusetts [privacy] statute, the school bus company was unable to learn of his record." Kronman, The Privacy Exemption to the Freedom of Information Act 38 n.108, Yale Law School, 23 July 1979.

[5] For example, an employer would presumably have to pay a higher salary to an employee who was required to take periodic lie-detector tests than to one who was not. If the additional information is not worth the extra salary, the employer is incurring an expense not justified by its benefits to him.

[6] See Rubin, *Government and Privacy: A Comment on "the Right of Privacy,"* 12 Ga. L. Rev. 505 (1978); Posner, note 1 *supra*, at 50–55.

[7] Warren & Brandeis, *The Right to Privacy*, 4 Harv. L. Rev. 193 (1890).

[8] Boyd v. United States, 116 U.S. 616 (1886).

Warren and Brandeis thought the existing legal protections of privacy too limited. Although the particular object of their concern—the newspaper gossip column—seems in retrospect a rather trivial one, their article successfully launched a movement to create a tort right of privacy that would reach beyond the limited protection for privacy afforded by the torts of trespass and conversion. The first fruit of this movement was the recognition that it was tortious to use a person's name or picture in commercial advertising without his consent. This branch of the privacy tort has come to be called the "right of publicity" because its primary use is not to protect shy people from unwanted publicity but to give celebrities a legally enforceable right in the advertising value of their name and likeness. Another branch of the tort forbids the media to present a person in a "false light" (as by embellishing a true story with details that distort the character or conduct of the person who is the subject of the story). The tort also forbids (*a*) wiretapping and related invasions of private communications; (*b*) obtrusive surveillance of the sort involved in the *Gallela v. Onassis* case; and (*c*) publicizing intimate facts about a person where the newsworthiness of the facts is outweighed by the embarrassment or humiliation that publicizing them would cause him.[9]

It was to be many years before the tort right of privacy came before the Supreme Court.[10] But long before then, the Court was faced with claims to the protections of privacy under the Fourth and Fifth Amendments. In most of these cases the explicit constitutional language—search and seizure, probable cause, self-incrimination, etc.—could be interpreted without reference to any underlying privacy objectives of the Amendments. *Olmstead v. United States*[11] was an exception. The question in that case was whether wiretapping by federal officers was subject to the Fourth Amendment. The answer logically depended on the precise privacy interest protected by the Fourth Amendment. If it was just physical privacy, then, as noted above, wiretapping should not be deemed subject to the Amendment, for it involves no substantive invasion of physical privacy (and often, as in *Olmstead* itself, not even a technical invasion—a trespass). But if a broader concept of privacy

---

[9] On the right of privacy in tort law, see PROSSER, HANDBOOK OF THE LAW OF TORTS ch. 20 (4th ed. 1971); Posner, note 4 *supra*, at 411–21.

[10] See text *infra*, at notes 86–97.

[11] 277 U.S. 438 (1928).

is implicit in the Fourth Amendment, then wiretapping might be within the scope of the Amendment.

The Court held that wiretapping was not subject to the Fourth Amendment. Its analysis was confused, however, because it focused on whether there was a trespass on the defendant's premises. If the Fourth Amendment protects only physical privacy, a trespass that does not disturb that privacy because it is unperceived should not violate the Amendment. But if the privacy interests protected by the Fourth Amendment are broader, the fact that there is no trespass and no invasion of physical privacy is immaterial. Thus the first question that had to be decided in *Olmstead* was precisely what privacy interest the Fourth Amendment was intended to protect, and the Court did not address that question. If physical privacy is not the only interest protected by the Fourth Amendment, the case for limiting wiretapping is strong even if one lacks enthusiasm for secrecy. The effect of wiretapping, at least when it is known to be employed on a wide scale, is probably less to obtain information and thus to compromise secrecy, which would often be a good thing, than, by inhibiting conversation, to make communication more costly than it would otherwise be.[12] Even this may be a tolerable—conceivably, a desirable—result where society wants to discourage communication, as it may when the communication is in furtherance of illegal activity. But law-enforcement officers cannot be trusted to confine their wiretapping to those communications, if only because they do not bear the costs (which I have suggested are more likely to take the form of less effective communication than of less secrecy) imposed on innocent people whose phones are tapped. Therefore there should be some external control, whether in the form of a tort remedy or a warrant or reasonableness requirement, over the discretion of the executive branch of government to tap phones.

However powerful this argument for limiting wiretapping may be, I am not certain that it should have prevailed in *Olmstead*. The usual view of *Olmstead* is that it was incorrectly decided because the only difference between conventional police searches and wiretapping is a technological difference that the framers of the Constitution could not have foreseen. I disagree with this view. The

[12] See Posner, note 1 *supra*, at 17–20; Posner, note 4 *supra*, at 401–03.

difference between the conventional search and wiretapping is the difference between seclusion and secrecy. Conceivably, the framers of the Fourth Amendment may have been concerned with protecting people's peace and quiet rather than with protecting the secrecy of their conversations.[13] If so, a technological advance that enabled the police to search a man's house with a microwave beam that emitted a loud noise would be subject to the Fourth Amendment, even though the framers had not foreseen this method of search, while wiretapping or "bugging" would not be subject to the Fourth Amendment at all.

The interest in peace and quiet may seem too trivial to be thought the only interest protected by the Fourth Amendment. But one has only to read Justice Douglas's catalog, in *United States v. United States District Court*, of the "gross invasions of privacy"[14] (privacy in the sense of seclusion) resulting from unlawful police searches to be convinced that it is not a trivial interest:[15]

> This Court has been the unfortunate witness to the hazards of police intrusions which did not receive prior sanction by independent magistrates. For example, in *Weeks* v. *United States*, 232 U.S. 383; *Mapp* v. *Ohio*, 367 U.S. 643; and *Chimel* v. *California*, 395 U.S. 752, entire homes were ransacked pursuant to warrantless searches. Indeed, in *Kremen* v. *United States*, 353 U.S. 346, the *entire contents* of a cabin, totaling more than 800 items (such as "1 Dish Rag") were seized incident to an arrest of its occupant and were taken to San Francisco for study by FBI agents. In a similar case, *Von Cleef* v. *New Jersey*, 395 U.S. 814, police, without a warrant, searched an arrestee's house for three hours, eventually seizing "several thousand articles, including books, magazines, catalogues, mailing lists, private correspondence (both open and unopened), photographs, drawings, and film." *Id.*, at 815. In *Silverthorne Lumber Co.* v. *United States*, 251 U.S. 385, federal agents "without a shadow of authority" raided the offices of one of the petitioners (the proprietors of which had earlier been jailed) and "made a clean sweep of all the books, papers and documents found there." Justice Holmes, for the Court, termed this tactic an "outrage."

---

[13] See note 30 *infra*. To be sure, the Amendment protects "papers" and "effects" as well as "persons" and "houses," but one cannot engage in one's activities uninterrupted while the police are rifling one's papers and effects in the course of a search.

[14] 407 U.S. 297, 326 (1972) (concurring opinion).

[15] *Id.* at 326–27.

Id. at 390, 391. In *Stanford* v. *Texas*, 379 U.S. 476, state police seized more than 2,000 items of literature, including the writings of Mr. Justice Black, pursuant to a general search warrant issued to inspect an alleged subversive's home.

The importance that the early search and seizure cases attach to the defendant's ownership of the property seized[16] is consistent with the view that the purpose of the Fourth Amendment is simply to protect peace and quiet from the disruptive consequences of police searches; for the seizure of one's own property is more likely to disturb one's peace and quiet than the seizure of someone else's property. *Hester v. United States*,[17] which held that the Fourth Amendment was not violated when officers secretly spied on the defendant, even if they were trespassing on his property, is also consistent with this view.[18] Thus, it is possible to explain the result in *Olmstead* on the theory that the only privacy interest protected by the Fourth Amendment is the interest in not having one's solitude, one's physical privacy, broken in on by the police. This may not be a correct interpretation of the Fourth Amendment, but it is intelligible and has nothing to do with technological change.

Justice Brandeis, in his dissenting opinion in *Olmstead*, recognized, as the majority did not, that the case properly turned on the nature of the privacy interest protected by the Fourth Amendment. The central passage in the opinion is therefore the one in which he explains the concept of privacy that he thinks the framers adopted:[19]

---

[16] For a review of these cases, see Warden v. Hayden, 387 U.S. 294, 303–04 (1967).

[17] 265 U.S. 57 (1924).

[18] *Hester* is of additional interest in relation to what might be called the property theory of the Fourth Amendment, *e.g.*, the theory visible in Justice Black's dissent in the *Katz* case, see text *infra*, at notes 34–36, that there must be a trespass to person or property for the Fourth Amendment to be violated. As *Hester* illustrates, the invasion of a property interest is not a sufficient condition for an invasion of privacy to be found. Is it a necessary condition? An affirmative answer would make sense only if there were no difference between acts committed by the government and acts by private individuals or firms. In that event the same standard should apply, and would apply if the Fourth Amendment were interpreted as requiring a violation of state property or tort law. But the justification and consequences of invasions of privacy by government and by private persons are different and argue for greater restrictions on the former than the latter, and thus for cutting the Fourth Amendment loose from the moorings of state property and tort law. I find nothing in the language and history of the Fourth Amendment to prevent this result.

[19] *Olmstead*, 277 U.S. at 478–79.

> The makers of our Constitution undertook to secure conditions favorable to the pursuit of happiness. They recognized the significance of man's spiritual nature, of his feelings and of his intellect. They knew that only a part of the pain, pleasure and satisfactions of life are to be found in material things. They sought to protect Americans in their beliefs, their thoughts, their emotions and their sensations. They conferred, as against the government, the right to be let alone—the most comprehensive of rights and the right most valued by civilized men. To protect that right, every unjustifiable intrusion by the Government upon the privacy of the individual, whatever the means employed, must be deemed a violation of the Fourth Amendment. And the use, as evidence in a criminal proceeding, of facts ascertained by such intrusion must be deemed a violation of the Fifth.

The first four sentences in this passage are probably an accurate description of the framers' ideals, but the fifth and key sentence "They conferred . . .") is a *non sequitur*. It does not follow that because the framers wanted to create conditions favorable to certain ideals of human life they created a "right to be let alone"[20] by government. There is no suggestion of such a right in the Constitution. There are simply particular rights to be free from specific forms of invasion of privacy.

Moreover, unless privacy is a synonym for freedom—and there is no evidence that Brandeis held such a view—a right to be let alone would protect much more than privacy.[21] For example, conscription would infringe the right to be let alone, though it might be saved from invalidation by the reference to justification in the next sentence of Brandeis's opinion.[22] But conscription would not invade privacy as earlier defined in this paper.

The Brandeis passage in *Olmstead* proved a harbinger of two important tendencies in contemporary Supreme Court privacy decisions. One is to declare a constitutional right of privacy that has

---

[20] The phrase apparently made its debut in the legal literature in COOLEY, A TREATISE ON THE LAW OF TORTS 29 (1888), where it was used solely in reference to the torts of assault and battery.

[21] See Kurland, *The Private I* 14 (1976), Ryerson Lecture, University of Chicago, published by The Center for Policy Studies.

[22] The objection to the quoted passage is not that Brandeis believed in an unlimited right to be let alone, but that even a limited right has no constitutional derivation.

no source in the constitutional text. The other is to broaden the right of privacy beyond seclusion and secrecy and make it a general right (though selectively, nonneutrally applied) to be free from governmental interference. It is surprising that so scrupulous and disciplined a judge as Justice Brandeis should have been its progenitor. The analytic method used in the passage quoted above is precisely that which he deplored in the Justices who believed that the Due Process Clause of the Fourteenth Amendment was a charter for the protection of a laissez-faire economy against state legislatures. Those Justices had no basis in the text or history of the Fourteenth Amendment for enacting their policy preferences into constitutional law. No more so did Justice Brandeis. The quoted passage contains no references to historical or other materials that would support the inference that the framers of the Constitution intended to create a right of privacy beyond the specific rights in the Third, Fourth, and Fifth Amendments.

Besides invoking the "right to be let alone," Brandeis's dissent in *Olmstead* made much of *Boyd v. United States*.[23] The Court in *Boyd* had held unconstitutional under the Fourth and Fifth Amendments a federal customs statute which provided that if a person refused to produce a document sought by federal authorities he would be deemed to admit the truth of any allegations concerning the contents of the document in any penalty suit brought against him under the revenue laws. Brandeis read the following language in *Boyd* as support for the position that wiretapping violates the Fourth Amendment:[24]

> It is not the breaking of his doors, and the rummaging of his drawers, that constitutes the essence of the offense; but it is the invasion of his indefeasible right of personal security, personal liberty and private property, . . . which underlies and constitutes the essence of Lord Camden's judgment [in *Entick v. Carrington*]. Breaking into a house and opening boxes and drawers are circumstances of aggravation; but any forcible and compulsory extortion of a man's own testimony or of his private papers to be used as evidence to convict him of crime or to forfeit his goods, is within the condemnation of that judgment. In this regard the Fourth and Fifth Amendments run almost into each other.

---

[23] 116 U.S. 616 (1886).

[24] 116 U.S. at 630, quoted at 277 U.S. at 474–75.

This language is pertinent, though somewhat obscurely, to the question whether the Fourth Amendment protects just the interest in seclusion, or whether it goes further and also protects the interest in secrecy or concealment. Lord Camden's opinion in *Entick v. Carington*,[25] from which the Court in *Boyd* quoted at length, treated the confidentiality of any papers seized in an unlawful search as a circumstance aggravating the basic unlawfulness, which in his view consisted of the unauthorized seizure of property. The intrusion was primary, the compromise of secrecy secondary. *Boyd* appears to reverse the sequence. But the appearance is misleading. For while the breaking in and rummaging are described as secondary, what is primary is the right of "personal security, personal liberty and private property," and the last surely, the first probably, and the second possibly also relate to the interest in seclusion. Moreover, *Boyd* involved the same kind of aggravating circumstances as in the traditional police search, if in attenuated form, for the statute in *Boyd* forced people to spend time sifting through their papers to comply with the production order.

To be sure, one cannot read the above passage from *Boyd* and think that all the Court was concerned about was the inconvenience of having to produce a document. It was also concerned with what seemed to it the compelling analogy between being forced to incriminate oneself by one's testimony and being forced to do so by one's documents. If the Court in *Boyd* was correct that the Fifth Amendment shields a man's documents from use in evidence, why not his phone conversations as well? It is not testimony, but neither was the invoice involved in *Boyd*.

The Fifth Amendment aspect of *Boyd* is no longer good law.[26] But what is more important so far as the bearing of that case on the right of privacy is concerned, the Fifth Amendment seems only tangentially involved in the protection of privacy.[27] Not only does the Amendment allow a person to be interrogated concerning matters, however private, that do not place him in jeopardy of a criminal prosecution (and thus the Amendment affords no protection to the

[25] 19 Howell's St. Tr. 1029 (1765).

[26] See Fisher v. United States, 425 U.S. 391, 408 (1976). See also Andresen v. Maryland, 427 U.S. 463 (1976).

[27] See Meltzer, *The Privilege against Self-Incrimination and the Hit-and-Run Opinions*, 1971 SUPREME COURT REVIEW 1, 21.

privacy of the innocent); but he can be forced to testify even as to incriminating matters so long as he is granted immunity from prosecution. Thus, even if wiretapping offends privacy, that is not in itself a compelling reason for invoking the Fifth Amendment. Nor does the Court's expansive interpretation of the Fifth Amendment in *Boyd* necessarily support an expansive concept of constitutionally protected privacy.

In suggesting that *Olmstead* could rationally be supported by reference to the difference between privacy as seclusion and privacy as secrecy and that the Brandeis dissent fails to make a persuasive case that the latter is also a protected interest, I do not mean to suggest that *Olmstead* was necessarily decided correctly. Colonial Americans were concerned not only with intrusions on their tranquillity and repose but also with the seizure of private information in circumstances where few or no elements of interference with peace and quiet were present—notably the unauthorized opening of mail.[28] While opening a letter may delay its arrival or increase the chances that it will be lost, these are minor consequences compared with the effect in compromising the confidentiality of the communication—or, in police searches of the home, the interference with peace and quiet. The background of the Fourth Amendment also includes the writs of assistance, which were used primarily to enforce mercantile statutes through searches of warehouses and other commercial buildings.[29] The principal objection to the writs of assistance was probably their effectiveness in ferreting out violations of the unpopular British mercantile statutes rather than the incidental disruptions of business that the searches under them sometimes caused.[30]

---

[28] See FLAHERTY, PRIVACY IN COLONIAL NEW ENGLAND (1972). An early case, Ex parte Jackson, 96 U.S. 727, 733 (1877), mentioned in passing in Brandeis's dissent, had suggested that it would violate the Fourth Amendment for the Post Office to spy on the mails.

[29] See, *e.g.*, LANDYNSKI, SEARCH AND SEIZURE AND THE SUPREME COURT 30–38 (1966).

[30] Yet it is significant to my basic argument, which is that the seclusion aspect of privacy has been neglected in discussions of the Fourth Amendment, that the colonists themselves focused on the disruptive effects of the writs of assistance, as in Samuel Adams's *The Rights of Colonists and List of Infringements and Violations of Rights* (1772): "Thus our houses and even our bed chambers, are exposed to be ransacked, our boxes chests & trunks broke open ravaged and plundered by wretches, whom no prudent man would venture to employ even as menial servants; whenever they are pleased to say they suspect there are in the house wares &c for which the dutys have not been paid. Flagrant instances of the wanton exercise

Let us jump ahead of our story to see how *Olmstead* has fared in the modern era. Consistently with the (implicit) distinction in *Olmstead* between protection of physical privacy and protection of secrecy, the Court in *Goldman v. United States*[31] held that electronic eavesdropping (in the form of "bugging" rather than wiretapping) was not subject to the Fourth Amendment. In *Silverman v. United States*,[32] a later bugging case, the Court reached a contrary conclusion. There, the bug was implanted in the wall of the defendant's premises, and *Goldman*, where the bug had simply been placed on the outside of the wall of the defendant's premises, was distinguished as involving no physical penetration. Finally, in *Katz v. United States*,[33] a case that involved tapping a phone in a public telephone booth, the Court, on the authority of *Silverman* and other intervening decisions, overruled *Goldman* and *Olmstead*.

---

of this power, have frequently happened in this and other sea port Towns. By this we are cut off from that domestick security which renders the lives of the most unhappy in some measure agreable. Those Officers may under colour of law and the cloak of a general warrant, break thro' the sacred rights of the Domicil, ransack mens houses, destroy their securities, carry off their property, and with little danger to themselves commit the most horred murders." 1 Schwartz, The Bill of Rights: A Documentary History 200, 206 (1971).

Before moving on, I would reply to a possible argument that the privacy interests protected by the Fourth Amendment cannot be very substantial since, in all of the cases I have discussed, the privacy protected is in fact that of wrongdoers. The impression that the Fourth Amendment protects criminals rather than law-abiding individuals is the result of the peculiar remedial scheme for enforcing the Amendment. Fourth Amendment claims are rarely advanced except by convicted criminals seeking to have their convictions overturned on the ground that evidence used at trial has been obtained in violation of the Fourth Amendment. Damage remedies for a violation of the Fourth Amendment exist but are rarely invoked. See Bivens v. Six Unknown Named Agents of the Bureau of Narcotics, 403 U.S. 388 (1971). Yet a useful way of apprehending the fundamental purposes of the Amendment is to imagine its being enforced exclusively through damage actions. Then police would be deterred from illegal searches by having to make the victim of such a search whole for any injury caused by the search to peace or quiet or to other interests protected by the Fourth Amendment. Whether the victim was later convicted of a crime based on evidence obtained in the search would be a detail. The damage remedy, to the extent the court was able to assess accurately the damages caused by an illegal search, would protect the privacy of criminals and the law-abiding alike. This would be true whether or not illegally seized evidence was used to convict a person. He would still be entitled to damages measured by the injury to any lawful privacy interest impaired by the search. By "lawful" interest, I mean to distinguish, for example, between the disturbance of the criminal's peace and quiet by an unlawful search and the punishment inflicted on him as a result of illegal activity discovered by the search and later used against him in a criminal proceeding. The punishment would not impair any lawful interest of his.

[31] 316 U.S. 129 (1942).

[32] 365 U.S. 505 (1961).

[33] 389 U.S. 347 (1967).

Justice Black, dissenting in *Katz*, was indignant that the majority had relied on *Silverman*, which unlike *Katz* (and *Goldman* and *Olmstead*) had involved a physical penetration of the defendant's premises and hence a trespass. But trespass is irrelevant. The trespass in *Silverman* involved no actual disturbance of the tranquillity of the defendant's premises. As in *Hester v. United States*,[34] where the Court had declined to subject unobtrusive surveillance to the Fourth Amendment notwithstanding that there was a trespass, the "spike mike" in *Silverman* was unobtrusive and so did not disturb the defendant's physical privacy. If the true basis for *Olmstead* is that the Fourth Amendment protects only the seclusion or physical-privacy aspect of privacy, then *Silverman* was indeed inconsistent with *Olmstead* because the Court in *Silverman* used the Fourth Amendment to protect secrecy rather than seclusion.

The Court in *Katz* overlooked the distinction between these two senses of privacy, seclusion and secrecy. It treated the meaning of privacy as too obvious to merit extended discussion. Most of the opinion deals with the question whether a telephone booth is within the scope of the Fourth Amendment's right of privacy and whether the tapping of the phone was unreasonable in the circumstances presented. Justice Black objected to the majority's loose invocation of the privacy concept:[35]

> By clever word juggling the Court finds it plausible to argue that language aimed specifically at searches and seizures of things that can be searched and seized may, to protect privacy, be applied to eavesdropped evidence of conversations that can neither be searched nor seized. Few things happen to an individual that do not affect his privacy in one way or another. Thus, by arbitrarily substituting the Court's language, designed to protect privacy, for the Constitution's language, designed to protect against unreasonable searches and seizures, the Court has made the Fourth Amendment its vehicle for holding all laws violative of the Constitution which offend the Court's broadest conception of privacy.

Save for his suggestion, which is not compelled by the language or history of the Fourth Amendment, that only seizures of tangibles

[34] See note 17 *supra*.

[35] 389 U.S. at 373.

are within its scope,[36] it is hard to quarrel with Justice Black. The majority did not attempt to define privacy and was apparently unaware that the result in *Olmstead* could be supported by reference to any principle other than the absence of a trespass.

Justice Black bolstered his asserted distinction between eavesdropping and searches and seizures by noting that eavesdropping existed at the time that the Bill of Rights was adopted—Blackstone's *Commentaries* had mentioned that eavesdropping was a misdemeanor at common law[37]—yet the framers had not sought to prohibit it, either in the Fourth Amendment or anywhere else in the Constitution. This point may not seem decisive, given the difference in effectiveness between personal and electronic eavesdropping and the fact that Blackstone's reference was to eavesdropping by "common scolds" rather than by law enforcers—until one reflects on the importance and effectiveness of one form of personal eavesdropping. I refer to the planting of undercover agents in a criminal gang or subversive group. Their use in law enforcement antedates the Bill of Rights by centuries, if not millennia. Their purpose is to eavesdrop.

The Supreme Court has steadfastly refused to hold that the use of undercover agents to gather leads and evidence of crime is subject to the Fourth Amendment.[38] It has based its refusal on the fiction of consent and has adhered to its view even when, as in *Osborn v. United States*,[39] the undercover agent carries a concealed microphone and records the interview with the suspect. The Court's approach was defensible in the *Olmstead* era when (except for the mails) arguably the only privacy right protected by the Fourth Amendment was the right not to be interrupted in what one was doing by police barging in to rifle one's desk or otherwise mess up one's house. But once the Fourth Amendment was held to protect privacy in the sense of secrecy, the step taken in *Silverman* and then

[36] The right declared in the Fourth Amendment "of the people to be secure in their persons" seems broadly enough stated to include a right to be free from unreasonable electronic surveillance.

[37] See 4 BLACKSTONE, COMMENTARIES ON THE LAWS OF ENGLAND *168.

[38] See, *e.g.*, Hoffa v. United States, 385 U.S. 293 (1966). For criticism of the Court's approach, see Stone, *The Scope of the Fourth Amendment: Privacy and the Police Use of Spies, Secret Agents and Informers*, 1976 AM. B. FOUND. RES. J. 1195.

[39] 385 U.S. 323 (1966).

in *Katz*, there was no longer a persuasive ground for treating the undercover agent as beyond the scope of the Fourth Amendment.[40] The undercover agent clearly invades the privacy-as-secrecy of the people whom he spies on. It is absurd to say that they "consent" to this invasion of privacy in any sense which the law would elsewhere respect; consent is vitiated by fraud. And it is circular to say that there is no invasion of privacy unless the individual whose privacy is invaded had a reasonable expectation of privacy; whether he will or will not have such an expectation will depend on what the legal rule is.[41] These are threadbare arguments.

To summarize, whether wiretapping and police spying are subject to the Fourth Amendment depends on whether the Fourth Amendment protects only privacy in the sense of seclusion or physical privacy—in which event these methods of gathering material should not be subject to the Fourth Amendment because, unlike physical searches of a person or his premises, they are unobtrusive—or whether it also protects privacy in the sense of secrecy, in which event they are clearly within the scope of the Fourth Amendment. Either way, the Court has decided the wiretapping and police spying cases inconsistently.

The Court's failure to recognize that there is a substantial question (on which the applicability of the Fourth Amendment to wiretapping and to undercover agents turns) whether only privacy in the sense of seclusion is actually protected by the Amendment is shared by the commentators. Some scholars of privacy seem not

[40] *Hoffa* and *Osborn* were decided after *Silverman* but before *Katz*, but the Court, in United States v. White, 461 U.S. 475 (1971), expressly declined to overrule the undercover agent cases in the light of *Katz*. I emphasize that it is not my argument that the logic of *Katz* requires that the use of undercover agents be banned, but only that such use should be subject to judicial control, as in the case of conventional searches. That the appropriate warrant would read differently from a warrant in a conventional search case is no more persuasive an objection than the notion that wiretapping is not subject to the Fourth Amendment because a wiretapping warrant reads differently from a conventional search warrant.

[41] See Amsterdam, *Perspectives on the Fourth Amendment*, 58 MINN. L. REV. 349, 384 (1974). The problem of circularity was recognized by Mr. Justice Rehnquist in his opinion for the Court in Rakas v. Illinois, 99 S. Ct. 421 (1978), where he stated that the expectation of privacy must be founded on property or other notions outside the Fourth Amendment doctrines themselves. *Id.* at 431 n.12. This is a very damaging admission so far as the Court's refusal to subject police spies to the Fourth Amendment is concerned, for an American citizen should have a reasonable expectation based on the customs and mores of a free society that people who represent themselves to him as being trustworthy friends are not in reality secret policemen or paid police informants.

to realize that seclusion is even a component of the concept of privacy.[42] Others understand the distinction but do not relate it to the Fourth Amendment.[43] Professor Geoffrey Stone, a forceful and persuasive advocate of extending the Fourth Amendment to undercover agents, does not adequately distinguish seclusion from secrecy as objects of protection of the Fourth Amendment. He writes:[44]

> The final possible absolute limitation on the scope of the amendment's protection of personal privacy would be to restrict its coverage to only those methods of obtaining information that intrude in some way upon the privacy of a "constitutionally protected area," such as a home or office. Such a limitation might at least arguably be justified if the framers' real concern in drafting the amendment was not with protection of the individual's general interest in keeping information about him out of the hands of government but, rather, with preservation of his related but more limited interest in being able to retreat to some special place of solitude where he can be free of unbridled government surveillance. The importance of this latter interest should not be underestimated, for a "sane, decent, civilized society must provide some such oasis, some shelter from public scrutiny" where the individual can safely store his most secret possessions and where he can relax, open his collar, and feel free to do all things he would not ordinarily "do in the same way at high noon in Times Square."
>
> Despite the importance of this core interest, it seems doubtful that the framers' desire to protect privacy was limited solely to the preservation of such special sanctuaries. Indeed, the framers' concern with the privacy of an individual's "papers" and "effects," wherever they be found, and their awareness of the interplay between freedom of expression and privacy seem to refute such a narrow view of their intent. It therefore seems reasonable to conclude, as did the Court in *Katz*, that in its concern with privacy, "the Fourth Amendment protects people, not places." And although there is good reason to be particularly wary of governmental intrusions into the privacy of homes and offices, the amendment's concern with privacy

---

[42] See Parker, *A Definition of Privacy*, 27 RUTG. L. REV. 275, 277 (1974); *cf*. Ely, *The Wages of Crying Wolf: A Comment on* Roe *v.* Wade, 82 YALE L.J. 920, 928–29 (1973).

[43] See Gross, note 1 *supra*, at 37; Bostwick, *A Taxonomy of Privacy: Repose, Sanctuary, and Intimate Decision*, 64 CALIF. L. REV. 1447, 1451–56 (1976).

[44] Stone, note 38 *supra*, at 1210–11.

> should properly be viewed more broadly as protecting the individual's interest in keeping information about him out of the hands of government.

The discussion begins promisingly with a reference to the interest in solitude, but it soon becomes clear that the relevance of solitude to Professor Stone is the freedom that it makes possible from surveillance, an interest that can be made to merge with a broader interest in keeping personal information from the government. There is, as I have been at pains to stress, a separate interest in not having one's solitude broken into: the interest invaded by an unwanted telephone solicitation or the blare of a sound truck as well as by a police search. It is conceivably—although improbably—the only privacy interest that was intended to be protected by the Fourth Amendment.

III. The Griswold Decision

As *Katz* illustrates the uncritical (not necessarily incorrect) expansion of the concept of privacy from privacy in the sense of physical privacy or seclusion to privacy in the sense of secrecy, so *Griswold v. Connecticut*[45] illustrates a further important expansion in the concept of privacy together with a shift in its constitutional foundations. The case involved the prosecution, as accessories in the violation of a state criminal statute prohibiting the use of contraceptives even by married people, of two members of a birth-control clinic who had been dispensing advice on the use of, and prescribing, contraceptives. In an opinion by Justice Douglas, the Supreme Court held that the statute violated a constitutional right of privacy created by the Bill of Rights.

After disposing of the standing question, the opinion begins apologetically by disclaiming any reliance on notions of "substantive due process" and continues by reminding the reader of how broadly the First Amendment has been interpreted. For example, although no right of association is mentioned in the First Amendment, such a right has been recognized as a matter of interpretation of the Amendment. On the basis of this example Justice Douglas concludes

---

[45] 381 U.S. 479 (1965). For a penetrating analysis of the *Griswold* case, see Bork, *Neutral Principles and Some First Amendment Problems,* 47 Ind. L. J. 7–11 (1971).

"that specific guarantees in the Bill of Rights have penumbras, formed by emanations from those guarantees that help give them life and substance."[46] The opinion notes that the First, Third, Fourth, and Fifth Amendments protect privacy and concludes that the "emanations" from these protections create a "penumbral" right of married people to use contraceptives.

The Court's invocation of the Third Amendment, which prohibits quartering troops in private homes in peacetime without the consent of the homeowner, is singularly inapt. The Third Amendment is the clearest example in the Constitution of a provision designed to protect privacy solely as seclusion—not even privacy in the sense of secrecy. A broader objection to this portion of the *Griswold* opinion is that the theory of "emanations" or peripheral rights implies a connection between core and periphery which is lacking in the case of a right to use contraceptives. One can conceive of a right of a pamphleteer to remain anonymous as being ancillary to his express First Amendment right to disseminate his opinions. But there is no such ancillary relationship between the right to use contraceptives and the core rights protected by the Third, Fourth, or Fifth Amendments.[47]

The nonspurious invocation of privacy as an ancillary right is illustrated by Douglas's dissenting opinion in *Public Util. Comm'n v. Pollack*.[48] The question in that case was whether the Public Utilities Commission (P.U.C.) of the District of Columbia had violated the Due Process Clause of the Fifth Amendment by allowing the District's trolley company to broadcast on its trolleys and buses. The majority agreed that the broadcasting invaded the passengers' right of privacy in the sense of seclusion but thought the invasion trivial. Justice Douglas disagreed, not on the ground that peace and quiet is itself an aspect of the liberty protected by the Due Process Clause, but on the ground that allowing the government (which is how he viewed the private trolley company because of the extensive regulation of it by the P.U.C.) to broadcast music to its

---

[46] 381 U.S. at 484.

[47] A feeble effort, destined to be abandoned in later cases, was made later in Justice Douglas's opinion to characterize the right to use contraceptives as being ancillary to the Fourth Amendment. See text *infra,* at notes 53–54.

[48] 343 U.S. 451 (1952).

captive audiences might lead eventually to sinister efforts by government to propagandize unwilling listeners.[49] In this view the invasion of the passengers' privacy was unconstitutional only because it posed a danger (a rather remote one, to be sure) of violating First Amendment freedoms. Privacy was an ancillary First Amendment right.

Another example where privacy could be regarded as an ancillary right is *Buckley v. Valeo*,[50] where the Court upheld against privacy objections the provisions of the federal campaign financing law that required public disclosure of the names of contributors—even of as little as $100—to candidates for public office. To be allowed to contribute anonymously to a political candidate could have been viewed as a right of privacy ancillary to the First Amendment, which protects freedom of expression primarily to the end of preserving political freedom; but it was not so viewed. The denial of such a right seems inconsistent with the right of anonymity of political pamphleteers,[51] and illustrative of the wavering manner of the Court's regard for privacy.

Griswold, in contrast, despite the talk of "penumbras" and emanations," elevates the right of privacy to independent constitutional significance. In doing so it uses privacy in a new sense, for the right to use contraceptives is not a right to seclusion—to be free from noise or interruption in home or office—or to conceal information. This point is obvious, but it is not an obvious objection to the result in *Griswold*. For it can be argued both that the Court is entitled to use ordinary language in a technical legal sense (compare, for example, the lay and legal meanings of so familiar a term as "assault") and that the right vindicated in *Giswold* resembles, or at least has roots similar to, the right of privacy in the sense of seclusion. The first argument can be bolstered by noting that one meaning of privacy is simply what is done in private—which certainly describes the ordinary use of contraceptives—so even the linguistic wrench is not that great. I accept for the moment this rather strained use of

---

[49] See *id.* at 468–69.

[50] 424 U.S. 1, 60–82 (1976).

[51] The pamphleteer's right of anonymity was upheld in Talley v. California, 362 U.S. 60 (1960); see also N.A.A.C.P. v. Alabama, 357 U.S. 449 (1958). Similar to *Buckley* in spirit is Laird v. Tatum, 408 U.S. 1, (1972), where the Court held that the Army's domestic surveillance program was not unconstitutional under the First Amendment despite its possible effect in "chilling" the expression of unpopular views.

language—but only for a moment, for the Court in cases subsequent to *Griswold* extended the right of privacy to embrace the sale of contraceptives and abortions, which are not private acts in the same sense as the use of contraceptives.

The second argument is more interesting. Whether one adopts a libertarian, economic, or I imagine any other view of human rights, both privacy as seclusion and privacy as the right of married people to use contraceptives are instrumental rather than final values, and the final values are similar, perhaps identical, in the two cases. Seclusion is valued because it enhances the quality of one's work or leisure. Contraception, by enabling the married couple to control the number of children they will have, enhances the quality of their marriage. Both seclusion and contraception are means to enhance liberty, but they can be distinguished on the basis of the difference between "freedom from" and "freedom to,"[52] or between negative and positive liberties. The claim of privacy as seclusion is a claim to be allowed to do in private, *i.e.*, alone, whatever tort or property or criminal law, or some other source of rights to act, allows one to do. It is not a claim to be allowed to do something more than the law allows. The claim in *Griswold* of a right to use contraceptives was a claim to do something a State had forbidden. One cannot conclude that because the Constitution protects the former kind of claim it also protects the latter. To be sure, the right to be free in one's home from noise or other interruptions would be worth little if the State forbade one to do the various things one wanted to do in the privacy of the home. But by the same token, to be free to do what one wants in the privacy of one's home would be worth little if one were poor and unhealthy. There is something wrong with a method of analysis that would allow one to extract a right to the good life from the Fourth Amendment. What is wrong is that it equates privacy with the purposes for which people want privacy.

An even more fundamental difficulty with defining the constitutional right of privacy in terms of the ends for which privacy is sought is that this procedure ignores the specific limitations of the relevant constitutional provisions. A conclusion that the Fourth Amendment is founded on the concept of privacy as seclusion would not justify the use of that concept to found rights which the lan-

---

[52] See Gross, note 1 *supra*, at 44.

guage in the Fourth Amendment clearly excludes from its protection. For example, the broadcasting of music to captive audiences in the *Pollak* case was an invasion—we will not worry about how serious a one—of the privacy, in the sense of seclusion, of the passengers, some of whose thinking or reading may have been disturbed. But not even the most generous interpretation of the terms search and seizure which delimit the scope of the Fourth Amendment will reach a broadcast. Similarly, even if the concept of privacy does include the right to use contraceptives, neither the Fourth Amendment nor any other provision of the Constitution can fairly be read to create a right to such use.

This point is further illustrated by the part of Justice Douglas's opinion in *Griswold* in which, perhaps to reinforce his "emanations" approach, he relates the right to use contraceptives to a more conventional notion of privacy by discussing a hypothetical mode of enforcing the Connecticut contraception statute—searching the bedroom for evidence of violations. Such a search would indeed be an invasion of privacy in a conventional sense. But it would be a justifiable invasion if the statute were not otherwise constitutionally objectionable. This can be seen by imagining that the statute in question forbade not contraception but murder and that the police had probable cause to believe that the suspected murderer had secreted the weapon in his mattress.

Furthermore, even if some methods of enforcing the Connecticut statute so offended privacy interests protected by the Fourth Amendment as to be impermissible though conducted pursuant to a warrant based on probable cause, that would mean only that the statute was difficult to enforce. Justice Harlan, in his dissenting opinion in *Poe v. Ullman*,[53] which anticipated this aspect of the Douglas opinion in *Griswold*, had suggested that there was no way of enforcing the Connecticut contraception statute without invading privacy. He was wrong. As the facts of *Griswold* show, the State could enforce the statute without invading anyone's privacy, simply by prosecuting, as accessories, the employees of birth-control clinics. It is no novelty for the primary violator of a statute to be beyond the effective reach of the law so that enforcement is possible only against accessories. There are, for example, areas of patent and copyright law where only the contributory infringer (the di-

[53] 367 U.S. 497, 548 (1961) (dissenting opinion).

rect infringer's supplier) is ever sued.[54] But even if there were no way to enforce the Connecticut contraceptive statute without violating a constitutionally protected interest in privacy, it would follow not that the statute violated anyone's right of privacy but only that the statute could not be enforced, a fate of many other statutes punishing "victimless" crimes. In any event, prosecution of employees of birth-control clinics is not a search.

The real objection that people have to the Connecticut contraception statute is not that it invades privacy but that prohibiting contraception, at least by married people, is an undue limitation of freedom of action. Whatever its weight, I do not see how this objection becomes more persuasive by being put in terms of privacy. Perhaps Justice Douglas chose to speak in those terms in order to avoid basing the decision explicitly on the concept of substantive due process.[55] Yet Justice Douglas did cite several cases limiting government regulation of the family. These cases either are irrelevant to the contraception question, such as *Skinner v. Oklahoma*,[56] which held that it was a violation of equal protection to sterilize thieves but not embezzlers, or are based explicitly on substantive due process, such as *Meyer v. Nebraska*.[57] *Meyer* held that a State's prohibition of the teaching of foreign (other than classical) languages to children in schools violated (as applied to private schools) a concept of liberty that included "the right of the individual to contract" and "to engage in the common occupations of life."[58] The opinion was by McReynolds and Holmes dissented.[59] Under the ostensible modern test of substantive due process, whereby a statute is invalid only if it bears no rational relationship to a permissible legislative ob-

---

[54] See, *e.g.*, Aro Mfg. Co. v. Convertible Top Replacement Co., 365 U.S. 336 (1961).

[55] This is the concept that the Due Process Clause protects rights not protected by any specific provision of the Constitution, such as the "right to liberty of contract" in the days when the Clause was used as a charter of freedom from economic regulation. See McCloskey, *Economic Due Process and the Supreme Court: An Exhumation and Reburial*, 1962 SUPREME COURT REVIEW 34.

[56] 316 U.S. 535 (1942). *Cf.* Loving v. Virginia, 388 U.S. 1 (1967) (invalidating miscegenation statute on equal protection grounds).

[57] 262 U.S. 390 (1923). See also Pierce v. Society of Sisters, 268 U.S. 510 (1925).

[58] 262 U.S. at 399. Justice Douglas quoted this very language from *Meyer* in the course of an opinion where he stated that the right to sexual privacy recognized in *Griswold* and later cases had "nothing to do" with substantive due process. Doe v. Bolton, 410 U.S. 179, 212 n.4, 214 (1973) (concurring opinion).

[59] The dissent appears in a companion case, Bartels v. Iowa, 262 U.S. 404, 412 (1923).

jective,[60] *Meyer* was incorrectly decided.[61] Douglas's citation of *Meyer* (which has been repeated in later "privacy" cases) is evidence of the survival of substantive due process despite frequent disclaimers. The contemporary Court has simply "deregulated" the family,[62] in the same way that its discredited predecessors prevented States from regulating business. One can agree with the policy preferences of either or both sets of Justices while questioning the constitutional basis for their actions.[63]

---

[60] For some examples of the Court's tolerance of statutes attacked as denials of substantive due process, see, *e.g.*, Kotch v. Board of River Port Pilot Comm'rs, 330 U.S. 552 (1947); Williamson v. Lee Optical Co., 348 U.S. 483 (1955). And for denial that there is even a rational-relationship requirement, see Ferguson v. Skrupa, 373 U.S. 726, 729 (1963).

[61] Holmes, in his dissenting opinion, discussed the "melting pot" philosophy which may have motivated the ban on the teaching of foreign languages to children and concluded that the statute was not irrational.

[62] Besides *Griswold*, see the cases discussed in the text *infra*, at notes 64, 67; Carey v. Population Services, Int'l, 431 U.S. 678 (1977); Zablocki v. Redhail, 434 U.S. 374 (1978).

[63] Still another objection to the procedure by which Douglas extracted a broad right of privacy from a number of constitutional amendments which protect particular aspects of privacy is that such a procedure assumes, what is doubtful, that a statute or constitution is animated by a coherent "spirit" which informs all of its provisions and enables one to decide cases not within the letter of the statute by reference to its spirit. This procedure treats individual statutory and constitutional provisions much like individual cases in a field of common law: from a study of the provisions, as of cases, the judge extracts some ruling principle that can be used to decide a new, previously unforeseen case. But as applied to either a statute or the Constitution this procedure rests on a failure to understand the difference between legislative enactments, including constitutions, and common-law decisions. See Posner, Economic Analysis of Law ch. 19 (2d ed. 1977). To a greater degree than common-law decisions, legislative enactments are the product of interest-group pressures. Insofar as those pressures prevail, an enactment may lack any "spirit" or rational unity that could provide guidance in areas not specifically covered by the enactment. See Kennedy, *Legal Formality*, 2 J. Legal Studies 351 (1973). Thus, the fact that there is one amendment to the Constitution in favor of the press and another against quartering troops in private homes and another establishing a right against being forced to incriminate oneself could be the result of the jockeying of interest groups represented at the Constitutional Convention rather than expressions of a consistent concept of the right to be left alone. At least this possibility should be considered (as Douglas failed to do) before separate Amendments are read as if they were common-law decisions expressing a uniform principle. Incidentally, if the Constitution has a "spirit," it is one of distrust of government. The modern welfare state is contrary to that spirit, a point to give pause to those who would create constitutional rights based on the Constitution's "spirit." I note also that Professor Charles Black, the outstanding advocate of what he calls "the method of inference from the structures and relationships created by the constitution in all its parts or in some principal part," Black, Structure and Relationship in Constitutional Law 7 (1969), does not suggest that *Griswold* illustrates that method.

IV. THE RIGHT OF PRIVACY IN THE SUPREME COURT SINCE THE *Griswold* CASE

Griswold was the first decision of the Supreme Court to announce a constitutional right of privacy divorced from the specific privacy-oriented guarantees of the Bill of Rights, as well as the first to interpret privacy in a broader sense than seclusion and secrecy. It appeared to usher in a new era, which I shall now describe, in the constitutional law of privacy.

I shall discuss the Court's principal privacy cases since *Griswold* in three groups: cases involving rights of marital or, more broadly, sexual privacy—the direct descendants of the *Griswold* decision; cases in which the right of privacy is in conflict with other constitutional rights such as freedom of the press; and cases in which the right of privacy is asserted in the context of governmentally required record keeping, a context in which defenders of privacy have expressed particular concern over the erosion of privacy. I shall not consider again the fourth important class of privacy cases, those from *Olmstead* to *Katz* in which the right of privacy is asserted against a police search or eavesdropping, to which reference was made earlier. Nor shall I consider the Court's nonconstitutional privacy cases.

A. SEXUAL PRIVACY

In *Eisenstadt v. Baird*,[64] the Court was presented with the question whether a State could forbid the distribution of contraceptives to unmarried persons. The Court held that it could not, on the ground that to treat unmarried people differently in this respect from married people, whose right to use contraceptives had been established in *Griswold*, would be arbitrary and hence violate the Equal Protection Clause of the Fourteenth Amendment. The heart of the opinion is the following passage:[65]

---

[64] 405 U.S. 438 (1972).

[65] *Id.* at 453. Students of the Supreme Court's citation practices may be interested to note what precedents the Court cited in support of the passage quoted in the text. There were three: Stanley v. Georgia, 394 U.S. 557 (1969), a First Amendment case (see text *infra*, following note 70); Skinner v. Oklahoma, 316 U.S. 535 (1942), an equal protection case which held that a State could not sterilize thieves without also sterilizing embezzlers (see text *supra*, at note 56); and Jacobson v. Massachusetts, 197 U.S. 11 (1905), which upheld the constitutionality of compulsory vaccination.

> It is true that in *Griswold* the right of privacy in question inhered in the marital relationship. Yet the marital couple is not an independent entity with a mind and heart of its own, but an association of two individuals each with a separate intellectual and emotional makeup. If the right of privacy means anything, it is the right of the *individual*, married or single, to be free from unwarranted governmental intrusion into matters so fundamentally affecting a person as the decision whether to bear or beget a child.

To say that the right of privacy means nothing if it does not allow an unmarried person to obtain contraceptives not only is hyperbole but shows how far the Court had moved by 1972 from any of the usual senses of the word "privacy." The Court in *Griswold* had at least attempted to relate the right to use contraceptives to familiar notions of privacy by speculating on the intrusive methods by which a statute banning the use of contraceptives might be enforced. This ground was unavailable in *Baird* because the statute there forbade not the use, but only the distribution, of contraceptives. *Baird* is thus a pure essay in substantive due process. It unmasks *Griswold* as based on the idea of sexual liberty rather than privacy.[66]

Once the Court, in *Baird*, had severed the right to use contraceptives from any concept of privacy as what people do in private, it was perhaps inevitable that the right of privacy would eventually be held to imply the right of a married or unmarried woman to have an abortion. Abortion is an alternative method to contraception for preventing an unwanted birth. To be sure, there are differences between the methods that may be relevant on the issue of the justification for government intervention; in particular, abortion may involve the taking of a human (or at least protohuman) life and contraception does not. But with regard to the question whether there is a constitutionally protected interest in being allowed to take measures to avoid giving birth to an unwanted child, as distinct from whether that interest is outweighed by competing interests, there is no difference between contraception and abortion. So perhaps it is not surprising that the Court in *Roe v. Wade*[67] devoted only one

---

[66] This point is recognized in Henkin, *Privacy and Autonomy*, 74 COLUM. L. REV. 1410 (1974), and approved as consistent with "constitutional modernization by the judiciary." *Id.* at 1424.

[67] 410 U.S. 113, 153 (1973).

sentence to the question whether the right of privacy includes the right to have an abortion.

Baird and *Wade* raise, even more acutely than *Griswold*, the question whether we have a written constitution, with the limitations thereby implied on the creation of new constitutional rights,[68] or whether the Constitution is no more than a grant of discretion to the Supreme Court to mold public policy in accordance with the Justices' own personal and shifting preferences. Nothing in the language, legislative history, or background of the Constitution, the Bill of Rights, or the Fourteenth Amendment shows any evidence of an intent to limit state regulation of the family, save perhaps when the regulation is along racial or otherwise invidious lines. This vacuum of relevant constitutional principle makes the issue in *Baird* and *Wade* quite different from that in *Olmstead* and *Katz*. The Fourth Amendment is based on a concept of privacy that may be broad enough to include the concealment of information even in circumstances where there is no invasion of physical privacy. But neither in the Fourth Amendment nor elsewhere in the Constitution is there reference to a policy of allowing people to engage in sexual activity without fear of giving birth. The Court has tried to bridge this gap by the purely verbal expedient of regarding as an aspect of "privacy" the freedom to engage in activity which the Supreme Court does not think should be regulated. What is private in this view is simply what the Court thinks should not be subject to public control. In this sense, however, the right to follow the occupation of one's choice without hindrance from government could equally well be regarded as an aspect of the right of privacy. The Justices who thought that the Constitution protected the right of employer and employee to set the terms of employment without government interference simply lacked the wit to justify their belief in the language of privacy.[69]

I close my discussion of the "sexual privacy" cases with a glance

---

[68] That we do not, that it is a good thing we do not, and that the sexual privacy cases show that we do not, is argued in Grey, *Do We Have an Unwritten Constitution?* 27 STAN. L. REV. 703, 713 nn.44, 46 (1975).

[69] At least one Justice apparently believes that there is a constitutional right to be let alone, applicable to the right of a policeman not to cut his hair to meet departmental requirements. See Marshall, J., dissenting, in Kelley v. Johnson, 425 U.S. 238, 253 (1976).

at *Stanley v. Georgia*,[70] where the Court held that a state statute forbidding the possession of obscene materials could not constitutionally be applied to the possession of such materials in the home. The primary basis of the decision was that the First Amendment allows people to read anything they want in their homes, and the reference in the opinion to "the privacy of one's own home"[71] seems therefore primarily decorative. It is, however, interesting to note that in distinguishing an earlier case upholding state regulation of obscenity the Court pointed out that enjoying pornography in the home does not create a danger presented by the public distribution of obscene materials, *i.e.*, of "intrud[ing] upon the sensibilities or privacy of the general public."[72] As we shall see, the Court's concern with the privacy-invasive characteristics of public distribution of sexually explicit materials was to be short-lived. It is also noteworthy that the Court in *Baird* (discussed earlier) cited *Stanley* for the proposition that the unmarried have a right to obtain contraceptives. This citation makes sense only if the Court conceives of the First Amendment as an instrument for achieving sexual freedom. Otherwise it is impossible to understand how a right to possess obscene materials is a basis for recognizing a right of unmarried people to obtain contraceptives. It is as if the right of people under the First Amendment to read about guns were a basis for holding that they have a First Amendment right to buy guns.

B. CONFLICTS WITH OTHER RIGHTS

The possibility of a collision between the right of privacy and other constitutional rights is not new. Long before *Griswold*, the Court had wrestled with the conflict between the First Amendment right to disseminate ideas by means of sound trucks or door-to-door solicitation and the right of householders to be free from the noise and interruptions caused by these methods. In 1951, the Court upheld a state law which forbade door-to-door solicitation in the absence of advance permission of owners or residents.[73] This ingenious accommodation of the rights of privacy and expression was later to save a statute that ordered the Post Office to take steps to stop de-

---

[70] 394 U.S. 557 (1969).

[71] *Id.* at 565.

[72] *Id.* at 567. See also Redrup v. New York, 386 U.S. 767, 769 (1967).

[73] Breard v. Alexandria, 341 U.S. 622 (1951). The opinion referred to the householder's interest in "privacy and repose." *Id.* at 625–26.

livery of direct-mail advertising of a sexual nature to people who filed a statement with the Post Office requesting that they not receive such mail.[74] But this accommodation was not available in the sound-truck cases.

In *Saia v. New York*,[75] the Court invalidated an ordinance requiring a permit for sound trucks. The Court stated: "In this case a permit is denied because some persons were said to have found the sound annoying. In the next one a permit may be denied because some people find the ideas annoying."[76] At first glance the parallel of annoying noise and annoying ideas appears to fail simply because the noise from a sound truck is an invasion of privacy and ideas are not. But this is a superficial distinction. Repose and tranquillity can be disturbed by ideas as well as by sounds. The true difference between noise and annoying ideas is that the former can be controlled without seriously restricting the dissemination of ideas, while the latter can be controlled—with some important exceptions[77] —only by forbidding their dissemination altogether. The First Amendment consequences are thus of a very different magnitude. The Court soon realized this and within a year virtually overruled *Saia* in an opinion which recognized that the blare of the sound truck was an invasion of "quiet and tranquillity."[78]

This conclusion was reached without any suggestion that there was a constitutional right to seclusion, although such a right would appear to have firmer roots in the Constitution, and specifically in the Fourth Amendment, than the right to use contraceptives which was asserted in the *Griswold* case. To be sure, the constitutional right of privacy recognized in that case was a right against governmental rather than private invasions of privacy. Nor is the distinction entirely a technical one, since there are reasons for distinguishing between governmental and private invasions of privacy, especially with regard to the secrecy aspect of privacy. But although the invasion of privacy that occurred in the sound-truck cases could

---

[74] Rowan v. Post Office Dept., 397 U.S. 728 (1970).

[75] 334 U.S. 558 (1948).

[76] *Id.* at 562.

[77] See *Rowan*, note 74 *supra; Erznoznik*, note 79 *infra;* and Cohen, note 82 *infra.*

[78] Kovacs v. Cooper, 336 U.S. 77, 87 (1949). Recent cases in the same spirit are Grayned v. City of Rockford, 408 U.S. 104 (1972), upholding an ordinance limiting noise in the vicinity of schools, and Village of Belle Terre v. Boraas, 416 U.S. 1, 9 (1974), upholding single-family-dwelling zoning designed to protect "quiet seclusion."

not have violated the Constitution, because the sound trucks were privately owned, the Court's declaration in *Griswold* of a constitutional right of privacy must surely say something about the Court's view of the importance of the underlying interests protected by the right; and unless the constitutional concept of privacy is to be wholly severed from the traditional meaning of privacy, those interests include tranquillity and repose. Therefore, now that the right of privacy has attained constitutional dignity, one might expect that the type of interest vindicated in *Breard* and *Kovacs* would fare even better in collisions with other constitutional rights. But, surprisingly, this has not been the case.

Erznoznik v. City of Jacksonville[79] involved a conflict between freedom of speech and, as in the sound-truck and solicitation cases, the right of privacy in its elemental sense of seclusion. The issue was the constitutionality of a city ordinance which forbade the showing of nude scenes on outdoor movie screens visible from a public highway or other public property. The basis of the ordinance was the interest—a privacy interest in a fundamental sense—in being able to drive without the distraction of immense nudes looming up before one on drive-in movie screens. The Court, in invalidating the ordinance, gave short shrift to the privacy issue. The key issue to the Court was whether the ordinance was overbroad in forbidding the showing of all nude scenes, whether or not obscene; and it held that it was. This approach is wide of the mark. A fifty-foot nude is a distraction whether or not so tastefully done, or so integral to a work of substantial artistic merit and intent, that it could not be suppressed under the obscenity laws. Some people find nude movie scenes offensive whether or not they violate any obscenity law, and some who do not still prefer not to expose their children to such scenes. One might have thought this interest in seclusion sufficiently substantial—to a Court that affects to believe that the right of privacy emanates from numerous provisions of the Bill of Rights—to outweigh the minor infringement of the interests of moviegoers caused by the ordinance. The ordinance did not ban the showing of nude scenes either in movie theaters generally or drive-in theaters in particular. It merely required that the screens be so located or shielded as not to be visible from public highways when nude scenes were shown. The necessary adjustments could probably have been made

[79] 422 U.S. 205 (1975).

at moderate cost, while alternative routing for those users of the public highways who did not wish to have their sensibilities invaded by nude scenes might have involved a cumulatively substantial inconvenience.

Some theater owners, to be sure, might have decided not to show movies containing nude scenes rather than take steps to shield the movie screen from users of the public highways. Even so, since not all drive-in movie screens—and no screens of indoor movie theaters—are visible from the highway, the impact on the audience for nude scenes would probably have been small. In the long run, the impact might well have been negligible, for the screens of drive-in theaters constructed after the ordinance was passed could probably, at moderate cost, be located or shielded to comply with the ordinance. The Court seemed aware of this possibility because it implied that a zoning ordinance regulating the location of drive-in movie theaters might not violate the First Amendment even if motivated by a desire to shield involuntary viewers from nude scenes.[80]

If the Court in *Erznoznik* had bothered to distinguish *Stanley v. Georgia*, which had remarked that public distribution of obscene materials could invade the privacy of the general public, it would probably have just repeated that not all nude scenes in movies are obscene. But privacy can be infringed by nonobscene as well as obscene nude movie scenes thrust on unwilling viewers. The out-

---

[80] *Id.* at 212 n.9. The restriction by zoning of the location of "adult" movie theaters was later upheld in Young v. American Mini Theatres, 427 U.S. 50 (1976), though without reference to a possible privacy interest which might support such zoning. Mr. Justice Powell was, however, sufficiently concerned with the apparent inconsistency between *Erznoznik* and *Young* to add a concurring opinion in *Young* in which he noted certain technical, and as it seems to me trivial, deficiencies of the ordinance invalidated in *Erznoznik*. See 427 U.S. at 873–84. For example, the ordinance contained no limitation on distance—and thus might be violated though the highway was so far from the movie screen that the latter had the apparent size of a postage stamp. Had such a case, purely hypothetical in the Powell opinion, ever arisen in the enforcement of the ordinance, it would have provided an appropriate vehicle for limiting the scope of its application. But it is too much to expect and require a city council to foresee and provide specifically for every remote application of its ordinances that the judicial imagination might conjure up. If that is the result required by the doctrines associated with such cases as Thornhill v. Alabama, 310 U.S. 88 (1940), and Smith v. California, 361 U.S. 147 (1959), that statutes regulating the expression of ideas are to be evaluated on their face rather than as applied—*i.e.*, by reference to hypothetical rather than actual cases—then the Court's refusal to recognize an exception to the doctrine in cases where the challenged legislation is based on a privacy interest entitles one to question whether the Court's devotion to privacy is as steadfast as the language of *Griswold* and of the other sexual-privacy cases seems to imply.

come in *Erznoznik* suggests the possibility that the right of privacy as conceived by the Supreme Court does not imply any right to be free from nude movie scenes but does imply the right of unmarried people to use contraceptives. This would be an inversion of the values associated with the term "privacy." In this view the Constitution is solicitous of the rights of theater owners to impose their nude scenes on an involuntary audience and of couples to fornicate without fear of conception but not of the feeling for privacy that leads a driver to be offended at the sight of fifty-foot nudes looming at the side of the road. *Erznoznik* confirms with painful clarity Professor Freund's remark of many years ago that "on the whole, the active proselyting interests have been given greater sanctuary than the quiet virtues or the right of privacy."[81]

Erznoznik is particularly interesting because it is a case where, although the invasion of seclusion is mental rather than physical, it was possible to protect a right of privacy without doing serious damage to First Amendment interests. A more difficult case is *Cohen v. California*,[82] where the Supreme Court held that a state statute which forbade conduct invading the "peace or quiet of any . . . person" could not constitutionally be applied to the wearing in a courthouse of a jacket on which was printed the legend: "F—— the Draft." Two sorts of invasion of peace and quiet can be distinguished in this case. One is the distress caused by the sentiment behind the legend—opposition to the draft and, by implication, to the then American policy in Vietnam. This distress provides an insufficient basis for regulation, even if one rejects the view that it is desirable to force unwanted ideas on people. The basic source of distress lies not in seeing opposition to the draft expressed on a jacket but knowing that people oppose the draft, and that knowledge cannot be prevented without preventing expression of opposition in any form.

The second affront to privacy in *Cohen* comes from the use of the obscene expletive as the vehicle for expressing opposition to the draft. The offensiveness of the manner of expression is separate

---

[81] FREUND, THE SUPREME COURT OF THE UNITED STATES 40 (1949). In this connection, one notes with alarm Professor Lawrence Tribe's remark, in a section of his treatise dealing with the right of privacy in its very extended modern constitutional sense, that "freedom to have impact on others . . . is central to any adequate conception of the self." TRIBE, AMERICAN CONSTITUTIONAL LAW 888 (1978).

[82] 403 U.S. 15 (1971).

from the content of the expression, as is shown by the fact that people who oppose the draft might still be offended by the use of the expletive to express opposition. For people, and there are still some, who find public use of obscene language offensive, the invasion of tranquillity and repose is as palpable as in the case of an unwanted telephone solicitation or the blare of a sound truck. Thus the ultimate question in *Cohen* was whether the invasion of privacy was substantial relative to the reduction in the effectiveness of communication brought about by disallowing the favorite term used by the vulgar and the inarticulate to express hostility.

In holding that it was not, the Court repeated an argument which it had made in *Erznoznik*, which it was to reject several years later in *F.C.C. v. Pacifica Foundation*,[83] and which exhibits insensitivity to the claims of privacy. It is the argument that the person who is offended by the obscene legend on the jacket (or the nude scene on the drive-in movie screen) can avert his eyes. Of course he can, and he will, but the damage will have been done. In denigrating the privacy claim in *Cohen* relative to that in the sound-truck cases, on the ground that people using the courthouse "could effectively avoid *further* bombardment simply by averting their eyes" and were thus only "briefly exposed" to an offensive sight,[84] the Court ignored every dimension of invasion of privacy except the duration of the invasion. The logic of the Court's argument is that a very loud noise heard for only ten seconds is inherently less invasive of privacy than a much softer noise heard for twenty seconds. The Court also disregarded the role of memory in prolonging an offensive sight or sound. It just is not possible to conclude a priori that the noise from a sound truck invades privacy more seriously than the sight of an obscene epithet or a nude movie scene.

The Court took a different approach to this question in *F.C.C. v. Pacifica Foundation*, which upheld, primarily on the basis of the privacy (seclusion) interest of the owners of radios and their families, the constitutionality of FCC regulation of the broadcasting of obscene expletives. Since it is no more difficult to change stations on a radio than to avert one's eyes (and one's children's eyes) from a drive-in screen while driving, the result in *Pacifica* is inconsistent with that in *Erznoznik* unless obscene expletives are not entitled to constitutional protection—contrary to *Cohen*—or unless the drive-

---

[83] 438 U.S. 726 (1978).

[84] *Id.* at 21–22. (Emphasis added.)

in theater is somehow regarded as a more worthy forum for the expression of opinion than the radio. The last may well be the true ground of distinction between *Pacifica* on the one hand and *Erznoznik* and *Cohen* on the other.[85]

Another area of conflict between privacy and the First Amendment is illustrated by *Time, Inc. v. Hill*,[86] which involved a collision between freedom of the press and the branch of the state tort law of privacy that protects people from being portrayed by the media in a "false light." The Court held that a State may constitutionally afford a tort remedy in a "false light" case only if the portrayal was made with "deliberate malice," *i.e.*, in deliberate or reckless disregard of the truth. It based this result on its holding in *New York Times Co. v. Sullivan*[87] that defamation suits by public figures were permissible under the First Amendment only if the defamation was deliberately or recklessly false. Although there is a close resemblance between the torts of defamation and of portraying someone in a false light, they are not identical. One difference is that the false-light tort requires publicity—wide dissemination—rather that just publication, which to support a defamation suit need be made to only one other person. Another difference is that in a false-light case, unlike a defamation case, the falsity need not injure the reputation of the plaintiff. One can summarize the difference between the torts in the following way: defamation protects an individual from losing advantageous transactions because his reputation is impaired, while the false-light privacy tort protects a person from unwanted attention—protects privacy in the sense of seclusion.[88]

Since defamation protects reputation and the false-light tort privacy, since the Court believes that there is a constitutional right of privacy but has never suggested that there is a constitutional right

---

[85] Radio and television have traditionally been accorded less protection under the First Amendment than the print media, *compare* National Broadcasting Co. v. United States, 319 U.S. 190 (1943), and Red Lion Broadcasting Co. v. F.C.C., 395 U.S. 367 (1969), *with* Miami Herald Pub. Co. v. Tornillo, 418 U.S. 241 (1974), on the basis of an economic fallacy discussed in Posner, note 63 *supra*, at 546–47.

I reject any suggestion that *Pacifica* can be distinguished from *Erznoznik* and *Cohen* on the ground that the right of privacy is limited to the home. Even in public places, people desire privacy and resent solicitations, jostling, loud noises, offensive language, and other interferences with their mental repose.

[86] 385 U.S. 374 (1967).

[87] 376 U.S. 254 (1964).

[88] Portraying a person in a false light could, of course, impair his ability to make advantageous transactions—could, that is, impair his reputation—but if so it would be actionable as defamation.

of reputation,[89] and since the plaintiff in *Sullivan* was a public figure and presumably therefore less sensitive to invasions of privacy than the average private citizen, one might have expected the Court to consider the issue whether to require proof of the defendant's actual malice a more difficult issue in *Hill* than in *Sullivan*. Yet the relevant part of the *Hill* opinion not only does not mention privacy but suggests that the case for tort liability was stronger in *Sullivan*, because that case involved the "additional state interest in the protection of the individual against damage to his reputation."[90] Reputation is put above privacy although the latter (one had been told by *Griswold*) has constitutional dignity and the former does not.

Similar misunderstanding and belittlement of the right of privacy under state tort law are evident in *Cox Broadcasting Corp. v. Cohn*,[91] which invalidated a state statute forbidding the publication or broadcast of the names of rape victims. The statute protected that aspect of the tort right of privacy which seeks to shield people from embarrassing, albeit truthful, publicizing of personal information. This aspect of the tort has been interpreted narrowly[92]—and rightly so, because, as noted earlier, a common motive for a person's concealing information about himself is to induce people to engage in transactions with him who would not do so if they knew the truth. Concealment so motivated is a species of fraud entitled *prima facie* to no greater protection than fraud in the market for goods. Not all concealment of personal information is so motivated, however, as the facts of the *Cox* case illustrate. The rape victim in question had been killed by the rapist, so one could hardly argue that knowledge that she had been raped might be material to someone contemplating future transactions with her. The motive for suppression of the rape victim's identity was to spare her parents grief, including unwanted attention from ghoulish members of the public—so that the interest in privacy as secrecy ran into the older interest in privacy as seclusion. Nor was the name of the victim vital, though it was relevant, to the information (or, for that matter, entertainment) value of an article or broadcast about the rape.

The Court paid no attention to the particular facts of the case

---

[89] The Court has stated that there is no constitutionally protected right to a good reputation. See Paul v. Davis, 424 U.S. 693, 711–12 (1975).

[90] 385 U.S. at 391.

[91] 420 U.S. 469 (1975).

[92] See Posner, note 4 *supra*, at 412–19.

which made it an attractive one for upholding the privacy claim. It invalidated the statute on the ground that the rape victim's identity was contained in court records open to public inspection and that the First Amendment entitles the press to publish any fact contained in such records. The Court suggested that the State might not have violated the First Amendment by denying all public access to the information; but having declined to go that far, the State was not entitled to prevent the information from being publicized in the media.[93]

This reasoning confronts the State with the unhappy choice of conducting rape trials *in camera* (assuming that this could be done without violating the defendant's right to a public trial)[94] or sacrificing the privacy of victims of rape. The State's approach which the Court invalidated protected the latter interest at a lower cost in impairment of the public-trial principle than the approach suggested by the Court would have done. The Court seemed to think that the State's willingness to allow the victim's name to appear in the public record of the trial showed it did not really care about privacy. This misses the fundamental distinction in the tort law of privacy between what is merely public and what is publicized. There is no violation of the tort right of privacy without publicity, *i.e.*, widespread dissemination, and conversely the right to complain about publicity should not be forfeited merely because the information in question is known to a few people.

Two recent defamation cases in which the Court has held that the "public figure" rule of *New York Times Co. v. Sullivan* does not extend to certain "involuntary" public figures suggest that the *Cox* decision may rest on shifting ground. In *Hutchinson v. Proxmire*[95] the Court held that a scientist who was ridiculed by a United States Senator could sue the Senator for defamation since the scientist had not sought publicity for his work outside of the scientific community. And in *Wolston v. Reader's Digest Ass'n*[96] the Court held that a man who had been convicted of contempt of Congress sixteen years earlier was not a public figure today. These cases evince a

[93] See 420 U.S. at 496.

[94] For the Court's most recent pronouncement on the Sixth Amendment's public-trial provision, see Gannett Co. v. DePasquale, 99 S. Ct. 2898 (1979).

[95] 99 S. Ct. 2675 (1979).

[96] 99 S. Ct. 2701 (1979).

sympathy for the involuntary recipient of media publicity that is absent in *Cox*.[97]

C. RECORD KEEPING

Warren and Brandeis's famous article on the right of privacy was apparently written in response to the rise of the newspaper gossip column, which they saw as threatening privacy. They overlooked the possibility that the gossip column was simply a substitute for the type of informal neighborhood surveillance that growing urbanization and increases in the value of time, coupled with growing literacy, had made a less efficient method of snooping.[98] Those who are concerned today with a possible loss of privacy focus not on the rise of the gossip column but on the progress of electronics, which has brought us not only efficient devices for eavesdropping (going well beyond the telephone tap) but also efficient techniques of data storage and retrieval, enabling much more information about people to be collected and disseminated than was once the case. Again it is possible that these developments have merely offset other factors, notably continued urbanization, which have tended to increase privacy, but that is not certain. What is certain is that modern

---

[97] With regard to one branch of the tort law of privacy, the "right of publicity," see text *supra*, at note 9, there is happily no conflict between state law and the First Amendment. In Zacchini v. Scripps-Howard Broadcasting Co., 437 U.S. 526 (1977), the issue was whether the broadcast on a news show of the entire act of a "human cannonball" could constitutionally be deemed tortious. The Court held that it could, noting that tort liability was unlikely to limit the dissemination of the human cannonball's act, since, of course, he desired publicity. See *id*. at 573. The Court could have put the point more strongly. Granting entertainers a property right—the effect of the state tort law in question—should, by encouraging the production of entertainments, increase rather than reduce the production and dissemination of ideas. But recall that in *Buckley v. Valeo*, note 50 *supra*, where First Amendment and privacy interests also coincided, the Court rejected the privacy claim.

I want to make clear that even if the notion of a general constitutional right to privacy is rejected, as a proper respect for the written Constitution would seem to require, it would not follow that privacy was not entitled to weighty consideration in First Amendment cases. Only dogmatists believe that the First Amendment should be interpreted literally. It is permissible to limit speech if the reasons for doing so are strong enough, and they need not be reasons found in the Constitution. The interests in liberty and security reflected in state tort law, including the tort law of privacy, are entitled to substantial consideration in determining whether a challenged law violates the First Amendment, whether or not those interests are independently protected by the Constitution against governmental invasion.

[98] See Posner, note 4 *supra*, at 396–97.

record keeping has been a focus of concern to all those who see themselves as the defenders of privacy—except the Supreme Court.

The Bank Secrecy Act of 1970[99] is a good example of the sort of legislation made possible by the progress of information storage that concerns the advocates of privacy. The Act, expressly for the purpose of facilitating law enforcement, requires banks to make and retain copies of all checks and other financial transfer instruments (though the implementing regulations have limited the copying and retention requirements to large transactions, such as checks in excess of $10,000) and to make these copies available to law-enforcement agencies. The record-keeping requirements of the Act were upheld against privacy and other challenges in *California Bankers Ass'n v. Shultz*,[100] and the production requirements in *United States v. Miller*,[101] where a law-enforcement agency had subpoenaed from a bank copies of the defendant's checks made and kept by the bank pursuant to the Bank Secrecy Act. In rejecting the privacy arguments made in these cases against the government-mandated creation and use for law-enforcement purposes of, in effect, a vast data bank containing intimate details of the financial lives of the nation's citizens, the Court resorted to artificial and casuistic arguments of a sort that would have received short shrift if the cases had instead involved the right of the unmarried to buy contraceptives. The Court placed particular emphasis on the fact that the records of bank transactions are the property of the bank rather than of the depositor or other bank customer. This would be a relevant consideration if the only aspect of privacy protected by the Constitution were seclusion, for one's physical privacy is not affected by the government's getting access to copies made by a bank. But once privacy is understood to include the confidentiality of private information, property notions become irrelevant, since our confidences are frequently reposed in another's files, be they a physician's, an employer's, or a bank's.[102]

The Court also stressed that checks are not confidential communications and that their privacy is in any event compromised by

---

[99] 12 U.S.C. § 1829b(d). [100] 416 U.S. 21 (1974). [101] 425 U.S. 435 (1976).

[102] Or a telephone company's: see Smith v. Maryland, 99 S. Ct. 2577 (1979), holding that police use of a "pen register" which records the phone numbers that a telephone subscriber dials does not violate the Fourth Amendment, on the highly artificial ground that the act of dialing discloses the number dialed to the phone company. Or an accountant's: see Crouch v. United States, 409 U.S. (1973).

the fact that they are read by the bank's employees. This is the same mistake the Court made in *Cox*. Privacy of information normally means the selective disclosure of personal information rather than total secrecy. (If it meant only the latter, wiretapping would not invade privacy.) A bank customer may not care that the employees of the bank know a lot about his financial affairs, but it does not follow that he is indifferent to having those affairs broadcast to the world or disclosed to the government. The consequences of disclosure depend on to whom disclosure is made.

Behind the Bank Secrecy Act cases lies the circular and even sinister doctrine of the old required-record cases, which, taken at face value, permitted privacy to be invaded with impunity by a simple two-stage procedure.[103] In the first stage the government requires the citizen to provide or make available to the government certain information; in the second the information is supplied to an enforcement agency. The individual has no remedy at either stage. He is entitled to object neither to being required to provide the information in the first place if the requirement is reasonable, nor to the release of the information by the agency that obtained it from him, since the agency is in lawful possession of the information.

Recent cases have held, to be sure, that an individual can invoke the Fifth Amendment to justify refusing to supply required information that would incriminate him.[104] But this makes it all the more surprising that the Court should have brushed aside the constitutional claim in *Miller*. Because the subpoena in *Miller* sought papers rather than an admission and because, as mentioned earlier, the suggestion in *Boyd v. United States* that the Fifth Amendment protects one's papers has been discredited, the claim in *Miller* had to be based on the Fourth rather than Fifth Amendment. But the Fourth Amendment is more clearly designed to protect privacy than the Fifth Amendment is.[105] One might have thought, therefore, that a subpoena which invaded privacy would be at least within the scope of the Fourth Amendment.

---

[103] See, *e.g.*, Shapiro v. United States, 335 U.S. 1 (1948); McKay, *Self-Incrimination and the New Privacy*, 1967 SUPREME COURT REVIEW 193, 214–24; Meltzer, *Required Records, the McCarran Act, and the Privilege against Self-Incrimination*, 18 U. CHI. L. REV. 687, 712 (1951).

[104] See Marchetti v. United States, 390 U.S. 39 (1968); Grosso v. United States, 390 U.S. 62 (1968).

[105] See text *supra*, at note 27.

A good sign that the Court lacks sympathy for a type of claim is its use of inconsistent reasoning to deny it. In *Miller* the fact that the defendant's financial transactions had been exposed to the scrutiny of the bank's employees before the challenged statute had been enacted persuaded the Court that he had no reasonable expectation of privacy that the statute might have destroyed. In *Whalen v. Roe*, where the Court upheld the constitutionality of a state law that required keeping records of the identity of people for whom certain dangerous but lawful drugs were prescribed by their physicians, the claim that the statute was an invasion of privacy was rejected in part because it limited disclosure of the private information collected to the employees of the state health agency.[106] This is just the sort of disclosure that was held in *Miller* to destroy a reasonable expectation of privacy. One would think that a statute which destroyed any reasonable expectation of privacy would thereby infringe the constitutional right of privacy.

To summarize, the Court has not indicated a serious concern with the danger to privacy posed by governmentally required record-keeping programs motivated by concern with crime and facilitated by modern advances in information storage and retrieval. The Court's attitude would be understandable if it believed that the Fourth Amendment protected only physical privacy and that the Constitution creates no general right of privacy. The former view would bar challenges to subpoenas in cases such as *Miller* and the latter would bar challenges to record keeping as in *Shultz* and *Whalen*. What makes the Court's attitude difficult to understand is that its members, including some who concurred in the Court's opinions in *Shultz*, *Whalen*, and *Miller*, believe the Fourth Amendment protects privacy in the sense of secrecy as well as in the sense of seclusion (*e.g.*, *Katz*), and also that the Constitution creates a general right of privacy uncabined by any specific language in the Constitution (*e.g.*, *Griswold*). The former belief implies that Miller should have had standing to object to the subpoena directed at the bank's copies of his financial records. The latter implies that analysis is not at an end even if the Fourth Amendment does not entitle a person to prevent the search of a bank's records of his financial transactions, since the constitutional right of privacy extends beyond the specific guarantees of the Fourth Amendment. The

[106] 429 U.S. 589, 602 (1977).

voluntary record-keeping practices of banks strike a balance between the privacy and other interests of their customers. That balance carries with it a presumption of optimality.[107] The Bank Secrecy Act shifted that balance against privacy and thereby it would seem infringed, at least *prima facie*, the general right of privacy formulated in *Griswold*.

There is no logical way to reconcile the Court's view of privacy in *Katz* with its view of privacy in *Miller*: the view that wiretapping is subject to the Fourth Amendment with the view that a statute which forces a bank to photograph its customers' checks and then to turn them over to a government agency for use in a criminal prosecution is not. And the only way to reconcile the sexual-privacy cases with the denial of a general right of privacy in the record-keeping cases is to narrow the concept of privacy so that it covers sexual freedom but not confidentiality: to stand the concept on its head. The Court did this in *Paul v. Davis*.[108] In holding that no constitutionally protected interest was invaded by the circulation of a flyer listing people who had been arrested (but not necessarily convicted) for shoplifting, the Court stated that the plaintiff was making no challenge to "the State's ability to restrict his freedom of action in a sphere contended to be 'private' " but only a "claim that the State may not publicize a record of an official act such as an arrest."[109] The periphery of the right of privacy is made the core, and the core is relegated to the periphery.

V. A Summary Assessment

The *Griswold* decision was heralded as inaugurating an era in which the Supreme Court would be a dependable bulwark of privacy.[110] That is not the way things have turned out. With the principal exception of *Katz*, which, overruling *Olmstead*, held that

---

[107] See text *supra*, at note 5.

[108] 424 U.S. 693 (1976).

[109] *Id.* at 713. Similarly, in Smith v. Daily Mail Pub. Co., 99 S. Ct. 2667 (1979), the Court, invalidating a statute forbidding newspapers to print the names of juvenile delinquents, remarked that "there is no issue here of privacy." *Id.* at 2672. On its facts, however, *Smith* is an easier case for invalidation of the challenged statute than *Cox* because the statute at issue in *Smith* was unaccountably limited to newspapers and did not apply to radio or television.

[110] See, *e.g.*, Beaney, *The Griswold Case and the Expanding Right to Privacy*, 1966 Wis. L. Rev. 979.

wiretapping is within the scope of the Fourth Amendment, the Court has evinced little regard for the protection of privacy as that term is ordinarily, even expansively, understood. Privacy in the sense of seclusion has fared particularly poorly, as cases like *Erznoznik* make clear; privacy in the sense of secrecy has also generally fared badly, as the bank-secrecy and undercover-agent cases make clear. *Cox* and *Hill* indicate the Court's reluctance to give much weight to the specific privacy values embodied in state tort law.

In only one area has the Court evinced a high regard for privacy, an area having nothing to do with privacy in any precise or principled sense of the term. The sexual-freedom cases, beginning with *Griswold*, have affirmed in the name of privacy the right of both married and unmarried people to use and to obtain contraceptives, the right of women to abortions, and the right of adults to possess obscene materials in the home. The objection to this line of cases is not merely that the rights they create have no basis in any meaningful conception of privacy or in any provision of the Constitution; it is also that when the rights of true privacy and the rights of those who invade privacy in the name of sexual freedom or the publicizing of sexual activity clash, it is generally the latter that prevail. It is *as if* (I emphasize the *as if*, because I do not consider it a fact) the Court had become infected with the student radicalism of the late 1960s and early 1970s with its emphasis on candor at the expense of privacy, its slogans of "doing your own thing" and "letting it all hang out."[111] *Erznoznik*, where the right of movie exhibitors to show nude scenes on drive-in screens visible from the public highways was held to prevail over the right of the user of the highway to prevent such invasions of his privacy and sensibilities, and *Cox*, where the right to publicize a dead rape victim's name was held to prevail over the right of the victim's parents to the privacy of their grief, when taken together with *Griswold* and the other sexual-privacy cases and with the suggestion in *Paul v. Davis* and *Smith v. Daily Mail*[112] that the right of privacy is a right to act and not a right to keep information private, suggest a tendency, surely unintended, on the part of a majority of the Supreme Court to confuse privacy with sexual freedom and display. It is also possible that the concept of privacy has been so abused in the sexual-privacy

[111] *Cf.* the quotation from Professor Tribe in note 81 *supra*.

[112] Note 109 *supra*.

cases that now some Justices have difficulty recognizing a legitimate privacy claim when it appears.

The decisions I have discussed cut across the change in the Court's membership associated with the transition from the "Warren Court" to the "Burger Court." They are evidence that the significance of this change for constitutional adjudication has been exaggerated, not least by some of the Justices themselves. Yet one might have inferred from a few recent decisions which I have discussed (*Pacifica*, *Hutchinson*, and *Wolston*) a growing sensitivity on the part of the Court to the claims of privacy in an intelligible sense, were it not for the decision last Term in *Bell v. Wolfish*,[113] with which I conclude. One of the issues in *Wolfish* was whether it was a violation of the Fourth Amendment for the custodians of a federal prison visually to search what are euphemistically termed the "body cavities" of male and female inmates after visits to an inmate by a person from outside the prison. These searches were conducted after every visit, whether or not there was any reason to believe that the visitors had conveyed a weapon or contraband to the inmate for concealment in the inmate's "body cavities." Among the inmates so searched were pretrial detainees, that is, persons who had not yet been convicted of the crime for which they were being detained; these were in fact the plaintiffs in the case.

The Court, in an opinion joined by Justices such as Blackmun who believe that it is an impermissible invasion of privacy to forbid the sale of contraceptives to children,[114] upheld body-cavity searches which suggests, in passing, that prison inmates, including pretrial detainees, who as I have said have not yet been convicted of the crime for which they are being detained, may have no Fourth Amendment rights whatever.[115] That the searches were not based upon probable cause, were "because of time pressures, . . . frequently conducted in the presence of other inmates,"[116] "caused some inmates to forego personal visits,"[117] and were employed despite elaborate screening of visitors and surveillance of the visits them-

---

[113] 99 S. Ct. 1861 (1979).

[114] See Carey v. Population Services Int'l, 431 U.S. 678, 691–99 (1977) (opinion of Mr. Justice Brennan, joined by Justices Stewart, Marshall, and Blackmun).

[115] See 99 S. Ct. at 1883–84.

[116] *Id.* at 1894 (Marshall, J., dissenting).

[117] *Ibid.*

selves, cut no ice with the Court. Perhaps, given the well-known security problems of American jails, the Court's decision in *Wolfish* was nevertheless correct. But it is not the decision of men who set a high value on privacy, and I have difficulty understanding the set of mind that brushes aside the privacy claims in cases like *Wolfish* and *Erznoznik* and *Cox* and *Miller* yet regards limiting the sale or use of contraceptives as deeply offensive to the idea of privacy.[118]

---

[118] In fairness to Mr. Justice Rehnquist, the author of the Court's opinion in *Wolfish,* it should be noted that he has dissented in all of the sexual-privacy cases in which he participated. He is at least consistent in his view of privacy, consistently hostile.

FREDERICK SCHAUER

"PRIVATE" SPEECH AND THE "PRIVATE" FORUM: GIVHAN v. WESTERN LINE SCHOOL DISTRICT

Short opinions, like "great" cases and "hard" cases,[1] often make bad law. A satisfactory judicial opinion need not be long. Concise prose and direct analysis are admirable if frequently ignored judicial virtues. They are not necessarily to be found in short opinions.

Constitutional adjudication, particularly by the Supreme Court, must to some extent be both prospective and advisory, anticipating problems to which the announced principles will be applied. No amount of academic prattle about holdings, dicta, and ratio decidendi can dispel the fact that, in courts other than the Supreme Court, the law is what the Supreme Court says by its words as much as it is what the Court holds by its decisions. If the Court were to say that two plus two equals five, as it so frequently does, then for the lower courts two plus two equals five, even when that assertion by the Court was unnecessary to its decision. Thus, brevity may be a judicial vice when it results in the pronouncement of broad prin-

Frederick Schauer is Associate Professor of Law, Marshall-Wythe School of Law, College of William and Mary.

The author is grateful for the assistance of Tom Collins, Mary Jane Morrison, and Doug Rendleman, all of whom provided cogent criticisms of an earlier draft of this article.

[1] "Great cases, like hard cases, make bad law." Northern Securities Co. v. United States, 193 U.S. 197, 400 (1904) (Holmes, J., dissenting).

ciples that are unqualified and unjustified. When explanation and qualification are lacking, the words of the Supreme Court may be used to support results neither intended by the Court nor covered by an inadequate rationale underlying the opinion.[2]

A recent example of this phenomenon is the Supreme Court's decision last Term in *Givhan v. Western Line Consolidated School District.*[3] In that case, a junior high school teacher had on numerous occasions complained to her principal, in the principal's office, about alleged racial discrimination in the school. These complaints antagonized the principal, and the teacher's contract was not renewed. The district court held that the dismissal violated the First Amendment.[4] The Fifth Circuit reversed that judgment, ruling that "private" speech such as that involved here was wholly outside the First Amendment.[5] A unanimous Supreme Court needed only a few pages to reject the Fifth Circuit's view of the First Amendment as "erroneous."[6] The Court held that the teacher's statements to the principal in his office could not, consistent with the First Amendment, be used to justify the teacher's dismissal. Mr. Justice Rehnquist, speaking for the Court, rejected any distinction between private and public speech, finding such a distinction supported neither by the words of the First Amendment nor by any of the Court's free speech cases.

There are difficult issues involved in the contrast between speech in a public forum and speech in private conversation, as well as in the extent to which the First Amendment protects a public employee who communicates his or her views on the employer's time and on the employer's premises. The complexity of these problems is

---

[2] The paradigm is perhaps Valentine v. Chrestensen, 316 U.S. 52 (1942). There a "casual, almost offhand" (Cammarano v. United States, 358 U.S. 498, 514 [1959] [Douglas, J., concurring]), statement of the commercial speech exception to the First Amendment established a principle that survived for twenty-four years, until its demise in Virginia State Board of Pharmacy v. Virginia Citizens Consumer Council, 425 U.S. 748 (1976).

[3] 99 S. Ct. 693 (1979).

[4] Ayers v. Western Line Consolidated School District, 404 F. Supp. 1225 (N.D. Miss. 1975). This opinion deals only with damages, interest, and attorneys' fees. Judge Smith's prior ruling on the merits is unreported.

[5] Ayers v. Western Line Consolidated School District, 555 F.2d 1309 (5th Cir. 1977).

[6] 99 S. Ct. at 695.

clouded more than it is illuminated by the Court's conclusory opinion in *Givhan.*

I. The Givhan Case

A. HISTORY

From 1963 until 1971 Bessie Givhan served as a junior high school teacher in three different schools in the Western Line Consolidated School District, which encompassed part of two counties near Greenville, Mississippi.[7] The school district lacked a tenure system, and she was employed under a series of one-year contracts. During this period, race relations was a subject of considerable significance and controversy both in the community and in the schools in which Bessie Givhan taught. Since 1969 the schools in the district had been operating under a desegregation order issued by the district court pursuant to the Fifth Circuit's decision in *Singleton v. Jackson Municipal Separate School District.*[8]

On frequent occasions during the 1970–71 school year Givhan objected to various practices within the school. Primarily, she contended that racial segregation existed in the appointment and assignment of nonprofessional employees such as administrative and clerical staff and lunchroom workers.[9] These objections were presented to the principal, Leach, in his office. Some complaints were presented orally and others in writing; all were characterized by Givhan as "requests" and by Leach as "demands."[10]

In 1971 Givhan was informed that she would not be rehired for the following academic year. In making that decision, the superintendent of schools had followed Leach's recommendation, which read in part as follows:[11]

---

[7] The Supreme Court's statement of the facts is elliptical. The facts here are derived from the Supreme Court opinion, the opinion of the Fifth Circuit, note 5 *supra*, the opinion on remedies of the district court, note 4 *supra*, and the unpublished district court opinion on the merits, Appendix to Petition for Certiorari, at 27a.

[8] 419 F.2d 1211 (5th Cir. 1969), *rev'd and remanded sub nom.* Carter v. West Feliciana Parish School Board, 396 U.S. 290 (1970), *on remand*, 425 F.2d 1211 (5th Cir. 1970).

[9] 555 F.2d at 1314.

[10] *Id.* at 1313.

[11] *Id.* at 1312.

> Ms. Givhan is a competent teacher, however, on many occasions she has taken an insulting and hostile attitude towards me and other administrators. She hampers my job greatly by making petty and unreasonable demands. She is overly critical for a reasonable working relationship to exist between us. She also refused to give achievement tests to her homeroom students.

Givhan sued the school district, alleging that her dismissal was impermissibly motivated by and based on her complaints to Leach, conduct she claimed was protected by the First Amendment. The district court agreed, finding that "the school district's motivation in failing to renew Givhan's contract was almost entirely a desire to rid themselves of a vocal critic of the district's policies and practices which were capable of interpretation as embodying racial discrimination."[12]

The Fifth Circuit reversed. The Court of Appeals did not find it necessary to consider the balancing analysis for speech by public employees mandated by *Pickering v. Board of Education*[13] and *Mt. Healthy City School District v. Doyle*.[14] In *Pickering* the Supreme Court held that a teacher could not be dismissed on the basis of a letter to the editor of a local newspaper in which the teacher criticized the board of education.[15] As long as the public expression by a teacher was not intentionally false,[16] the speech was presumptively protected, although it remained necessary to balance the free speech rights involved against the interests of the school as employer in preserving close working relationships, confidentiality, and professional competence.[17] In 1977 the Court held in *Mt. Healthy*

[12] *Id.* at 1314, quoting the unreported opinion of the district court.

[13] 391 U.S. 563 (1968).

[14] 429 U.S. 274 (1977).

[15] Pickering had sent a letter to a local newspaper in connection with a proposed tax increase. The letter was critical of the way that both the board of education and the superintendent of schools had handled previous revenue proposals. He was dismissed because his letter was found to be "detrimental to the efficient operation and administration of the schools of the district." 391 U.S. at 564.

[16] *Pickering* specifically adopted the standard of New York Times Co. v. Sullivan, 376 U.S. 254 (1964). 391 U.S. at 573–74.

[17] 391 U.S. at 568–72. The Court in *Pickering* did little more than hint at ways in which other cases might be differently decided if the speech were different or the nature of the relationship were different. One commentator has gleaned from the *Pickering* opinion fourteen different factors that go into the balance. Zillman, *Free Speech and Military Command*, 1977 UTAH L. REV. 423, 450–51. On *Pickering* generally, see Van Alstyne, *The Constitutional Rights of Teachers and Professors*, 1970 DUKE L.J. 841, 848–54.

that, where a teacher had been dismissed on the basis of the kinds of statements held protected in *Pickering*, the dismissal could still be upheld if the school board could demonstrate by a preponderance of the evidence that it would have dismissed the teacher even in the absence of the protected expression.[18]

The Fifth Circuit did not apply this balancing analysis because it did not find Givhan's actions covered in any way by the First Amendment. *Pickering* and *Mt. Healthy* come into play only when the teacher has engaged in First Amendment conduct and when that conduct has played a part in the dismissal. If no First Amendment conduct is involved, then the *Pickering–Mt. Healthy* issues are never reached. The Fifth Circuit disposed of the case at this threshold stage:[19]

> The strong implication of [*Pickering*, *Mt. Healthy*, and *Perry* v. *Sindermann*[20]] is that private expression by a public employee is not constitutionally protected. . . . Neither a teacher nor a citizen has a constitutional right to single out a public employee to serve as the audience for his or her privately expressed views, at least in the absence of evidence that the public employee was given that task by law, custom, or school board decision.

The Fifth Circuit's decision is thus based on two distinct but related grounds. First, speech in the "private forum" is not covered by the First Amendment. Second, the First Amendment does not protect the speaker who forces his views on an unwilling listener.

B. THE SUPREME COURT OPINION

The Supreme Court found *Givhan* an easy case. The Fifth Circuit had made an obvious and fundamental error in First Amendment doctrine. For a unanimous Court, Mr. Justice Rehnquist said that it was mistaken to view the activity in question as outside the scope

---

[18] 429 U.S. at 287. The burden shifts to the school board after the teacher has met the burden of showing that he engaged in constitutionally protected conduct and that that conduct was a "substantial factor" or "motivating factor" in the decision to dismiss or not to rehire. *Ibid*. The relevant conduct in *Mt. Healthy* was a telephone call to a radio station. *Id*. at 281–84.

[19] 555 F.2d at 1318–19.

[20] 408 U.S. 593 (1972). *Perry* is best known as the procedural due process case dealing with *de facto* tenure. The opinion also makes it clear, however, that *Pickering* applies to the decision not to retain a nontenured teacher. *Id*. at 598.

of the First Amendment merely because it occurred in the principal's private office. Although the speech in *Pickering*, *Perry*, and *Mt. Healthy* had indeed taken place in the public forum, the fact of the public forum was irrelevant to the holdings in those cases.[21] And once the distinction between Givhan's complaints in the principal's office and Pickering's letter to a newspaper is removed, Bessie Givhan's case falls squarely within the principles of *Pickering* and *Mt. Healthy*.[22] The dismissal can then only be sustained if the school board can involve one of the special justifying reasons found in *Pickering*,[23] or if the school board can demonstrate by a preponderance of the evidence that it would have dismissed her even in the absence of the constitutionally protected conduct. The Court's opinion very strongly suggests that, as to the quality of the speech justifying removal, the result must be the same as in *Picker-*

---

[21] "This Court's decisions in *Pickering*, *Perry*, and *Mt. Healthy* do not support the conclusion that a public employee forfeits his protection against governmental abridgment of freedom of speech if he decides to express his views privately rather than publicly. While those cases each arose in the context of a public employee's public expression, the rule to be derived from them is not dependent on that largely coincidental fact." 99 S. Ct. at 695–96.

[22] In holding that *Pickering* protection was not lost by the private or personal or limited nature of the speech, *Givhan* was consistent with virtually all lower court decisions addressing this issue. The most extensive discussion is in Pilkington v. Bevilacqua, 439 F. Supp. 465 (D.R.I. 1977). "Certainly his criticisms do not lose the protection of the First Amendment by reason of their being prudently directed to his co-employees and superiors . . . instead of to the public at large." *Id.* at 474–75. See also Jannetta v. Cole, 493 F.2d 1334, 1337 n.4 (4th Cir. 1974); Hostrop v. Board of Junior College District No. 515, 471 F.2d 488, 493 n.13 (7th Cir. 1972); Smith v. Losee, 485 F.2d 334, 338 (10th Cir. 1973); Ring v. Schlesinger, 502 F.2d 479, 489 (D.C. Cir. 1974); Downs v. Conway School District, 328 F. Supp. 338 (E.D. Ark. 1971); Phillips v. Puryear, 403 F. Supp. 80, 87–88 (W.D. Va. 1975); Johnson v. Butler, 433 F. Supp. 531, 535 (W.D. Va. 1977). The strongest precedent for the Fifth Circuit's exclusion of private speech is Roseman v. Indiana University of Pennsylvania, 520 F.2d 1364, 1368 (3d Cir. 1975). Some of the foregoing cases dealt with private complaints quite similar to those in *Givhan*. Others dealt with the circulation of petitions or complaints among a number of colleagues. While neither is fully public, the latter seems clearly more so. See Rosado v. Santiago, 562 F.2d 114 (1st Cir. 1977) (holding the circulation of a letter among colleagues to be protected speech, but specifically reserving the issue of whether a purely private letter to one's superior is protected).

[23] See note 17 *supra*. Among the most important of these reasons, as suggested in *Pickering*, are a particular threat to internal discipline, 391 U.S. at 569; a particular threat to harmony among co-workers, *ibid.*; jeopardizing a close working relationship with an immediate superior, *id.* at 570; preserving a special need for confidentiality, *id.* at 570 n.3, 572; or statements "so without foundation" as to call into question a teacher's fitness for the position, *id.* at 573 n.5.

ing, where none of the proffered justifications were found acceptable.[24] But as to the second factor—independent grounds for dismissal—the record was less clear. The case had been tried in the district court before *Mt. Healthy* was decided, and thus the school board had neither reason nor opportunity to attempt to prove that it would not have rehired Givhan even without the presence of the constitutionally protected criticism. The Supreme Court therefore remanded the case so that the district court could make the appropriate findings on this aspect of the *Mt. Healthy* analysis.[25]

The Supreme Court rejected the Fifth Circuit's conclusion that the principal was a captive and unwilling audience. "Having opened his office door to petitioner, the principal was hardly in a position to argue that he was the '*unwilling* recipient' of her views."[26] The reversal on this point is almost wholly factual. Nothing in the Court's opinion suggests any expansion of the very limited circumstances in which the presence of an unwilling audience diminishes the extent of free speech protection. *Cohen v. California*[27] and *Erznoznik v. Jacksonville*[28] emerge untouched,[29] and so do *Rowan v. Post*

[24] In commenting on the conclusion by the Court of Appeals that Givhan's statements may have jeopardized a close working relationship with her immediate superior, the principal, the Court said that "we do not feel confident that the Courts of Appeals' decision would have been placed on that ground notwithstanding its view that the First Amendment does not require the same sort of *Pickering* balancing for the private expression of a public employee as it does for public expression." 99 S. Ct. at 696 (footnote omitted).

[25] Givhan had allegedly engaged in several acts of insubordination not involving First Amendment questions, such as a refusal to give certain standardized tests to her students. 99 S. Ct. at 694 n.1, 695 n.2. The Court's opinion suggests that some of these acts, if substantiated, might support a finding that she would not have been rehired even were it not for the complaints. *Id.* at 697 n.5. The brief concurring opinion of Mr. Justice Stevens, directed solely to this point, takes the position that the previous proceedings most likely preclude a successful *Mt. Healthy* claim by the school board. *Id.* at 697–98.

[26] 99 S. Ct. at 696.

[27] 403 U.S. 15 (1971).

[28] 422 U.S. 205 (1975).

[29] *Erznoznik* had to some extent been qualified by Young v. American Mini Theatres, Inc., 427 U.S. 50 (1976). See Friedman, *Zoning "Adult" Movies: The Potential Impact of* Young v. American Mini Theaters, 28 Hastings L.J. 1293 (1977); Schauer, *The Return of Variable Obscenity?* 28 Hastings L.J. 1275 (1977). And both *Cohen* and *Erznoznik* were called into question on this point by the Court's reliance on captive audience reasoning in F.C.C. v. Pacifica Foundation, 438 U.S. 726 (1978). The Court in *Pacifica* suggested that the distinction may turn on whether the speech takes place inside or outside the home, *id.* at 732 n.5. But by specifically referring to a "balance between the offensive speaker and the unwill-

Office Department[30] and *Lehman v. City of Shaker Heights.*[31]

The Court did say that time, place, and manner restrictions on teacher complaints would be permissible and that a violation of such restrictions by a teacher could constitutionally be cause for dismissal.[32] In this sense *Givhan* is based upon impermissible content regulation,[33] as were both *Erznoznik* and *Chicago Police Department v. Mosley*.[34] Just as *Mosley* suggests that a content-neutral prohibition on speech near a school would be permissible, so too does *Givhan* suggest that the principal could limit the access of teachers to his office.[35] Only by opening his office to complaints and then basing his action on the substance of those complaints did the principal run afoul of the First Amendment.[36] The most relevant

---

ing audience," *ibid.* the Court left the entire area of offensive speech and intrusive speech wide open for further development and clarification. *Compare* Feinberg, *Pornography and the Criminal Law*, 40 U. PITT. L. REV. 567 (1979), *with* Schauer, *Pornography and the First Amendment*, 40 U. PITT. L. REV. 605 (1979); see also Haiman, *Speech v. Privacy: Is There a Right Not to Be spoken To?* 67 NW. U. L. REV. 153 (1972); Kaufman, *The Medium, the Message and the First Amendment*, 45 N.Y.U.L. REV. 761 (1970); Rutzick, *Offensive Language and the Evolution of First Amendment Protection*, 9 HARV. CIV. RTS. CIV. LIB. L. REV. 1 (1974).

[30] 397 U.S. 728 (1970).

[31] 418 U.S. 298 (1974). As with *Cohen* and *Erznoznik*, the validity of *Lehman* may be in question on other grounds. *Lehman* is not a content regulation case only because commercial advertising was not in 1974 held to be within the First Amendment. Thus, the creation of a forum for commercial advertising would not then be considered to be the creation of a public forum in First Amendment terms. But if, as is now the case, commercial advertising is within the First Amendment, it may not be possible to avoid creating a public forum by accepting commercial material.

[32] 99 S. Ct. at 696 n.4.

[33] See TRIBE, AMERICAN CONSTITUTIONAL LAW 672–74 (1978); Karst, *Equality as a Central Principle in the First Amendment*, 43 U. CHI. L. REV. 20 (1976).

[34] 408 U.S. 92 (1972). See Grayned v. City of Rockford, 408 U.S. 104 (1972). The virtually unqualified abhorrence of content regulation in *Mosley* (see Karst, note 33 *supra*) seems now in decline, a development primarily the product of Mr. Justice Steven's opinions in *Young* and *Pacifica*. This in turn seems consistent with Mr. Justice Stevens's flexible approach to constitutional adjudication that eschews distinct categories, rigid rules, and unqualified doctrines. See, *e.g.*, Craig v. Boren, 429 U.S. 190, 211 (1976) (Stevens, J., concurring). It is theoretically possible that distinguishing among forms of speech will increase the amount of First Amendment protection. Note, *Public Figures, Private Figures and Public Interest*, 30 STAN. L. REV. 157, 181 (1977). But the results in *Pacifica* and *Young* belie such as possibility.

[35] 99 S. Ct. at 696 n.4.

[36] A school principal who said that his office was off limits might be on safe constitutional ground. But a principal who totally eliminated access of any kind, by teachers or parents, might be in difficulty under the Petition Clause of the First Amendment.

precedent on this point may be *Southeastern Promotions, Ltd. v. Conrad*.[37] Chattanooga need not build a civic center, and thus need not create this particular forum for speech. But having done so it must treat all speech equally. So too must Leach, having created this forum by opening his office door, treat all speech equally. The complainer may not be fired while the apple-polisher is promoted.

A principal could still under some circumstances base a decision, including a termination decision, on what is said in his office. As with the teacher who speaks out in public, the teacher who speaks out in the principal's office is still a teacher. The *Pickering* balancing approach rather than the more absolute principles of *Mosley* provides the framework for the analysis. The principal's voluntary action in opening his office turns the office into the equivalent of a public forum, but it does not remove Givhan's status as a teacher. It does not therefore diminish the extent to which under *Pickering* a teacher may still be disciplined or dismissed for speaking out.[38]

This approach works, however, only if the forum so created is indeed a First Amendment forum, notwithstanding its cloistered location and notwithstanding that the public at large not only was not invited, but also would not have been permitted entrance. Here the Court relies on its rejection of the distinction between public and private speech. Givhan argued that a complaining teacher might be more prudent in voicing her complaints in the principal's office than in public. It would be anomalous, she claimed, if the more prudent action could result in less constitutional protection.[39] This argument appears to have helped persuade the Court that a distinction between public and private speech is untenable.

C. A NOVEL SOURCE FOR FIRST AMENDMENT DOCTRINE

My initial remarks about the brevity of the opinion in *Givhan* were prompted not so much by the length of the entire opinion as by the fact that the discussion of the distinction between public speech and private speech is contained in only three sentences:[40]

---

[37] 420 U.S. 546 (1975). *See* Karst, *Public Enterprise and the Public Forum: A Comment on* Southeastern Promotions, Ltd. v. Conrad, 37 OHIO ST. L.J. 247 (1976).

[38] See text *supra*, at notes 17 and 23.

[39] Brief for Petitioner, at 16–17.

[40] 99 S. Ct. at 696–97.

> The First Amendment forbids abridgment of the "freedom of speech." Neither the amendment itself nor our decisions indicate that this freedom is lost to the public employee who arranges to communicate privately with his employer rather than to spread his views before the public. We decline to adopt such a view of the First Amendment.

That is it. Nothing about why private communications falls into the same category as spreading one's views before the public, with the exception of one rather unusual source for First Amendment doctrine. The Court looked at and relied on the text of the First Amendment![41] In the past the text has hardly been a popular source for free speech methodology. Of course, most of our First Amendment doctrine is based on the very strong wording of that amendment, but it is rarely suggested that the amendment gives much guidance to its application in hard cases.[42] For that heretofore we have looked elsewhere.

The Court here uses the text to say that a particular distinction is untenable. The distinction between public speech and private speech is indeed not suggested by the words "freedom of speech." But neither is the distinction between commercial speech and po-

---

[41] Mr. Justice Rehnquist's punctuation is intriguing to those of us who labor under the handicap of an exposure to linguistic philosophy. Note that the opinion places the quotation marks after the word "the," although the words in the First Amendment are "the freedom of speech," not "freedom of speech." The inclusion of the word "the" allows a wider range of interpretation than would the words "freedom of speech" standing alone. Mr. Justice Rehnquist's conclusion that the distinction between public speech and private speech is not supported by the text is buttressed by his selective extraction of relevant words. Moreover, even the phrase "freedom of speech" standing alone is far from clear and far from absolute. See Schauer, *Speech and "Speech": Obscenity and "Obscenity"—an Exercise in the Interpretation of Constitutional Language*, 67 GEO. L.J. 899 (1979); Note, *The Speech and Press Clause of the First Amendment as Ordinary Language*, 87 HARV. L. REV. 374 (1973).

[42] Neither of the two most prominent textual arguments has prevailed. The first is the Douglas-Black argument for an absolute interpretation of the First Amendment. See, *e.g.*, Barenblatt v. United States, 360 U.S. 109, 143–44 (1959) (Black, J., dissenting); Roth v. United States, 354 U.S. 476, 514 (1957) (Douglas, J., dissenting). The other is the textual argument for special protection for the press. See Lange, *The Speech and Press Clauses*, 23 U.C.L.A. L. REV. 77 (1975); Nimmer, *Introduction—Is Freedom of the Press a Redundancy: What Does It Add to Freedom of Speech?*, 26 HASTINGS L.J. 639 (1975); Nimmer, *Speech and Press: A Brief Reply*, 23 U.C.L.A. REV. 120 (1975); Stewart, "*Or of the Press*," 26 HASTINGS L.J. 631 (1975); Van Alstyne, *The Hazards to the Press of Claiming a "Preferred Position*," 28 HASTINGS L.J. 761 (1977); see also First National Bank v. Bellotti, 435 U.S. 765 (1978) (Burger, C.J., concurring).

litical speech,[43] the distinction between defamatory speech and non-defamatory speech,[44] the distinction between the broadcast media and other forms of communication,[45] or the distinction between public figures and private individuals,[46] all distinctions well established in contemporary free speech doctrine. The text tells us only that the distinction between public speech and private speech is not supported by the wording of the text. It does not tell us that the distinction cannot be found in history, in the intent of the drafters, in the philosophical underpinnings of the concept of freedom of speech, or in the vast realm of constitutional policy. If textual silence regarding a distinction mandates rejection of that distinction, then free speech theory is in need of a major overhaul. And if textual silence is not dispositive, then we need to know why the other sources of First Amendment doctrine do not either command or support this distinction, an inquiry totally absent from the reasoning in *Givhan.*

D. A QUESTION OF COVERAGE

The treatment of private speech by the Court becomes more understandable upon closer examination of the opinion of the Fifth Circuit. The Court of Appeals did not say that Bessie Givhan's words were not protected by the First Amendment. It said that her words were not even covered by the First Amendment.[47]

This distinction between coverage and protection is of major importance in First Amendment theory.[48] There are some activities

---

[43] Ohralik v. Ohio State Bar Association, 436 U.S. 447 (1978); Virginia State Board of Pharmacy v. Virginia Citizens Consumer Council, Inc., 425 U.S. 748, 771 n.24 (1976). See Schiro, *Commercial Speech: The Demise of a Chimera,* 1976 SUPREME COURT REVIEW 45.

[44] Gertz v. Robert Welch, Inc., 418 U.S. 323 (1974).

[45] F.C.C. v. Pacifica Foundation, 438 U.S. 726 (1978); Red Lion Broadcasting Co. v. F.C.C., 395 U.S. 367 (1969).

[46] Time, Inc. v. Firestone, 424 U.S. 448 (1976); Gertz v. Robert Welch, Inc., 418 U.S. 323 (1974).

[47] The point is highlighted by the concurring opinion of Judge Roney, in which he agreed that the error was in even "casting this case in the First Amendment terms." 555 F.2d at 1322.

[48] The distinction has been emphasized primarily by the "definitional balancers," who use the distinction to argue that the First Amendment can be absolute in

that are totally outside the First Amendment. Such conduct includes not only a wide range of nonverbal conduct, such as killing, maiming, speeding, and polluting, but also some linguistic or pictorial conduct, such as verbal betting, price-fixing, acceptance of a contract, extortion, perjury, and hard-core pornography.[49] In each of these instances the conduct at issue, whether verbal or not, is not taken to be speech in the First Amendment sense, and thus First Amendment modes of analysis are inappropriate.[50] It is more than the mere use of words that triggers First Amendment considerations.[51] Constitutional law has swallowed enough of the law school curriculum as it is without having to encompass almost all of contract and commercial law.

The key point here is that conduct that is covered is not necessarily protected. Defamatory speech is covered by the First Amendment, but it is not protected if it is false and if it is published either negligently, in the case of private individuals, or with knowledge of falsity, in the case of public figures and public officials.[52] Speech having political content is plainly covered, but it is not protected if it "is directed to inciting or producing imminent lawless action and is likely to incite or produce such action."[53] Nonprurient offensive speech is covered by the First Amendment but is not protected when

---

terms of protection without being absolute in terms of coverage. See EMERSON, THE SYSTEM OF FREEDOM OF EXPRESSION (1970); Frantz, *The First Amendment in the Balance*, 71 YALE L.J. 1424 (1962); Nimmer, *The Right to Speak from* Times *to* Time: *First Amendment Theory Applied to Libel and Misapplied to Privacy*, 56 CALIF. L. REV. 935 (1968); Kauper, *Book Review*, 58 MICH. L. REV. 619 (1960). But these theories obscure the point that coverage and protection are different even if protection is not absolute. The distinction shows us that the governmental burden of justification is higher within the First Amendment arena than outside it, but it does not command that the burden inside the First Amendment must be insurmountable. See DWORKIN, TAKING RIGHTS SERIOUSLY 260–61 (1977), in which Dworkin describes the same distinction as a distinction between the range of a principle (coverage) and the force of a principle (protection).

[49] See Schauer, note 41 *supra*.

[50] The First Amendment is of course relevant in drawing the line between that which is covered and that which is not. This is most apparent in the obscenity cases. See Schauer, *Reflections on "Contemporary Community Standards": The Perpetuation of an Irrelevant Concept in the Law of Obscenity*, 56 N. CAR. L. REV. 1 (1978).

[51] "[T]he First Amendment . . . cannot have been, and obviously was not, intended to give immunity for every possible use of language." Frohwerk v. United States, 249 U.S. 204, 206 (1919) (Holmes, J.).

[52] Gertz v. Robert Welch, Inc., 418 U.S. 323 (1974).

[53] Brandenburg v. Ohio, 395 U.S. 444, 447 (1969).

broadcast over the airwaves[54] nor protected from content-based zoning regulation.[55] Commercial speech is now covered by the First Amendment[56] (although it was not under *Valentine v. Chrestensen*),[57] but it is not protected if false or misleading or deceptive.[58]

Pickering applies this same analytic structure to public speech by school teachers. The speech is covered, but it is not protected if it can be shown to hamper a close working relationship with an immediate supervisor, if it can be shown to call into question the teacher's competence as a scholar or teacher, if it breaches a legitimate interest in confidentiality, or if it is outweighed by any of a number of other qualifying factors suggested in *Pickering*. The significance of the Fifth Circuit opinion in *Givhan* is that it does not treat private speech merely as unprotected. It treats it as not covered. The First Amendment is not even relevant. The Court of Appeals could alternatively have said that private speech was covered, but that when presented in this manner and under these circumstances the protection was lost. Indeed, the Supreme Court endorsed such an approach, since it said that the private nature of the speech might suggest additional factors in applying the "*Pickering* calculus."[59]

Viewed in this way, the issue is clearly drawn. Is private speech the type of communication to which the First Amendment is addressed? It is this question to which the Fifth Circuit loudly answered "No" and to which the Supreme Court more loudly answered "Yes." And it is that "Yes" answer that requires more analysis than is afforded in *Givhan*.

II. The Problem of Private Speech

A. The Meaning of "Private Speech"

To weigh the protection afforded to private speech, it is necessary to determine precisely what the Court did and did not hold

[54] F.C.C. v. Pacifica Foundation, 438 U.S. 726 (1978).

[55] Young v. American Mini Theatres, Inc., 427 U.S. 50 (1976).

[56] Virginia State Board of Pharmacy v. Virginia Citizens Consumer Council, Inc., 425 U.S. 748, 762 (1976).

[57] 316 U.S. 50 (1942).

[58] See Pitofsky, *Beyond Nader: Consumer Protection and the Regulation of Advertsing*, 90 Harv. L. Rev. 661 (1977).

[59] 99 S. Ct. at 696 n.4.

in *Givhan*. It is apparent that the Court did not hold that private speech is per se protected by the First Amendment. There is no suggestion in *Givhan* that private speech is more protected than public speech. In holding that speaking publicly is not a necessary condition for the First Amendment protection, the Court did not hold that speaking privately is a sufficient condition.

Since the Court did not hold that private speech is protected by reason of its privacy, it necessarily did not hold that all private speech is protected. Those restrictions that are permissible for public speech remain permissible for private speech, except in those situations where the public nature of the speech provides the justification for the restriction, as with public offensiveness or the provocation of an angry crowd.[60] If I approach an individual whom I know to be on the verge of committing a political assassination and, with the intent of causing that assassination, specifically urge him to carry out his plan, then this private speech may be punished just as could public counseling of murder in circumstances where it is likely that murder will immediately ensue.

What the Court did hold in *Givhan* is that private speech is not for that reason alone excluded from either the coverage or the protection of the First Amendment. If a certain form of speech would be protected if delivered in print, or to a public audience, then that same speech is equally protected if spoken or published in a closed office, in a living room, or at a table in a quiet restaurant. This implies that the distinction between public speech and private speech is never relevant in First Amendment adjudication, an implication that derives much support from the unqualified nature of the Court's opinion as well as from the Court's statement that the lack of such a distinction is derived directly from the text of the First Amendment.

Several unexplained distinctions serve to obscure the Court's conclusions about private speech. Thus, the public-private distinction discussed here is not the same as the distinction between speech that is in the public interest and speech that concerns only the private personal interests of the speaker or the listener. We are not dis-

[60] Crowd reaction may be relevant whether the crowd is sympathetic or hostile. Brandenburg v. Ohio, 395 U.S. 444 (1969); Feiner v. New York, 340 U.S. 315 (1951). There may not be much left of *Feiner*. Smith v. Collin, 436 U.S. 953 (1978); Gregory v. Chicago, 394 U.S. 111 (1969); Edwards v. South Carolina, 372 U.S. 229 (1963).

cussing private speech in the sense in which Meiklejohn distinguished private speech from public speech.[61] The issue here and in *Givhan* involves the forum and the audience, not the subject matter. Bessie Givhan's complaints plainly related both to the operation of the public schools and to race relations in a community in which satisfactory race relations were vitally important. However narrowly one wishes to define the notion of "speech in the public interest," the speech in *Givhan* is undoubtedly included.[62] The holding in *Givhan* does not support the conclusion that the same result might have been reached if Bessie Givhan devoted her time in the principal's office to spreading rumors about the private behavior of mutual acquaintances.[63]

Any distinction between public or important speech and private or trivial speech may be unworkable.[64] There is certainly such a suggestion in the rejection of *Rosenbloom v. Metromedia, Inc.*[65] by *Gertz v. Robert Welch, Inc.*[66] But the impact of *Gertz* on this issue is lessened not only by *Time, Inc. v. Firestone*[67] but also by *Young*

---

[61] MEIKLEJOHN, FREE SPEECH AND ITS RELATION TO SELF-GOVERNMENT (1948); Meiklejohn, *The First Amendment Is an Absolute*, 1961 SUPREME COURT REVIEW 245. For similar distinctions, see BeVier, *The First Amendment and Political Speech: An Inquiry into the Substance and Limits of Principle*, 30 STAN. L. REV. 299 (1978); Bork, *Neutral Principles and Some First Amendment Problems*, 47 IND. L.J. 1 (1971).

[62] Indeed, the firing of Bessie Givhan for complaining may not be all that dissimilar to a prosecution for sedition. The ultimate question is the value of loyalty, whether to a nation or to an employer. See Kalven, *The New York Times Case: A Note on "The Central Meaning of the First Amendment,"* 1964 SUPREME COURT REVIEW 191.

[63] I am not saying that such a distinction could be supported by current doctrine, only that *Givhan* itself stands as no barrier to the adoption or application of this type of distinction.

[64] See Shiffrin, *Defamatory Non-Media Speech and First Amendment Methodology*, 25 U.C.L.A. L. REV. 915, 936 (1978); see also Chafee, Book Review, 62 HARV. L. REV. 891 (1949).

[65] 403 U.S. 29 (1971).

[66] 418 U.S. 323 (1974).

[67] 424 U.S. 448 (1976). The import of *Time* is that at least some degree of legitimate public importance is part of the determination of who is a public figure. It is arguably beyond the human capacity to comprehend all of the different ways in which the Supreme Court has used the word "public." Since "private" is the most obvious antonym for "public," it is not surprising to find the varying use of that word as well.

There is a similar distinction embodied in the "newsworthiness" standard applied in actions for invasion of privacy. See Kalven, *The Reasonable Man and the First Amendment: Hill, Butts, and Walker*, 1967 SUPREME COURT REVIEW 267, 283. Although the Supreme Court has yet to speak to the constitutionality of a true (as

v. American Mini Theatres, Inc.[68] "[F]ew of us would march our sons and daughters off to war to preserve the citizen's right to see 'Specified Sexual Activities' exhibited in the theaters of our choice."[69] But the theoretical wisdom or practical workability of distinctions like this is not at issue here. The subject matter of Givhan's speech did pertain to public issues, and this sense of the public-private distinction is not what is involved in *Givhan.*

Exclusion of the subject-matter sense of "private" still leaves several different concepts of private speech. One is the distinction between face-to-face communication and less personal forms of speech. In upholding constitutional protection for client solicitation by lawyers in *In re Primus*[70] and denying such protection in *Ohralik v. Ohio State Bar Association,*[71] the Court drew some support from the presence of "in-person" solicitation in *Ohralik,* a factor absent in *Primus.*[72] The Court suggests that in-person solicitation might either be less central to the purposes of the First Amendment or at least more susceptible to abuse. But the letter in *Ohralik* is also directed to one person only and is as much if not more inaccessible to the public at large. Thus it is hard to see how *Ohralik* and *Primus* can turn on a public-private distinction, although in-person communication is one of the earmarks of the type of speech at issue in *Givhan.* Mr. Justice Rehnquists's dissent in *Primus* questions the distinction between face-to-face and other forms of communication,[73] and there may be a relationship between this dissent and his opinion in *Givhan.* But the concurrence of the entire Court in *Givhan* leads to the conclusion that the rejection of the public-private distinction there leaves the distinction between in-person and more distant speech intact.

Alternatively, private speech may be taken to mean speech directed to only one person, rather than to a group, or to the general public, or to anyone who cares to listen. Speech that is private in this sense would include both face-to-face communication and a

---

opposed to false-light) privacy case, the newsworthiness standard has provided the relevant distinction in most such cases in the lower courts. See, *e.g.,* Briscoe v. Reader's Digest Association, 4 Cal.3d 529 (1971).

[68] 427 U.S. 50 (1976).

[69] *Id.* at 70; see also *id.* at 61.

[70] 436 U.S. 412 (1978).

[71] 436 U.S. 447 (1978).

[72] *Id.* at 464–66.

[73] 436 U.S. at 445 (Rehnquist, J., dissenting).

personal letter, but would exclude a speech to a large audience, a mass mailing, or the publication of a book, newspaper, or magazine. Such a distinction is suggested by the current formulation of the "fighting words" doctrine.[74] The Court has strongly implied that the crucial demarcation between regulable fighting words and protected inflammatory words is the extent to which the former are directed at particular individuals.[75] Standing on a platform and proclaiming that all police officers are pigs is protected, even if a police officer is in the audience.[76] But yelling "You're a pig!" to a particular officer may be the subject of prosecution.[77] Although Paul Cohen has the right to wear a jacket bearing the words "Fuck the Draft,"[78] he may not have the right to say "Fuck you!" to a particular individual.

To the extent that *Givhan's* rejection of the public-private distinction can be interpreted as a rejection of a distinction between speech directed to the public at large and speech directed at a particular individual, this aspect of the fighting words cases is called into question. This is an issue to which I will return later, since a distinguishing principle seems available.[79] There is less question about the effect on another area of First Amendment doctrine. The holding in *Givhan* certainly casts grave doubts on the extent to which the principles of *Gertz v. Robert Welch, Inc.* are limited to publications by the media. Such a limitation is supported by the Court's repeated references to the mass media in the *Gertz* opinion.[80] A num-

---

[74] See, *e.g.*, Gooding v. Wilson, 405 U.S. 518 (1972); Rosenfeld v. New Jersey, 408 U.S. 901 (1972); Lewis v. New Orleans, 408 U.S. 913 (1972); Brown v. Oklahoma, 408 U.S. 914 (1972); Lewis v. New Orleans, 415 U.S. 130 (1974); Plummer v. City of Columbus, 414 U.S. 2 (1973). The Court's cryptic decisions in these cases, generally on overbreadth or vagueness grounds, make it difficult to say whether or not there is anything worthy of the title "doctrine." See TRIBE, note 33 *supra*, at 617–18.

[75] Gooding v. Wilson, 405 U.S. 518 (1972).

[76] Brown v. Oklahoma, 408 U.S. 914 (1972).

[77] See Cincinnati v. Karlan, 39 Ohio St.2d 107 (1974).

[78] Cohen v. California, 403 U.S. 15 (1971).

[79] See text *infra*, at note 103.

[80] See Shiffrin, *supra* note 64; Collins & Drushal, *The Reaction of the State Courts to* Gertz v. Robert Welch, Inc., 28 CASE WEST. RES. L. REV. 306, 328–34 (1978); Eaton, *The American Law of Defamation through* Gertz v. Robert Welch, Inc. *and Beyond: An Analytical Primer*, 61 VA. L. REV. 1349, 1403–08, 1416–19 (1975); Note, *First Amendment Protection against Libel Actions: Distinguishing Media and Non-Media Defendants*, 47 SO. CAL. L. REV. 902 (1974) (written before *Gertz*).

ber of lower courts that have been called upon to apply *Gertz* to nonmedia speech have in fact held *Gertz* inapplicable.[81] Recent decisions of the Supreme Court negate the notion that *Gertz* applies only to the organized press.[82] A majority of the Court has consistently refused to distinguish between the press and other forms of communication, and one can say with a fair degree of confidence that this same majority would apply *Gertz* to public orations as well as to printed or broadcast publications.[83] But speech directed to a limited number of identified individuals is more problematic. What if *A* tells *B* that *C* is having an affair with *D*'s wife? The implication in *Givhan* is that this is subject to the same protection as would obtain if *A*'s charges against *C* were published in the *New York Times* or announced on the Boston Common.[84] The resolution of this lingering issue in the law of defamation may or may not have been the Court's oblique intention, but it is quite likely that that is the result.

A distinction between public speech and private speech may instead (or in addition) be a distinction based on the location of the speech. Some speech takes place in cloistered locations, such as living rooms or private offices. Other speech is more open, taking place in the streets, the parks, or the mass media. The Court does not make clear in *Givhan* whether the speech was private in the sense that it was directed only to the principal or in the sense that it was made in the principal's closed office. It is likely but not certain that the Court rejected both distinctions.

Both the audience-directed and location-directed notions of private speech turn on the concept of who is invited.[85] A meeting

---

[81] *E.g., compare* Calero v. Del Chemical Corp., 68 Wis.2d 487 (1975), *with* Jacron Sales Co. v. Sindorf, 276 Md. 580 (1976).

[82] This conclusion is drawn from the Court's refusal to recognize a distinct privilege for the press, often on the grounds that no distinguishing features can be developed in any principled manner. See, *e.g.*, Branzburg v. Hayes, 408 U.S. 665 (1972); Zurcher v. Stanford Daily, 436 U.S. 547 (1978); Houchins v. KQED, Inc., 438 U.S. 1 (1978); Pell v. Procunier, 417 U.S. 817 (1974); Saxbe v. Washington Post Co., 417 U.S. 843 (1974).

[83] *See* Eaton, note 80 *supra*, at 1406.

[84] It is true that this hypothetical case involves speech that is purely private in the subject-matter sense. But there is absolutely no suggestion in *Gertz* that the constitutionalized negligence requirement would not apply to all mass media defamation regardless of subject matter.

[85] If I have a conversation with a friend in my living room, it is private in that

of the American Bar Association from which the press is excluded is in both senses private, although the audience could be large. The speaker knows the identity of the audience and can also limit the audience.

This suggests that privacy as used here is a complex rather than a simple notion. Its very complexity may suggest a rejection of the public-private distinction on pragmatic rather than theoretical grounds.[86] It is perhaps best to look at private speech in the context of a paradigm example. In all senses other than the subject-matter sense the truly private speech is a two-person face-to-face conversation in a private living room closed to everyone except the two participants. If we can say that this speech is within the First Amendment, then we can say that forms of speech in some sense less private are within the First Amendment as well.

B. THE VALUE OF PRIVATE SPEECH

Unraveling the different senses of a distinction between public speech and private speech helps in understanding the import of *Givhan* and in applying it to other situations. It remains, however, to examine the Court's conclusion that the distinction is not relevant. Does speech that is private in some or all senses have less First Amendment value?

A distinction between public speech and private speech in the extent of either coverage or protection is least justified under a First Amendment theory derived in whole or in part from some concept of democracy or self-government. The Meiklejohn theory is the most famous,[87] although it is neither the first nor the only articula-

---

no one else is invited into my living room to participate. But if I have the conversation with the same friend on a bench in a park, the conversation is every bit as private even though the location is in some senses public. But the important fact is that the conversation is private in either case. It is in all cases restricted to the participants, whether by reason of the laws of private property or by reason of the fact that we will stop talking if anyone comes too close. Aficionados of bad movies or television police shows know that if you want to take out a contract on someone you do not do it in a private house; you do it in a public park. Privacy may be created by crowds or by anonymity as much as by seclusion. It all depends on what you mean by "private," and the Court in *Givhan* does not tell us what it means.

[86] See Shiffrin, note 64 *supra*.

[87] See note 61 *supra*.

tion of such a theory.[88] Under any such theory it is difficult to distinguish between speech in public and speech in private. As much as we may talk about the public forum, we must not avoid recognizing that a great deal of political speech takes place outside of the public forum. To find the "true" forum for political discussion and commentary in this country, we should not journey to the theaters, the parks, or the streets, or read newsapers, magazines, placards, posters, or billboards. Rather, we must go to the pool halls, the factories, the bars, the private offices, the barbershops, and the proverbial living room in Peoria. Although many of these are "public" places, they are all locations where particular conversations are limited to a known, invited, and usually quite small audience. But it is here that politics and public matters are discussed and minds are changed. It is here that arguments about politics and personalities take place.

The public forum is indeed the catalyst for much discussion of public matters. But the public forum is not the end of the process. The culmination of the process is to be found in the discussion among people in much more cloistered settings. The town meeting model so stressed by Meiklejohn relies on dialogue and participation. To see that process outside of the New England town meeting we should look at a forum for discussion and argument, not a forum for unilateral speechmaking and passive listening. This forum for discussion and argument is much more likely to be limited rather than open to all. It may be one sign of a totalitarian society that people are imprisoned for what they say in public, especially if they are criticizing government, its policies, or its leaders.[89] But the ultimate affront to the notion of a free society occurs when people are imprisoned for what they say in their living rooms. We are in danger when the informer is one member of a large audience, but we are in greater danger when the informer is our next-door neighbor.

From this perspective, we can see that the rejection of the public-

---

[88] See Kant, On the Old Saw: That May Be Right in Theory But It Won't Work in Practice 72 (E. B. Ashton trans. 1974); Spinoza, Tractatus Theologico-Politicus chap. 20 (1670); Hume, *Of the Liberty of the Press,* in Essays, Moral, Political and Literary 8 (Oxford ed. 1963); see also Gilbert v. Minnesota, 254 U.S. 325, 337–38 (1920) (Brandeis, J., dissenting).

[89] See Kalven, note 69 *supra.*

private distinction is also supported by the "self-expression"[90] and "catharsis"[91] values often said to justify the principles of freedom of speech. It may be that free speech theories derived from the concept of the marketplace of ideas,[92] or the search for truth,[93] or the principles of self-government,[94] are theories derived from societal rather than individual interests.[95] They are directed more toward the interests of society, and also to the interests of the listeners, than they are toward the interests of the speaker. Under such theories we protect speakers only instrumentally in the service of these broader interests. From this point of view one can imagine granting less protection to private speech, since the closed setting reduces the number of listeners and thereby reduces the impact on society at large. But if, instead, we look at free speech as providing a catharsis, an outlet for frustration short of violence, then we should acknowledge that this may occur as easily with private speech as with public speech.

Similarly, if we look to the value to the speaker of communicating ideas to others, then the size or location of the audience may again be of little importance. Indeed, the value to the speaker may be increased as the size of the audience and the openness of the location decrease. Although self-expression in general is not a First

---

[90] See, *e.g.*, TRIBE, note 33 *supra* at 576–736; Dworkin, *Introduction*, in DWORKIN, ED., PHILOSOPHY OF LAW 1, 13–16 (1977); Baker, *Scope of the First Amendment Freedom of Speech*, 25 U.C.L.A. L. REV. 964 (1978); Richards, *Free Speech and Obscenity Law: Toward a Moral Theory of the First Amendment*, 123 U. PA. L. REV. 45 (1974).

[91] See, *e.g.*, Emerson, *Toward a General Theory of the First Amendment*, 72 YALE L.J. 877, 884 (1963); LASKI, A GRAMMAR OF POLITICS, 121 (4th ed. 1938).

[92] See Red Lion Broadcasting Co. v. F.C.C., 395 U.S. 367 (1969); Abrams v. United States, 250 U.S. 616, 630 (1919) (Holmes, J., dissenting).

[93] MILL, *On Liberty*, in ESSENTIAL WORKS OF JOHN STUART MILL 268–304 (Lerner ed. 1961); MILTON, AREOPAGITICA 78, 126 (Suffolk ed. 1968); LOCKE, A LETTER CONCERNING TOLERATION 151 (Gough ed. 1948); Bagehot, *The Metaphysical Basis of Toleration*, in 2 LITERARY STUDIES 422, 425 (Hutton ed., 3d ed., 1884); Jefferson, *First Inaugural Address*, in THE COMPLETE JEFFERSON 384 (Padover ed. 1943); United States v. Associated Press, 52 F. Supp. 372 (S.D.N.Y. 1943) (L. Hand, J.); See Gunther, *Learned Hand and the Origins of Modern First Amendment Doctrine: Some Fragments of History*, 27 STAN. L. REV. 719 (1975).

[94] See notes 61 and 86 *supra*.

[95] On this distinction in the context of freedom of speech, see 3 POUND, JURISPRUDENCE 63–67, 313–17 (1959).

Amendment value,[96] self-expression by communication has been so regarded in numerous opinions of the Supreme Court.[97] And so long as this value remains as one core of free speech theory, then it follows that the interests of the speaker are independently deserving of First Amendment protection. When we focus on the interests of the speaker, it is difficult to say that these interests are necessarily diminished by the smallness or seclusion of the audience.

Moreover, there may be societal or listener interests even where there is an individual listener receiving the message other than in the public forum. One of the values of freedom of speech is its function in helping to correct and challenge accepted beliefs.[98] This is a value that obtains under both the self-government and marketplace-of-ideas arguments. Here the proper focus is on the identity of the listener rather than the number of listeners. Criticism of the President of the United States does more than allow the populace to remove or fail to reelect an unsatisfactory President. It does more than mobilize public opinion in such a way that the President may respond with deeds or reply with words. There is a more direct argument. Criticism of the President is valuable because the President himself may hear the particular criticism and may as a result modify or reject an erroneous policy.

From this perspective the Free Speech Clause merges with the First Amendment right to petition the government for a redress of grievances. One of the *amicus* briefs in *Givhan* relied as much on the right to petition the government as it did on freedom of speech.[99]

---

[96] See Schauer, note 41 *supra*.

[97] See First National Bank of Boston v. Bellotti, 435 U.S. 765, 777, 783 (1978); Garrison v. Louisiana, 379 U.S. 64, 74–75 (1964).

[98] See POPPER, THE OPEN SOCIETY AND ITS ENEMIES (5th ed. 1966). A forceful criticism of Mill and Popper is Kendall, *The "Open Society" and Its Fallacies*, 54 AM. POL. SCI. REV. 972 (1960).

[99] Brief Amicus Curiae of the American Association of University Professors, at 15–20. See also Brief for Petitioner, at 19 n.14. The relationship between the Free Speech Clause and the Petition Clause was suggested by Justice Rutledge in Thomas v. Collins, 323 U.S. 516, 530 (1945). This is particularly interesting here because some of the activities in *Thomas* could be characterized as "private" solicitation. The Court recognized that private solicitation of a single individual might create different issues, *id.* at 528–29, and used the combination of the Free Speech and Petition Clauses to suggest that private solicitation would be for one reason or another protected by the First Amendment. *Id.* at 533–34.

The right to petition plainly encompasses administrative bodies as well as legislative ones. California Motor Transport Co. v. Trucking Unlimited, 404 U.S. 508,

The argument also has some textual support. Because it is impossible to petition the government for a redress of grievances without at the same time speaking, the Petition Clause would be a redundancy if it did not give particular protection for direct criticism of public officials, without regard to whether the criticism is made by public speech, private letter, or private audience.[100] The Free Speech Clause protects my right to stand in Lafayette Park and announce that the President and his policies are demented. It may be the Petition Clause that gives me the right to write him a letter containing the same message.

Regardless of whether the source is the Free Speech Clause or the Petition Clause, it would certainly be odd if some part of the First Amendment[101] did not protect the right to criticize a governmental official to his face. Private communication with an officer of government may in many respects be the most effective way of calling that officer to task or pointing out mistakes in judgment that can be corrected. The more the Court continues to rely on arguments about democracy to support the concept of freedom of speech,[102] the more it can be said that direct criticism of public officials lies at the core of First Amendment theory. And, as we increasingly identify this as a core free speech value, a blanket exclusion of private speech appears ever more anomalous.

Of course, there may in many instances be advantages in the kind of public speech that is directed to a large and possibly anonymous

---

510 (1972). The Petition Clause has been used on numerous occasions in the lower courts to overturn discharges of complaining employees. See, *e.g.*, Jackson v. United States, 428 F.2d 844 (Ct. Cl. 1970); Swaaley v. United States, 376 F.2d 857, 861 (Ct. Cl. 1967); Jannetta v. Cole, 493 F.2d 1334, 1337 n.5 (4th Cir. 1974); Los Angeles Teachers Union v. Los Angeles City Board of Education, 455 P.2d 827, 832 (1969).

[100] Direct communication has frequently been considered to be the special concern of the Petition Clause. See Pell v. Procunier, 417 U.S. 817, 828–29 n.6 (1974); Bridges v. California, 314 U.S. 252, 302–03 (1941) (Frankfurter, J., dissenting).

[101] The Court has frequently relied on the connection between the Free Speech and Petition Clauses to hold that conduct is protected by one, the other, or both. See United Mine Workers v. Illinois Bar Association, 389 U.S. 217, 222 (1967); Brotherhood of Railroad Trainmen v. Virginia State Bar, 377 U.S. 1 (1964); Edwards v. South Carolina, 372 U.S. 229, 235 (1963); Thomas v. Collins, 323 U.S. 516, 530–31 (1945).

[102] See Brennan, *The Supreme Court and the Meiklejohn Interpretation of the First Amendment*, 79 HARV. L. REV. 1 (1965); Polsby, Buckley v. Valeo: *The Special Nature of Political Speech*, 1976 SUPREME COURT REVIEW 1.

group. It is a mistake to assume that there is only one core to First Amendment theory. Freedom of speech is more properly regarded as a bundle of different but interrelated concepts, joined together under the oversimplifying rubric of "freedom of speech." One core value of the First Amendment is personal or face-to-face criticism of public officials. But this does not exclude as another core value the right to stand in the public forum, or the right to publish criticism of government for public consumption. The soapbox, the parade, the demonstration, the newspaper, the book, and the magazine all occupy special places in our society, places recognized as special by contemporary First Amendment doctrine. These are all forms of "mass" speech, and their effectiveness increase in direct proportion to the size of the audience.

To the extent that free speech is a societal rather than an individual interest, forms of speech that reach large segments of society may have advantages not possessed by speech that is private in the sense now under discussion. But merely because public speech is in some respects more important than private speech does not mean that in other respects private speech may not be equally if not more important. As long as we realize that free speech is more than one concept, these two positions are not inconsistent. Since the value of public speech may be derived in large part from the private speech that it provokes and fosters, a theory that places public speech above private speech in the First Amendment hierarchy is on shaky ground indeed.

The foregoing lends support to the conclusion that the Court was correct in saying that the private context of the speech did not dispose of *Givhan* (and this is all the Court decided) and to the corollary conclusion that *Gertz* cannot be limited to the mass media. But what then of the fighting words cases, where a similar distinction seems established? The answer seems to come from an examination of the other side of the First Amendment question. On the one hand, we look at the value of the particular speech or at the value of a particular category of speech. But on the other hand, we look at the justifications for the asserted restriction. In developing categories and approaches to First Amendment analysis, we look at the interests in regulation as well as the interests in free speech. From this vantage point we see in *Ohralik* the interest in preventing potentially coercive and misleading solicitation. In many cases we look at the interests in public order and safety that justify content-neutral time, place, and manner regulations.[103] In the fighting words case we look at the interest in preventing "idea-less" provocation.[104]

In all of these situations it is the context of speech that governs its regulability. The justification for regulation in these and other situations depends on the context in which the speech exists. This is not the place to analyze each instance of permissible regulation of speech in which the extent of that permission varies with the context. The important point is that there are such instances, although they do not exhaust the category of permissible restrictions.[105] In those instances in which context is established as being the relevant or dispositive factor it would be foolish to say that context may be considered but that the public or private nature must be ignored. The location of the speech may very well give the speech the impact that justifies its regulation. So too with the size of the audience. In the fighting words cases the "privateness" increases the impact of the very factor that justifies the regulation. Private verbal assaults are more likely to provoke violent reactions.[106] The distinction between public speech and private speech may indeed be relevant in determining the extent of protection where the principles that permit regulation would, without the public-private distinction, allow a consideration of context. The private context, as has been seen, cannot create the justification. But where the principles of regulation lead us to context, the location of the speech and the identity of the audience are factors to be considered. This conclusion is supported by the Court's observation that under some circumstances the setting may be relevant to the "*Pickering* calculus,"[107] but the principles extend far beyond *Pickering* alone.

In some instances of regulation justified by context the private

---

[103] See, *e.g.*, Kovacs v. Cooper, 336 U.S. 77 (1949); Cox v. New Hampshire, 312 U.S. 569 (1941).

[104] See Chaplinsky v. New Hampshire, 315 U.S. 568 (1942).

[105] Permissible restrictions on defamatory speech, *e.g.*, are largely independent of context.

[106] The more the speech is directed at a particular individual, the more he is likely to react violently. But it is possible that, once the speech is directed at a particular individual, the likelihood of violent reaction increases with the number of observers. Part of the cause of violent reaction may very well be humiliation, which requires an audience.

[107] 99 S. Ct. at 696 n.4.

setting may argue for increased protection. This may be the case in *Givhan*, for the private audience may produce better results with fewer unpleasant side effects. And in *Pickering* the Court suggested that under some circumstances a teacher might be required to make a complaint internally before going public with the complaint.[108] But instances also exist where it is possible that the private setting may decrease the available protection. Fighting words again seem the best example.

With this vital qualification regarding context, we can both justify and qualify the holding in *Givhan*. The private setting alone does not result in forfeiture of First Amendment coverage or protection, but the private setting is indeed relevant to the extent of protection where the extent of protection is to be determined by the context of the utterance at issue.

III. The Private Citizen and the Public Employee

We have seen several senses of the public-private distinction, one in terms of subject matter, another in terms of the forum, and a third in terms of the audience. But there is still another sense, one that leads to a consideration of the other important facet of *Givhan*. For Bessie Givhan was not only a private citizen; she was also a public employee. *Pickering* was decided in large part in reliance on the fact that Pickering was speaking out not as a public employee but as a private citizen.[109] The same is true of both the situation and the Court's opinions in *Perry*,[110] in *Mt. Healthy*,[111] and in *City of Madison, Joint School District No. 8 v. Wisconsin Employment Relations Commission*.[112] In all of these cases it could as easily have been a private citizen not employed by the State who was speaking.

These cases leave undecided the extent of free speech protection where the individual speaks not *qua* citizen but *qua* public employee. *Givhan* is far from illuminating on this issue, but it provides some signposts for exploring this difficult constitutional terrain.

The cases before *Givhan* all involve speech in forums open to the

---

[108] 391 U.S. at 572 n.4.

[109] *Id.* at 574, noting that the employment "is only tangentially and insubstantially involved in the subject matter of the public communication made by a teacher."

[110] 408 U.S. at 598.

[111] 429 U.S. at 282.

[112] 429 U.S. 167 (1976).

general public. In each case the Court took pains to point out that it was the teacher as citizen that provided the focal point of the analysis. "He addressed the school board not merely as one of its employees but also as a concerned citizen, seeking to express his views on an important decision of his government."[113] This language would clearly have been controlling in *Givhan* if Bessie Givhan's complaints about racial discrimination in the schools had been expressed in a letter to the editor of a local newspaper, in a speech in a public park, or at a board of education meeting open to the general public.[114] But by expressing her complaints in the principal's office, she utilized a forum not open to the general public. It was open to her solely by virtue of her employment as a teacher.

When a teacher or other public employee speaks out as a teacher, or as a public employee, additional considerations come into play, some of which were suggested in *Pickering*.[115] The speech may jeopardize a necessarily close working relationship, it may breach a valid interest in confidentiality, or it may call into question a teacher's very fitness for the position. I have the right to believe that the world is flat or that astrology tells us more than the theories of Newton and Einstein. I also have the right to express these views to anyone foolish enough to listen. But if I am the head of the physics department at a major state research university, I can hardly deny that such public utterances might validly cause my superiors to wonder if perhaps I am in the wrong line of work and to take appropriate action. As a citizen I have the right to interest myself in and comment upon the fortunes of the New York Yankees. But as a teacher of constitutional law I do not have the right to devote my entire course in constitutional law to evaluating the performances of Reggie Jackson and Ron Guidry in the 1978 World Series. It is this latter situation that more closely relates to the facts in *Givhan*. Bessie Givhan was not only speaking out as a teacher, she

---

[113] *Id.* at 174–75.

[114] In *City of Madison* it was the fact that the meeting was open to the public rather than a closed bargaining session that was determinative. *Ibid.*

[115] "At the same time it cannot be gainsaid that the State has interests as an employer in regulating the speech of its employees that differ significantly from those it possesses in connection with regulation of the speech of the citizenry in general. The problem in any case is to arrive at a balance between the interests of the teacher, as citizen, in commenting upon matters of public concern and the interest of the State, as an employer, in promoting the efficiency of the public services it performs through its employees." 391 U.S. at 568.

was speaking out on her employer's premises and on her employer's time. Regardless of whether a modern-day McAuliffe might have the right to talk politics on his own time,[116] it is clear that he could be legitimately dismissed for delivering a political oration when he was supposed to be directing traffic.

Transposing this to the academic setting, we can see that virtually all of the Supreme Court's references to academic freedom have been little more than excess verbiage. In the most prominent "academic freedom" cases, from *Keyishian v. Board of Regents*[117] and *Wieman v. Updegraff*[118] to *Pickering* and *Perry*, the speech took place outside of the school and on the teacher's own time. These are not academic freedom cases—they are free speech cases. The issue is only whether a public employee can be penalized for exercising a citizen's right of free speech. The full application of the principle in these cases to public employees who are not teachers demonstrates that the principle is only that dismissal from public employment is just one of many impermissible penalties on protected speech.[119] If it is academic freedom that protects a teacher's right to join an organization, or speak out in public, then one who is not an academic has no claim to such rights. Surely this is not true. Pickering's right to criticize the school board is no greater than the streetcleaner's right to criticize the sanitation department.[120]

---

[116] McAuliffe v. Mayor of New Bedford, 155 Mass. 216 (1892) (Holmes, J.). "The petitioner may have a constitutional right to talk politics, but he has no constitutional right to be a policeman." *Id.* at 220. The accepted wisdom is that *McAuliffe* is the prototypical example of the now discredited right-privilege distinction. See Van Alstyne, *The Demise of the Right-Privilege Distinction in Constitutional Law*, 81 HARV. L. REV. 1439 (1968). But *McAuliffe* might not necessarily be decided differently today. See Civil Service Commission v. National Association of Letter Carriers, 413 U.S. 548 (1973); United Public Workers v. Mitchell, 330 U.S. 75 (1947).

[117] 385 U.S. 589 (1967).

[118] 344 U.S. 183 (1952). See also Elfbrandt v. Russell, 384 U.S. 11 (1966); Shelton v. Tucker, 364 U.S. 479 (1960); Fellman, *Academic Freedom in American Law*, 1961 WIS. L. REV. 3; Jones, *The American Concept of Academic Freedom*, in JOUGHIN, ED., ACADEMIC FREEDOM AND TENURE 224 (1967); Murphy, *Academic Freedom—an Emerging Constitutional Right*, 28 L. & CONT. PROB. 447 (1963); Van Alstyne, *The Constitutional Rights of Teachers and Professors*, 1970 DUKE L.J. 841; Wright, *The Constitution on the Campus*, 22 VAND. L. REV. 1027 (1969); Schauer, *School Books, Lesson Plans, and the Constitution*, 78 W. VA. L. REV. 287 (1976).

[119] See O'Neil, *Unconstitutional Conditions: Welfare Benefits with Strings Attached*, 54 CALIF. L. REV. 443 (1966); Van Alstyne, *The Constitutional Rights of Employees: A Comment on the Inappropriate Uses of an Old Analogy*, 16 U.C.L.A. L. REV. 751 (1969).

[120] On applications of *Pickering* to nonacademic positions, see, *e.g.*, Donahue

Talk of academic freedom is therefore pointless unless there is something about academic freedom that is special or different. Academic freedom is a meaningful concept only if it protects activities not otherwise protected by the general concept of free speech.[121] Unless academic freedom adds something to freedom of speech its deployment serves only to confuse the analysis.

If there is an independent concept of academic freedom, it is surely derived not only from the First Amendment, in general, but also from the doctrine of freedom of speech, in particular. Yet this does not mean that the two are the same. The values of the intellectual marketplace and of open inquiry into even the most accepted beliefs are arguably served in a special way within the setting of an academic institution. It can also be said that the academic institution has a special responsibility to instill the spirit of inquiry that enables the general notion of free speech to function. If this is true, then the First Amendment may generate a distinct institutional protection for the academy.

Drawing this distinction makes it possible to see *Givhan* in a different light. Prior to *Givhan* there had been only one "true" academic freedom case in the Supreme Court, *Sweezy v. New Hampshire*.[122] Without the concept of academic freedom there is nowhere in constitutional law an exception to the principle that during working hours employees are to do what their employers tell them to do. But in *Sweezy* the Court suggested that activities in the classroom might be protected, a seeming exception to this general principle. After *Sweezy*, the State as employer is to some extent limited in the extent to which it can mandate what the university teacher as employee can do in the classroom. But this is a somewhat obscure

---

v. Staunton, 471 F.2d 475 (7th Cir. 1972) (chaplain at mental hospital); Commonwealth of Pennsylvania ex rel. Rafferty v. Philadelphia Psychiatric Center, 356 F. Supp. 500 (E.D. Pa. 1973) (psychiatric nurse); Jannetta v. Cole, 493 F.2d 1334 (4th Cir. 1974) (fireman). In *Rafferty* the court suggested that, if the plaintiff's superiors in the community mental health center were that sensitive to criticism, they perhaps ought to be the patients rather than the supervisors.

[121] By far the best exposition of this distinction is Van Alstyne, *The Specific Theory of Academic Freedom and the General Issue of Civil Liberties*, 404 ANNALS 140 (1972).

[122] 354 U.S. 234 (1957), in which a state investigation into a lecture delivered in a class at the University of New Hampshire was held invalid. Epperson v. Arkansas, 393 U.S. 97 (1968), involved classroom activity, but the case was decided on establishment of religion grounds. Mr. Justice Stewart's concurrence did suggest a possible academic freedom–free speech path to the same result. *Id.* at 116.

dictum in *Sweezy*, and there has been little more guidance from the Supreme Court.[123]

The paucity of precedent has not deterred the proliferation of an extensive literature on this subject.[124] There have been several notable lower court cases, most prominently Judge Johnson's opinion in *Parducci v. Rutland*.[125] But the Supreme Court has said very little about the extent to which either academic freedom or freedom of speech protects utterances on school time and on school property. In *Tinker v. Des Moines Independent Community School District*,[126] the Court said that "[i]t can hardly be argued that either students or teachers shed their constitutional rights to freedom of speech or expression at the schoolhouse gate,"[127] but the Court there did little more than protect only those exercises of constitutional rights that are not inconsistent with the educational function. It said nothing about whether freedom of speech is part of the educational function.

To answer this question it is necessary to look closely at the educational process. This is a task that is not manageable here and would be quite far afield from what can be gleaned from *Givhan*. There is also the independent and equally difficult question whether the recognition of such a distinct institutional right can be found in the First Amendment and, also, whether its recognition would be

[123] Two additional cases are helpful. In Healy v. James, 408 U.S. 169, 180–81 (1972), it was suggested that the classroom was a marketplace of ideas. And in Regents of the University of California v. Bakke, 438 U.S. 265 (1978), Mr. Justice Powell talked of academic freedom: "Academic freedom, though not a specifically enumerated constitutional right, long has been viewed as a special concern of the First Amendment. The freedom of a university to make its own judgments as to education includes the selection of its student body." 438 U.S. at 312. Since the selection of students is not speech, Mr. Justice Powell's opinion goes a long way toward recognizing that academic freedom protects activities not otherwise protected by the concept of free speech.

[124] In addition to the authorities cited at note 118 *supra*, see Goldstein, *The Asserted Constitutional Right of Public School Teachers to Determine What They Teach*, 124 U. Pa. L. Rev. 1293 (1976); Miller, *Teachers' Freedom of Expression within the Classroom: A Search for Standards*, 8 Ga. L. Rev. 837 (1974); Nahmod, *Controversy in the Classroom: The High School Teacher and Freedom of Expression*, 39 Geo. Wash. L. Rev. 1032 (1971); Note, *Academic Freedom in the Public Schools: The Right to Teach*, 48 N.Y.U.L. Rev. 1176 (1973).

[125] 316 F. Supp. 352 (M.D. Ala. 1970). See also Keefe v. Geanakos, 418 F.2d 359 (1st Cir. 1969); Mailloux v. Kiley, 323 F. Supp. 1387 (D. Mass. 1971), *aff'd*, 448 F.2d 1242 (1st Cir. 1971).

[126] 393 U.S. 503 (1969).

[127] *Id*. at 506.

consistent with the Court's rejection of independent institutional rights for the organized press.[128] But if there is such an independent concept of academic freedom, a freedom to teach or to choose class materials, it arguably varies with the type and level of education involved.[129] For central to the recognition of classroom academic freedom is acceptance of the classroom as more of a public forum than a state-controlled agency for indoctrination. It is not at all unreasonable to suggest that the classroom shifts from indoctrinative to exploratory with the increasing age and sophistication of the students.

But *Givhan* is not a classroom case. It must not be read to suggest that Bessie Givhan's complaints are to be tolerated if she uses the classroom rather than the principal's office as the forum for her grievances. *Givhan* is the intermediate case, dealing with speech out of the classroom but in the school and on school time.[130] In holding that this was indeed a forum for speech activities, the Court goes at least part of the way toward recognizing an independent concept of academic freedom. Albeit obliquely, it suggests as well that the internal critic has a constitutionally protected position.

Various theories might support these conclusions. First, there is the very real problem in government that critics may be singled out for especially unfavorable treatment. In protecting the internal critic, the gadfly, the Court partially commits itself to a philosophy of workplace democracy. Harmony, uniformity, and obedience may not be the only important values in public employment. The marketplace of ideas is moved from the public forum into the working environment and the employment relationship. This is again quite far from most of the commonly accepted core principles of freedom of speech. But as a question of policy there is much to commend such a theory. If our assumptions about the value of criticism and the value of free interchange of ideas are justified, then those assumptions apply with special force to those, such as em-

---

[128] See notes 42 and 82 *supra*.

[129] *Compare Developments in the Law—Academic Freedom*, 81 Harv. L. Rev. 1045, 1053 (1968); Schauer, note 118 *supra;* and Goldstein, note 124 *supra, with* Note, note 124 *supra, and Le Clerscq, The Monkey Laws and the Public Schools: A Second Consumption*, 27 Vand. L. Rev. 209, 235 (1974).

[130] For such intermediate cases, see, *e.g.*, Clark v. Holmes, 474 F.2d 928 (7th Cir. 1972); Whitsel v. Southeast Local School District, 484 F.2d 1222 (6th Cir. 1973).

ployees, who have a particular expertise and a particular concern with the matters at hand. Reference to this special expertise is found in *Pickering* as well.[131] But let there be no mistake. The constitutionalization of the workplace makes it clear, as the procedural due process cases had done earlier, that public employment and private employment are becoming increasingly dissimilar.

This constitutionalized openness may inure to the benefit of the public in several ways. Not only may it be said that the public benefits when institutions are structured on more open lines, but the public may also benefit more directly when public employees can inform the electorate about the business of their agencies without necessarily proceeding through cumbersome and hierarchical grievance structures. By strongly intimating in *Givhan* that the public employee has free speech rights *qua* public employee, the Court takes the first step toward constitutional protection for the "whistle-blower," an increasingly common phenomenon in American public life.[132]

Finally, *Givhan* may say something special about schools. Possibly much of the foregoing applies only or with stronger force in schools, rather than in public employment generally. When Dwight Eisenhower was president of Columbia University, he addressed the faculty as "employees of the university," only to be interrupted by a senior faculty member who observed that "We are not *employees* of this university. We *are* this university."[133] This may strike a responsive chord in those who have witnessed the increasing bureaucracy and hierarchical structure of the American university. The extent to which openness and internal criticism are as valuable in primary and secondary schools as they are in the university is very possibly a quite different matter. The Court, however, may be speaking in more general terms. One may infer from *Givhan* the view that schools are to a degree special, that traditional organization charts and hierarchical structures may be inconsistent with the

---

[131] 391 U.S. at 571–72.

[132] See Comment, *Government Employee Disclosures of Agency Wrongdoing: Protecting the Right to Blow the Whistle*, 42 U. CHI. L. REV. 530 (1975); *The Whistleblowers, a Report on Federal Employees Who Disclose Acts of Governmental Waste, Abuse, and Corruption*, prepared for Senate Committee on Governmental Affairs, 98th Cong., 2d Sess. (Feb. 1978); GOVERNMENT ACCOUNTABILITY PROJECT, A WHISTLEBLOWER'S GUIDE TO THE FEDERAL BUREAUCRACY (1977).

[133] ADAMS, THE ACADEMIC TRIBES 15 (1976).

openness that some consider inherent in the processes of education and academic inquiry. This is undoubtedly quite far afield from what is directly found in the opinion in *Givhan*. Yet if these observations about the implications of *Givhan* are correct, the Court may have taken the first step toward recognizing academic freedom as a principle and not a platitude. But, like the issue of public speech and private speech, the Court tells us little and leaves much for speculation.

IV. Conclusion

On closer analysis, the opinion in *Givhan*, in rejecting the distinction between public speech and private speech, and in further extending free speech principles within the walls of the schoolhouse, has much to commend it. But the implications of *Givhan* are considerable, and the opinion raises more questions than it answers. The opinion is, thus, both too clear and too obscure. A reading of the opinion may lead lower courts to ignore the extent to which the public-private distinction remains relevant in applying certain accepted justifications for restricting speech. In this sense the words say too much. On the other hand, a reading of *Givhan* may lead lower courts to underestimate its effect on the issue of academic freedom and on the issue of freedom of speech in the academic setting. On both the issue of private speech and the issue of speech in the schools much more remains to be said. We can do little more than guess as to the extent to which the Court will follow the implications of *Givhan*. It is a pity that the brevity of the opinion leaves so much to speculation.

HENRY J. BOURGUIGNON

THE SECOND MR. JUSTICE HARLAN: HIS PRINCIPLES OF JUDICIAL DECISION MAKING

The aim of this article is to reconstruct the frame of reference for judicial decision making utilized by one particularly articulate Justice of the Supreme Court, the second Mr. Justice Harlan. Like almost all who reached his judicial eminence, he never published in any one place an expression of his personal judicial philosophy. Nevertheless, he was deeply committed to legal norms or principles which he believed should guide a judge in rendering decisions. These basic, firmly held convictions, these judicial principles, must be gleaned from his many opinions and other published writings.[1] Harlan certainly rejected the Realist contention that judges are not bound by any legal rules or principles.[2] Although he was a firm believer in judicial restraint, he felt that his decisions were con-

Henry J. Bourguignon is Professor of Law, University of Toledo College of Law.

[1] For a collection of some of Harlan's opinions and others writings, see HARLAN, THE EVOLUTION OF A JUDICIAL PHILOSOPHY (Shapiro, ed. 1969).

[2] See Llewellyn, *A Realistic Jurisprudence—the Next Step*, 30 COLUM. L. REV. 431, 464 (1930); LLEWELLYN, THE BRAMBLE BUSH 12 (1930); FRANK, LAW AND THE MODERN MIND 102–06, 130 (1930). For a general discussion of legal realism, see Purcell, *American Jurisprudence between the Wars: Legal Realism and the Crisis of Democratic Theory*, 75 AM. HIST. REV. 424 (1969); White, *From Sociological Jurisprudence to Realism*, 58 VA. L. REV. 999 (1972). For some raised eyebrows about the realist position, see Hart, *American Jurisprudence through English Eyes: The Nightmare and the Noble Dream*, 11 GA. L. REV. 969, 972–78 (1977).

trolled by legal principles, rather than that his acts of judgment were limited only by a personal sense of self-restraint. For him, certain objective legal norms limited the scope of his judicial decision making.

In his seventeen years on the Supreme Court, Harlan wrote, in addition to 168 opinions for the Court, 296 dissenting opinions and 149 concurring opinions. For seven Terms, he wrote more dissenting opinions than any other Justice. Of course, no attempt can be made to state all the principles expressed in these many opinions. My major concern here will be to delineate the essential contours of Harlan's judicial philosophy, the canons which he said led him to his legal conclusions. Necessarily, any Justice who has written so large a number of opinions will leave behind the problem of reconciling the rationales for all of them and for establishing the hierarchy among the principles that purported to guide him. Few, if any, of the cases that come before the Court do not invoke more than one value. It is the conflict among competing values that gives rise to most of the cases that the Court takes for adjudication. What is distinctive about Harlan's opinions is the weight that he attributed to each principle and the intensity with which he insisted on its application.

I. Respect for Legitimate State Interests

Justice Harlan clearly believed that, barring clear constitutional violation, the States should be allowed to solve their own problems, determine their own policies, govern their own court systems, and establish their own criminal justice procedures. He placed this principle of federalism at the peak of his hierarchy of constitutional values.[3] In his dissent in *Chapman v. California*, he stated:[4]

> For one who believes that among the constitutional values which contribute to the preservation of our free society none ranks higher than the principles of federalism, and that this Court's responsibility for keeping such principles intact is no less than its responsibility for maintaining particular constitutional rights, the doctrine announced today is a most disturbing one.

[3] For an evaluation of Harlan's commitment to federalism, see Wilkinson, *Justice John M. Harlan and the Values of Federalism*, 57 Va. L. Rev. 1185 (1971).

[4] 386 U.S. 18, 57 (1967).

Harlan found the genius of the federal system in the achievement of national solidarity and unparalleled strength while keeping governmental authority workably diffused.[5] The crucial benefit derived from the decentralization is personal liberty. Harlan revealed his classical view of dual federalism when he said:[6]

> Our federal system, though born of the necessity of achieving union, has proved to be a bulwark of freedom as well. We are accustomed to speak of the Bill of Rights and the Fourteenth Amendment as the principal guarantees of personal liberty. Yet it would surely be shallow not to recognize that the structure of our political system accounts no less for the free society we have. Indeed, it was upon the structure of government that the founders primarily focused in writing the Constitution. Out of bitter experience they were suspicious of every form of all-powerful central authority and they sought to assure that such a government would never exist in this country by structuring the federal establishment so as to diffuse power between the executive, legislative, and judicial branches. The diffusion of power between federal and state authority serves the same ends and takes on added significance as the size of the federal bureaucracy continues to grow.

When he thought the Court had violated the federalism principle, Harlan objected that its action was "unnecessary, undesirable, and constitutionally all wrong," since it manifested the Court's "peculiar insensitivity to the need for seeking an appropriate constitutional balance between federal and state authority."[7] He warned the Court that upsetting the constitutional balance between the state and the national government ran grave risks. "A constitutional democracy which in order to cope with seeming needs of the moment is willing to temporize with its basic distribution and limitation of governmental powers will sooner or later find itself in trouble."[8] A viola-

---

[5] Harlan, *Dedicatory Address*, 111 U. PA. L. REV. 920, 922 (1963).

[6] Harlan, *Thoughts at a Dedication: Keeping the Judicial Function in Balance*, 49 A.B.A.J. 943–44 (1963). In his dissent in Duncan v. Louisiana, 391 U.S. 145, 173 (1968), Harlan stated that the Framers "were wont to believe . . . that the security of liberty in America rested primarily upon the dispersion of governmental power across a federal system." For this proposition he relied on Madison's *Federalist No. 51*. For a demonstration of the wide variety of meanings given the term federalism in our history, see Scheiber, *American Federalism and the Diffusion of Power: Historical and Contemporary Perspectives*, 9 U. TOL. L. REV. 619 (1978).

[7] United Mine Workers v. Illinois Bar Ass'n, 389 U.S. 217, 233–34 (1967) (dissenting).

[8] Carrington v. Rash, 380 U.S. 89, 99 (1965) (dissenting).

tion of the federalism principle was "an unacceptable intrusion into a matter of state concern."[9]

An obvious corollary of the principle of federalism is that federal courts have a "a duty to respect state legislation."[10] "[T]he Court must give the widest deference to legislative judgments that concern the character and urgency of the problems with which the State is confronted."[11] The state legislature is empowered to establish the norms and plans of action for the State. As long as the legislature does not venture beyond the limits set by the Constitution, its policy determinations should not be disturbed by the Supreme Court.

Diversity is bound, of course, to result from allowing each state legislature freedom to define its own public policy. For Harlan there was a significant, positive value in this diversity. He objected vigorously when a Supreme Court decision, in his view, placed the States in a constitutional straitjacket.[12] "The States have been put in a federal mold with respect to this aspect of criminal law enforcement, thus depriving the country of the opportunity to observe the effects of different procedures in similar settings."[13] In an apportionment case in which the Court applied the one-person, one-vote principle to the election of the trustees of a consolidated junior college district, Harlan again protested, "The facts of this case afford a clear indication of the extent to which reasonable state objectives are to be sacrificed on the altar of numerical equality."[14]

Even where Harlan thought the particular state statute was unwise or outmoded, he objected when the Supreme Court held it unconstitutional:[15]

> Property and poll-tax qualifications, very simply, are not in accord with current egalitarian notions of how a modern

[9] Konigsberg v. State Bar of California, 353 U.S. 252, 312 (1957) (dissenting).

[10] NAACP v. Button, 371 U.S. 415, 469 (1963).

[11] In re Gault, 387 U.S. 1, 70 (1967) (concurring and dissenting).

[12] Ker v. California, 374 U.S. 23, 45 (1963).

[13] Coolidge v. New Hampshire, 403 U.S. 443, 490 (1971) (concurring). This opinion, one of the last he wrote, reveals his faithful adherence to the principle of federalism to the end of his judicial career.

[14] Hadley v. Junior College District, 397 U.S. 50, 63 (1970) (dissenting).

[15] Harper v. Virginia Bd. of Elections, 383 U.S. 663, 686 (1966) (dissenting); see also Griffin v. Illinois, 351 U.S. 12, 29 (1956) (dissenting).

> democracy should be organized. It is of course entirely fitting that legislatures should modify the law to reflect such changes in popular attitudes. However, it is all wrong, in my view, for the Court to adopt the political doctrines popularly accepted at a particular moment of our history and to declare all others to be irrational and invidious, barring them from the range of choice by reasonably minded people acting through the political process.

The state legislatures should be left free to experiment with different solutions to problems which faced many States. All the States then could benefit by discovering the success or failure of the experiment in one State. In *Duncan v. Louisiana*, Harlan wrote:[16]

> We have before us, therefore, an almost perfect example of a situation in which the celebrated dictum of Mr. Justice Brandeis should be invoked. It is, he said, "one of the happy incidents of the federal system that a single courageous State may, if its citizens choose, serve as a laboratory. . . ." *New State Ice Co.* v. *Liebmann*, 285 U.S. 262, 280, 311 (dissenting opinion). This Court, other courts, and the political process are available to correct any experiments in criminal procedure that prove fundamentally unfair to defendants. That is not what is being done today: instead, and quite without reason, the Court has chosen to impose upon every State one means of trying criminal cases; it is a good means, but it is not the only fair means, and it is not demonstrably better than the alternatives States might devise.

Harlan insisted on the principle of federalism most frequently in the area of criminal justice. During the years when the Supreme Court was imposing broader constitutional standards on the States'

[16] 391 U.S. 145, 193 (1968) (dissenting). Harlan had expressed the same idea in Roth v. United States, 354 U.S. 476, 505 (1957) (concurring and dissenting): "It has often been said that one of the great strengths of our federal system is that we have, in the forty-eight States, forty-eight experimental social laboratories. 'State statutory law reflects predominantly this capacity of a legislature to introduce novel techniques of social control. The federal system has the immense advantage of providing forty-eight separate centers for such experimentation.' Different States will have different attitudes toward the same work of literature. The same book which is freely read in one State might be classed as obscene in another. And it seems to me that no overwhelming danger to our freedom to experiment and to gratify our tastes in literature is likely to result from the suppression of a borderline book in one of the States, so long as there is no uniform nation-wide suppression of the book, and so long as other States are free to experiment with the same or bolder books." (The inner quotation is from Hart, *The Relations between State and Federal Law*, 54 COLUM. L. REV. 489, 493 (1954).) See also Memoirs v. Massachusetts, 383 U.S. 413, 456 (1966) (dissenting); California v. Green, 399 U.S. 149, 172 (1970) (dissenting).

criminal procedures, Harlan repeatedly reminded the Court that "A state criminal conviction comes to us as the complete product of a sovereign judicial system."[17] He urged the Court not to seek procedural symmetry and administrative convenience at the price of disfiguring the boundaries between state and federal courts. Patience was called for by those who might like to see the States move faster in reforming their criminal justice systems.[18] Precisely because of the vast differences across the country, the Court simply did not know whether the cities and towns were prepared to cope with the new constitutional rules of criminal procedure, or whether these rules were necessary in each locality to protect fundamental liberties.[19]

Harlan derived the principle of federalism from the constitutional structure which divided governmental powers between state and federal governments. These principles were reinforced by other constitutional norms, the distinction between the Fourteenth Amendment (limitation on the States) and the Bill of Rights (limitation on the national government). Harlan insisted that the Bill of Rights should not become a limitation upon the States by wholesale or piecemeal incorporation into the Fourteenth Amendment. It did not trouble him that different standards would, consequently, be applied to federal government and state governments. The Bill of Rights restricted only federal action. Only the vague limitations of the Due Process Clause of the Fourteenth Amendment bound the States. Harlan stated his position in *Berger v. New York*:[20]

> The Court in recent years has more and more taken to itself sole responsibility for setting the pattern of criminal law enforcement throughout the country. Time-honored distinctions between the constitutional protections afforded against federal authority by the Bill of Rights and those provided against state action by the Fourteenth Amendment have been obliterated, thus increasingly subjecting state criminal law enforcement policies to oversight by this Court.

---

[17] Mapp v. Ohio, 367 U.S. 643, 682 (1961) (dissenting).

[18] *Id.* at 680–82.

[19] Chimel v. California, 395 U.S. 752, 769 (1969) (concurring).

[20] 388 U.S. 41, 89 (1967) (dissenting). Harlan's two-tiered approach was also applied in obscenity cases. See, *e.g., Roth*, note 16 *supra;* Interstate Circuit v. Dallas, 390 U.S. 676, 707 (1968) (concurring and dissenting).

The fact that Harlan read the Constitution to impose different standards on the States from those which applied to the national government intensified his views on the principle of federalism. Any incongruity in applying different standards were at the heart of the federal system. "The powers and responsibilities of the State and Federal Governments are not congruent, and under the Constitution they are not intended to be."[21]

Federalism provided the fundamental premise from which Harlan argued against undue Supreme Court interference with the States in the administration of their criminal justice systems:[22]

> It should not be forgotten that in this country citizens must look almost exclusively to the States for protection against most crimes. The States are charged with responsibility for marking the area of criminal conduct, discovering and investigating such conduct when it occurs, and preventing its recurrence. . . . Limitations on the States' exercise of their responsibility to prevent criminal conduct should be imposed only where it is demonstrable that their own adjustment of the competing interests infringes rights fundamental to decent society.

The Supreme Court does not possess "some sort of supervisory power over state courts"; the members of the Court "are not free to disturb a state conviction simply for reasons that might be permissible were we sitting on the state court of last resort."[23]

Harlan's principle of federalism was central to his discussions of the adequate and independent state ground doctrine. The Supreme Court lacks jurisdiction to review federal questions involved in a case, if the state judgment rested on state law broad enough to provide a foundation for the judgment independent of any federal ground. In the first opinion Harlan wrote as a Supreme Court Justice, he applied this adequate nonfederal ground doctrine. He wrote for the majority in dismissing a writ of certiorari as improvidently granted, because the New York Court of Appeals was

---

[21] Griffin v. California, 380 U.S. 609, 616 (1965) (concurring).

[22] Jackson v. Denno, 378 U.S. 368, 439 (1964) (dissenting); see also Griffin v. Illinois, 351 U.S. 12, 29 (1956) (dissenting); Fahy v. Connecticut, 375 U.S. 85, 92 (1963) (dissenting); Malloy v. Hogan, 378 U.S. 1, 14 (1964) (dissenting); Spencer v. Texas, 385 U.S. 554 (1962).

[23] Giles v. Maryland, 386 U.S. 66, 113, 119 (1967) (dissenting).

justified, under state procedures, in refusing to pass upon a federal constitutional issue not properly pleaded.[24]

His position on the adequate state ground doctrine was most fully expressed in *Fay v. Noia*.[25] The majority had held that a federal court could grant Noia habeas corpus relief although he had never appealed his conviction. The state procedural ground, the failure to appeal, only barred the Supreme Court's revision of the state court judgment on direct review, the Court said. It did not prevent federal courts from collateral habeas corpus review of the legality of the prisoner's detention.[26]

In *Noia*, Harlan strongly dissented; he found the majority opinion "one of the most disquieting that the Court has rendered in a long time."[27] Noia's detention by New York violated no federal right. It was "pursuant to a conviction whose validity rests upon an adequate and independent state ground which the federal courts are required to respect."[28] Harlan concluded that on direct review it is a "rule . . . of constitutional dimensions going to the heart of the division of judicial powers in a federal system."[29] If the Supreme Court were to ignore the adequate state ground doctrine on direct review, it would "assume full control over a State's procedures for the administration of its own criminal justice. This is and must be beyond [its] power if the federal system is to exist in substance as well as form."[30] Harlan found it just as clearly an encroachment of state authority for the Court to allow a federal court to grant a writ of habeas corpus where an adequate state ground for disposition of the case existed.[31]

Two years after *Noia*, Harlan again invoked the principle of federalism when he concluded the Court was expanding *Noia* to reach a case on direct review. In *Henry v. Mississippi*[32] Harlan objected to the Court's review of a state court conviction when review should have been barred by the State's rule requiring contemporaneous objection to the introduction of evidence.[33] He con-

---

[24] Ellis v. Dixon, 349 U.S. 458 (1955). See also Harlan's opinion for the Court in Department of Mental Hygiene v. Kirchner, 380 U.S. 194 (1965).

[25] 372 U.S. 391 (1963).

[26] *Id.* at 429–34.

[27] *Id.* at 448.

[28] *Ibid.*

[29] *Id.* at 464.

[30] *Id.* at 466.

[31] *Id.* at 469.

[32] 379 U.S. 443 (1965).

[33] *Id.* at 457.

cluded that "to all who believe the federal system as we have known it to be a priceless aspect of our Constitutionalism, the spectre implicit in today's decision will be no less disturbing than what the Court has already done in *Fay* v. *Noia*."[34] An adequate state procedural ground prevented the Supreme Court from reviewing a state court judgment, unless the procedural rule was fundamentally unfair or was applied by the state court with a "purpose to defeat federal constitutional rights."[35] To ignore this doctrine, Harlan said, "open[ed] the door to further excursions by the federal judiciary into state judicial domains."[36]

Harlan found other forms of federal court incursions into state judicial domains equally unacceptable, equally violative of the principle of federalism. A federal court should not be allowed to enjoin a federal agent from testifying and providing evidence for a state criminal prosecution, even though the agent's evidence was obtained in an illegal search.[37] Such a holding departed "from the concepts which have hitherto been considered to govern state and federal relationships in this area."[38] Nor should a federal court enjoin a state official from giving evidence in pending state criminal proceedings, where his testimony and evidence were derived from an illegal search and questioning conducted by a federal official.[39] Harlan found such interference by a federal court with a state proceeding undermined the principle of federalism. "Such direct intrusion in state processes does not comport with proper federal-state relationships."[40]

The abstention doctrine also has its roots in the proper respect due a state court's interpretation of its own law. It is hardly surprising, therefore, that Harlan frequently insisted on the application of the doctrine. The abstention doctrine required federal courts to decline

---

[34] *Id.* at 465.

[35] Chapman v. California, 386 U.S. 18, 56 (1967) (dissenting).

[36] *Id.* at 57. See also Sullivan v. Little Hunting Park, 396 U.S. 229, 241 (1969) (dissenting), where Harlan found no bar to Supreme Court review because of an unanticipated, novel application of a state procedural rule.

[37] Rea v. United States, 350 U.S. 214, 218 (1956) (dissenting).

[38] *Id.* at 218.

[39] Cleary v. Bolger, 371 U.S. 392 (1963); see also Atlantic Coast Line R. Co. v. Brotherhood of Locomotive Engineers, 398 U.S. 281, 297 (1970) (concurring).

[40] 371 U.S. at 401.

to pass upon the constitutionality of state statutes "fairly open to interpretation until the state courts have been afforded a reasonable opportunity to pass upon them."[41] Abstention "is aimed at the avoidance of unnecessary interference by the federal courts with proper and validly administered state concerns, a course so essential to the balanced working of our federal system."[42] When the Supreme Court was assessing the constitutionality of a state statute, "the construction given the statute by the State's courts is conclusive of its scope and meaning. . . . This principle is ultimately a consequence of the differences in function of the state and federal judicial systems."[43] Should there be any doubt about the correct construction of a state statute, the case should be returned to the state court for clarification.[44]

Harlan amplified his discussion of the federalism basis for the abstention doctrine in *Dombrowski v. Pfister*.[45] The majority held that the district court had erred in abstaining. The Court argued that abstention is inappropriate where a state statute regulating speech is properly attacked as unconstitutional on its face. Abstention, the Court noted, could well result in delay and futility for efforts to assert First Amendment rights. Harlan, in dissent, again showed the depth of his conviction that a state court should have the first say in interpreting its own laws:[46]

> The basic holding in this case marks a significant departure from a wise procedural principle designed to spare our federal system from premature federal judicial interference with state statutes or proceedings challenged on federal constitutional grounds. This decision abolishes the doctrine of federal judicial abstention in all suits attacking state criminal statutes for vagueness on First Amendment grounds. As one who considers that it is a prime responsibility of this Court to maintain federal-state court relationships in good working order, I cannot subscribe to a holding which displays such insensitivity to the legitimate demands of those relationships under our federal system. I see no such incompatibility between the absten-

[41] Harrison v. NAACP, 360 U.S. 167, 176 (1959).

[42] *Ibid*. Harlan would also have ordered abstention in Chicago v. Atchison, Topeka & S.F. R. Co., 357 U.S. 77, 89 (1958) (dissenting).

[43] Berger v. New York, 388 U.S. 41, 91 (1967) (dissenting).

[44] Garner v. Louisiana, 368 U.S. 157, 189 (1961) (concurring).

[45] 380 U.S. 479 (1965).

[46] *Id*. at 498.

> tion doctrine and the full vindication of constitutionally protected rights as the Court finds to exist in cases of this kind.

The underlying premise of the Court's position, Harlan asserted, was the fear that state courts would be less prone than federal courts to vindicate federal constitutional rights promptly and effectively. "We should not assume that [state] courts would not be equally diligent in construing the statutes here in question in accordance with the relevant decisions of this Court."[47]

For Harlan, state courts, state administrators, state legislators have their own proper roles to play in government. Federal courts should be sensitive to these roles and should not deprive state officials of necessary breathing room to make their own decisions, to establish their own policies, and even to make their own mistakes. However, there were obvious limits to Harlan's respect for state autonomy. In exploring other canons of his philosophy of judicial decision making, we shall see that he often implicitly had to balance these principles against each other. Basic as federalism was to his philosophy, it did not always prevail in this balancing process.

Two good examples of cases where federalism principles did not prevail are *Street v. New York*[48] and *Cohen v. California*.[49] In both cases Harlan wrote for the majority. In both, his vote was essential to constitute a majority since the Court split five to four. In both, Harlan agreed that a state statute had been unconstitutionally applied. Both involved free expression values which had to be balanced against the legitimate state interests involved.

Street had been prosecuted under a New York statute making it a misdemeanor publicly to mutilate "or defy, . . . or cast contempt upon [any flag of the United States], either by words or act."[50] Street had been convicted for publicly burning an American flag. Harlan held that Street's conviction was unconstitutional, since it "may have rested on a form of expression, however distasteful, which the Constitution tolerates and protects."[51] The dissenters ac-

[47] *Id.* at 499. Abstention should not be required where there is no room for statutory construction that would obviate the need for a decision on the constitutional issue. Zwickler v. Koota, 389 U.S. 241, 255 (1967) (concurring); United Pipe Line Gas Co. v. Ideal Cement Co., 369 U.S. 134, 140 (1962) (dissenting).

[48] 394 U.S. 576 (1969).

[49] 403 U.S. 15 (1971).

[50] 394 U.S. at 576 and n.1.

[51] *Id.* at 594.

cused Harlan of misreading the facts and of overriding legitimate state interests.[52]

Similarly in *Cohen*, Harlan cast the decisive vote to hold that the California statute had been unconstitutionally applied. Cohen had been convicted for disturbing the peace. He had appeared in a county courthouse wearing a jacket bearing the words "Fuck the draft." Harlan concluded that "[a]bsent a more particularized and compelling reason for its actions, the State may not, consistently with the First and Fourteenth Amendments, make the simple public display here involved of this single four-letter expletive a criminal offense."[53] The four dissenters objected that Harlan had ignored the most recent interpretation of the statute by the California Supreme Court.[54] Again Harlan thought that factors other than federalism tipped the balance. There were other cases in which Harlan might have found the federalism interests paramount but did not.[55]

Justice Harlan adhered strongly to his belief in the necessity for allowing the States to function as autonomous, self-governing entities, unless some other more weighty principles compelled him to decide against a State's action in a particular case. Mere pragmatic considerations, such as achieving needed political reforms promptly, did not convince Harlan that the Court should act to make reforms possible where the States had failed to act. The Constitution as interpreted by the Court, Harlan thought, should not be made the cutting edge of reform even though other avenues for change might be foreclosed. In a tribute to Justice Robert H. Jackson, Harlan commented:[56]

> [T]he important thing, I think, is not so much whether the particular changes themselves are good or bad as it is the fundamental shift such changes evince in the current judicial approach to federal-state relationships. This shift must be recog-

---

[52] *Id.* at 594 (Warren dissenting); *id.* at 609 (Black dissenting); *id.* at 610 (White dissenting); *id.* at 615 (Fortas dissenting).

[53] 403 U.S. at 26.

[54] 403 U.S. at 27 (Blackmun, J., dissenting, joined by Justices Burger, Black, and White).

[55] *E.g.*, NAACP v. Alabama, 357 U.S. 449 (1958); NAACP v. Alabama, 377 U.S. 288 (1964); Lane v. Brown, 372 U.S. 477 (1963) (concurring); Poe v. Ullman, 367 U.S. 497, 522 (1961) (dissenting); In re Gault, 387 U.S. 1, 65 (1967) (concurring and dissenting); Epperson v. Arkansas, 393 U.S. 97, 114 (1968) (concurring).

[56] Harlan, *Introduction, Robert H. Jackson's Influence on Federal State Relationships*, 23 RECORD 7, 9–10 (1968).

> nized as involving something more than mere differences among judges as to where the line should be drawn between state and federal authority in particular cases arising under the Fourteenth Amendment. It reflects, I believe, at bottom a distrust in the capabilities of the federal system to meet the needs of American society in these fast-moving times, and a readiness on the part of the federal judiciary to spearhead reform without circumspect regard for constitutional limitations upon the manner of its accomplishment. To those who see our free society as dependent primarily upon a broadening of the constitutional protections afforded to the individual, these developments are no doubt considered to be healthy. To those who regard the federal system itself as one of the mainsprings of our political liberties, this increasing erosion of state authority cannot but be viewed with apprehension. There can be little doubt, I venture to say, that were Mr. Justice Jackson still here, he would be found among the latter.

There can be no doubt that he would have been joined by Harlan in this attitude.

II. Deference to Coordinate Branches of Government

Justice Harlan also insisted that the national judiciary should maintain proper respect for the other branches of the national government. Though the question seldom arose, Harlan followed the traditional doctrine of avoiding conflict with or possible embarrassment of the President in his handling of foreign affairs.[57] Similarly, courts should not interfere with the President's discretionary power where his decisions involved "elements not susceptible of ordinary judicial proof nor within the general range of judicial experience."[58]

More frequently Harlan had occasion to discuss the proper relationship between the national judiciary and Congress. Precisely "because of the Court's inherent incapacity to deal with the problem in the comprehensive and integrated manner which would doubtless characterize [Congress's] legislative treatment . . . [the Court] should heed the limitation on [its] own capacity and authority."[59] The Court traditionally had declared that any congressional statute

[57] Banco Nacional de Cuba v. Sabbatino, 376 U.S. 398 (1964).

[58] United Steelworkers v. United States, 361 U.S. 39, 58 (1959) (concurring with Frankfurter in separate opinion).

[59] Mitchell v. Trawler Racer, Inc., 362 U.S. 539, 572–73 (1960) (dissenting).

comes before it with a presumption of constitutionality. In *Flemming v. Nestor*,[60] however, Harlan bent over backward to avoid finding a constitutional objection to a provision of the Social Security Act. He declared that where Congress withheld a noncontractual benefit under the social security program, "we must recognize that the Due Process Clause can be thought to interpose a bar only if the statute manifests a patently arbitrary classification, utterly lacking in rational justification."[61] Even though the individual deprived of the benefits could point to strong suggestions of a punitive purpose of Congress, Harlan insisted that only the clearest proof of such purpose would suffice as a reason for holding the Act unconstitutional. "Judicial inquiries into Congressional motives are at best a hazardous matter, and when that inquiry seeks to go behind objective manifestations it becomes a dubious affair indeed."[62]

Harlan at times found that Congress had gone beyond its constitutional limits. His views on congressional authority come out quite clearly in the line of cases dealing with the power of Congress to authorize military courts to try civilian dependents overseas. The cases involved the trial for murder of two wives who killed their servicemen spouses. Under pressure of the closing days of the Term, Harlan voted, initially, with the majority to uphold congressional authority to establish military courts outside the United States to try civilian dependents for capital offenses.[63] Harlan rethought his position over the summer recess and voted for rehearing. The murder convictions of the military wives were then overturned, with Harlan concurring separately.[64] He concluded that Congress did have the power to establish courts-martial and that these courts could try civilian dependents abroad, but not in capital cases. Contrary to the plurality opinion of Justice Black, Harlan argued that congressional power to make laws for the regulation of the military should be amplified by the Necessary and Proper Clause. "Subjection of civilian dependents overseas to court-martial jurisdiction can in no wise be deemed unrelated to the power of Congress to make all necessary and proper laws to insure the effective

[60] 363 U.S. 603 (1960). [61] *Id.* at 611. [62] *Id.* at 617.

[63] Kinsella v. Krueger, 361 U.S. 470 (1956); Reid v. Covert, 361 U.S. 487 (1956). Harlan discussed the unusual sequence of events in his dissenting opinion in McElroy v. United States, 361 U.S. 281 (1960). Harlan's dissent is at 361 U.S. at 249.

[64] Reid v. Covert, 354 U.S. 1 (1957).

governance of our overseas land and naval forces."[65] Harlan, therefore, gave a broad interpretation to Congress's legislative powers. He ultimately concluded, however, that other provisions of the Constitution imposed limits on this congressional power. For capital cases, and only for such cases, he was "ready to say that Congress' power to provide for trial by court-martial of civilian dependents overseas is limited by Article III and the Fifth and Sixth Amendments."[66]

When the Court confronted cases involving overseas military trials for civilian dependents accused of noncapital offenses, Harlan reiterated his position that Congress had the power to authorize such trials.[67] He required only a showing of a rational, appropriate basis to uphold the congressional exercise of its power. He expressed his fundamental conviction in assuring that Congress and the Supreme Court each function without interference by the other in its own sphere:[68]

> I think it unfortunate that this Court should have found the Constitution lacking in enabling Congress to cope effectively with matters which are so intertwined with broader problems that have been engendered by present disturbed world conditions. Those problems are fraught with many factors that this Court is ill-equipped to assess, and involve important national concerns into which we should be reluctant to enter except under the clearest sort of constitutional compulsion. That such compulsion is lacking here has been amply demonstrated by the chequered history of the past cases of this kind in the Court.

When Justice Harlan had an opportunity to write a word of praise for his former colleague, Justice Frankfurter, he described the characteristics which he thought made Frankfurter great. One trait Harlan observed was Frankfurter's "scrupulous observance of the boundaries between the executive, legislative, and judicial branches of the government."[69] Harlan's own deep regard for the principle of separation of powers derived from his conviction that the political

---

[65] *Id.* at 73.

[66] *Id.* at 76.

[67] Kinsella v. Singleton, 361 U.S. 234, 249 (1960).

[68] *Id.* at 258. See O'Callahan v. Parker, 395 U.S. 258, 274 (1969), where Harlan, in dissent, objected to the Court's holding that servicemen could not be tried by court-martial for crimes not connected with military service or on military bases.

[69] Harlan, *The Frankfurter Imprint as Seen by a Colleague*, 76 Harv. L. Rev. 1, 2 (1962).

process is more likely to breed better solutions to society's problems than judicial fiat. Faithful to the Frankfurter tradition, Harlan voiced his opposition to the view that the Supreme Court should exercise its power of review of Acts of Congress to abrogate unwise, harsh, or out-of-date legislation. As Harlan saw it, the consequences of such a policy would be disastrous:[70]

> For in the end what would eventuate would be a substantial transfer of legislative power to the courts. A function more ill-suited to judges can hardly be imagined, situated as they are, and should be, aloof from the political arena and beholden to no one for their conscientious conduct. Such a course would also denigrate the legislative process, since it would tend to relieve legislators from having to account to the electorate. The outcome would inevitably be a lessening, on the one hand, of judicial independence and, on the other, of legislative responsibility, thus polluting the blood stream of our system of government. We should be on guard against any such deliberate or unwitting folly.

Harlan acknowledged that the Constitution imposed limits on the authority of Congress. These constitutional limits, however, should not be manipulated by the Court to accomplish goals the Court in its wisdom thought desirable. The political process, functioning through Congress, should be allowed to explore all possibilities, consider alternatives, and finally impose solutions, limited only by the clear prohibitions of the Constitution. "For the establishment by this Court," Harlan wrote, "of a rigid constitutional rule in a field where Congress has attempted to strike a delicate balance between competing economic forces, and in circumstances where we cannot know how the controversy would be settled by Congress' chosen instrument, may also have a considerable disruptive effect."[71]

Harlan repeatedly demonstrated his respect for the proper sphere of Congress by the sensitive manner in which he considered congressional legislation. The Court should make every effort to grasp the meaning of a statute which Congress intended, to understand the law as Congress understood it. In *Welsh v. United States*, Harlan wrote:[72]

---

[70] Harlan, note 6 *supra*, at 944.

[71] Amalgamated Food Employees Union Local 590 v. Logan Valley Plaza, 391 U.S. 308, 337 (1968) (dissenting).

[72] 398 U.S. 333, 346–47 (1970) (concurring). The case involved the Court's

> It is Congress' will that must here be divined. In that endeavor it is one thing to give words a meaning not necessarily envisioned by Congress so as to adapt them to circumstances also uncontemplated by the legislature in order to achieve the legislative policy, . . . [citation omitted]; it is a wholly different matter to define words so as to change policy. The limits of this Court's mandate to stretch concededly elastic congressional language are fixed in all cases by the context of its usage and legislative history, if available, that are the best guides to congressional *purpose* and the lengths to which Congress enacted a policy.

When the majority used legislative history to arrive at a meaning of the statute Harlan could not accept, he analyzed the sources himself to show the inadequacy of the majority's interpretation. In *Jones v. Alfred H. Mayer Co.*,[73] the majority concluded that § 1 of the Civil Rights Act of 1866 prohibited private as well as governmental discrimination in the sale or rental of property. Harlan in dissent carefully studied the congressional debates to show that they "do not, as the Court would have it, overwhelmingly support the result reached by the Court, and in fact that a contrary conclusion may equally well be drawn."[74] After his analysis, he concluded that the legislative history, as well as the general historical context of the period, strongly suggested that the majority had misconstrued the intent of Congress:[75]

> The foregoing analysis of the language, structure, and legislative history of the 1866 Civil Rights Act shows, I believe, that the Court's thesis that the Act was meant to extend to purely private action is open to the most serious doubt, if in-

interpretation of the congressional requirement that conscientious objector status for selective service purposes was available only to individuals who "by reason of religious training and belief" opposed participation in war. Harlan, recanting his position in United States v. Seeger, 380 U.S. 163 (1965), concluded that the Court had exceeded proper bounds in interpreting the statute to avoid constitutional questions. He thought the Court should face the First Amendment issue. *Id.* at 354. For an analysis of Harlan's approach to this case, see Comment, *The Legitimacy of Civil Law Reasoning in the Common Law: Justice Harlan's Contribution*, 82 Yale L.J. 258 (1972).

[73] 392 U.S. 409 (1968).

[74] *Id.* at 454.

[75] *Id.* at 473. Professor Fairman's analysis of the Civil Rights Act of 1866 shows that Harlan came closer to the original intent than did the majority. See Fairman, Reconstruction and Reunion, 1864–88, VI History of the Supreme Court of the United States 1207–59 (1971). For a view that Harlan's position was in error, see Kohl, *Civil Rights Act of 1866, Its Hour Come Round at Last*, 55 Va. L. Rev. 272 (1969).

> deed it does not render that thesis wholly untenable. Another, albeit less tangible, consideration points in the same direction. Many of the legislators who took part in the congressional debate inevitably must have shared the individualistic ethic of their time, which emphasized personal freedom and embodied a distaste for governmental interference which was soon to culminate in the era of laissez-faire. It seems to me that most of these men would have regarded it as a great intrusion on individual liberty for the Government to take from a man the power to refuse for personal reasons to enter into a purely private transaction involving the disposition of property, albeit those personal reasons might reflect racial bias. It should be remembered that racial prejudice was not uncommon in 1866, even outside the South.

For Harlan, legislative history involved a serious endeavor to grasp the original meaning and purpose of the statute. He tried to avoid the typical law office form of historical research which starts from the conclusion and then rummages through the sources for all the data which support that conclusion.

By grasping the intent of Congress, Harlan could feel confident that the Court was appropriately implementing congressional policy determinations, rather than devising policy for itself. In *United States v. Sisson*,[76] he dealt in extended metaphor, quite unlike his usual style, on this fundamental function of legislative history. "Were we to throw overboard the ballast provided by the statute's language and legislative history, we would cast ourselves adrift, blind to the risks of collision with other policies that are the buoys marking the safely navigable zone of our jurisdiction."[77]

Utilizing a drastically different metaphor, Harlan observed in *Rosado v. Wyman*[78] that the background of the statute under consideration "reveals little except that we have before us a child born of the silent union of legislative compromise." In such a situation the Court could exercise broader discretion in interpreting statutory language:[79]

> Thus, Congress, as it frequently does, has voiced its wishes in muted strains and left it to the courts to discern the theme in the cacophony of political understanding. Our chief resources in this undertaking are the words of the statute and

[76] 399 U.S. 267 (1970).

[77] *Id.* at 299.

[78] 397 U.S. 397, 412 (1970).

[79] *Ibid.*

> those common-sense assumptions that must be made in determining direction without a compass.

In numerous other cases Harlan strove to pierce the veil of the statute's language, not to arrive at a meaning he considered wise or currently appropriate, but to approach as near as possible to the meaning Congress had intended to express.[80]

Of course, even the most thorough legislative history often leads only to the conclusion that Congress had never considered the particular question. This too Harlan understood and objected when the Court found clarity in a legislative record which he read as opaque. "We are thus left with a legislative history," he wrote, "which, on the precise point at issue, is essentially negative, which shows with fair conclusiveness only that Congress was not squarely faced with the problem these cases present."[81] In this case he preferred to have Congress face the issue itself rather than have the Court make the policy determination.

The constitutional protection of individual rights provided a limit on congressional power which Harlan thought must be respected.[82] When other basic constitutional principles intervened, Harlan also strenuously opposed deferring to the determination of Congress. In *Katzenbach v. Morgan*[83] the Court upheld the constitutionality of § 4(e) of the Voting Rights Act of 1965. That section prohibited the States from denying any person who had completed the sixth grade in a non-English-speaking school in Puerto Rico the right to vote in any election because of his inability to read or write English. The Court found the source of congressional authority in § 5 of the Fourteenth Amendment which grants Congress power to enforce, by appropriate legislation, the provisions of that Amendment.

---

[80] See DeSylva v. Ballentine, 351 U.S. 570 (1956); United States v. Mississippi Valley Generating Co., 364 U.S. 520, 567 (1961) (dissenting); Scales v. United States, 367 U.S. 203 (1961); Rusk v. Cort, 369 U.S. 367, 383 (1962) (dissenting); Sanders v. United States, 373 U.S. 1, 23 (1963) (dissenting); Pure Oil Co. v. Suarez, 384 U.S. 202 (1966); Tooahnippah v. Hickel, 397 U.S. 598, 611 (1970) (concurring); Chandler v. Judicial Council of the Tenth Circuit, 398 U.S. 74, 89 (1970) (concurring); Adickes v. Kress & Co., 398 U.S. 144 (1970); United States v. Vuitch, 402 U.S. 62, 81 (1971) (dissenting).

[81] National Woodwork Mfrs. Ass'n v. N.L.R.B., 386 U.S. 612, 649 (1967) (separate memorandum).

[82] See, *e.g.*, Marchetti v. United States, 390 U.S. 39 (1968).

[83] 384 U.S. 641 (1966).

Although Harlan had no quarrel with the purposes Congress sought to achieve, he was convinced that § 4(e) of the statute violated the principle of federalism. The separation of powers principle was also violated, here by congressional intrusion into the sphere reserved to the judiciary. Harlan in his dissent sought to protect the judicial power from encroachment by Congress. He argued that this statutory provision was not "appropriate remedial legislation to cure an established violation of a constitutional command,"[84] and thus not within Congress's power to enforce the provisions of the Fourteenth Amendment. It is the appropriate function of the judiciary to determine when the Fourteenth Amendment has been violated by the States. Congress, pursuant to § 5 of the Amendment, can legislate to cure such violations. But Congress cannot define the substantive meaning of the Amendment, as the majority's opinion would, in effect, allow. If Congress were permitted to assume this essentially judicial function, Harlan saw no reason why Congress could not enact statutes which would dilute the Equal Protection or Due Process Clause decisions of the Supreme Court. It is a judicial role, not a function of Congress, to determine whether or not there has been a denial by a State of equal protection or due process. When Congress steps beyond its proper sphere, the deference ordinarily due its enactments is no longer appropriate. Harlan concluded, therefore, that § 4(e) should be held unconstitutional:[85]

> Thus, we have here not a matter of giving deference to a congressional estimate, based on its determination of legislative facts, bearing upon the validity *vel non* of a statute, but rather what can at most be called a legislative announcement that Congress believes a state law to entail an unconstitutional deprivation of equal protection. Although this kind of declaration is of course entitled to the most respectful consideration, coming as it does from a concurrent branch and one that is knowledgeable in matters of popular political participation, I do not believe it lessens our responsibility to decide the fundamental issue of whether in fact the state enactment violates federal constitutional rights.

Katzenbach reveals the balancing Harlan undertook. The courts, he agreed, must give deference to congressional statutes. "However, it is also a canon of judicial review that state statutes are given a similar presumption."[86] The Court, there, must either uphold the

[84] *Id.* at 667.

[85] *Id.* at 669.

[86] *Id.* at 670.

state law and declare the congressional law unconstitutional, or vice versa. Merely giving the Act of Congress greater weight is not a satisfactory resolution of the dilemma. Harlan stated the considerations which in his mind tipped the balance against the principle of deference to Congress:[87]

> [I]t should be recognized that while the Fourteenth Amendment is a "brooding omnipresence" over all state legislation, the substantive matters which it touches are all within the primary legislative competence of the States. Federal authority, legislative no less than judicial, does not intrude unless there has been a denial by state action of Fourteenth Amendment limitations, in this instance a denial of equal protection. At least in the area of primary state concern a state statute that passes constitutional muster under the judicial standard of rationality should not be permitted to be set at naught by a mere contrary congressional pronouncement unsupported by a legislative record justifying that conclusion.

The principle of federalism, in Harlan's view, here outweighed the deference ordinarily due to Congress, especially since Congress had in this Act intruded into the sphere properly reserved to the judiciary, that of defining the substantive content of the Fourteenth Amendment.

Finally, the mere failure of Congress to exercise its undoubted power (for example, to reapportion congressional districts) did not, in Harlan's mind, give the Supreme Court authorization to step in to fill the gap. This is especially true where Congress deliberately decides not to reapportion. As he reminded his brethren in *Wesberry v. Sanders*:[88]

> This Court, no less than all other branches of the Government, is bound by the Constitution. The Constitution does not confer on the Court blanket authority to step into every situation where the political branch may be thought to have fallen short. The stability of this institution ultimately depends not only upon its being alert to keep the other branches of government within constitutional bounds but equally upon recognition of the limitations on the Court's own functions in the constitutional system.

---

[87] *Ibid*. Harlan reiterated this argument in Oregon v. Mitchell, 400 U.S. 112, 152, 204 (1970) (dissenting).

[88] 376 U.S. 1, 48 (1964) (dissenting).

Harlan's sense of the proper relationship between Congress and the Supreme Court, therefore, often drew its force from other principles, the canon of federalism and his convictions on the inherent limits of the judicial capability. He was willing to read congressional powers broadly, upholding legislation unless Congress had itself clearly overstepped the boundaries protecting state autonomy, or individual rights, or the proper role of the judiciary. The Court, however, must avoid usurping Congress's power to legislate. Judicial restraint was also an important canon of Harlan's judicial philosophy. The principle of separation of powers was discussed by Harlan less frequently and was perhaps somewhat less basic to his judicial philosophy than the principle of federalism.

III. Consideration of Historical Tradition

In contrast to the intense convictions Harlan revealed when he saw breaches of the canons of federalism and separation of powers, he approached the historical tradition with more subdued feelings. Harlan insisted, however, that the Court should at least consider historical tradition as one factor in its decision-making process. "I think that the dictates of history, even though the Court has seen fit to disregard them for the purpose of determining whether it should get into the matter at all, should cause the Court to take a hard look before striking down a traditional state policy in this area as rationally indefensible."[89] Harlan, for instance, expected such a hard look in evaluating the historical tradition of the jury process. The Court, in *Williams v. Florida*,[90] had upheld the constitutionality of a state statute providing for criminal trials by a six-man jury. Harlan, in dissent, objected. "The historical argument by which the Court undertakes to justify its view that the Sixth Amendment does not require 12-member juries is, in my opinion, much too thin to mask the true thrust of this decision."[91] History itself is usually not determinative: "history should not imprison those broad guarantees of the Constitution whose proper scope is to be determined in a given instance by a blend of historical understanding and the adaptation of purpose to contemporary circumstances."[92] But a common-law jury is not a term whose meaning should be adapted

[89] Carrington v. Rash, 380 U.S. 89, 99 (1965) (dissenting).

[90] 399 U.S. 78 (1970).

[91] *Id.* at 118.

[92] *Id.* at 124–25.

to uncontemplated circumstances. "[T]he right to a trial by jury . . . has no enduring meaning apart from historical form."[93] Severing the "umbilical cord that ties the form of the jury to the past"[94] will lead to continuing uncertainty as to what form is constitutionally required.

It was important to Harlan's dissent in *Harper v. Virginia Board of Elections*[95] that "[p]roperty qualifications and poll taxes have been a traditional part of our political structure." Similarly, only by a thorough review of the historical background of the statutory term "arrest of judgment" could the Court interpret the statute in *United States v. Sisson.*[96] "Congress acted against a common-law background that gave the statutory phrase a well-defined and limited meaning."[97]

Harlan would not try to compress contemporary reality merely to fit it into outmoded legal forms. With a touch of sarcasm, Harlan noted that "Legal history has been stretched before to satisfy the deep needs of society."[98] The Court should at least pause, however, before it makes a drastic break with the past. "[A] decision which finds virtually no support in more than a century of this Court's experience should certainly be subject to the most careful scrutiny."[99] Harlan had enough sensitivity to tradition to object when the Court "improvise[d] a rule necessarily based on pure policy that largely shrugs off history."[100] In *Spevack v. Klein*[101] he traced the tradition of judicial supervision of lawyers' fitness to practice all the way to the courts of Edward I. He strongly disagreed with the Court's action in overruling the disbarment of a lawyer, since he thought that the state court was merely continuing the efforts of courts for centuries to protect the systems of justice from abuse and to enhance public confidence in lawyers as officers of the court.

When Harlan had researched a point of legal history, he felt confident in rejecting a contrary conclusion of a scholar.[102] He had

93 *Id.* at 125.

94 *Ibid.*

95 383 U.S. 663, 684 (1966).

96 399 U.S. 267 (1970).

97 *Id.* at 280.

98 Miranda v. Arizona, 384 U.S. 436, 515 (1966) (dissenting).

99 Fay v. Noia, 372 U.S. 391, 463 (1963) (dissenting).

100 Cheff v. Schnackenberg, 384 U.S. 373, 383 (1966) (concurring and dissenting).

101 385 U.S. 511, 520 (1967) (dissenting).

102 California v. Green, 399 U.S. 149, 172 (1970) (concurring).

no qualms about rejecting a doctrine of ancient English vintage when his careful analysis led him to the conclusion that it was ill-suited to the contemporary American situation.[103] Mere blessing of age was insufficient reason for preserving such a legal anomaly. When a party argued from legal history, Harlan took the trouble to meet the contention on its own ground.[104] The point is, however, that he repeatedly showed a sensitivity in approaching legal history; he kept his ears attuned to the voices of the past even if in the end he might not always accept their message.

Harlan expressed his fundamental rationale for fidelity to historical tradition in his dissent in *Poe v. Ullman*.[105] Harlan derived content for the cryptic term "due process" in large part from "[t]he balance struck by this country, having regard to what history teaches are the traditions from which it developed as well as the traditions from which it broke."[106] Historical tradition, therefore, was an integral part of Harlan's judicial philosophy. Though the lessons of the past are not, by themselves, determinative, they should at least be understood. They can be ignored only at the risk of losing a dimension of ourselves as a nation.

Constitutional history carried even greater weight for Harlan. When he was convinced that the Court had distorted the meaning of the Constitution intended by its framers, his dissenting voice rose to assure that his objections would be heard. The majority, for instance, in *Wesberry v. Sanders* had held that Art. I, § 2, "construed in its historical context," required that in congressional elections "by the People of the several states," one person's vote must be worth as much as another's.[107] In his dissent Harlan expressed shock. "I had not expected to witness the day when the Supreme Court of the United States would render a decision which casts grave doubt on the constitutionality of the composition of the House of Representatives."[108] He was hesitant even to discuss the history of Art. I, § 2, since its language was so clear. "There is dubious propriety in turning to the 'historical context' of constitutional provisions which speak so consistently and plainly. But, as one might expect when the Constitution itself is free from ambiguity, the surrounding his-

---

[103] Moragne v. States Marine Lines, 398 U.S. 375 (1970).

[104] Green v. United States, 356 U.S. 165 (1958).

[105] 367 U.S. 497 (1961).

[106] *Id.* at 542.

[107] 376 U.S. 1, 7 (1964).

[108] *Id.* at 20.

tory makes what is already clear even clearer."[109] After carefully sifting the available historical data, he concluded:[110]

> The upshot of all this is that the language of Art. I, §§ 2 and 4, the surrounding text, and the relevant history are all in strong and consistent direct contradiction of the Court's holding. The constitutional scheme vests in the States plenary power to regulate the conduct of elections for Representatives, and, in order to protect the Federal Government, provides for congressional supervision of the States' exercise of their power. Within this scheme, the appellants do not have the right which they assert, in the absence of provision for equal districts by the Georgia Legislature or the Congress. The constitutional right which the Court creates is manufactured out of whole cloth.

Again in *Oregon v. Mitchell*,[111] Harlan demonstrated his deep concern that the original meaning of a constitutional provision should not be ignored by the Court. "From the standpoint of the bedrock of the constitutional structure of this Nation, these cases bring us to a crossroad that is marked with a formidable 'Stop' sign."[112] In the 1970 Voting Rights Act Amendments, Congress had lowered the minimum age of voters in federal and state elections to eighteen. It had also barred the use of literacy tests in all elections for five years and forbade the States from disqualifying voters in presidential elections for failure to meet the state residency requirements. The fragmented Court in *Mitchell* could not agree on a majority opinion. Piecing together different majorities which agreed with different parts of his opinion, Black was able to cast the decisive vote on the most controversial issues and announce the judgment of the Court. The Court, in this unsatisfactory manner, held that Congress had the power to lower the voting age to eighteen for federal but not for state elections, to suspend literacy tests, and to set residency requirements for presidential elections.[113]

Harlan prefaced his historical analysis with a quotation from Senator Charles Sumner which he completely endorsed. Sumner in 1866 had stated:[114]

---

[109] *Id.* at 30.

[110] *Id.* at 41–42. *Cf.* Harlan's dissent in Afroyim v. Rusk, 387 U.S. 253, 268 (1967).

[111] 400 U.S. 112 (1970). [112] *Id.* at 152. [113] *Id.* at 117.

[114] *Id.* at 154, citing Cong. Globe 677, 39th Cong., 1st Sess. (1866).

> Every Constitution embodies the principles of its framers. It is a transcript of their minds. If its meaning in any place is open to doubt, or if words are used which seem to have no fixed signification, we cannot err if we turn to the framers; and their authority increases in proportion to the evidence which they have left on the question.

Harlan felt sure that the history of the Fourteenth Amendment made it clear beyond doubt that no part of the Voting Rights Act of 1970 could be upheld as within congressional power to legislate under that Amendment. The opposite conclusion could be reached only by "those who are willing to close their eyes to constitutional history in making constitutional interpretations or who read such history with a preconceived determination to attain a particular constitutional goal."[115]

Harlan discussed at considerable length what he considered the relevant historical information. He then confronted the objection that the historical analysis was, after all, inconclusive. After attempting to refute the arguments which some claimed showed the inconclusiveness of history, Harlan concluded: "[I]f the consequences for our federal system were not so serious, the contention that the history is 'inconclusive' would be undeserving of attention. And, with all respect, the transparent failure of attempts to cast doubt on the original understanding is simply further evidence of the force of the historical record."[116] This historical record, Harlan thought, was free from the usual ambiguities "which bedevil most attempts to find a reliable guide to present decision in the pages of the past."[117]

Where the historical record so clearly demonstrated the original meaning of the Fourteenth Amendment intended by its framers, it should control subsequent judicial interpretation. Yet for some members of the Court this clear record made no difference. "I must confess to complete astonishment," Harlan wrote, "at the position of some of my Brethren that the history of the Fourteenth Amendment has become irrelevant."[118] History was too important to Harlan to be cast into the discard. He realized that the Constitution must be a living document continually interpreted to suit contemporary needs. Totally ignoring the meaning originally intended,

[115] 400 U.S. at 154.

[116] *Id.* at 200.

[117] *Ibid.*

[118] *Id.* at 201.

however, effectively gave the Court the power to rewrite the Constitution. In a passage which sums up much of his basic belief in the importance of a historical grasp of the Constitution, Harlan wrote:[119]

> It must be recognized, of course, that the amending process is not the only way in which constitutional understanding alters with time. The judiciary has long been entrusted with the task of applying the Constitution in changing circumstances, and as conditions change the Constitution in a sense changes as well. But when the Court gives the language of the Constitution an unforeseen application, it does so, whether explicitly or implicitly, in the name of some underlying purpose of the Framers. This is necessarily so; the federal judiciary which by express constitutional provision is appointed for life, and therefore cannot be held responsible by the electorate, has no inherent general authority to establish the norms for the rest of society. It is limited to elaboration and application of the precepts ordained in the Constitution by the political representatives of the people. When the Court disregards the express intent and understanding of the Framers, it has invaded the realm of the political process to which the amending power was committed, and it has violated the constitutional structure which it is its highest duty to protect.

IV. Fidelity to Judicial Precedent

Closely related to Justice Harlan's careful consideration of legal history is his concern that the Court not needlessly overrule or ignore its prior decisions. Harlan realized that judicial precedents of the Court can no more be irrevocably binding than can other aspects of historical tradition. He agonized over the principle of *stare decisis*, particularly where he had strongly disagreed with the decision when it was first decided. He found it painful to be bound by such a precedent.

Harlan discussed his basic conviction of the need for fidelity to judicial decisions in *Williams v. Florida*.[120] The Court there had upheld the constitutionality of a six-member criminal jury. Harlan, in dissent, after discussing the need to keep the common-law jury tied to its historical roots, objected further that the Court was showing "cavalier disregard" for its prior decisions which had required that a Sixth Amendment jury should consist of twelve men,

---

[119] *Id.* at 202.

[120] 399 U.S. 78 (1970).

neither more nor less.[121] Precedent should not so lightly be ignored even if it was not so sacred that it could never be touched. "The principle of *stare decisis* is multifaceted," Harlan stated:[122]

> It is a solid foundation for our legal system; yet care must be taken not to use it to create an unmovable structure. It provides the stability and predictability required for the ordering of human affairs over the course of time and a basis of "public faith in the judiciary as a source of impersonal and reasoned judgments." . . . Woodenly applied, however, it builds a stockade of precedent that confines the law by rules, ill-conceived when promulgated, or if sound in origin, unadaptable to present circumstances. No precedent is sacrosanct and one should not hesitate to vote to overturn this Court's previous holdings—old or recent—or reconsider settled dicta where the principles announced prove either practically . . . or jurisprudentially . . . unworkable, or no longer suited to contemporary life. . . . Surely if the principle of *stare decisis* means anything in the law, it means that precedent should not be jettisoned when the rule of yesterday remains viable, creates no injustice, and can reasonably be said to be no less sound than the rule sponsored by those who seek change, let alone incapable of being demonstrated wrong.

Where possible, the Court should further the elusive goal of certainty in the law. It should follow past precedents and not inject greater "uncertainties into a field already plagued by excessive refinements,"[123] leaving to Congress the task of law reform. The Court should remain faithful to its precedents especially when Congress, in subsequent legislation,[124] or the States, in administering their criminal laws,[125] have relied on them. Prior decisions of the Court should not be discarded merely because of a change of membership on the Court.[126] Harlan would not overrule a prior judicial interpretation of a statute unless it appeared beyond doubt that the statute had been previously misinterpreted by the Court.[127] He spoke out when the Court relied on cases which were not relevant

---

[121] *Id.* at 126.

[122] *Id.* at 127 (citations omitted).

[123] Detroit v. Murray Corp., 355 U.S. 489, 510 (1958) (concurring and dissenting).

[124] Lee v. Madigan, 358 U.S. 228, 237 (1959) (dissenting); Lee v. Florida, 392 U.S. 378, 388 (1968) (dissenting).

[125] Mapp v. Ohio, 367 U.S. 643, 676 (1961) (dissenting).

[126] *Id.* at 677.

[127] Monroe v. Pape, 365 U.S. 167, 192 (1961) (concurring).

to its conclusions,[128] as he did when the Court paid too little heed to relevant precedent.[129]

Harlan's belief in the principle of *stare decisis* was put to the test when the prior controlling precedent was one with which he had disagreed when originally decided. He followed the precedent, but not without an audible note of displeasure. He frequently mentioned, usually in a brief concurrence, that he felt obliged to go along with the Court's opinion because of the binding precedent of the previous decision from which he had dissented. One can sense his annoyance as he wrote in *Burns v. Richardson*,[130] a case involving reapportionment of Hawaii's legislature. "Because judicial responsibility requires me, as I see things, to bow to the authority of *Reynolds* v. *Sims* . . . despite my original and continuing belief that the decision was constitutionally wrong . . . I feel compelled to concur in the Court's disposition of this case."[131] The same discomfort was apparent in *Coleman v. Alabama*, where the Court had held that state-appointed counsel must be provided for the indigent defendant at a preliminary hearing.[132] Harlan again concurred, but only because bound by prior decisions:[133]

> If I felt free to consider this case upon a clean slate I would have voted to affirm these convictions, But—in light of the lengths to which the right to appointed counsel has been carried in recent decisions of this Court . . .—I consider that course is not open to me with due regard for the way in which the adjudicatory process of this Court, as I conceive it, should work.

Harlan's usual practice was to continue for the duration of a Term to adhere to his positions expressed in dissents.[134] After the

---

[128] Donovan v. Dallas, 377 U.S. 408, 414 (1964) (dissenting).

[129] Elkins v. United States, 364 U.S. 206, 251 (1960) (separate memorandum); Miranda v. Arizona, 384 U.S. 436, 504 (1966) (dissenting).

[130] 384 U.S. 73 (1966).

[131] *Id.* at 98 (citations omitted). See also Gibson v. Thompson, 355 U.S. 18, 19 (1957) (concurring); Stinson v. Atlantic Coast Line R. Co., 355 U.S. 62 (1957) (concurring); Jordan v. Silver, 381 U.S. 415 (1965) (concurring); United States v. General Motors Corp., 384 U.S. 127, 148 (1966) (concurring); S.E.C. v. New England Electric System, 390 U.S. 207, 221 (1968) (concurring); Cipriano v. Houma, 395 U.S. 701, 707 (1969) (concurring); Coolidge v. New Hampshire, 403 U.S. 443, 490 (1971) (concurring).

[132] 399 U.S. 1 (1970).

[133] *Id.* at 19 (citation omitted).

[134] North Carolina v. Pearce, 395 U.S. 711, 744 (1969) (concurring and dissenting).

end of the Term he would consider himself bound by the precedent he had originally opposed. He continued, however, to express his basic dissatisfaction with the precedent. For instance, Harlan had dissented at length from the Court's decision in *Miranda v. Arizona,* in which the Court, relying on the Fifth Amendment, had held that specific warnings must be given by the police to a suspect subjected to custodial interrogation or else his confession would be inadmissible at trial.[135] When *Miranda* was applied in subsequent Terms, Harlan reluctantly felt bound by it. "The passage of time," he wrote, "has not made the *Miranda* case any more palatable to me than it was when the case was decided."[136] He nonetheless could find no acceptable way of escape from the distasteful precedent, so, "purely out of respect for *stare decisis*,"[137] he followed it. When the Court itself had refused to apply this precedent, Harlan felt obliged by *stare decisis* to dissent again. "As one who has never agreed with the *Miranda* case," he wrote, "but nonetheless felt bound by it, I now find myself in the uncomfortable position of having to dissent from a holding which actually serves to curtail the impact of that decision."[138]

By way of exception, Harlan refused to be bound by recent precedents in *Oregon v. Mitchell.*[139] In that case, as indicated above, the Court, by divided vote, had upheld portions of the Voting Rights Act of 1970. Harlan's dissent, based on his analysis of the historical evidence concerning the power of Congress under the Fourteenth Amendment, has been discussed. He concluded with a frank acknowledgment that *stare decisis* should have led him to vote with those members of the Court who thought that Congress had the authority to lower the voting age and abolish state residency requirements in presidential elections. He nevertheless refused to be controlled by these precedents. He viewed fidelity to the original intent of the framers of the Fourteenth Amendment as more compelling than the principle of *stare decisis:*[140]

> After much reflection I have reached the conclusion that I ought not to allow *stare decisis* to stand in the way of casting

[135] 384 U.S. 436, 504 (1966).

[136] Orozco v. Texas, 394 U.S. 324, 327 (1969) (concurring).

[137] *Id.* at 328.

[138] Jenkins v. Delaware, 395 U.S. 213, 222 (1969) (dissenting).

[139] 400 U.S. 112 (1970).

[140] *Id.* at 218.

> my vote in accordance with what I am deeply convinced the Constitution demands. In the annals of this Court few developments in the march of events have so imperatively called upon us to take a fresh hard look at past decisions, which could well be mustered in support of such developments, as do the legislative lowering of the voting age and, albeit to a lesser extent, the elimination of state residential requirements in presidential elections. Concluding, as I have, that such decisions cannot withstand constitutional scrutiny, I think it my duty to depart from them, rather than to lend my support to perpetuating their constitutional error in the name of *stare decisis.*

No precedent was so carved in stone that it could not be reversed. Though Harlan obviously thought long before he voted to overrule a prior decision, he did on occasion so vote.[141] He set out in *Moragne v. State Marine Lines, Inc.*,[142] the policy considerations which he thought should be balanced in determining whether to overrule a precedent. By looking to the rationale which justified the principle of *stare decisis*, he could evaluate whether these factors had lost their significance in a particular case:[143]

> Very weighty considerations underlie the principle that courts should not lightly overrule past decisions. Among these are the desirability that the law furnish a clear guide for the conduct of individuals, to enable them to plan their affairs with assurance against untoward surprise; the importance of furthering fair and expeditious adjudication by eliminating the need to relitigate every relevant proposition in every case; and the necessity of maintaining public faith in the judiciary as a source of impersonal and reasoned judgments. The reasons for rejecting any established rule must always be weighed against these factors.

V. Scrupulous Regard for Procedural Detail

Justice Harlan, in his work as a judge, insisted on crossing *t*'s and dotting *i*'s. No one could ever accuse him of producing slipshod opinions. What the layman might call technical details mattered very much to him. For him, they were not mere technical details. He believed that lawyers and judges must turn square corners

---

[141] See, *e.g.*, Swift & Co. v. Wickham, 382 U.S. 111, 124 (1965); Zschernig v. Miller, 389 U.S. 429, 443, 457 (1968) (concurring); Lear, Inc. v. Adkins, 395 U.S. 653, 671 (1969); Marchetti v. United States, 390 U.S. 39, 54 (1968).

[142] 398 U.S. 375 (1970).

[143] *Id.* at 403.

when it came to such procedural rules. Certainly the Supreme Court should not ignore them to suit its convenience. Harlan never discussed this concern for accuracy in procedural detail as a separate principle. It is in what he did rather than what he said that this principle appears.

A look at Harlan's attitude toward the final judgment rule reveals his concern for mitered corners in dealing with judicial procedures. A majority of the Court frequently took a relaxed, pragmatic approach to the finality rule, riddling it with exceptions to meet the occasion. Harlan, however, regarded it as a fixed barrier to Supreme Court jurisdiction. Only rarely did he agree that the rule did not apply. He dissented repeatedly, often alone, when the Court created broad exceptions to it.

Early in Harlan's career on the Court he stated the standard final judgment rule in *Parr v. United States*.[144] The government, after its attempts to have a criminal case transferred to another court were unsuccessful, had obtained a new indictment in a different district and had the original indictment dismissed. The defendant sought review of the dismissal in the court of appeals, which dismissed the appeal for want of a final judgment in the district court. The Supreme Court affirmed. Harlan explained for the majority that a judgment is final for purposes of appeal only when it ends the litigation on the merits and leaves nothing to be done by the trial court except to execute the judgment. Here the order dismissing the first indictment was but an interlocutory step in this prosecution. Its review must await the conclusion of the litigation. The initial dismissal would still be reviewable if the defendant should be convicted under the second indictment. "To hold this order 'final' at this stage of the prosecution would defeat the longstanding statutory policy against piecemeal appeals."[145]

Harlan took care to distinguish this case from *Cohen v. Beneficial*

---

[144] 351 U.S. 513 (1956). The final judgment rule is stated in two statutory provisions of the Judicial Code. Supreme Court review of state courts is limited by 28 U.S.C. § 1257 to "final judgments or decrees rendered by the highest court of a State in which a decision could be had." United States Courts of Appeals, with certain exceptions provided by statute, 28 U.S.C. § 1292, "have jurisdiction of appeals from all final decisions of the district courts of the United States." 28 U.S.C. § 1291. The Supreme Court has largely ignored the potential distinctions between "final judgments" in § 1257 and "final decisions" in § 1291 and has cited opinions relating to one in cases involving the other.

[145] 351 U.S. at 519.

Industrial Loan Corp.,[146] in which the Court had agreed that the court of appeals could hear an appeal from an interlocutory order, treating the order there as if it were a final judgment. He pointed out that in *Cohen* the interlocutory order had been held appealable because it "related to matters outside the stream of the main action and would not be subject to effective review as part of the final judgment in the action."[147] As an attorney Harlan had been counsel for Beneficial Industrial Loan and had briefed and argued the *Cohen* case. He had argued for Beneficial that the district court's order was appealable because it had determined a controversy separate and distinct from the main action and because effective appellate review of this issue would not be available if Beneficial had to await entry of final judgment.[148] His argument had prevailed. But thereafter, when he sat on the Court, he consistently objected to the creation of further exceptions to the final judgment rule. We would not expect an attorney's approach to such a rule, when representing a client, to be the same as a judge's attitude toward the rule. His repeated and strenuous insistence on the rule, however, indicates the importance he attached to it.

When the Court had applied the *Cohen* exception to allow review of a different type of interlocutory order, Harlan revealed these strong convictions:[149]

---

[146] 337 U.S. 541 (1949). The *Cohen* case involved a shareholder derivative action alleging a conspiracy to enrich corporate officers and directors at the expense of the corporation and its shareholders. Federal jurisdiction was based exclusively on diversity of citizenship. The trial court had held that a New Jersey statute requiring plaintiffs in derivative actions to post security for costs and attorneys' fees was not applicable in this suit in New Jersey. This interlocutory order was appealed to the Court of Appeals under 28 U.S.C. § 1291, see note 144 *supra*, and that court reversed the trial court judgment. The Supreme Court held that the order was appealable although not a final decision because it "appears to fall in that small class which finally determine claims of right separable from, and collateral to, rights asserted in the action, too important to be denied review and too independent of the cause itself to require that appellate consideration be deferred until the whole case is adjudicated." *Id.* at 546.

[147] 351 U.S. at 519.

[148] See Respondent's Brief in Opposition and Brief on the Merits, in *Cohen v. Beneficial Industrial Loan Corp.*, note 146 *supra*.

[149] Mercantile National Bank v. Langdeau, 371 U.S. 555, 572 (1963) (dissenting). Harlan's opinion also applied to a companion case, Construction Laborers v. Curry 371 U.S. 542, 553 (1963) (concurring). The interlocutory order in *Curry* was a denial of a temporary injunction by a state trial court in a labor dispute as beyond its jurisdiction. The order had been reversed by the state supreme court. The interlocutory order in *Langdeau* was a denial by the state trial court of a plea to the court's venue.

> That requirement is more than a technical rule of procedure, yielding when need be to the exigencies of particular situations. Rather, it is a long-standing and healthy federal policy that protects litigants and courts from the disruptions of piecemeal review and forecloses this Court from passing on constitutional issues that may be dissipated by the final outcome of a case, thus helping to keep to a minimum undesirable federal-state conflicts.

Harlan made clear that the case under review was "wholly different from *Cohen*."[150] He concluded that the Court's decision threw "the law of finality into a state of great uncertainty and will, I am afraid, tend to increase future efforts at piecemeal review."[151] In another case Harlan objected again that the Court had approved the "loose practices sanctioned by the Court of Appeals"[152] which had reviewed a nonfinal order. "This case," he wrote, "thus presents a striking example of the vice inherent in a system which permits piecemeal litigation."[153] He again distinguished *Cohen*, since in that case the interlocutory order was not a step toward the final judgment in which it would be merged.[154] He was particularly upset that the Court had argued that the eventual costs would be less if it decided the legal issues presented rather than sending the case back with those issues undecided. "Essentially such a position," Harlan retorted, "would justify review here of any case decided by a court of appeals whenever this Court, as it did in this instance, erroneously grants certiorari and permits counsel to brief and argue the case on the merits. That, I believe, is neither good law nor sound judicial administration."[155]

In *Mills v. Alabama*,[156] Harlan declared that the congressionally imposed final judgment rule should not be ignored by the Court. "I continue to believe," he stated, "that constitutionally permissible limitations on the jurisdiction of this Court . . . should be respected

---

[150] 371 U.S. at 574.

[151] *Id.* at 575.

[152] Gillespie v. U.S. Steel Corp., 379 U.S. 148, 167 (1964) (dissenting). The interlocutory order struck those parts of the complaint relying on a state statutory action for negligence and one for unseaworthiness, while sustaining a claim under the Jones Act.

[153] *Id.* at 167–68.

[154] *Id.* at 169.

[155] *Id.* at 170. *Cf.* Hudson Distributors v. Eli Lilly, 377 U.S. 386, 395 (1964) (dissenting).

[156] 384 U.S. 214 (1966).

and not turned on and off at the pleasure of its members or to suit the convenience of litigants. If the traditional federal policy of 'finality' is to be changed, Congress is the body to do it."[157]

Harlan clung tenaciously to the final judgment rule. He thought insistence on the essential integrity of the rule important enough to justify separate opinions whenever the Court tampered with it. Accuracy in detail, exactness about procedural rules, were important to Harlan's unstated judicial philosophy.

Another procedural rule that Harlan considered important was the Supreme Court's own "rule of four." This nonstatutory rule means that if four members of the Court vote to review a case, the entire Court will hear it, even though a majority of the Court thinks that the case does not merit the Court's attention.[158] This is hardly the type of rule which provokes frequent debate on the Court. Harlan, nevertheless, considered it so significant in *Rogers v. Missouri Pacific Railroad Co.*[159] that he wrote a separate opinion strongly criticizing the way his colleague, Justice Frankfurter, had voted.

Four cases, captioned as *Rogers*, had been received by the Supreme Court. Three involved recovery for injuries to railroad employees under the Federal Employers' Liability Act, while the fourth involved recovery for injury by a seaman under the parallel Jones Act. In all four the trial court had awarded a judgment, based on a jury verdict or directed verdict, for the injured worker. The verdicts had been challenged by the employers in the appellate courts. The state supreme court in one case and the federal courts of appeals in two had reversed the verdicts on the ground of insufficiency of the evidence. The Supreme Court reviewed the cases and in all four upheld the original awards to the injured workmen.[160]

---

[157] *Id.* at 223 (separate opinion). See also Organization for a Better Austin v. Keefe, 402 U.S. 415, 420 (1971) (dissenting); Brown Shoe Co. v. United States, 370 U.S. 294, 357 (1962) (concurring and dissenting); Avery v. Midland County, 390 U.S. 474, 486 (1968) (dissenting).

[158] Though the "rule of four" properly applies to certiorari cases, where the Court's review is discretionary, the same rule seems to be applied to appeals where jurisdiction is supposed to be nondiscretionary. See Ohio ex rel. Eaton v. Price, 360 U.S. 246 (1959) (Brennan, J., separate opinion).

[159] 352 U.S. 500, 559 (1957) (concurring and dissenting).

[160] Rogers v. Missouri Pacific R. Co., 352 U.S. 500 (1957); Webb v. Illinois Cent. R. Co., 352 U.S. 512 (1957); Herdman v. Pennsylvania R. Co., 352 U.S. 518 (1957); Ferguson v. Moore-McCormack Lines, Inc., 352 U.S. 521 (1957).

Frankfurter dissented in a lengthy opinion. He objected to the Court's action in these cases as wholly inconsistent with its certiorari policy. He voted to dismiss as improvidently granted the petitions for certiorari which had been granted under the rule of four. The Court, he was convinced, had no business reviewing cases in which the sole issue was the sufficiency of the evidence submitted to a jury. He argued that the integrity of the certiorari policy did not require him to vote on the merits of these cases, even though four Justices had voted to grant review. He pointed out the impossibility and undesirability of giving the same attention to the initial question of granting or denying review as was demanded by the decision on the merits. Furthermore, each Justice should have a right to express his dissenting vote.[161]

Harlan wrote a separate opinion expressing basic agreement with Frankfurter's arguments on the Court's willingness to review such cases where the only issue was the sufficiency of the evidence for jury consideration. "I think," he wrote, that "the Court should not have heard any of these four cases."[162] After this initial admission of basic agreement with Frankfurter's position, Harlan thought it important to develop at length his reasons for disagreeing with the way Frankfurter had cast his vote, to dismiss the writ as improvidently granted rather than merely dissenting on the merits. Once the Court, by the rule of four, decided to take the cases, Harlan conceived it to be a duty to consider them on their merits:[163]

---

[161] 352 U.S. at 524.

[162] *Id.* at 559.

[163] *Ibid.* Harlan discussed the rule of four in the context of his *Rogers* opinion in a talk to the Association of the Bar of the City of New York: "It must also be recognized, however, that this 'rule of four,' if not administered with the utmost respect for the purposes and traditional limits of certiorari jurisdiction, may operate to bring cases to the Court which should not be there. That possibility is illustrated by the sharp division in the Court, already a matter of public record, as to the wisdom of bringing up those cases under the Federal Employers' Liability Act or the Jones Act which present essentially only factual issues. So far, however, all but one of the Justices who believe that the review of such cases is not a profitable expenditure of the Court's time have nevertheless adhered to the view that once before the Court under the 'rule of four' such a case should be disposed of on the merits, rather than by dismissal of the writ as 'improvidently granted' by a majority vote after the case has been argued. This view rests on the premise that unless the argument reveals factors which were not known or fully appreciated at the time certiorari was granted, such course would in effect amount to undoing the 'rule of four' in this class of cases." 13 Record 541, 556 (1958). Harlan repeated essentially the same comments in *Some Aspects of the Judicial Process in the Supreme Court of the United States*, 33 Aust. L. J. 108, 112 (1959); see also *A Glimpse of the Supreme Court at Work*, 34 Okla. Bar J. 1649, 1650 (1963).

I cannot reconcile voting to dismiss the writs as "improvidently granted" with the Court's "rule of four." In my opinion due adherence to that rule requires that once certiorari has been granted a case should be disposed of on the premise that it is properly here, in the absence of considerations appearing which were not manifest or fully apprehended at the time certiorari was granted. In these instances I am unable to say that such considerations exist, even though I do think that the arguments on the merits underscored the views of those of us who originally felt that the cases should not be taken because they involved only issues of fact, and presented nothing of sufficient general importance to warrant this substantial expenditure of the Court's time.

I do not think that, in the absence of the considerations mentioned, voting to dismiss a writ after it has been granted can be justified on the basis of an inherent right of dissent. In the case of a petition for certiorari that right, it seems to me—again without the presence of intervening factors—is exhausted once the petition has been granted and the cause set for argument. Otherwise the "rule of four" surely becomes a meaningless thing in more than one respect. *First*, notwithstanding the "rule of four," five objecting Justices could undo the grant by voting, after the case has been heard, to dismiss the writ as improvidently granted—a course which would hardly be fair to litigants who have expended time, effort, and money on the assumption that their cases would be heard and decided on the merits. . . . *Second*, permitting the grant of a writ to be thus undone would undermine the whole philosophy of the "rule of four," which is that any case warranting consideration in the opinion of such a substantial minority of the Court will be taken and disposed of. It appears to me that such a practice would accomplish just the contrary of what representatives of this Court stated to Congress as to the "rule of four" at the time the Court's certiorari jurisdiction was enlarged by the Judiciary Act of 1925. In effect the "rule of four" would, by indirection, become a "rule of five." *Third*, such a practice would, in my opinion, be inconsistent with the long-standing and desirable custom of not announcing the Conference vote on petitions for certiorari. For in the absence of the intervening circumstances which may cause a Justice to vote to dismiss a writ as improvidently granted, such a disposition of the case on his part is almost bound to be taken as reflecting his original Conference vote on the petition. And if such a practice is permissible, then by the same token I do not see how those who voted in favor of the petition can reasonably be expected to refrain from announcing their Conference votes at the time the petition is acted on.

Harlan concluded by responding directly to Frankfurter's defense of his practice. Certainly Harlan felt strongly about the integrity of the certiorari process and the Court's rule of four. Again we see him insisting on the exact and faithful compliance with a procedural rule as he understood it. On several other occasions he briefly noted his opposition to the practice of voting to dismiss certiorari as improvidently granted when no special factors had intervened.[164] When Harlan did vote to dismiss a writ as improvidently granted, he made it a practice to note specifically the intervening factors which, in his mind, justified such a vote. He voted to dismiss cases because of a massive stale record,[165] because of lack of a record,[166] because question of leave to amend the complaint was best left to the Courts of Appeals,[167] because of the need to avoid establishing a rigid constitutional rule in a field where Congress had tried to strike a balance between economic forces,[168] because of recent passage of an Act of Congress,[169] because of recent repeal of an Act of Congress.[170] He tried to remain consistent with the views he had so forcefully expressed in *Rogers*.

VI. Need for Principled Decision Making

In his Holmes Lecture at Harvard Law School Professor Wechsler, in 1959, expressed his views on the need for neutral principles in constitutional adjudication.[171] Wechsler argued that there

---

[164] See Gibson v. Thompson, 355 U.S. 18, 19 (1957) (separate memorandum); The Monrosa v. Carbon Black Export, Inc., 359 U.S. 180, 184 (1959) (dissenting); Rudolph v. United States, 370 U.S. 269, 270 (1962) (separate opinion); Holt v. Allegheny Corp., 384 U.S. 28 (1966) (dissenting).

[165] Protective Committee v. Anderson, 390 U.S. 414, 454 (1968) (dissenting); Grunenthal v. Long Island R. Co., 393 U.S. 156, 163 (1968) (dissenting).

[166] Hicks v. District of Columbia, 383 U.S. 252 (1966) (concurring); *cf.* Wainwright v. New Orleans, 392 U.S. 598 (1968) (concurring).

[167] Foman v. Davis, 371 U.S. 178, 183 (1962) (separate opinion).

[168] Amalgamated Food Employees v. Logan Valley Plaza, 391 U.S. 308, 333 (1968) (dissenting).

[169] Jones v. Alfred H. Mayer Co., 392 U.S. 409, 449 (1968) (dissenting); Sullivan v. Little Hunting Park, 396 U.S. 229, 241 (1969) (dissenting).

[170] Triangle Improvement Council v. Ritchie, 402 U.S. 497 (1971) (concurring).

[171] Wechsler, *Toward Neutral Principles of Constitutional Law*, 73 Harv. L. Rev. 1 (1959). See White, *The Evolution of Reasoned Elaboration: Jurisprudential Criticism and Social Change*, 59 Va. L. Rev. 279 (1973).

should be criteria for judicial decision making, applicable both to the members of the Supreme Court and its critics, which "can be framed and tested as an exercise of reason and not merely as an act of willfulness or will."[172] An act of willfulness, an *ad hoc evaluation,* if tolerable in the realm of politics ought not to afford a basis to reduce constitutional principles to mere tools for judges to accomplish personal goals. More should be expected of the judicial process.

Judicial decision making "must be genuinely principled, resting with respect to every step that is involved in reaching judgment on analysis and reasons quite transcending the immediate result that is achieved."[173] Judicial decisions should rest on "grounds of adequate neutrality and generality," especially since courts determine issues which are inescapably political, involving a choice of societal values. The obligation to support its choice of competing values by a reasoned or principled explanation of the grounds for the choice is intrinsic to the judicial function, while such an explanation is not expected of the executive or legislative branches. "A principled decision," Wechsler concluded, "in the sense I have in mind, is one that rests on reasons with respect to all the issues in the case, reasons that in their generality and their neutrality transcend any immediate result that is involved."[174] A corollary of Wechsler's demand for articulated, neutral decision making is a doctrine of judicial restraint, as he understood it. A court should not intervene in the political process unless it was capable of rendering a reasoned, principled choice between competing values. "[T]he courts ought to be cautious to impose a choice of values on the other branches or a state, based upon the Constitution, only when they are persuaded, on an adequate and principled analysis, that the choice is clear."[175]

Justice Harlan was a striking example of a Justice who consistently strove for the goal of neutral, principled decision making. This is implicit in much of his judicial work. The Supreme Court's decisions ought not be mere *ad hoc* determinations imposing upon the political process the personal preferences or personal sense of justice of the individual members of the Court.

In speeches he delivered from time to time, he adumbrated these views. In one address he remarked, "Our scheme of ordered liberty

[172] Wechsler, note 171 *supra,* at 11.

[173] *Id.* at 15. [174] *Id.* at 19. [175] *Id.* at 25.

is based, like the common law, on enlightened and uniformly applied legal principle, not on *ad hoc* notions of what is right or wrong in a particular case."[176] The Supreme Court, he repeatedly insisted, is not "a tribunal where correction of every sort of legal wrong may be sought . . . a final court of errors and appeals"[177] like a state supreme court. The Court should not be concerned so much with the rightness or wrongness of a decision of a lower federal court. This merely affects the immediate parties to the litigation. The Court should rather be concerned with the "proper and uniform development of the federal law" and the vindication of constitutional rights.[178]

In his opinions, Harlan occasionally suggested the need for neutral, rational principles as the basis of judicial decision making. For example, in *Carrington v. Rash*,[179] he chastized the majority for further extending the reapportionment cases into the States' political affairs:[180]

> I deplore the added impetus which this decision gives to the current tendency of judging constitutional questions on the basis of abstract "justice" unleashed from the limiting principles that go with our constitutional system. Constitutionally principled adjudication, high in the process of which is due recognition of the just demands of federalism, leaves ample room for the protection of individual rights.

Harlan frequently objected when he thought the majority's opinion was unleashed from principles. In a case in which the majority

[176] Harlan, note 6 *supra*, at 944.

[177] Harlan, *Address*, 58 LAW LIB. J. 372, 373 (1965); see also Harlan, *Manning the Dikes*, 13 RECORD 541, 549 (1958); Harlan, *Some Aspects of the Judicial Process in the Supreme Court of the United States*, 33 AUST. L. J. 108, 112 (1959).

[178] 58 LAW LIB. J. at 373.

[179] 380 U.S. 89 (1965).

[180] *Id.* at 98–99 (dissenting). The fact that Harlan insisted on principles in judicial decision making should not be taken to mean that questions of policy were not involved. In Bivens v. Six Unknown Fed. Narcotics Agents, 403 U.S. 388, 407 (1971) (concurring), he explicitly stated: "In resolving that question, it seems to me that the range of policy considerations we may take into account is at least as broad as the range of those a legislature would consider with respect to an express statutory authorization of a traditional remedy." This certainly suggests that Harlan does not fit the description of the ideal judge, "Hercules," a creature of Professor Dworkin's. TAKING RIGHTS SERIOUSLY 81–130 (1978). Harlan relied on policy arguments in many of his decisions. See, *e.g.*, *Flast v. Cohen*, 392 U.S. 83, 116 (1968) (dissenting); Lear v. Adkins, 395 U.S. 653 (1969); Hellenic Lines Ltd. v. Rhoditis, 398 U.S. 306, 311 (1970) (dissenting).

held a provision of the Nationality Act of 1940 unconstitutional, Harlan retorted that its interpretation of the Constitution rested, "in the last analysis, simply on the Court's *ipse dixit*, evincing little more, it is quite apparent, than the present majority's own distaste for the expatriation power."[181] Similarly, he was opposed to the action of the Court overturning an agency determination where the Court had only "substituted its own preferences for the discretion given by Congress"[182] to the agency. When the majority held that a state-required teacher's loyalty oath was unconstitutional, Harlan thought the State would rightly be baffled by the Court's decision based on "reasoning that defies analysis. . . . The only thing that does shine through the opinion of the majority is that its members do not like loyalty oaths."[183]

In *Flast v. Cohen*,[184] the Court held that federal taxpayers had standing to challenge the constitutionality of a federal expenditure of tax funds as an aid to religious schools. Harlan, in dissent, noted that the specific issue of standing was narrow and quite abstract. Nonetheless, "the principles by which [the issue] must be resolved involve nothing less than the proper functioning of the federal courts, and so run to the roots of our constitutional system."[185] Viewing the appropriate principles as basic, he was sharply critical of the Court's inadequate criteria for resolving this issue and its reasoning, which he found circular. "Apparently the Court," he caustically observed, "having successfully circumnavigated the issue, has merely returned to the proposition from which it began. A litigant, it seems, will have standing if he is 'deemed' to have the requisite interest, and 'if you . . . have standing, then you can be confident you are' suitably interested."[186]

Harlan firmly believed that the Supreme Court's function in its discretionary jurisdiction was not to give the defeated party in the lower court another day in court. This jurisdiction did not exist merely for the benefit of the individual litigant. The Court's power existed to settle issues which were of public importance. The human

---

[181] Afroyim v. Rusk, 387 U.S. 253, 293 (1967) (dissenting).

[182] Udall v. F.P.C., 387 U.S. 428, 454 (1967) (dissenting).

[183] Whitehill v. Elkins, 389 U.S. 54, 62–63 (1967) (dissenting); see also Harper v. Virginia Board of Elections, 383 U.S. 663, 680 (1966) (dissenting).

[184] 392 U.S. 83 (1968).

[185] *Id.* at 116.

[186] *Id.* at 130.

appeal of the individual's request for relief should not mislead the Court into ignoring legal principles.[187]

One fruit of principled decision making should be proper guidance for the lower courts and members of the legal community. In a dissent from the majority's opinion in an obscenity case, Harlan observed that anyone who took the trouble to read the Court's own recent decisions in obscenity cases "would find himself in utter bewilderment."[188] He objected that the Court was demanding far more precise language from legislatures in defining obscenity offenses than the Court itself had been able to achieve. Again in reapportionment cases he criticized the Court for "leaving the state legislatures, the lower courts, and even Congress without meaningful guidance."[189] In the area of the constitutional authority of military courts, Harlan objected in one opinion that "the Court has thrown the law in this realm into a demoralizing state of uncertainty."[190]

Similarly, Harlan insisted that the Court must rethink the entire question of retroactivity, that is, the question of which newly developed constitutional principles affecting the rights of the accused should be applied retroactively. He objected to the "doctrinal confusion" which characterized the Court's prior opinions on the question.[191] Resolution by the Court of questions of retroactivity "must be determined upon principles that comport with the judicial func-

---

[187] Jones v. Alfred H. Mayer Co., 392 U.S. 409, 479 (1968) (dissenting); Peak v. United States, 353 U.S. 43, 52 (1957) (concurring and dissenting); see also United States v. Mississippi Valley Generating Co., 364 U.S. 520, 572 (1961) (dissenting).

[188] Interstate Circuit v. Dallas, 390 U.S. 676, 707 (1968).

[189] Rockefeller v. Wells, 389 U.S. 421, 423 (1967) (dissenting); see also Scholle v. Hare, 369 U.S. 429, 430 (1962) (dissenting); W.M.C.A. v. Simon, 370 U.S. 190, 191 (1962) (dissenting).

[190] O'Callahan v. Parker, 395 U.S. 258, 275 (1969) (dissenting).

[191] Desist v. United States, 394 U.S. 244, 258 (1969) (dissenting): "Matters of basic principle are at stake. In the classical view of constitutional adjudication, which I share, criminal defendants cannot come before this Court simply to request largesse. This Court is entitled to decide constitutional issues only when the facts of a particular case *require* their resolution for a just adjudication on the merits. . . . We do not release a criminal from jail because we like to do so, or because we think it wise to do so, but only because the government has offended constitutional principle in the conduct of his case. And when another similarly situated defendant comes before us, we must grant the same relief or give a principled reason for acting differently. We depart from this basic judicial tradition when we simply pick and choose from among similarly situated defendants those who alone will receive the benefit of a 'new' rule of constitutional law."

tion, and not upon considerations that are appropriate enough for a legislative body."[192]

Harlan again pointed out the unavoidable confusion for lawyers and judges when the Supreme Court overturned a lower court judgment a year and a half after it had denied certiorari and despite its subsequent denial of two petitions for rehearing. The Court thereby violated the principle that litigation must at some definite point be ended. "I can think of nothing more unsettling to lawyers and litigants, and more disturbing to their confidence in the evenhandedness of the Court's processes, than to be left in the kind of uncertainty which today's action engenders, as to when their cases may be considered finally closed in this Court."[193]

The Court's summary dispositions of controversial cases often triggered Harlan's dissents. If reasoned decision making was the goal, such summary actions hardly fulfilled the Court's chief function:[194] "These matters bristle with difficult and important questions, that touch the nerve centers of the sound operation of our federal and state judicial and political systems. They involve, among other things, the right of a federal court to order that one house of a state legislature shall temporarily be of greater size than is permitted by the State Constitution. Surely such questions are deserving of plenary consideration and reasoned explication."

When Harlan rethought a particular question and changed his mind, he carefully noted the change. After all, reasoned analysis meant a judge should strive to eliminate unnecessary contradictions and conflicts between decisions. As he stated in *Welsh v. United States*,[195]

---

[192] Mackey v. United States, 401 U.S. 667, 677 (1971) (concurring and dissenting); *cf.* United States v. Estate of Donnelly, 397 U.S. 286 295 (1970) (concurring).

[193] United States v. Ohio Power Co., 353 U.S. 98, 111 (1957) (dissenting); see also Sanders v. United States, 373 U.S. 1, 23 (1963) (dissenting); Gondeck v. Pan American World Airways, Inc., 382 U.S. 25, 30 (1965) (dissenting).

[194] Travia v. Lomenzo, 381 U.S. 431, 434 (1965) (dissenting); see also National Motor Freight Traffic Ass'n v. United States, 372 U.S. 246, 247 (1963) (dissenting); Hughes v. W.M.C.A., Inc., 379 U.S. 694 (1965) (dissenting); Columbia Artists Management, Inc. v. United States, 381 U.S. 348 (1965) (dissenting); Kennecott Copper Corp. v. United States, 381 U.S. 414 (1965) (dissenting); Damico v. California, 389 U.S. 416, 417 (1967) (dissenting); United States v. Chicago, 400 U.S. 8, 11 (1970) (dissenting).

[195] 398 U.S. 333, 344 (1970) (concurring) (citations omitted); see also Wyandotte Transportation Co. v. United States, 389 U.S. 191, 210 (1967) (concurring); Carafas v. LaFallee, 391 U.S. 234, 242 (1968) (concurring); Grunenthal v. Long Island

> Candor requires me to say that I joined the Court's opinion in *United States* v. *Seeger*, only with the gravest misgivings as to whether it was a legitimate exercise in statutory construction, and today's decision convinces me that in doing so I made a mistake which I should now acknowledge.

Harlan also showed his insistence on explicitly reasoned decisions by writing a separate concurring opinion providing the careful analysis which he found lacking in the majority's opinion.[196] He would not tolerate carelessly drafted opinions which failed to provide the level of professional workmanship he thought essential to the role of a member of the Court.

Harlan firmly believed that judicial restraint was a prime virtue of a Supreme Court Justice.[197] Like Wechsler, Harlan opposed the active assertion of judicial power to solve society's problems because of the institutional limitations on the Court's ability to articulate fully principled decisions. In a dissent to the majority's opinion upholding a plaintiff's standing to sue, Harlan wrote:[198]

> Swept up in a constitutional revolution of its own making, the Court has a tendency to lose sight of the principles that have traditionally defined and limited its role in our political system. Constitutional adjudication is a responsibility we cannot shirk. But it is a grave and extraordinary process, one of last resort. And when it cannot legitimately be avoided, it is a function that must be performed with the utmost circumspection and precision, lest the Court's opinions emanate radiations which unintentionally, and spuriously, indicate views on matters we have not fully considered.

Harlan also argued for judicial restraint on grounds of the broader principles of separation of powers and federalism which constitute constitutional limitations on the Court's authority. He stated his objections to judicial activism most forcefully in *Reynolds v. Sims*, where he wrote:[199]

R. Co., 393 U.S. 156, 163 (1968) (dissenting); F.T.C. v. Texaco, 393 U.S. 223, 231 (1968) (concurring); Dutton v. Evans, 400 U.S. 74, 93 (1970) (concurring).

[196] *E.g.*, Chandler v. Judicial Council of the Tenth Circuit, 398 U.S. 74, 89 (1970) (concurring); Schacht v. United States, 398 U.S. 58, 65 (1970) (concurring).

[197] See, *e.g.*, Harlan, note 69 *supra;* Harlan, *Mr. Justice Black—Remarks of a Colleague*, 81 Harv. L. Rev. 1 (1967); Harlan, note 56 *supra.*

[198] Jenkins v. McKeithen, 395 U.S. 411, 433 (1969) (dissenting).

[199] 377 U.S. 533, 624 (1964) (dissenting); see also Shapiro v. Thompson, 394 U.S. 618, 655 (1969) (dissenting).

> [T]hese decisions give support to a current mistaken view of the Constitution and the constitutional function of this Court. This view, in a nutshell, is that every major social ill in this country can find its cure in some constitutional "principle," and that this Court should "take the lead" in promoting reform when other branches of government fail to act. The Constitution is not a panacea for every blot upon the public welfare, nor should this Court, ordained as a judicial body, be thought of as a general haven for reform movements. The Constitution is an instrument of government, fundamental to which is the premise that in a diffusion of governmental authority lies the greatest promise that this Nation will realize liberty for all its citizens. This Court, limited in function in accordance with that premise, does not serve its high purpose when it exceeds its authority, even to satisfy justified impatience with the slow workings of the political process. For when, in the name of constitutional interpretation, the Court *adds* something to the Constitution that was deliberately excluded from it, the Court in reality substitutes its view of what should be so for the amending process.

This canon of reasoned decision making fits closely with the canon of meticulous care for procedural details previously discussed. Together they provide a skeleton outline of that legal craftsmanship for which Harlan has often been praised. Judge Henry Friendly of the Second Circuit stated in tribute to Harlan: "I believe, and I have measured these words, that there has never been a Justice of the Supreme Court who has so consistently maintained a high quality of performance or, despite differences in views, has enjoyed such nearly uniform respect from his colleagues, the inferior bench, the bar, and the academy."[200] Harlan's careful insistence on precise accuracy and his constant effort to express fully and rationally the neutral principles on which he relied, have made many of his decisions models for judicial writing.

VII. Deference to Lower Court Determinations

Harlan thought the Supreme Court's role as a finder of fact should be very limited. Fact finding is a function of the trial court, with limited review by intermediate appellate courts. Generally the

---

[200] Friendly, *Mr. Justice Harlan, as Seen by a Friend and Judge of an Inferior Court*, 85 Harv. L. Rev. 382, 384 (1971).

Supreme Court's inquiry should rest on the record. Where violations of constitutional rights have been asserted, the Court can draw its own inferences from the facts determined below but it should give due weight to the lower court's findings. In review of state court judgments, Harlan observed:[201]

> [This] distinction between facts and inferences may often be difficult to draw, but the guiding principle for this Court should be that when a question is in doubt and demeanor and credibility of witnesses, or contemporaneous understandings of the parties, have a part to play in its resolution, this Court should be extremely slow to upset a state court's inferential findings. The impetus for our exercising *de novo* review of the facts comes from the attitude that unless this Court can fully redetermine the facts of each case for itself, it will be unable to afford complete protection for constitutional rights. But when the "feel" of the trial may have been a proper element in resolving an issue which is unclear on the record, our independent judgment should give way to the greater capability of the state trial court in determining whether a constitutional right has been infringed. Proper regard for the duality of the American judicial system demands no less.

Thus, Harlan objected when the Court, in his view, merely substituted its view on a factual question for that of the state court.[202] What he called, based on his own extensive experience as a trial lawyer, the "feel" of the trial was an important factor in the fact-finding process, unavailable to the Supreme Court. In *Mesarosh v. United States*,[203] the Solicitor General had called to the attention of the Supreme Court the unreliability of the testimony of one of the government's informants and requested a remand for a hearing to determine the truthfulness and credibility of the witness. The Court, instead, reversed the convictions on its own and remanded for a new trial. Harlan, in dissent, believed the reversal of the convictions represented "an unprecedented and dangerous departure from sound principles of judicial administration."[204] He explained why the trial court should have been allowed to make the necessary factual determinations:[205]

---

[201] Beck v. Ohio, 379 U.S. 89, 100 (1964) (dissenting).

[202] Darwin v. Connecticut, 391 U.S. 346, 350 (1968) (concurring and dissenting).

[203] 352 U.S. 1 (1956).

[204] *Id.* at 20.

[205] *Id.* at 22–23.

> The District Court was the proper forum for the kind of investigation which should have been conducted here. This Court, and for that matter the Courts of Appeals, are ill-equipped for such a task. We need say no more than that appellate courts have no facilities for the examination of witnesses; nor in the nature of things can they have that intimate knowledge of the evidence and "feel" of the trial scene, which are so essential to sound judgment upon matters of such complexity and subtlety as those involved here, and which are possessed by the trial court alone.

Generally the Supreme Court should not review the evidence of a criminal trial to determine whether it is sufficient to support the verdict. Harlan, however, writing for the Court, did exactly that in *Scales v. United States*[206] and *Noto v. United States*,[207] in which the Court for the first time reviewed convictions under the membership clause of the Smith Act. He was careful to explain that this review of the sufficiency of the evidence was extraordinary, but was justified in these cases "not only to make sure that substantive constitutional standards have not been thwarted, but also to provide guidance for the future to the lower courts in an area which borders so closely upon constitutionally protected rights."[208] Harlan clearly appreciated the fact that, where the trial court had the last word in determining the facts, constitutional rights could easily be lost. Even in such cases, however, he usually inclined to defer to the greater fact-finding ability of the trial court.[209]

---

[206] 367 U.S. 203 (1961). [207] 367 U.S. 290 (1961). [208] 367 U.S. at 230.

[209] Time, Inc. v. Pape, 401 U.S. 279, 293 (1971) (dissenting). A Chicago police officer had brought a libel suit against a magazine for reporting certain police brutality as a finding rather than as an allegation of the Commission on Civil Rights. The trial court directed a verdict for the defendant but the Court of Appeals reversed, holding that the question of "malice" should have been submitted to the jury. The Supreme Court, reviewing the evidence for itself, reversed the Court of Appeals. Harlan wrote, *id.* at 294: "While it is true, of course, that this Court is free to reexamine for itself the evidentiary bases upon which rest decisions that allegedly impair or punish the exercise of Fourteenth Amendment freedoms, this does not mean that we are of necessity always, or even usually, compelled to do so. Indeed, it is almost impossible to conceive how this Court might continue to function effectively were we to resolve afresh the underlying factual disputes in all cases containing constitutional issues. Nor can I discern in those First Amendment considerations that led us to restrict the States' powers to regulate defamation of public officials any additional interest that is not served by the actual-malice rule of *New York Times* . . . , but is substantially promoted by utilizing this Court as the ultimate arbiter of factual disputes in those libel cases where no unusual factors, such as allegations of harassment or the existence of a jury verdict resting on erroneous instructions . . . are present. While I am confident that the Court does not intend its decision to have any such broad reach, I fear that what is done today may open a door that will prove difficult to close."

Harlan expressed his views repeatedly and vigorously on the appropriate deference due to lower courts in cases involving compensation by employers for injuries to their employees. The trial court primarily, and where necessary the lower appellate courts, had the responsibility of controlling the fact-finding process of a jury in such cases. Where these lower courts had overturned jury verdicts as unsupported by the evidence, the Supreme Court had no business intervening. Since appellate courts were involved, Harlan could no longer rely on the "feel" of the trial scene. He objected to what he viewed as efforts by the Supreme Court merely to assure recovery for the injured party, regardless of the lack of evidence to sustain the verdict. This long series of separate opinions by Harlan focused especially on the Federal Employers Liability Act and the Jones Act. He stated his position in *Rogers v. Missouri Pacific Railroad Co.*[210] Harlan reproached the Court for merely substituting its reading of the evidence for the conclusions of the lower appellate courts. "In my view we should not interfere with the decisions of these three courts in the absence of clear legal error, or some capricious or unreasonable action on their part."[211] "No scientific or precise yardstick," he continued, "can be devised to test the sufficiency of the evidence in a negligence case. The problem has always been one of judgment, to be applied in view of the purposes of the statute."[212] Verdicts in negligence cases must be based on more than a mere scintilla of evidence, there must be enough evidence to enable a reasonable man "to infer both negligence and causation *by reasoning from the evidence*."[213] The trial court, or if necessary, the appellate court, should see to it that a jury observes such a standard and that verdicts are based on reason, not on will or sheer speculation. In these cases, Harlan contended, the Court had departed from these standards. It had reversed lower appellate courts and upheld verdicts based on evidence insufficient to convince a reasoning man. This "departure from a wise rule of law"[214] was unacceptable.

Harlan had many occasions after *Rogers* to reiterate his point. "Cases involving only factual issues and which are of no general

---

[210] 352 U.S. 500 (1957). See text *supra*, at notes 159–60.

[211] *Id.* at 562.

[212] *Id.* at 563.

[213] *Id.* at 564.

[214] *Ibid.*

importance have no legitimate demands upon our energies."[215] He thought that the trial courts and intermediate courts of appeals should supervise jury verdicts. It was not merely a question of saving time and energy for the Supreme Court, but was also a question of maintaining a reasoned, principled approach to control of jury verdicts. After *Rogers* and its sequels, Harlan became convinced that the Supreme Court was interfering too much with the lower courts, eliminating in the process any meaningful norms for supervision of jury verdicts by the lower courts:[216]

> I fear that this decision confirms my growing suspicion that the real but unarticulated meaning of *Rogers* is that in FELA cases anything that a jury says goes, with the consequence that all meaningful judicial supervision over jury verdicts in such cases has been put at an end. . . . If so, I think the time has come when the Court should frankly say so. If not, then the Court should at least give expression to the standards by which the lower courts are to be guided in these cases. Continuance of the present unsatisfactory state of affairs can only lead to much waste motion on the part of lower courts and defense lawyers.

In this whole line of employer's liability cases, all the Supreme Court was doing, according to Harlan, was to "second-guess, one step further removed from the actual events, the District Court and the Court of Appeals."[217] This was not an appropriate use of the Supreme Court's time. It made more sense to Harlan to rely more fully on the lower court's review of the record and determination of such factual issues. Furthermore, some rational standard or norm

---

[215] Harris v. Pennsylvania R. Co., 361 U.S. 15, 25 (1959) (dissenting).

[216] *Id.* at 27 (citation omitted); see also Gibson v. Thompson, 355 U.S. 18, 19 (1957) (separate memorandum); Sinkler v. Missouri Pac. R. Co., 356 U.S. 326, 332 (1958) (dissenting); Honeycutt v. Wabash R. Co., 355 U.S. 424 (1958) (separate memorandum); Moore v. Terminal R.R. Ass'n of St. Louis, 358 U.S. 31, 32 (1958) (concurring); Ward v. Atlantic Coast Line Co., 362 U.S. 396, 400 (1960) (dissenting); Gallick v. Baltimore & O. R. Co., 372 U.S. 108, 122 (1963) (dissenting); Basham v. Pennsylvania R. Co., 372 U.S. 699, 701 (1963) (dissenting); Dennis v. Denver & R.G.W.R. Co., 375 U.S. 208, 212 (1963) (dissenting); Davis v. Baltimore & O. R. Co., 379 U.S. 671, 672 (1965) (concurring); see also Michalic v. Cleveland Tankers, Inc., 364 U.S. 325 (1960); Senko v. LaCrosse Dredging Corp., 352 U.S. 370, 374 (1957) (dissenting); Crumady v. The Joachim Hendrick Fisser, 358 U.S. 423, 429 (1959) (dissenting); Mitchell v. Trawler Racer, 362 U.S. 539, 570 (1960) (dissenting); Guzman v. Pichirilo, 369 U.S. 698, 703 (1962) (dissenting); Salem v. United States Lines, 370 U.S. 31, 38 (1962) (concurring and dissenting); Reed v. The Yaka, 373 U.S. 410, 416 (1963) (dissenting); Tipton v. Socony Mobil Oil Co., 375 U.S. 34, 37 (1963) (dissenting).

[217] Mercer v. Theriot, 377 U.S. 152, 156 (1964) (dissenting).

should be preserved to allow lower courts to assure that jury verdicts were not mere gifts to the unfortunate injured party at the expense of the employer.

Beside these cases dealing with the limits of the Supreme Court's role in the fact-finding process, Harlan also urged the Court to show deference to the lower courts on other issues. In *United States v. Loew's, Inc.*,[218] for instance, the Court, in the last part of its decision, modified the terms of the trial court's remedial decree in an antitrust suit to achieve "greater precision in the operation of the decrees." Harlan concurred with most of the Court's opinion but objected to this tampering with the trial court's decree. It was inappropriate for the Court "to concern itself at all with such comparatively trivial remedial glosses upon the District Court's decree," Harlan stated:[219]

> I think it distorts the proper relationship of this Court to the lower federal courts, whose assessment of a particular situation is bound to be more informed than ours, for us to exercise revisory power over the terms of antitrust relief, except in instances where things have manifestly gone awry. This is not such a case, as the meticulous handling of it by the District Court abundantly shows. In my view its decree should be left undisturbed.

Similarly, the Supreme Court should not itself determine the scope of the trial judge's discretion in assessing the amount of costs to be taxed against the unsuccessful litigant. This type of question should, in Harlan's view, be decided by the courts of appeals.[220] The trial judge's power to punish for contempt for disorder in the courtroom likewise should be reviewed only by the the courts of appeals, not by the Supreme Court.[221] The Court should not "strip the district courts of all discretion to exercise their common sense."[222]

Harlan's insistence on proper deference to the lower court's determinations undoubtedly influenced him as he considered how to decide a particular case. Purely factual determinations should not

[218] 371 U.S. 38, 55 (1962) (concurring and dissenting).

[219] *Id.* at 56.

[220] Farmer v. Arabian American Co., 379 U.S. 227, 239 (1964) (dissenting).

[221] In re McConnell, 370 U.S. 230, 237 (1962) (dissenting).

[222] Rodriguez v. United States, 395 U.S. 327, 334 (1969) (concurring and dissenting).

ordinarily be reviewed *de novo* by the Supreme Court. In obscenity cases, however, where factual and constitutional issues are necessarily intertwined, Harlan was convinced that the Court should provide individualized adjudication, reviewing and determining for itself whether the material was obscene.[223] But he thought it inappropriate, in most cases, for the Supreme Court to expend its time reviewing factual questions. If the Court insisted on intervening in such questions, it should at least do so in a reasoned, principled manner which would provide guidance for the lower courts in the future. This principle of deference to lower court determinations is thus closely related to the principle of neutral, reasoned decision making. The pathetic situation of an individual litigant should not lead the Court to ignore appropriate legal principles and intervene in a purely factual dispute. In one of his talks Harlan said:[224]

> The cornerstone of a petition for certiorari in a federal case is a showing that the question sought to be reviewed is one of *general* importance. Review by certiorari is "in the interest of the law, its appropriate exposition and enforcement, not in the mere interest of the litigants." The fact that a case may have been wrongly decided as between the parties is not, standing alone, enough to assure certiorari.

VIII. Protection of the Individual's Right to Fundamental Fairness

In Justice Harlan's judicial philosophy, the right of the individual to due process of law operated as a core principle. In the tradition of Justices Cardozo and Frankfurter, he interpreted the Due Process Clause of the Fourteenth Amendment as a demand that the States meet a standard of fundamental fairness in dealing with individuals. He refused to read the Due Process Clause as a shorthand expression of the more specific protections of the Bill of Rights. His insistence on a clear distinction between Fourteenth Amendment Due Process and the Bill of Rights led to his application of a double standard in the protection of individual rights: rights asserted by the individual against the State were measured by a dif-

---

[223] Kingsley International Pictures Corp. v. Regents, 360 U.S. 684, 702 (1959) (concurring).

[224] Harlan, *Manning the Dikes*, 13 Record 541, 551 (1958).

ferent standard (the Fourteenth Amendment) than rights asserted against the federal government (the Bill of Rights).

Harlan discussed his position on procedural due process most fully in his dissent in *Duncan v. Louisiana*.[225] Gary Duncan, a nineteen-year-old black, had been convicted of simple battery, which under Louisiana law was a misdemeanor punishable by a maximum of two years' imprisonment and a $300 fine. He was actually sentenced to serve sixty days and fined $150. Duncan had sought a trial by jury, but the state constitution allowed jury trials only in cases in which capital punishment or imprisonment at hard labor could be imposed. The trial court, therefore, denied his request. The state supreme court found no error of law and denied review. The Supreme Court heard the case and held that the State had denied Duncan his constitutional right to a jury trial. It held that the right to a jury trial guaranteed by the Sixth Amendment as a limitation on the federal government was also a limitation on the States by reason of the Due Process Clause of the Fourteenth Amendment.

The Court, in Harlan's view, was wrong not only in its conclusion, but also in the method it employed to reach it. The State was not prohibited from trying charges of simple battery without a jury either by the Fourteenth Amendment or, even more emphatically, by the Sixth Amendment. Harlan, always attuned to questions of federalism, began by reflecting on the proper allocation of authority over the criminal justice system between the States and the national government. Primary responsibility had always belonged to the States to operate the criminal justice system within their borders and to adapt it to local needs. The States must meet the requirements of the Due Process Clause that their criminal procedures be "fundamentally fair in all respects."[226] This requirement, however, did not impose nationwide uniformity, command fidelity to older methods, or require conformance of state procedures to those in federal courts.

The heart of Harlan's position was that "the first section of the Fourteenth Amendment was meant neither to incorporate, nor to be limited to, the specific guarantees of the first eight Amendments."[227] If the content of the Fourteenth Amendment is not

[225] 391 U.S. 145 (1968).

[226] *Id.* at 172.

[227] *Id.* at 174.

supplied by the Bill of Rights, Harlan had to look elsewhere to discover a sufficiently clear and specific meaning to serve as a limitation upon the States. As he expressed it, the method of analysis of the Due Process Clause:[228]

> is to start with the words "liberty" and "due process of law" and attempt to define them in a way that accords with American traditions and our system of government. This approach, involving a much more discriminating process of adjudication than does "incorporation," is, albeit difficult, the one that was followed throughout the 19th and most of the present century. It entails a "gradual process of judicial inclusion and exclusion," seeking, with due recognition of constitutional tolerance for state experimentation and disparity, to ascertain those "immutable principles . . . of free government which no member of the Union may disregard."

Historical tradition and the principle of federalism offered Harlan the tools he needed to probe the meaning of the Fourteenth Amendment's Due Process Clause. Due process was not restricted to any precise, past statement of rules such as the first eight Amendments. This would eliminate all possibility of growth of the law to meet changing circumstances. Nor did the Fourteenth Amendment command the elimination of diversity among the States within the federal system. Harlan sought instead to get a broad sense of the nation's historical tradition, which was derived from many sources, including its long-standing commitment to the more specific protections in the Bill of Rights:[229]

> The relationship of the Bill of Rights to this "gradual process" seems to me to be twofold. In the first place it has long been clear that the Due Process Clause imposes some restrictions on state action that parallel Bill of Rights restrictions on federal action. Second, and more important than this accidental overlap, is the fact that the Bill of Rights is evidence, at various points, of the content Americans find in the term "liberty" and of American standards of fundamental fairness.

He looked to examples where the Court from the first eight Amendments had derived evidence of America's traditional commitment to liberty and procedural fairness:[230]

---

[228] *Id.* at 176 (citation omitted).

[229] *Id.* at 177.

[230] *Id.* at 179.

> In all of these instances, the right guaranteed against the States by the Fourteenth Amendment was one that had also been guaranteed against the Federal Government by one of the first eight Amendments. The logically critical thing, however, was not that the rights had been found in the Bill of Rights, but that they were deemed, in the context of American legal history, to be fundamental.

Harlan based his approach to the Due Process Clause on that of Justice Cardozo. He analyzed Cardozo's opinion in *Palko v. Connecticut*[231] to demonstrate his fidelity to Cardozo's philosophy. Cardozo had read the Fourteenth Amendment as imposing upon the States, not all the limitations of the Bill of Rights which restricted the federal government, but only those limitations which were "of the very essence of a scheme of ordered liberty."[232] Harlan fully concurred in Cardozo's rejection of any theory which incorporated the Bill of Rights into the Fourteenth Amendment.

After clarifying the proper meaning of the Due Process Clause, Harlan concluded his *Duncan* dissent by reframing the issue: "[T]he question before this Court, in my view, is whether [the criminal defendant] was denied any element of fundamental procedural fairness."[233] He cited cases to show that the Court in the past had held that a jury trial was not an essential requisite of criminal due process. Time had not altered the situation or exposed significant new evidence. "The virtues and defects of the jury system have been hotly debated for a long time, and are hotly debated today."[234] Trial by jury was not the prevailing mode of determining guilt either in England or in this country. It is not the only fair method. Throughout British and American history, summary procedures have been used for trial of lesser crimes. The point in considering these summary criminal trials, without juries, as Harlan saw it, was not that:[235]

> [M]any offenses that English-speaking communities have, at one time or another, regarded as triable without a jury are more serious, and carry more serious penalties, than the one involved here. The point is rather that until today few people would have thought the exact location of the line mattered very much. There is no obvious reason why a jury trial is a

[231] 302 U.S. 319 (1937).

[232] *Id.* at 325.

[233] 391 U.S. at 183.

[234] *Id.* at 186.

[235] *Id.* at 192–93.

> requisite of fundamental fairness when the charge is robbery, and not a requisite of fairness when the same defendant, for the same actions, is charged with assault and petty theft. The reason for the historic exception for relatively minor crimes is the obvious one: the burden of jury trial was thought to outweigh its marginal advantages. Exactly why the States should not be allowed to make continuing adjustments, based on the state of their criminal dockets and the difficulty of summoning jurors, simply escapes me.

In addition to *Duncan*, Harlan had many occasions to scrutinize the procedures employed in particular cases to determine whether they satisfied the norm of fundamental fairness. In *In re Gault*,[236] Harlan was forced to draw a distinction between those procedural safeguards for a juvenile proceeding which he thought were required by Fourteenth Amendment and other more ample safeguards which the majority thought were necessary. Harlan's process of analysis revealed again his struggling effort to express the due process principle in a clear and intelligible manner. The majority had concluded that the following procedures were constitutionally necessary to protect the accused individual in a juvenile proceeding to determine delinquency: advance written notice of the charges; the right to be represented by counsel; the right to court-appointed counsel in cases of indigency; the privilege against self-incrimination; assurance that confessions are voluntary and, absent a valid confession, the requirement of confrontation of witnesses and sworn testimony with the possibility of cross-examination. Harlan accepted some, but not all, of these requirements. He concluded that only four procedural safeguards were required in state juvenile courts by the Due Process Clause: timely notice to the parents and children of the nature of the proceeding which may affect their rights; timely notice of the right to be represented by counsel; in cases where the child may be confined, notice that the court will appoint counsel for indigent parties; and the maintenance of a written record of the proceedings adequate to permit effective review.

Harlan thus had distingushed in *Gault* certain rights required by due process from the broader range of rights which the majority had held necessary. He knew that such a distinction must be based on the proper rational methodology for analyzing the Due Process Clause. He would have been the first to reject the notion that he

---

[236] 387 U.S. 1 (1967).

was merely expressing his own subjective values and preferences. He labored, therefore, to state the objective, neutral, rational principles which provided a basis for this distinction between the lesser demands he derived from the Due Process Clause and the more extensive requirements of the majority. "The central issue here," Harlan insisted, "is the method by which the procedural requirements of due process should be measured."[237]

To determine the precise requirements of procedural due process in the context of the State's interest in the juvenile proceedings, Harlan adopted a balancing approach. The Court should, Harlan thought:[238]

> measure the requirements of due process by reference both to the problems which confront the State and to the actual character of the procedural system which the State had created. The Court has for such purposes chiefly examined three connected sources: first, the "settled usages and modes of proceeding," . . . second, the "fundamental principles of liberty and justice which lie at the base of all our civil and political institutions," . . . and third, the character and requirements of the circumstances presented in each situation. . . . Each of these factors is relevant to the issues here, but it is the last which demands particular examination.
>
> The Court has repeatedly emphasized that determination of the constitutionally required procedural safeguards in any situation requires recognition both of the "interests affected" and of the "circumstances involved." . . . In particular, a "compelling public interest" must, under our cases, be taken fully into account in assessing the validity under the due process clauses of state or federal legislation and its application. . . . Such interests would never warrant arbitrariness or the diminution of any specifically assured constitutional right, . . . but they are an essential element of the context through which the legislation and proceedings under it must be read and evaluated.

Harlan refined the balancing approach by analyzing the public interest of the States in establishing specialized juvenile courts organized with their own rules and distinctive consequences. On the one hand, the Supreme Court should give the widest deference to the judgments of the state legislatures in determining substantive policy. On the other hand, where these legislative judgments touched the necessity and wisdom of procedural guarantees, the

---

[237] *Id.* at 68.

[238] *Ibid.* (citations omitted).

legislature had entered a sphere of particular competence of the courts. Viewing this substantive-procedural dichotomy as an indispensable tool of analysis, Harlan concluded:[239]

> Courts are thus obliged both by constitutional command and by their distinctive functions to bear particular responsibility for the measurement of procedural due process. These factors in combination suggest that legislatures may properly expect only a cautious deference for their procedural judgments, but that, conversely, courts must exercise their special responsibility for procedural guarantees with care to permit ample scope for achieving the purposes of legislative programs. Plainly, courts can exercise such care only if they have in each case first studied thoroughly the objectives and implementation of the program at stake; if, upon completion of those studies, the effect of extensive procedural restrictions upon valid legislative purposes cannot be assessed with reasonable certainty, the court should necessarily proceed with restraint.

This sensitive approach to the state legislature's policy determinations led Harlan to suggest the criteria by which the procedural requirements of due process should be measured:[240]

> [F]irst, no more restrictions should be imposed than are imperative to assure the proceedings' fundamental fairness; second, the restrictions which are imposed should be those which preserve, so far as possible, the essential elements of the State's purpose; and finally, restrictions should be chosen which will later permit orderly selection of any additional protections which may ultimately prove necessary. In this way, the Court may guarantee the fundamental fairness of the proceeding, and yet permit the State to continue development of an effective response to the problems of juvenile crime.

This carefully measured, balancing approach, with sensitivity to the State's legislatively chosen policies, is vintage Harlan: just enough procedural requirements to ensure fundamental fairness, but not enough to intrude unnecessarily upon the State's legislative policy. When Harlan applied these criteria, he concluded that only the four procedural requirements already mentioned must be imposed upon the state juvenile proceedings in the name of due process.

The *Duncan* and *Gault* cases demonstrate the interrelationship between the principles already discussed and Harlan's analysis of

---

[239] *Id.* at 71.

[240] *Id.* at 72.

the content of procedural due process. Federalism, deference to the legislature, and fidelity to precedent and historical tradition were all critical factors as he tried to articulate in a reasoned, neutral expression the meaning of due process. His careful balancing of the State's legitimate interests in *Gault* against the demands of due process for the individual juvenile enabled him to give some idea of what he meant by fundamental fairness. The Fourteenth Amendment required the States to comply only with those procedural guarantees "imperative to assure fundamental fairness," while allowing the States "to develop without unnecessary hindrance their systems of juvenile courts."[241]

Harlan returned repeatedly to the fundamental fairness test for due process. This provided the touchstone by which he determined in particular cases whether or not there had been a denial of due process. In the following cases Harlan concluded that the individual had been denied due process of law.

Where an individual, unrepresented by counsel, faced enhanced punishment as a multiple offender and had been given no advance notice of the charges made in the multiple-offense accusation until he appeared in open court and learned on which convictions the State had relied, it was a denial of due process to expect him to plead then and there and state his defense. "One who is untutored in the law cannot help but be bewildered by this sudden presentation of the charges against him and the demand for an immediate response."[242]

It was likewise a denial of due process to hold a labor union's lawyer in contempt where he was deprived of the opportunity to prove that it had been agreed on among the parties to use contempt proceedings against the pickets as a test of the state court's jurisdiction.[243] Due process, in Harlan's view, was also denied where one accused of a felony was denied court appointed counsel.[244] This reversal of a prior rule was necessary, Harlan thought, because the prior rule had long been eroded by exceptions. It was unhealthy to pay lip service to a rule which was ignored in practice.

Testimony against the accused from a preliminary hearing at

---

[241] *Id.* at 76.

[242] Chewning v. Cunningham, 368 U.S. 443, 458 (1962) (concurring).

[243] In re Green, 369 U.S. 689, 693 (1962) (concurring and dissenting).

[244] Gideon v. Wainwright, 372 U.S. 335, 349 (1963) (concurring).

which accused was not represented by counsel and did not cross-examine the witness cannot be used at the trial to convict the accused when the witness was unavailable to testify. Harlan concluded that "this state judgment must be reversed because a right of confrontation is 'implicit in the concept of ordered liberty' . . . reflected in the Due Process Clause of the Fourteenth Amendment independently of the Sixth."[245]

Harlan concluded that the Due Process Clause likewise prohibited the State, over defendant's objection, from employing television in the courtroom to televise a criminal trial of widespread interest. Though the State had argued there had been no specific prejudice to the defendant, Harlan insisted:[246]

> I do not believe that the Fourteenth Amendment is so impotent when the trial practices in question are instinct with dangers to constitutional guarantees. I am at a loss to understand how the Fourteenth Amendment can be thought not to encompass protection of a state criminal trial from the dangers created by the intrusion of collateral and wholly irrelevant influences into the courtroom.

Harlan also saw a due process violation in the State's inability to employ its compulsory process to obtain the relevant testimony of a defense witness who was serving time in a state prison, especially where such a witness would not have been barred from testifying for the prosecution.[247] The Due Process Clause also barred a State from ignoring an accused's request to be promptly brought to trial merely because he was incarcerated in another jurisdiction.[248]

In a juvenile proceeding to determine delinquency, Harlan was convinced that due process required the proof of guilt beyond a reasonable doubt, not merely proof by a preponderance of the evidence:[249]

> I view the requirement of proof beyond a reasonable doubt in a criminal case as bottomed on a fundamental value determination of our society that it is far worse to convict an innocent man than to let a guilty man go free. It is only because of the

[245] Pointer v. Texas, 380 U.S. 400, 408 (1965) (concurring).

[246] Estes v. Texas, 381 U.S. 532, 593 (1965) (concurring).

[247] Washington v. Texas, 388 U.S. 14, 23 (1967) (concurring).

[248] Smith v. Hooey, 393 U.S. 374, 383 (1969) (separate opinion).

[249] In re Winship, 397 U.S. 358, 372 (1970) (concurring).

> nearly complete and long-standing acceptance of the reasonable-doubt standard by the States in criminal trials that the Court has not before today had to hold explicitly that due process, as an expression of fundamental procedural fairness, requires a more stringent standard for criminal trials than for ordinary civil litigation.

Finally, in a noncriminal case, Harlan concluded that due process was denied by garnishment of wages without notice and prior hearing.[250]

These cases demonstrate that Harlan did find in the fundamental fairness test for due process a significant limitation upon a State's powers in dealing with individuals. In some of these cases the due process principle overrode the federalism principle on which Harlan had so often insisted. In the cases which follow, on the other hand, Harlan concluded that there had been no denial of due process. He undoubtedly was swayed in these cases by the principle of federalism as well as by his interpretation of due process as fundamental fairness.

In one such case Harlan concluded that due process was satisfied by the State's procedure to determine the sanity of a convict before his execution. The State imposed a continuing duty upon the warden to check on the mental condition of condemned prisoners and to commence proceedings for a sanity determination whenever he found ground to believe the prisoner had become insane. The condemned person had no right to initiate the proceedings himself. "This procedure," Harlan thought, "satisfies the test of fundamental fairness."[251]

Harlan likewise found that due process was satisfied where the Justice in charge of a state judicial inquiry into alleged improper practices of the local bar had required counsel retained by the private detectives and investigators being questioned to remain outside the hearing room while they were interrogated. The Justice, however, had been ready to suspend the hearing whenever the detectives wished to consult with counsel.[252]

Where criminal defendants, convicted by the trial court, had been denied court-appointed counsel on appeal, Harlan thought that the state procedure did not deny due process. The state appellate court

[250] Sniadach v. Family Finance Corp., 395 U.S. 337, 342 (1969) (concurring).

[251] Caritativo v. California, 357 U.S. 549, 550 (1958) (concurring).

[252] Anonymous v. Baker, 360 U.S. 287 (1959).

had reviewed the record and concluded that no good could be served by appointment of counsel. Harlan revealed the limited approach he took to the due process issue by the way he framed the issue. Since due process did not require appellate review at all, Harlan wrote, "the question presented is the narrow one whether the State's rules with respect to the appointment of counsel are so arbitrary or unreasonable, *in the context of the particular appellate procedure that it has established*, as to require their invalidation."[253]

Due process, in Harlan's view, did not bar a State from applying its harmless error rule in a criminal trial where evidence obtained through an unconstitutional search and seizure had been erroneously admitted.[254] Harlan did not find a due process violation in a trial judge's failure, on his own initiative, to conduct a competency hearing for a criminal defendant since the facts known to the judge did not forcefully suggest the defendant's incompetency.[255]

In another case, eight members of the Supreme Court had held that prejudicial statements by the bailiff necessitated reversal of the conviction. Harlan in dissent concluded that the statements, though prejudicial in nature, had not had a prejudicial effect. He would require "a substantial showing of prejudice in fact . . . before a due process violation can be found."[256]

Still another case in which Harlan held that due process was satisfied involved the Texas recidivist statute. The jury there had been fully informed of the defendant's previous criminal convictions but was charged by the court that such matters were not to be taken into account in determining the defendant's guilt or innocence on the primary charge. Harlan manifested the close interrelationship in his thinking between the federalism principle and the principle of fundamental fairness. In the opinion for the Court, he stated:[257]

---

[253] Douglas v. California, 372 U.S. 353, 365 (1963) (dissenting).

[254] Fahy v. Connecticut, 375 U.S. 85, 92 (1963) (dissenting); see also Chapman v. California, 386 U.S. 18, 50 (1967) (dissenting): "[T]he record is barren of any showing that the California courts, which have been in the vanguard in the development of individual safeguards in criminal trials, are using their harmless-error rule to destroy or dilute constitutional guarantees. If the contrary were the case and the harmless-error rule itself were shown to have resulted in a course of convictions significantly influenced by constitutionally impermissible factors, I think it clear that constitutional due process could not countenance the continued application of the rule."

[255] Pate v. Robinson, 383 U.S. 375, 387 (1966) (dissenting).

[256] Parker v. Gladden, 385 U.S. 363, 368 (1966) (dissenting).

[257] Spencer v. Texas, 385 U.S. 554, 563–64 (1967) (citations omitted).

> Cases in this Court have long proceeded on the premise that the Due Process Clause guarantees the fundamental elements of fairness in a criminal trial. . . . But it has never been thought that such cases establish this Court as a rule-making organ for the promulgation of state rules of criminal procedure. And none of the specific provisions of the Constitution ordains this Court such authority. In the face of the legitimate state purpose and the long-standing and widespread use that attend the procedure under attack here, we find it impossible to say that because of the possibility of some collateral prejudice the Texas procedure is rendered unconstitutional under the Due Process Clause as it has been interpreted and applied in our past cases. As Mr. Justice Cardozo had occasion to remark, a state rule of law "does not run foul of the Fourteenth Amendment because another method may seem to our thinking to be fairer or wiser or to give a surer promise of protection to the prisoner at bar."

Finally, where the Supreme Court held that the trial court record did not disclose that the defendant's guilty plea was voluntarily and intelligently made and that the conviction must be reversed, Harlan again dissented. In his view due process was not denied by the state court's failure to develop an adequate record to establish that the defendant had knowingly pleaded guilty, especially since the defendant had never alleged that his guilty plea was involuntary.[258]

In these cases there would seem to be no clear line separating those situations in which Harlan found a denial of due process and those where he concluded that due process had been satisfied. The narrow channel he navigated was marked only by dim beacons barely visible through the mist. Harlan groped to express, as clearly as he could, the methodology he used in determining the content of fundamental fairness. He clearly evaluated each case individually, wrestled with the facts in the record, and tried to determine whether the individual had been treated in a fundamentally fair manner. In spite of his effort to articulate neutral, objective principles to determine whether due process had been satisfied, it is doubtful whether anyone, even those accepting Harlan's approach to due process, would have agreed with him in all its applications.

Only a few related questions remain to complete the outline. Harlan consistently rejected the theory, espoused by most members

[258] Boykin v. Alabama, 395 U.S. 238, 244 (1969).

of the Court, that the more defined restrictions of the first eight amendments provided content for the amorphous concept of due process. This incorporation theory was presented in two forms, either absolute or selective incorporation. Justice Black believed in the absolute incorporation of all provisions of the Bill of Rights into the Fourteenth Amendment. For Black, the Fourteenth Amendment imposed on the States the same limitations, neither broader nor narrower, that the Bill of Rights imposed on the national government. As Black said in *Adamson v. California*:[259] "My study of the historical events that culminated in the Fourteenth Amendment . . . persuades me that one of the chief objects that the provisions of the Amendment's first section, separately, and as a whole, were intended to accomplish was to make the Bill of Rights, applicable to the states." Black rejected what he called the natural law theory of the Constitution. By this theory Black feared the Supreme Court could periodically expand or contract constitutional standards such as due process "to conform to the Court's conception of what at a particular time constitutes 'civilized decency' and 'fundamental liberty and justice.' "[260]

Most members of the Court rejected Black's absolute incorporation theory. Instead they incorporated specific provisions of the Bill of Rights selectively, as applicable to the case then under consideration. Rather than accept Black's wholesale incorporation, they looked to the particular clause of the Bill of Rights to determine whether it should be embraced within the Due Process Clause of the Fourteenth Amendment as a limitation upon the States.[261] If a Clause of the Bill of Rights was incorporated in the Fourteenth Amendment, the same provision, presumably with identical metes and bounds, restricted both the federal and state governments.

As we have seen, Harlan rejected the incorporation theory,

---

[259] 332 U.S. 46, 71 (1947) (Black, J., dissenting). Harlan's grandfather, the first Mr. Justice Harlan, also thought that the Fourteenth Amendment had been intended to make the Bill of Rights applicable as a limitation on the States. O'Neil v. Vermont, 144 U.S. 323, 366 (1892) (dissenting); Maxwell v. Dow, 176 U.S. 581, 605 (1900) (dissenting). Justice Frankfurter referred to the first Mr. Justice Harlan in this regard as an "eccentric exception." Adamson v. California, 332 U.S. at 62.

[260] 332 U.S. at 69; see also Rochin v. California, 342 U.S. 165, 174 (1952) (Black, J., concurring).

[261] See, *e.g.*, Mapp v. Ohio, 367 U.S. 643 (1961); Duncan v. Louisiana, 391 U.S. 145 (1968).

whether absolute or selective. In *Duncan*, he stressed the historical reason for rejecting the incorporation theories. Relying on an article by Professor Charles Fairman,[262] he concluded that the drafter and ratifiers of the Fourteenth Amendment simply did not think they were incorporating the Bill of Rights. The very breadth and generality of the Fourteenth Amendment's terms suggested that its authors intended the conceptions of "liberty" and "due process" would evolve with the "increasing experience and evolving conscience of the American people."[263] Freezing the meaning of these terms by restricting them to the various provisions of the Bill of Rights was foreign to the intent of the framers of the Fourteenth Amendment. "In short, neither history, nor sense, supports using the Fourteenth Amendment to put the States in a constitutional straitjacket with respect to their own development in the administration of criminal or civil law."[264]

Besides this historical argument, Harlan turned to prior judicial interpretation of the Fourteenth Amendment to demonstrate the jarring shift implied in the incorporation theories. He repeatedly cited Justice Cardozo to show that the current majority had repudiated the previously accepted reading of the Amendment:[265]

> [T]hat this Court should have apparently become so impervious to the pervasive wisdom of the constitutional philosophy embodied in *Palko*, and that it should have felt itself able to attribute to the perceptive and timeless words of Mr. Justice Cardozo nothing more than a "watering down" of constitutional rights, are indeed revealing symbols of the extent to which we are weighing anchors from the fundamentals of our constitutional system.

In rejecting the incorporation theories, Harlan argued that the Fourteenth Amendment Due Process Clause limits the States by the norm of fundamental fairness, "whose content in any given instance is to be judicially derived not alone, as my colleague [Black] believes it should be, from the specifics of the Constitution, but also,

---

[262] Fairman, *Does the Fourteenth Amendment Incorporate the Bill of Rights? The Original Understanding*, 2 STAN. L. REV. 5 (1949).

[263] 391 U.S. at 175.

[264] *Id.* at 175–76.

[265] Benton v. Maryland, 395 U.S. 784, 809 (1969) (dissenting). Harlan also relied on Cardozo's interpretation of the Fourteenth Amendment in Duncan v. Louisiana, 391 U.S. 145, 179 (1968) (dissenting); Malloy v. Hogan, 378 U.S. 1, 14 (1964) (dissenting); and Pointer v. Texas, 380 U.S. 400, 408 (1965) (concurring).

as I believe, from concepts which are part of the Anglo-American legal heritage."[266]

Justice Black feared that the Cardozo-Harlan approach allowed a Justice to read his own personal social philosophy and sense of right and wrong into the "nebulous standards" of the Due Process Clause.[267] Harlan could hardly ignore this gauntlet. He firmly believed that a judge should not impose his social philosophy upon the nation in the name of constitutional interpretation; he too had read Holmes's dissent in *Lochner v. New York*.[268] He insisted, however, that fidelity to historical tradition and the principles of federalism and separation of powers provided a framework for interpreting Fourteenth Amendment Due Process which mitigated the risk of judicially dictated philosophies:[269]

> While I could not more heartily agree that judicial "self restraint" is an indispensable ingredient of sound constitutional adjudication, I do submit that the formula suggested for achieving it is more hollow than real. "Specific" provisions of the Constitution, no less than "due process," lend themselves as readily to "personal" interpretations by judges whose constitutional outlook is simply to keep the Constitution in supposed "tune with the times" . . . .
>
> Judicial self-restraint will not, I suggest, be brought about in the "due process" area by the historically unfounded incorporation formula long advanced by my Brother BLACK, and now in part espoused by my Brother STEWART. It will be achieved in this area, as in other constitutional areas, only by continual insistence upon respect for the teachings of history, solid recognition of the basic values that underlie our society, and wise appreciation of the great roles that the doctrines of federalism and separation of powers have played in establishing and preserving American freedoms. . . . Adherence to these principles will not, of course, obviate all constitutional differences of opinion among judges, nor should it. Their continued recognition will, however, go farther toward keeping most judges from roaming at large in the constitutional field than will the interpolation into the Constitution of an artificial and largely illusory restriction on the content of the Due Process Clause.

---

[266] Sniadach v. Family Finance Corp., 395 U.S. 337, 342 (1969) (concurring).

[267] Rochin v. California, 342 U.S. 165, 175 (1952) (Black, J., concurring).

[268] 198 U.S. 45, 74 (1905).

[269] Griswold v. Connecticut, 381 U.S. 479, 501 (1965) (concurring).

Harlan thus reverted to his philosophy of federalism and his reliance on history in repudiating the incorporation theories. In his view incorporation implied the application to the States of a particular Clause of the Bill of Rights with all its prior judicial construction in federal cases, "thereby making the former applicable lock, stock, and barrel to the States."[270] Harlan saw two consequences of incorporation, both equally objectionable. In the first place, deriving the content of Fourteenth Amendment Due Process from the provisions of the Bill of Rights disregarded "all relevant differences which may exist between state and federal criminal law and its enforcement. The ultimate result is compelled uniformity, which is inconsistent with the purpose of our federal system."[271] Harlan viewed the Constitution as tolerating, indeed encouraging, differences between state and federal law enforcement, but "[t]he philosophy of 'incorporation' . . . subordinates all such state differences to the particular requirements of the Federal Bill of Rights."[272]

On the other hand, Harlan feared that the incorporation theories would lead to a dilution of federal protection under the Bill of Rights in order to allow the States greater flexibility in ordering their criminal justice systems. When the Court held that the Sixth Amendment, made applicable to the States by the Fourteenth Amendment, tolerated a six-person jury, Harlan pointed out, "The necessary consequence of this decision is that 12-member juries are not *constitutionally* required in *federal* criminal trials either."[273]

Harlan's double standard based on the distinction between constitutional restrictions on the States in the Fourteenth Amendment and those limiting the national government was espoused most explicitly in a pair of obscenity cases which the Court decided at the same time. In one case in which the national government had brought

[270] Benton v. Maryland, 395 U.S. 784, 801 (1969) (dissenting).

[271] Malloy v. Hogan, 378 U.S. 1, 16 (1964) (dissenting).

[272] Pointer v. Texas, 380 U.S. 400, 409 (1965) (concurring).

[273] Williams v. Florida, 399 U.S. 78, 118 (1970) (concurring). Throughout his years on the Court, Harlan objected to the incorporation theories in many opinions. See, *e.g.*, Gideon v. Wainwright, 372 U.S. 335, 349 (1963) (concurring); Griffin v. California, 380 U.S. 609, 615 (1965) (concurring); Parker v. Gladden, 385 U.S. 363, 366 (1966) (dissenting); Washington v. Texas, 388 U.S. 14, 23 (1967) (concurring); Smith v. Hooey, 393 U.S. 374, 383 (1969) (separate opinion); Dickey v. Florida, 398 U.S. 30, 38 (1970) (concurring). See Rogge, *Williams v. Florida: End of a Theory*, 16 VILL. L. REV. 411, 424 (1971).

the obscenity prosecution, Harlan concluded that the federal statute violated the letter and the spirit of the First Amendment.[274] The other case involved a prosecution by a State under its obscenity statute. Here Harlan thought that the statute's constitutionality should be determined by inquiring "whether the state action so subverts the fundamental liberties implicit in the Due Process Clause that it cannot be sustained as a rational exercise of power."[275] Reflecting a classical view of federal-state relations, Harlan made his position explicit:[276]

> The Constitution differentiates between those areas of human conduct subject to the regulation of the States and those subject to the powers of the Federal Government. The substantive powers of the two governments, in many instances, are distinct. And in every case where we are called upon to balance the interest in free expression against other interests, it seems to me important that we should keep in the forefront the question of whether those other interests are state or federal. Since under our constitutional scheme the two are not necessarily equivalent, the balancing process must needs often produce different results. Whether a particular limitation on speech or press is to be upheld because it subserves a paramount governmental interest must, to a large extent, I think, depend on whether that government has, under the Constitution, a direct substantive interest, that is, the power to act, in the particular area involved.

Harlan saw no anomaly in applying a different constitutional norm to the States and to the national government.

The *Roth* and *Alberts* cases introduce the question of substantive due process. Harlan was one of the few recent Justices who explicitly justified the use of the Due Process Clause as a substantive limitation on legislation.

In many ways Harlan's dissent in *Poe v. Ullman*[277] was a remarkable performance. A Connecticut statute imposed criminal penalties on the use of any contraceptive device. A majority of the Supreme Court voted to dismiss the appeal since the State had not enforced the statute and thus the cases were not justiciable. Justice Frank-

[274] Roth v. United States, 354 U.S. 476, 496 (1957) (dissenting).

[275] Alberts v. California, 354 U.S. 476, 501 (1957) (concurring).

[276] 354 U.S. at 503–04. See also Mapp v. Ohio, 367 U.S. 643, 672 (1961).

[277] 367 U.S. 497 (1961).

furter, for a plurality of the Court, stressed the principle of avoidance of unnecessary constitutional adjudication. Quoting from a prior decision, Frankfurter stated, " 'the best teaching of this Court's experience admonishes us not to entertain constitutional questions in advance of the strictest necessity.' "[278] Harlan, in a lengthy dissenting opinion, contended that the Court was wrong in sidestepping the constitutional issue. Since he thought the cases justiciable, he proceeded to express his reasons why the state statute should be held unconstitutional.

Throughout his years on the Court, Harlan, like Frankfurter, had often reminded his colleagues of the principle of avoidance of constitutional determination.[279] In other cases, Harlan did not feel bound by this principle and expressed his views on constitutional issues not decided by the Court.[280] His opinion in *Poe* showed how far he would depart from this principle by determining a constitutional issue which could have been avoided: "While ordinarily I would not deem it appropriate to deal, in dissent, with Constitutional issues which the Court has not reached, I shall do so here because such issues, as I see things, are entangled with the Court's conclusion as to the nonjusticiability of these appeals."[281]

Harlan obviously felt deeply the need to state his conviction that the Connecticut statute, making it a crime for married couples to use contraceptives, was an intolerable and unreasonable invasion of privacy. In spite of the fact that the Constitution speaks nowhere of a right of privacy, nor of an abstract right to be free from unreasonable laws, Harlan proceeded to confront the constitutional issues. In this realm of uncertain constitutional guideposts, he felt obliged to lay the groundwork for his position with care and clarity. In the

---

[278] *Id.* at 503, quoting from Parker v. County of Los Angeles, 338 U.S. 327, 333 (1949).

[279] Griffin v. Illinois, 351 U.S. 12, 29 (1956) (dissenting); Chicago v. Atchison, T. & S. F. R. Co., 357 U.S. 77, 89 (1958) (dissenting); Burton v. Wilmington Parking Authority, 365 U.S. 715, 728 (1961) (dissenting); Communist Party v. Catherwood, 367 U.S. 389 (1961); Zschernig v. Miller, 389 U.S. 429, 443 (1968) (concurring); Jones v. Alfred H. Mayer Co., 392 U.S. 409, 449 (1968) (dissenting); Jenkins v. McKeithen, 395 U.S. 411, 433 (1969) (dissenting); Benton v. Maryland, 395 U.S. 784, 801 (1969) (dissenting).

[280] Lathrop v. Donohue, 367 U.S. 820, 848 (1961) (concurring); Baker v. Carr, 369 U.S. 186, 330 (1962) (dissenting); Wiseman v. Massachusetts, 398 U.S. 960 (1970) (dissenting from denial of certiorari); Welsh v. United States, 398 U.S. 333, 344 (1970) (concurring).

[281] Poe v. Ullman, 367 U.S. 497, 524 (1961).

process of trying to express his reasons for this extraordinary decision, Harlan provided the clearest insight of his view on substantive due process and on the decision-making process itself.

State police power legislation, Harlan had said so often when insisting on the principle of federalism, can be invalidated by the Supreme Court only to the extent the Constitution compelled interference. Harlan had no hesitation in acknowledging that the solution to this question of constitutional limits to the State's police powers was derived from a rational analysis. In *Poe* he said, "[T]he basis of judgment as to the Constitutionality of state action must be a rational one, approaching the text . . . as the basic charter of our society, setting out in spare but meaningful terms the principles of government."[282] Especially in giving meaning to the broad prohibitions of the Fourteenth Amendment against deprivation of life, liberty, or property without due process of law, "the rational process in Constitutional adjudication" is essential.[283]

Although the Due Process Clause, on its face, seems limited to a guarantee of procedural fairness, Harlan argued that this was too narrow a reading. Conscious of the past abuses by the Court in applying the Clause as a substantive prohibition against arbitrary state legislation, Harlan nonetheless insisted that substantive interpretation was essential:[284]

> Were due process merely a procedural safeguard it would fail to reach those situations where the deprivation of life, liberty or property was accomplished by legislation which by operating in the future could, given even the fairest possible procedure in application to individuals, nevertheless destroy the enjoyment of all three. . . . Thus the guaranties of due process, though having their roots in Magna Carta's "per legem terrae" and considered as procedural safeguards "against executive usurpation and tyranny," have in this country "become bulwarks also against arbitrary legislation."

Harlan, thus, rejected the theories which would discover the content of the Due Process Clause outside of and independent of his own reasoning process. A judge should not expect to find its meaning spelled out in the first eight Amendments or anywhere else. But this rational analysis is not an open invitation for the judge to

[282] *Id.* at 540.

[283] *Ibid.*

[284] *Id.* at 541 (citations omitted).

read into the Constitution his own subjective philosophies or prejudices. It is, for Harlan, a structured reasoning process. The judge is obliged by his judicial office to confront and balance all the relevant principles. Harlan equally rejected both overly simple solutions: he was aware that a judge did not discover already existing law, but at the same time he insisted that the judge was not merely engaging in a pure exercise of will. The principles of judicial decision making provided a heuristic structure, a framework within which the judge must search for answers and ultimately decide:[285]

> Due process has not been reduced to any formula; its content cannot be determined by reference to any code. The best that can be said is that through the course of this Court's decisions it has represented the balance which our Nation, built upon postulates of respect for the liberty of the individual, has struck between that liberty and the demands of organized society. If the supplying of content to this Constitutional concept has of necessity been a rational process, it certainly has not been one where judges have felt free to roam where unguided speculation might take them. The balance of which I speak is the balance struck by this country, having regard to what history teaches are the traditions from which it developed as well as the traditions from which it broke. That tradition is a living thing. A decision of this Court which radically departs from it could not long survive, while a decision which builds on what has survived is likely to be sound. No formula could serve as a substitute, in this area, for judgment and restraint.
>
> [The liberty assured by the Due Process Clause, therefore,] is not a series of isolated points pricked out in terms [of the Bill of Rights.] . . . It is a rational continuum which, broadly speaking, includes a freedom from all substantial arbitrary impositions and purposeless restraints . . . and which also recognizes, what a reasonable and sensitive judgment must, that certain interests require particularly careful scrutiny of the state needs asserted to justify their abridgment.

The meaning of the Due Process Clause, therefore, must be derived from a consideration of the purposes of the Constitution's terms, from the reasons for their statement by the Framers, not from any ready-made mechanical answers. In this rational process of developing the meaning of Due Process in a new context, the judge exercises "limited and sharply restrained judgment . . . . The de-

[285] *Id.* at 542–43.

cision of an apparently novel claim must depend on grounds which follow closely on well-accepted principles and criteria."[286] He knew that a judge must search not for already existing content for a term like due process. In reaching a decision he was necessarily imposing new content on the concept, but only within the structure provided by controlling principles. The judicial decision-making process, whether for substantive due process or for other unsettled areas of the law, is structure, not content. The principles, some of which we have seen, provide the structure. Harlan was well aware that as a judge he was obliged to weigh and evaluate the structuring principles, to consider and fully to face up to all the relevant principles, in order to arrive at a decision in each case. The answers did not pop out automatically; the judge's duty is to judge.

Having laid this far-reaching foundation, Harlan proceeded to analyze the relevant principles. He considered the State's significant interest in preserving the moral soundness of its people. He concluded that, even though the Constitution nowhere speaks of privacy, the concept of liberty in the Fourteenth Amendment embraced a right of privacy of the home. He derived this right of privacy from a "common understanding throughout the English-speaking world";[287] from the special constitutional protection of the home in the Third and Fourth Amendments; from "the rational purposes, historical roots, and subsequent developments"[288] of the Due Process Clause; and from prior judicial interpretations of the Clause. He carefully restricted this right of privacy to include only the intimate relations of husband and wife, which the State could have no legitimate interest in criminalizing. He excluded other private acts between individuals which the State in his view can regulate, such as adultery, homosexuality, fornication, and incest. He concluded that the Court should have adjudicated this issue and declared the Connecticut law unconstitutional. Four years after *Poe*, the Court in *Griswold v. Connecticut*[289] finally reached the same conclusion, though based largely on different reasoning, and held the Connecticut birth control statute unconstitutional.

Substantive due process was a fundamental principle in Harlan's judicial philosophy. He strongly preferred employing this due

[286] *Id.* at 544.

[287] *Id.* at 548.

[288] *Id.* at 549.

[289] 381 U.S. 479 (1965).

process analysis to the use of the Equal Protection Clause except in the area of racial inequality. He considered the new equal protection analysis a subjective judicial judgment as to the fundamental fairness of state legislation. He said in *Williams v. Illinois*:[290]

> Under the rubric of "equal protection" this Court has in recent times effectively substituted its own "enlightened" social philosophy for that of the legislature no less than did in the older days the judicial adherents of the now discredited doctrine of "substantive" due process. I, for one, would prefer to judge the legislation before us in this case in terms of due process, that is to determine whether it arbitrarily infringes a constitutionally protected interest of this appellant.

He objected to the judicial rhetoric of "equalizing" which failed to analyze the rationality of the legislative choice. Characteristically, he tried to articulate his reasons for preferring substantive due process analysis to new equal protection analysis:[291]

> An analysis under due process standards, correctly understood, is, in my view, more conducive to judicial restraint than an approach couched in slogans and ringing phrases, such as "suspect" classification or "invidious" distinctions, or "compelling" state interest, that blur analysis by shifting the focus away from the nature of the individual interest affected, the extent to which it is affected, the rationality of the connection between legislative means and purpose, the existence of alternative means for effectuating the purpose, and the degree of confidence we may have that the statute reflects the legislative concern for the purpose that would legitimately support the means chosen.

IX. Conclusion

Some might think of Harlan as a conservative[292] or a formalist,[293] or even a positivist. Harlan's philosophy of the judicial process

---

[290] 399 U.S. 235, 259 (1970) (concurring).

[291] *Id.* at 260. See Harper v. Virginia Board of Elections, 383 U.S. 663, 680 (1966) (dissenting); Shapiro v. Thompson, 394 U.S. 618, 655 (1969) (dissenting); *cf.* Boddie v. Connecticut, 401 U.S. 371 (1971). See also Clune, *The Supreme Court's Treatment of Wealth Discriminations under the Fourteenth Amendment*, 1975 Supreme Court Review 289.

[292] White, The American Judicial Tradition 343 (1976).

[293] See Clune, note 291 *supra*, at 292, where Harlan's approach is seen as a model of the Burger Court's tendency to formalism.

merits serious consideration without reference to such labels; it can be derived from what he did and said. His implicit and explicit position concerning his responsibility as a judge was subtle and complex, based on deeply held convictions.

The canons discussed, of course, were not the only principles in Harlan's judicial philosophy. He had strong views on freedom of expression,[294] freedom of association,[295] the responsibility of the legal profession,[296] and the role of the national government in regulating business activity.[297] I have focused on a manageable number of the key principles which were basic to his thought and which he developed, interrelated, and balanced against each other in his opinions and public addresses. Precisely by working within the heuristic structure provided by these principles, Harlan tried to avoid the subjectivity of the realists. Thus his process of judicial decision making involved a structured evaluation of all the questions raised by the relevant principles. He clearly assumed responsibility for the result of this rational process, the judicial decision. It was not, he knew, solely the necessary conclusion from legal premises, the one correct decision derived from rules of law brooding in the sky. He felt confident, however, that he was not merely reading his subjective values and preferences into the law since he insisted on honestly considering the implications of these structuring principles.

The limitations of Harlan's effort to refrain from imposing his own subjective values on the law can be briefly pointed out. Certainly there is a strong appeal in a jurist struggling to achieve the goal of a reasoned, neutral expression of the law. The judge who

---

[294] *E.g.*, Roth v. United States, 354 U.S. 476, 496 (1957) (concurring and dissenting); Kingsley Pictures Corp. v. Regents, 360 U.S. 684, 702 (1959) (concurring); Manual Enterprises v. Day, 370 U.S. 478 (1962); Memoirs v. Massachusetts, 383 U.S. 413, 455 (1966) (dissenting); Ginzburg v. United States, 383 U.S. 463, 493 (1966) (dissenting); Curtis Publishing Co. v. Butts, 388 U.S. 130 (1967); Street v. New York, 394 U.S. 576 (1969); Cohen v. California, 403 U.S. 15 (1971).

[295] *E.g.*, NAACP v. Alabama 357 U.S. 449 (1958); NAACP v. Alabama, 377 U.S. 288 (1964); Shelton v. Tucker, 364 U.S. 479, 496 (1960) (dissenting); Scales v. United States, 367 U.S. 203 (1961); NAACP v. Button, 371 U.S. 415, 448 (1963) (dissenting).

[296] *E.g.*, Konigsberg v. State Bar, 366 U.S. 36 (1961); Cohen v. Hurley, 366 U.S. 117 (1961); NAACP v. Button, 371 U.S. 415, 448 (1963) (dissenting); Spevack v. Klein, 385 U.S. 511, 520 (1967) (dissenting); United Mine Workers v. Illinois Bar Ass'n, 389 U.S. 217, 225 (1967) (dissenting); United Transportation Union v. State Bar of Michigan, 401 U.S. 576, 586 (1971) (concurring and dissenting).

[297] See ADAMS, JUSTICE JOHN MARSHALL HARLAN AND THE ANTITRUST LAWS (1977).

seems to derive his decisions from controlling legal principles creates a strong impression of objectivity and fairness. Is it, after all, just an illusion?

Any framework of legal principles runs the risk of remaining static and losing touch with the constantly changing social and moral realities of life. Law, it seems, must always remain in a state of tension; striving, on the one hand for an objective, principled articulation, yet on the other hand, adjusting, adapting previously stated legal rules to the ceaselessly changing developments in society. It is helpful to recall that the Supreme Court's most disastrous decision had the surface appearance of an application of reasoned, neutral principles. Although Chief Justice Taney in his *Dred Scott* opinion[298] undoubtedly reached out for broad issues which might have been left undecided, he clearly tried to convince all readers of his scrupulous concern for procedural details, fidelity to historical tradition (at least to his own satisfaction), strict adherence to precedent and the intent of the Framers, and preservation of the spirit of federalism. No case, however, shows more clearly that these norms, woodenly applied, can be tragically inadequate. The Supreme Court must be able to recognize when the demands of justice, or fundamental fairness, not merely to an individual litigant, but for the whole social context, demand a new beginning, a break from the rigid framework created by the past.

We can raise the same point by asking whether Harlan, had he been on the Court, would have dissented in *Brown v. Board of Education.*[299] Undoubtedly not. But if he had, he could have derived a basis for his dissent from his usual framework of principles: precedent, historical tradition, and the original meaning of the Fourteenth Amendment.

The fact is that Harlan was willing to create new dimensions in the law; he was at times sensitive to the fact that something was askew with the existing legal framework. His dramatically striking dissent in *Poe v. Ullman,*[300] for instance, could never have seen the light of day had Harlan remained inflexibly restricted by the structural norms he so often invoked. In *Poe* he showed his strong sense of moral outrage at the irrationality and arbitrariness of a state law

[298] Dred Scott v. Sanford, 19 How. 393 (1857).

[299] 347 U.S. 483 (1954).

[300] See text *supra*, at notes 281–89.

criminalizing the use of birth control instruments even by married couples. He analyzed the case within the familiar structural framework of federalism, historical tradition, the purposes of the Framers, and due process. Yet, despite his accustomed insistence on judicial restraint, his conclusions went well beyond what these principles demanded if applied narrowly to the case. For Harlan the societal and moral implications of the state law cried out for a new constitutional principle; he responded with his opinion in *Poe*. He showed here an ability and a willingness to derive what was surely new out of the standard, oft-repeated principles so basic to his philosophy. In other cases also he demonstrated an expansiveness in deriving new, unexpected conclusions while always striving to maintain a fidelity to the same structural principles.[301]

One can only wonder why Harlan so seldom made a similarly expansive response in the ordinary criminal law cases which came before the Court in such large numbers during the years he sat. Did the ghost of his past experience as a prosecutor remain too much with him?[302] Over the years it seems clear that Harlan was much more likely than the Court's majority to cast his vote against the criminal defendant. It is possible, of course, that Harlan, in his reluctance to constitutionalize criminal procedure, was more consistently right than the Court. In at least one of these cases, however, the larger social context seemed to call for the same type of creative response Harlan gave in *Poe*. This example will clarify the point.

In *Duncan v. Louisiana*[303] Harlan dissented from the Court's opinion, which held that the Sixth Amendment, incorporated into the Fourteenth, required the States to provide a jury trial for a criminal defendant charged with a serious crime. Harlan uncharacteristically ignored some crucial facts and the broader context of the case. Gary Duncan, a nineteen-year-old black, was driving down a highway in Plaquemines Parish, Louisiana, when he noticed two younger cousins confronted by four white boys off the shoulder of the road.

---

[301] See, *e.g.*, Street v. New York, 394 U.S. 576 (1969); Welsh v. United States, 398 U.S. 333, 344 (1970) (concurring); Moragne v. States Marine Lines, 398 U.S. 375 (1970); Cohen v. California, 403 U.S. 15 (1971).

[302] Harlan served in 1928 as Chief Assistant to Emery R. Buckner as Special Prosecutor and from 1951 to 1953 as Special Assistant Attorney General and Chief Counsel to the New York State Crime Commission. See HARLAN, note 1 *supra*, at xix–xxii.

[303] 391 U.S. 145, 171 (1968).

The cousins had recently transferred, because of a federal court order, to a previously all-white school. There had been threats and some violence during this period of transfer to the new school. Duncan stopped, asked the six boys what they were doing, and after some bickering back and forth, told his cousins to get into the car. He told the white boys to go home and either touched or slapped the elbow of one of the white boys. For this incident, Duncan was charged with simple battery, a misdemeanor punishable by a maximum of two years imprisonment or a $300 fine or both. The trial court, following Louisiana law, denied a jury trial, and Duncan after conviction was sentenced to sixty days in the parish prison and a fine of $150.[304]

Harlan often observed that the Supreme Court should not overturn lower courts' factual determinations merely to assure justice to the individual—an arguable position. But surely, in this highly charged context of court-ordered integration in the South, the Court, even by Harlan's due process analysis, should have been concerned to assure the appearance and the reality of fundamental fairness. Even if he had strongly disagreed with the majority's selective incorporation approach, he could have concurred on due process grounds. If not the trial procedure, at least the excessive sentence could have been mitigated on the basis of fundamental fairness. The whole societal milieu in *Duncan* cried out for an appropriate response by the Supreme Court. The haunting question is, why was Harlan so expansive, even daring, in *Poe* and so insensitive to the larger moral implications in *Duncan?* In *Poe*, Harlan demonstrated that he did not always believe the judiciary should stand by impotent when faced with gross unfairness and irrationality. This modest degree of judicial activism seems to vanish when Harlan turned to the ordinary criminal case.

It is, one surmises, precisely in this difference in approach between *Poe* and *Duncan* that one perceives the breakdown of Harlan's strenuous efforts to avoid the subjectivism of Realism. Something beyond his structural principles must have been operative. Perhaps when scholars have access to Harlan's unpublished papers they can determine the outlines of his personal system of values, preferences, and biases. Many unique influences must have shaped his judicial

[304] *Id.* at 146–47. See also transcript at 30, 44, 47, 53, 56, 78.

philosophy: growing up with his father a lawyer and his grandfather a Supreme Court Justice, study of law at Oxford with little legal education in an American law school, marriage to the daughter of a prominent historian, the years of successful practice as a trial attorney in a prominent New York law firm, his experience as a prosecutor, to mention but a few. Only a careful, detailed judicial biography can explain in what ways these and many other factors shaped his philosophy of the role of a judge and swayed his judgment in individual cases.

Rather than end on this negative note of the limitations of Harlan's philosophy, an effort to compose a portrait of the Justice at work seems more appropriate. We get the image of a thoughtful, reflective man, complex, probing, and subtle in addressing a legal problem, a man of deeply held convictions yet with great self-control; an advocate, but not rancorous. He had developed habits of thorough research, precise care for detail, and an unusual ability to convey his intricate, nuanced thought in a clear, direct, and often graceful writing style. He ordinarily insisted on taking account of the full complexity of the legal and factual issues; seldom did he gloss over untidy questions. He approached historical tradition and judicial precedent with a perceptive openness which enabled him to view the past on its own terms, not as a quarry from which to gather materials to bolster preconceived arguments. Because he took the trouble to understand the past, he felt free at times to reject its teachings. His classical stand on federalism permeated much of his judicial thinking. He had clearly defined views of the role of the judiciary and of the legal profession because of which he was willing to defer to the political branches for political judgments and to the lower courts for fact finding. Though he recalled frequently the essentially limited scope of the judicial process, he was not bashful about using the judicial power to the full when necessary to contain Congress or the States within constitutional bounds. He consistently made an honest effort to express the reasons for his decisions in a principled, neutral manner which would provide guidance for future judges and lawyers. He often stretched to the ultimate his effort to express precisely the weight he gave to competing considerations. Perhaps the very complexity of the diverse factors he evaluated at times rendered it less feasible for his decisions to serve as principled guides for future decision making. When he concluded he had been wrong, he went out of his way to admit that he was changing his position. He rejected anything that appeared as simplistic or subjective in judicial decisions. His entire judicial philosophy repudiated the notion that he could give free reign to a hunch or some intuitive sense of right to the individual litigant. He grappled with subtle constitutional concepts like fundamental fairness, trying to avoid imposing merely his own sense of values and yet conscious of the fact that he was not acting as a ventriloquist's dummy in expressing already formulated legal rules. If Justice Harlan was not always completely successful, it is well to recall that even Homer nodded.

ROBERT A. BURT

THE CONSTITUTION OF THE FAMILY

Family relations have become a substantial part of the Supreme Court's constitutional concerns. In the 1978 Term alone, the Court addressed the constitutional rights of pregnant children to obtain abortions without parental consent,[1] of illegitimate children to intestate inheritance under state law,[2] of fathers to bar adoption of their illegitimate children,[3] of mothers to obtain federal Social Security support for their illegitimate children,[4] and of husbands to equal claims to alimony from their wives in divorce proceedings.[5] The Court's repeated attention during the past decade to abortion and gender discrimination,[6] as well as adoption and foster placement proceedings[7] and disputes between children, parents, and school authorities,[8] has elaborated new constitutional doctrine to adjudicate relations both within the family and between the family unit and outsiders.

Robert A. Burt is Professor of Law, Yale University.

[1] Bellotti v. Baird, 99 S. Ct. 3035 (1979).

[2] Lalli v. Lalli, 99 S. Ct. 518 (1978).

[3] Caban v. Mohammed, 99 S. Ct. 1760 (1979).

[4] Califano v. Boles, 99 S. Ct. 2767 (1979).

[5] Orr v. Orr, 99 S. Ct. 1102 (1979).

[6] See text *infra*, at notes 124 *et seq.*

[7] See note 82 *infra*.

[8] See text at notes 27 *et seq.*

One case decided last Term illuminates central aspects of the Court's contemporary work. In *Parham v. J.R.*,[9] the Court considered whether the Constitution constrains parents who want to confine their children in mental institutions. Though the Court acknowledged the child's "substantial liberty interest" in avoiding unjustified hospitalization,[10] it held that due process protections against parental impositions could adequately be provided through "informal traditional medical investigative techniques" presided over by "physicians and behavioral specialists."[11] The Court rejected the lower courts' requirement of formal adversarial hearing before a "law-trained or a judicial or administrative officer" to protect children,[12] though constitutional norms would require such process for an adult who protested or who (like most children) lacked capacity to consent to such confinement.[13]

Chief Justice Burger, writing for the Court, rested this holding on "Western Civilization concepts of the family as a unit with broad parental authority over minor children."[14] Mr. Justice Brennan, in dissent, was prepared to give special constitutional homage to family status only by postponing adversarial hearings for a "limited period" after a child was admitted to the institution.[15] Beyond this concession, he argued that both children and adults had the same constitutional claims for protection against hospitalization.

Parham points to the broader context of the Court's family jurisprudence. Though the dispute most directly concerned the prerogatives of parents over children, the case arose only because a professional caretaking bureaucracy agreed with parents' requests to take custody of their children. Though the Chief Justice wrote glowingly of the traditional deference owed to parental authority, those claims came to the Court enmeshed with the authoritative validation of medical professionals and bureaucratic officials. The case thus directly implicates a long-existent dispute over the proper judicial role in confronting executive claims for deference on grounds of supposed expertise supported by expansive legislative

[9] 99 S. Ct. 2493 (1979), decided in conjunction with Secretary of Public Welfare of Penna. v. Institutionalized Juveniles, 99 S. Ct. 2523 (1979).

[10] 99 S. Ct. at 2503.

[11] *Id.* at 2507.

[12] *Id.* at 2506.

[13] *Cf.* Addington v. Texas, 99 S. Ct. 1804 (1979); O'Connor v. Donaldson, 422 U.S. 563 (1975).

[14] 99 S. Ct. at 2504.

[15] *Id.* at 2519.

delegation. The combatants in this dispute have come to be popularly characterized as proponents of judicial activism and restraint. Whatever the inelegance of this labeling, the Court divided in *Parham* along the ideological lines that the popular characterization would predict: the four Nixon appointees on one side and Justices Brennan and Marshall on the other. (Three "swing" Justices were in effect evenly distributed, Mr. Justice White with the majority opinion, Mr. Justice Stevens with the dissent, and Mr. Justice Stewart joining the majority judgment but writing for himself alone.)

A different aspect of the case heightens its ideological significance from the perspective of the Court's contemporary politics. Socially disruptive conduct is a common reason that parents seek, and behavioral professionals accept, psychiatric hospitalization for children.[16] The case thus has a "law-and-order" cast which generally claims special scrutiny from judicial activists and special deference from their opponents. The Court's ruling supports governmental claims to combat antisocial conduct without detailed judicial scrutiny.

Parham thus reveals a central aspect of the Court's contemporary construction of a family jurisprudence: that the Court is fundamentally concerned with addressing conflicting claims of individual and community, of liberty and authority. Though the Court may speak of a crisis in family structure and authority, and may find a sympathetic response in popular attitudes, that shared perception is part of a broader concern in our society. Indeed, current historians who have only recently made the family a subject for rigorous inquiry cast doubt on the accuracy of contemporary claims for an earlier "golden age" of unquestioned familial authority and stability.[17] This scholarship suggests that current lamentations regarding the decline of parental authority and of familial bonds is an unacknowledged proxy for a different social concern regarding the strength and legitimacy of communal authority.

The Court's constitutional jurisprudence of the family developed during the past decade can most coherently be understood in this

[16] See Miller & Burt, *Children's Rights on Entering Therapeutic Institutions*, 134 AM. J. PSYCH. 153, 156 (1977).

[17] See FISCHER, GROWING OLD IN AMERICA 230 (1978); Elder, *Approaches to Social Change and the Family*, in DEMOS & BOOCOCK, eds., TURNING POINTS: HISTORICAL AND SOCIOLOGICAL ESSAYS ON THE FAMILY 57 (1978).

light. Though speaking of the proper role of law in regulating family relations, the Justices have implicitly, and occasionally explicitly, addressed the definition of legitimate social authority, asking how legitimacy can be recognized and what is the proper role of the courts and constitutional adjudication in that recognition. The two popularly identifiable ideological blocs on the Courts—the "conservatives" and "liberals," to use typically opaque terminology[18] have approached these questions in distinctive ways. Exploring the critical differences and agreements between the blocs in the family relations cases may not only clarify the dispute between majority and dissenters in *Parham* but may illuminate the contemporary Court's constitutional jurisprudence.

I. The Conservative Justices: Suppressing Conflict by Force of Authority

The Court spoke in *Parham* as if it were upholding parental prerogatives against governmental intrusions. Chief Justice Burger acknowledged that some parents harm their children and that state intervention can be justified when children's "physical or mental health is jeopardized." Nonetheless, he said, "the statist notion that governmental power should supersede parental authority in *all* cases because *some* parents abuse and neglect children is repugnant to American tradition."[19] This is an odd way to describe the issue at stake in *Parham*. Parents there were not seeking to resist governmental power over their children; they were invoking that power by attempting to confine their children in state psychiatric institutions.

This paean to parental prerogatives would have had greater relevance if state officials had sought to impose behavioral controls on children against their parents' wishes. The Court did consider a case two years earlier that directly implicated that question. School officials had administered corporal punishment to children. The Court majority, composed of the same conservative nucleus as in *Parham* (here joined by Mr. Justice Stewart but with Mr. Justice

[18] On the contemporary Court, the Nixon-appointed "conservatives" are Chief Justice Burger (appointed in 1969), and Justices Blackmun (1970), Powell (1972), and Rehnquist (1972); the "liberals" are Justices Brennan (an Eisenhower appointment, 1956) and Marshall (a Johnson appointment, 1967).

[19] 99 S. Ct. at 2504.

White in dissent), ruled that school officials were free to disregard parental objections to this form of behavior control on their children.[20] Mr. Justice Powell spoke for the Court:[21]

> Although the early cases viewed the authority of the teacher as deriving from the parents, the concept of parental delegation has been replaced by the view—more consonant with compulsory education laws—that the State itself may impose such corporal punishment as is reasonably necessary "for the proper education of the child and for the maintenance of group discipline."

So much for the American tradition—paraded in *Parham* as well as "the early cases"—that "governmental power should [not] supersede parental authority."

The conservative nucleus in *Parham* also spoke quite differently in 1971 about placing the evidentiary presumption between "governmental power" and "parental authority" in judging the best interests of children. In *Wyman v. James*[22] the Court ruled that state officials could demand home entry as a condition for welfare eligibility without submitting that demand to judicial scrutiny upon an applicant's protest. Mr. Justice Blackmun[23] there observed that the purpose of the home inspection was to protect children. "There is no more worthy object of the public's concern. The dependent child's needs are paramount, and only with hesitancy would we relegate those needs, in the scale of comparative values, to a position secondary to what the mother claims as her rights."[24] The Court here assumed a conflict of interest between parent and child without any specific showing that the parent might be acting harmfully. In *Parham*, Chief Justice Burger appeared to reject this position by requiring a showing of "the likelihood of parental abuse" before the traditional rights of parents might be limited by some governmental official purporting to protect the child. He stated, "Simply because the decision of a parent . . . involves risks [of harm to a child] does not automatically transfer the power to make that decision from the parents to some agency or officer of the state."[25]

---

[20] Ingraham v. Wright, 430 U.S. 651 (1977).

[21] *Id.* at 662.

[22] 400 U.S. 309 (1971).

[23] The Court's majority included the Chief Justice and Justices Black, Harlan, Stewart, and White; Justices Douglas, Brennan, and Marshall dissented.

[24] 400 U.S. at 318.

[25] 99 S. Ct. at 2504.

In *Wyman*, the Court had characterized the mother as claiming "her rights" without acknowledging that those rights could be understood to include authority to rear her child without inappropriate state interference, that her privacy claim was not simply individualistic but encompassed both her own and her child's right to privacy in their familial relationship.

In *Wyman*, of course, the mother was inviting some state participation in her child-rearing conduct; she was requesting state financial assistance. The Court construed this supplicant posture as a general waiver of the mother's ordinary claims to personal or family privacy.[26] But in *Parham*, the parents were also requesting state assistance in their child rearing by seeking admission of their children to state institutions. The Court did not construe this request as a waiver of individual or parental prerogatives; it characterized this parental wish in the high rhetoric of "Western Civilization concepts of the family as a unit with broad parental authority over minor children." The Court apparently saw no irony in its invocation of this rhetoric to vindicate parents' decision to relinquish their authority to a state psychiatrist.

An underlying consistency can be seen, however, in comparing *Parham* with *Wyman* and the school corporal punishment case. In each case, state-employed behavioral professionals–psychiatrists, teachers, welfare workers–had opinions regarding proper techniques of child rearing. In *Parham* the parents agreed with those opinions; in the other cases, the parents disagreed. The Court–that is, the conservative bloc constituting the majority nucleus in those cases–supported the parents' decision only in *Parham*. In all three cases the professionals' opinions prevailed. These three cases are not the whole of the Court's or its conservative bloc's family jurisprudence. Neither the Court nor this bloc consistently defers to professionals' child-rearing views any more than they give consistent deference to parental views. The conservative Justices' attitude toward behavioral experts in these cases does, however, point toward a unified viewpoint that can be seen in other family decisions.

[26] The Court observed: "One who dispenses purely private charity naturally has an interest in and expects to know how his charitable funds are utilized and put to work. The public, when it is the provider, rightly expects the same." 400 U.S. at 319.

The Court's (including its conservative bloc's) ruling in *Wisconsin v. Yoder*[27] appears as a clear victory for parents' opposition to the views of state child-rearing professionals. *Yoder* upheld the religiously based claims of Amish parents to resist state requirements that their children attend school beyond the eighth grade. Chief Justice Burger for the Court rested the decision both on notions of religious freedom and on the "enduring American tradition" of the "primary role of the parents in the upbringing of their children."[28] Justice Douglas dissented alone on the ground that the Court should protect only the child's right, and not his parents' rights as such, against state compulsion.[29] The Chief Justice responded that the case record showed no conflict between the children and parents in their resistance to state demands;[30] Justices Stewart and Brennan concurred in the Court's opinion on this understanding.[31] And the Chief Justice spoke further to this point:[32]

> Recognition of the claim of the State [to support children's opposition to their parents' wishes] . . . would, of course, call into question traditional concepts of parental control over the religious upbringing and education of their minor children recognized in this Court's past decisions. It is clear that such an intrusion by a State into family decisions in the area of religious training would give rise to grave questions of religious freedom. . . . On this record we neither reach nor decide those issues.

Unlike *Yoder*, the record in *Parham* did reveal explicit opposition between parents and children. The Court in *Parham* did not hold, however, that state officials were obliged to honor the parents' wishes in this conflict or even to give special weight to those wishes. The Court ruled only that deference was required from judges. The state physicians in *Parham* were not only free, in the Court's view, to take the child's side against his parents' wishes for hospitalization; the Court ruled that constitutional due process norms required the psychiatrists to evaluate independently the propriety of the child's hospitalization, to be "neutral and detached trier[s] of fact" in this parent-child dispute.[33] Does this then mean that, if the Court had seen explicit opposition between the Amish parents

---

[27] 406 U.S. 205 (1972).

[28] *Id.* at 232.

[29] *Id.* at 243.

[30] *Id.* at 232.

[31] *Id.* at 237.

[32] *Id.* at 231–32.

[33] 99 S. Ct. at 2506.

and children regarding school attendance, the parents' wishes could be overridden? It seems clear from the tone of the Court's opinions in the two cases that this result would not follow, at least for the Chief Justice who wrote both opinions. But if not, why not?

The cases might appear different because the Amish parents' wishes were clearly rooted in religious beliefs while parents' choice for psychiatric hospitalization carries only secular implications. But here we must take account of another recent Court decision adjudicating conflict between parents and children. In *Planned Parenthood v. Danforth*[34] the Court ruled that state law cannot prohibit an abortion for a pregnant minor solely because of her parents' wishes. Mr. Justice Blackmun wrote for the Court with only Justices White and Stevens dissenting; thus the conservative nucleus was prepared here to override parental authority on a question that clearly implicates passionately held religious convictions for some parents. Many parents might oppose abortion on secular grounds, but many parents might oppose compulsory education on such grounds. The Court in *Yoder* took care to restrict its dispensation to parental objections based explicitly on religious belief;[35] in *Danforth* no such exemption was given.

Withholding a requested abortion would seem to have more profound and irreversible consequences for a child than withholding attendance at a public secondary school. The differential severity of consequences might thus afford a consistent explanation for the conservative bloc's willingness to defer to parental authority in one case and not the other. Reliance on this difference seems to underlie the positions of the liberal bloc members, Justices Brennan and Marshall, who joined the Court majority in both *Yoder* and *Danforth*. But if the conservatives also relied on this difference, they would have joined with the dissenting liberals in *Parham* to honor the child's objection to his parents' wish for his psychiatric hospitalization. The psychological trauma of this enforced confinement and its potentially life-long stigma are surely more analogous to the harmful potential of enforced childbearing for an objecting minor than to the harmfulness of barring a student from public high school in deference to his parents' wishes.[36]

---

[34] 428 U.S. 52 (1976).

[35] 406 U.S. at 235–36.

[36] See Mr. Justice Brennan's dissent in *Parham*, 99 S. Ct. at 2519.

Chief Justice Burger distinguished *Danforth* in his *Parham* opinion, however, on the ground that state law gave an "absolute parental veto" over the child's abortion, while parents could commit their children to mental institutions only when physicians "exercise independent [concurring] judgment as to the child's need for confinement."[37] This distinction points to the underlying decisional principle for the conservative bloc—a principle whose visibility is only occasionally clouded by their rhetoric of deference to parental authority. The clouds clearly part, however, in a case decided just twelve days after *Parham.*

Massachusetts law provided that a pregnant child whose parents would not allow an abortion could seek permission from a state judge. The Court, in *Bellotti v. Baird,*[38] ruled that the state law was unconstitutional only because it required the child to inform her parents of her wishes and to solicit their consent before asking the judge for his permission. Mr. Justice Powell, in a plurality opinion joined by the Chief Justice and Justices Rehnquist and Stewart, wrote that state law could constitutionally provide that a pregnant minor who wanted an abortion without her parents' consent or knowledge must persuade a judge (or some other state officer) that her wishes were "mature and well-informed" or if immature and ignorant were "nevertheless . . . in her best interest."[39] The Court had invalidated the parental consent law in *Danforth* on the ground that the State could not "give a third party [the parents] an absolute, and possibly arbitrary, veto of the decision over the physician and his patient [the pregnant child] to terminate his patient's pregnancy."[40] Mr. Justice Powell was, however, clearly prepared to give this veto power to a state official while withholding it from parents. Does he assume that parents are "possibly arbitrary" but that judges or other state officials are not? That judges can discern a child's maturity or best interests while her parents cannot? That judges' possible arbitrariness can be constrained, while parents'

[37] 99 S. Ct. at 2505.

[38] 99 S. Ct. 3035 (1979).

[39] 99 S. Ct. at 3050. In *Baird,* alone among the cases discussed thus far, the four Nixon appointees were not united; Mr. Justice Blackmun voted to invalidate judicial supervision of the minor's abortion decision. He has, more than his conservative colleagues, been consistently opposed to any governmental restriction on abortions for adults or children. See Beal v. Doe, 432 U.S. 438 (1977); Maher v. Roe, 432 U.S. 464 (1977); Poelker v. Doe, 432 U.S. 519 (1977).

[40] 428 U.S. at 74.

cannot, by the crystalline clarity of the "maturity" and "best interests" standard that he posits?

These assumptions may inform Mr. Justice Powell's position. But there is a consistent principle uniting the conservative bloc Justices' positions in these family cases that does not rest on these questionable assumptions. The principle is not that parental authority as such warrants respect. Rather, the authority over children that commands constitutionally mandated respect is that which is backed by force clearly promising effective control over children's disruptive impulses. On this view, parents occasionally embody such force. But when parents in fact fail to control their child, then their authority no longer commands respect in principle. Parents whose effective authority has failed can rehabilitate themselves and their claim to constitutionally mandated respect only by invoking some extrafamilial authority to buttress their weakened force—a psychiatrist who will institutionalize their child, a teacher who will paddle their child, a judge who will rule their child.

When one of the conservative Justices extols the American tradition of respect for parental authority, he is not commanding deference for the status of parenthood. The operative principle that gives consistency to this bloc's various decisions is rather that only parental authority exercised in a traditional authoritarian format requires constitutional deference. This principle dominates the *Yoder* decision. As noted, the strength of Amish parents' religious conviction does not adequately explain why their child-rearing wishes command state deference; otherwise, the minor's abortion cases are inexplicable. Nor can the case be explained by the intensity of the Amish parents' belief in the psychic damage inflicted on their children by the public school teachers; otherwise, the school corporal punishment cases are inexplicable. The Amish parents do not command respect from the conservative Justices for the strength of any of their beliefs. They command respect because of their effective strength in imposing those beliefs on their children and obtaining apparently conforming conduct from them. Throughout his opinion for the Court, Chief Justice Burger repeatedly and lavishly praises Amish parents' child-rearing techniques on this score:[41]

> The testimony . . . showed that the Amish succeed in preparing their high school age children to be productive members of

[41] 406 U.S. at 212–13, 222, 233–34.

> the Amish community. [One expert witness] described their system of learning-through-doing the skills directly relevant to their adult roles in the Amish community as "ideal" and perhaps superior to ordinary high school eduction. The evidence also showed that the Amish have an excellent record as law-abiding and generally self-sufficient members of society....
>
> The State attacks [the parents'] position as one fostering "ignorance" from which the child must be protected by the State. No one can question the State's duty to protect children from ignorance but this argument does not square with the facts disclosed in the record. Whatever their idiosyncrasies as seen by the majority, this record strongly shows that the Amish community has been a highly successful social unit within our society, even if apart from the conventional "mainstream." Its members are productive and very law-abiding members of society; they reject public welfare in any of its usual modern forms. . . . To be sure, the power of the parent, even when linked to a free exercise claim, may be subject to limitation . . . if it appears that parental decisions will jeopardize the health or safety of the child, or have a potential for significant social burdens. But in this case, the Amish have introduced persuasive evidence undermining the arguments the State has advanced to support its claims in terms of the welfare of the child and society as a whole. The record strongly indicates that . . . [upholding Amish parents' claims here] will not impair the physical or mental health of the child, nor result in an inability to be self-supporting or to discharge the duties and responsibilities of citizenship, or in any other way materially detract from the welfare of society.

If parental authority warrants deference only when the parents are "productive and . . . reject public welfare in any of its usual modern forms," then it is obvious why the claims to family and personal privacy of the welfare-applicant mother in *Wyman v. James* were overridden. If parental child-rearing decisions forfeit respect, as a matter of constitutional principle, when those decisions would "result in [the child's] inability to be self-supporting," then no deference is owed parents' refusal to authorize an abortion for their pregnant unmarried daughter. (The state laws in *Danforth* and *Baird* provided that, if she were married, the pregnant minor was deemed an adult and thus could reach her abortion decision without parental or judicial supervision.)[42] And if parental authority must be honored only when parents succeed (as the Court found

---

[42] 428 U.S. at 72; 99 S. Ct. at 3039.

that "the Amish succeed") in bringing obedient social conformance from their children, then no honor is due to parents who have failed to keep their child from premarital intercourse and pregnancy.[43]

This is the thread that can be traced into a coherent pattern among the votes of the conservative bloc Justices in the cases discussed thus far—that a specific, authoritarian style of parenting rather than the status of parent itself warrants constitutional deference. Mr. Justice Powell espoused this position in an opinion, joined only by the other conservative Justices, dissenting from the Court's imposition of some procedural formality on school suspensions in *Goss v. Lopez.*[44] Mr. Justice Powell stated:[45]

> Education in any meaningful sense includes the inculcation of an understanding in each pupil of the necessity of rules and obedience thereto. This understanding is no less important than learning to read and write. One who does not comprehend the meaning and necessity of discipline is handicapped not merely in his education but throughout his subsequent life. In an age when the home and church play a diminishing role in shaping the character and value judgments of the young, a heavier responsibility falls upon the schools.

This "heavier responsibility" appears to fall not merely on school officials, in Mr. Justice Powell's view, but equally on other public officers including Supreme Court Justices. The Court in his view should not limit application of any "of the traditional means . . . used to maintain discipline in the schools"[46] but rather should preach their propriety and necessity from the pulpit of the Court.

Propounding a rule that the Supreme Court must, in common with other state officials, defer to any parent's choice regarding child rearing would not accomplish this purpose because, in Mr. Justice Powell's view, many modern parents themselves must be taught this lesson. He observed in his *Goss* dissent: "There is, no doubt, a school of modern psychological or psychiatric persuasion that maintains that *any* discipline of the young is detrimental. Whatever one may think of the wisdom of this unproved theory, it hardly affords dependable support for a *constitutional* decision."[47] The

---

[43] I owe this observation, and am generally indebted, to Anne Shere Wallwork (J.D. Yale University, 1979) and her unpublished paper, The Most Authoritarian Alternative: Parents, Children, and the State before the Burger Court.

[44] 419 U.S. 565 (1975).

[45] *Id.* at 593.

[46] *Id.* at 591.

[47] *Id.* at 598 n.19.

Justice obviously thinks very little of the wisdom of this theory, but he apparently finds "support for a *constitutional* decision" in a different theory of child rearing.

That theory, as he describes it, has one central attribute that applies equally to children and to Supreme Court Justices: that discipline administered by traditional authorities should not be questioned. Thus Mr. Justice Powell prescribes for students:[48]

> When an immature student merits censure for his conduct, he is rendered a disservice if appropriate sanctions are not applied or if procedures for their application are so formalized as to invite a challenge to the teacher's authority—an invitation which rebellious or even merely spirited teenagers are likely to accept.

The Powell prescription for his brethren is:[49]

> In mandating due process procedures [in school disciplinary suspensions] the Court misapprehends the reality of the normal teacher-pupil relationship. There is an ongoing relationship, one in which the teacher must occupy many roles—educator, adviser, friend, and, at times, parent-substitute. It is rarely adversary in nature except with respect to the chronically disruptive or insubordinate pupil whom the teacher must be free to discipline without frustrating formalities.

In a subsequent opinion, in *Ingraham v. Wright*,[50] Mr. Justice Powell identified a problem of central concern to him that could result from such "frustrating formalities": "If a prior hearing, with the inevitable attendant publicity within the school, resulted in rejection of the teacher's recommendation, the consequent impairment of the teacher's ability to maintain discipline in the classrom would not be insubstantial."[51] His concern here was not limited to the ability of teachers to maintain discipline. In the penultimate footnote in his *Ingraham* opinion he observed:[52]

> The need to maintain order in a trial courtroom raises similar problems. In that context, this Court has recognized the power of the trial judge "to punish summarily and without notice or hearing contemptuous conduct committed in his presence and observed by him." . . . The punishment so imposed may be as severe as six months in prison.

---

[48] *Id.* at 593.

[49] *Id.* at 594.

[50] 430 U.S. 651 (1977).

[51] *Id.* at 681 n.50.

[52] *Id.* at 682 n.54.

Mr. Justice Powell wrote for the Court in *Ingraham*. As in *Goss v. Lopez*, he was joined by his three conservative colleagues, but Mr. Justice Stewart deserted the *Goss* majority here to make the Powell opinion the Court's opinion. In *Ingraham*, the Court refused to require even an informal prior notice or hearing opportunity before administration of corporal punishment and refused to impose Eighth Amendment constraints on corporal punishment no matter how brutal—how cruel, unusual, or punitive—those beatings might appear to an untutored eye.[53]

It would be unfair, however, to portray the Court in *Ingraham* or its conservative nucleus as intending to condone or encourage brutality by teachers, parents, or judges. This nucleus intends to encourage an unquestioning attitude toward, and a reciprocally firm and self-confident attitude by, constituted authority. An idealized image of conflict-free interpersonal relations appears to lie beneath this intention. Mr. Justice Powell reveals this in his *Goss v. Lopez* dissent:[54] "The role of the teacher in our society historically has been an honored and respected one, rooted in the experience of decades that has left for most of us warm memories of our teachers, especially those of the formative years of primary and secondary education." It might thus appear an insult to these honored memories if the Supreme Court were now to abandon "[our reliance] for generations upon the experience, good faith and dedication of those who staff our public schools."[55]

Mr. Justice Blackmun in his opinion for the Court in *Wyman v. James* offers the same romantic vision of the relationship between authority (there the social worker) and dependent (the welfare applicant):[56]

> The [challenged home] visit is not one by police or uniformed authority. It is made by a caseworker of some training whose primary objective is, or should be, the welfare, not the prosecution, of the aid recipient for whom the worker has profound responsibility. . . . [T]he program concerns dependent children and the needy families of those children. It does not deal with crime or with the actual or suspected perpetrators of crime. The caseworker is not a sleuth but rather, we trust, is a friend to one in need.

---

[53] See Burt, *Children as Victims*, in VARDIN & BRODY, ED., CHILDREN'S RIGHTS: CONTEMPORARY PERSPECTIVES 37–38 (1979).

[54] 419 U.S. at 594 n.12.

[55] *Id.* at 595.

[56] 400 U.S. at 322–23.

Mr. Justice Blackmun's invocation of "trust" here has many meanings. The caseworker must be a trusting "friend" and "not a sleuth" to the welfare recipient. The welfare applicant qualifies as a worthy dependent only if she is willing to trust the worker's good intentions. And "we trust," *i.e.*, the Court trusts, that the caseworker will deserve trust.[57] Mr. Justice Blackmun appears to assume that if the Court sees conflict between caseworker and welfare recipient, and mandates adversarial process based on that perception, that this Court perception will itself create, or at least exacerbate, conflict and thus in itself defeat the ideal of conflict-free relations.

Chief Justice Burger in *Parham* expresses the same vision regarding parent-child relations:[58]

> [The law] historically . . . has recognized that natural bonds of affection lead parents to act in the best interests of their children [citing Blackstone and Kent]. . . . That some parents "may at times be acting against the interests of their child" . . . creates a basis for caution, but is hardly a reason to discard wholesale pages of human experience that teach that parents generally do act in the child's best interests.

The Chief Justice is not denying the possibility of conflict between parent and child, any more than his conservative colleagues are denying that possibility between teacher and student or welfare worker and recipient. These Justices are, however, united in the belief that the Court must view these relations as if they were conflict-free in order to encourage a trusting, even childlike, deference without which—as they see it—no wholesome relationship is possible between children and parents, or among their social surrogates. The Court, in the eyes of these Justices, has a special role in holding this ideal aloft in legitimizing authority by teaching the populace to ignore—as they would have the Court ignore—the conflict-ridden aspects of their contemporary social relations.

In his paean to the Amish way of life, Chief Justice Burger appears to see Amish success in leading children into law-abiding, productive, and self-reliant adulthood as arising from their achievement of this heavenly goal: "Old Order Amish communities [have] devotion to a life in harmony with nature and the soil, as exempli-

---

[57] See Burt, *Forcing Protection on Children and Their Parents: The Impact of* Wyman v. James, 69 MICH. L. REV. 1259, 1261–64 (1971).

[58] 99 S. Ct. at 2504.

fied by the simple life of the early Christian era that continued in America during much of our early national life."[59] The Chief Justice may have an inaccurate vision of conditions in contemporary Amish communities;[60] he certainly has a historically inaccurate conception of the successful achievement of this simple, harmonious life in early American history.[61] He is correct to see this ideal for community and for family life as a normative goal espoused throughout our national history, sometimes more and sometimes less emphasized.

The Chief Justice and his conservative colleagues clearly believe that our contemporary national life is ridden with profound and socially harmful divisions. Mr. Justice Powell, in the school discipline cases, repeatedly notes "[t]he seriousness of the disciplinary problems in the Nation's public schools"[62]—problems which, he states, have "increased significantly in magnitude in recent years."[63] Our recent years have been marked not simply by conflict in particular classrooms. Students have seized and barricaded universities; many public secondary schools resemble armed camps, with violence common among students and between teachers and students. These recent years have seen bloody urban riots and assassinations of national political leaders.

The Court inevitably acts against the background of such transfixing events, attempting to place them in proper perspective and to evaluate its institutional role in responding to them. In its family cases, the conservative nucleus has clearly set its agenda with reference to larger social events. These Justices have concluded that our contemporary national life is so fractionated that any challenge to constituted authority undermines the legitimacy of all authority, that we must recapture an earlier social attitude of unquestioning deference to authority which alone can create a stable precondition for belief in the legitimacy of any authority.

Like other lost faiths, however, unquestioning belief cannot be revived simply by exhortation. There are other possible techniques

---

[59] 406 U.S. at 210.

[60] Justice Douglas in his *Yoder* dissent pointed to evidence of defections from Amish communities and of high suicide rates, adolescent drinking, and "rowdyism and stress" in them. 406 U.S. at 245 n.2, 247 n.5.

[61] See Fischer, note 17 *supra*, at 66–76.

[62] 430 U.S. at 681 n.53.

[63] 419 U.S. at 592.

for resolving doubts about the good faith or legitimacy of authorities—whether parents or judges—beyond suppressing those doubts, pretending that we have none. The liberal Justices offer an apparently different technique to this end in these family cases and more generally in their jurisprudence. On ultimate analysis, however, their technique depends on an uncomfortably transparent pretense that has more in common with their conservative brethrens' stance than either bloc likes to admit.

II. The Liberal Justices: Suppressing Conflict by Force of Reason

The modern Court's concern for a jurisprudence of the family originated in *In re Gault*, decided in 1967.[64] This was only the second juvenile court case to reach Supreme Court adjudication,[65] though such courts had been established for some fifty years in virtually every State.[66] The central characteristic of these courts was informality: no clearly defined offenses, no clear separation of prosecutorial and adjudicatory roles, no defense attorneys adversarially committed to a juvenile client. The juvenile court was instead conceived as if it were a Victorian family with the juvenile as rebellious lad moved to repentance and reformation by the imprecation and example of the stern but kindly *paterfamilias*.

This court's legitimacy depended ostentatiously on unquestioning trust in the benevolence of authority. The architects of the juvenile court, writing around the turn of the century, made this clear.[67] Adversarial representation and other constitutionally mandated attributes of the adult criminal justice system were excluded from the juvenile court because they were premised on conflict of interest between individual and State and concomitant mistrust of state authority. These premises had no proper application, the argument went, to relations between children and adults—whether

[64] 387 U.S. 1 (1967).

[65] The first was Kent v. United States, 383 U.S. 541 (1966), a case originating in the District of Columbia Juvenile Court which the Supreme Court resolved on statutory grounds.

[66] See President's Comm'n on Law Enforcement and Administration of Justice, Task Force Report: Juvenile Delinquency and Youth Crime 2–3 (1967).

[67] See Ryerson, The Best-laid Plans: America's Juvenile Court Experiment 35–56 (1978).

those adults were biological parents or state officials acting as *parens patriae* (the latinism adopted as their characterizing catchphrase by the architects of the juvenile court movement).

The juvenile court was thus built on the mutually reinforcing assumptions that conflict of interest did not exist between adults and children and that proper child rearing required adults and children to suppress any suspicion of actual or potential conflict. A further related assumption rested beneath these—that there was no conflict (or no properly perceived conflict) between state officials and parents in child-rearing matters. The juvenile court movement took hold at the same time that compulsory education laws became enacted in almost every State and that other protectively intended measures, such as child labor laws, became extensively advocated.[68] Though these laws on their face appear to express mistrust of parental conduct toward children, this does not mean that these laws were recognized as symptomatic of conflicting interests between parents and state officials. Rather, these laws coincided with a widely articulated sense of mistrust by middle-class parents of their own child-rearing capacities and a concomitant willingness, even eagerness, among these parents to find support from some extrafamilial source of expertise and authority.

Social historians have pointed to the distinctive emergence in the late nineteenth century of popular child-rearing manuals.[69] With the development of Freudian psychology exalting the significance of early childhood experience for adult life and the transportation of that psychology into its distinctive American ameliorative-interventionist format beginning in the 1920s and 1930s, the notion that good parents were obliged to seek out and defer to child-rearing experts became firmly enshrined as a middle-class norm.[70] During this same time, lower-class immigrant families were expected to deliver their children to state officials for "Americanization." Though the nativist proponents of this policy frequently portrayed themselves as at odds with the socially disruptive aliens

---

[68] See WIEBE, SEARCH FOR ORDER: 1877–1920, 169–71 (1967).

[69] See Demos, *The American Family in Past Times*, 43 AMERICAN SCHOLAR 422, 439 (1974); ROTHMAN, WOMAN'S PROPER PLACE: A HISTORY OF CHANGING IDEALS AND PRACTICES, 1870 TO THE PRESENT 97–106 (1978).

[70] See SCHNEIDER & SMITH, CLASS DIFFERENCES AND SEX ROLES IN AMERICAN KINSHIP AND FAMILY STRUCTURE 46–49 (1973).

who had suddenly appeared in such numbers,[71] the immigrant parents themselves were frequently eager to deliver their children and even themselves to the apostles of Americanism.[72] Thus here too the parents addressed by state child-rearing interventions tended, for their own reasons, to mute any sound of conflict between parents, children, and state authority.

By 1967, when *Gault* was decided, such conflicts could no longer be so readily obscured. The reasons for this are not clear. It may be that, as racially identifiable urban immigrants succeeded the earlier ethnic immigrants as the most visible lower-class targets of state intervention,[73] these new targets were no longer so eager, or even so ambivalent, in their acceptance of the official middle-class child-rearing norms. Or it may be—and I think it more likely—that by 1967 the officials presiding over state interventions, including Supreme Court Justices, could no longer suppress conscious awareness of familial or social conflict with the easy aplomb of their predecessors. The officials of 1967 had come into maturity during the Great Depression and World War II—events which must have sharpened their awareness of, though not necessarily their tolerance for, the prevalence of social conflict.

Gault does more than signal this awareness in the modern Court's jurisprudence; it also epitomizes the liberal bloc Justices' characteristic response to social conflict generally. *Gault* ruled specifically that the procedural informality that had marked the juvenile court from its inception would not satisfy constitutional norms—that juveniles must be given clear notice of the offense charged, opportunity to defend themselves against state intervention, and the right to an attorney who could be adversarially committed to protect them against interventions. The Court majority—then in its most confidently liberal heyday—rejected the vision of social fact and norm on which the juvenile court's informality had rested; it

---

[71] See ROTHMAN, note 69 *supra*, at 101–03.

[72] Compare Irving Howe's account of Jewish immigrant attitudes: "In the main . . . the immigrant Jews looked up to the school system as an agency meriting respect and a little fear—since it was a power that, through incomprehensible edicts, could satisfy or destroy all one's hopes for one's children." WORLD OF OUR FATHERS: THE JOURNEY OF THE EAST EUROPEAN JEWS TO AMERICA AND THE LIFE THEY FOUND AND MADE 278–79 (1976).

[73] See MYRDAL, AN AMERICAN DILEMMA: THE NEGRO PROBLEM AND MODERN DEMOCRACY 191–97 (1944).

ruled that actual or potential conflict between child and State must not be ignored but rather must be structurally expressed in the procedures of the court.

Conservative critics of the *Gault* ruling argued that this structuralization would itself create, or at least intensify, conflict between children and State.[74] The liberals dismissed this objection, but not because they espoused the propriety of such conflict. The liberals rested their case on a further assumption—that not only was such conflict inevitable but that its open admission and structural expression would permit the best possible resolution of that conflict.

The liberals conceived that the juvenile court posed a question to itself: Should the State intervene in the life of this child? Juvenile court procedure, the liberals posited, should be framed to answer this question. This conception was, to the early architects of the juvenile court, equivalent to asking whether a child should be subject to adult authority—a question that to them answered itself.

This fundamental difference in the conception of the question explains one apparent paradox in the historical development of the juvenile court—a paradox that impressed the *Gault* majority and appeared to blunt the force of the dissent's argument. The paradox was that interventionist claims of the juvenile court appeared to rest on behavioral expertise while the court personnel, whether judge or supporting staff, was nude of any credentialed claims to such expertise.[75] By 1967, the child-rearing claims of behavioral experts had become so expansive, and parental reliance on such experts had become so widely expected, that the *Gault* majority could reduce the juvenile court's claim to expertise and, from this reduction, easily argue that an adversarial mode is best adapted to test the experts' claims.

In this constricted vision, the role of the juvenile court judge assumed a different face. The *Gault* majority saw him as an umpire presiding over a clash of views regarding the propriety of state intervention for the child. The juvenile court judge was not the reflexive embodiment of state power or, that is, a representative of adult authority indistinguishable from all other adults who control

[74] See Mr. Justice Blackmun's plurality opinion in McKeiver v. Pennsylvania, 403 U.S. 528 (1971), and Chief Justice Burger's dissent in In re Winship, 397 U.S. 358, 376 (1970).

[75] *Gault*, 387 U.S. at 14–15 n.14.

children. He was to stand outside the conflict between state or adult authority and children, to serve as neutral adjudicator of the claims of each. The pretensions of the behavioral experts appeared to give substantive content to this umpireal judicial role—that rules for proper child rearing could be identified and applied by objective observers. Thus comforted, the *Gault* majority readily mandated that the juvenile court judge must act as the majority Justices conceived themselves in confronting more general social conflict: as adjudicators committed to protect minority rights (or, in this case, the rights of minors) against impositions by state authority.

The readiness with which the *Gault* majority portrayed children in the same conceptual mold as other minority groups warranting judicial protection against majoritarian state power was evident in the rhetoric of its opinion. The Court spoke consistently of vindicating children's rights, though the facts of the *Gault* case made clear that both the child and his parents were united in resisting juvenile court jurisdiction.[76] The Court's failure to seize on these facts, and to portray the dispute as between State and family unit, was not an oversight; this failure was a central aspect of the liberal majority's vision of the case.

This choice of characterization—children's rights rather than family rights—assumed even greater significance in a case decided two years after *Gault*, with the liberal majority of the Warren years still the dominant voice of the Court. In *Tinker v. Des Moines Independent School District*,[77] the Court ruled that school authorities violated constitutional norms by forbidding students from wearing black armbands in class to protest the Vietnam War. The Court, in an opinion by Mr. Justice Fortas (who also wrote the *Gault* opinion), viewed the state authorities as violating the First Amendment speech rights of the schoolchildren and wholly ignored the question whether the school's imposition of an ideological orthodoxy on the children transgressed their parents' child-rearing rights.

This analytic omission had more direct significance here than in *Gault*. Justice Black dissented in *Tinker* on the ground that the children's black armbands more reflected their parents' antiwar views than their own. He noted, among other things, that one of the demonstrating children originally expelled from the Des Moines

[76] *Id.* at 5–7.

[77] 393 U.S. 503 (1969).

school was only eight years old.[78] Even assuming with Justice Black that the children had no discernible or "maturely" independent views, it does not necessarily follow that the school's imposition is to be preferred to the parents'.[79] The *Tinker* majority could have used Justice Black's factual characterization to posit a "family right" against state-imposed ideological conformity. But the liberal majority in *Tinker* was not interested in the family unit as such. They saw the family as discrete individuals with traditionally individualistic rights against state authority to be vindicated by umpireal judges who stood apart from the State.

Just as family unity was not relevant for the liberal majority in *Gault* and *Tinker*, family discord was not analytically significant for the liberal remnant in *Parham*. Mr. Justice Brennan's dissent argued that adversarial process, presided over by a judgelike officer, should protect children's rights against unjustified psychiatric hospitalization whether or not parents joined with state officials in such imposition. While Mr. Justice Brennan was willing to accept "short term in-patient treatment" at parental direction without prior judicialized hearing, this concession appeared dictated only by "practical implications" that parents should not be unduly deterred by adversarial formalities from initially seeking psychiatric hospitalization for their children.[80] When the hospitalization became a significant imposition, after a "limited period," his willingness to defer to parental sensitivities yielded to his individualistic and judicial-umpireal conception of the dispute and disputants.

For the liberal dissenters in *Parham* the familial guise of authority over children was not significant in principle. Authority required judicialized process to assure its legitimacy for the liberal Justices, whether that authority was exercised by parents, teachers, psychiatrists, or police. The liberals thus share with their conservative brethren an essentially unitary conception of authority in society. While the conservatives view authority as legitimized by unques-

---

[78] *Id.* at 516. Justice Black also observed that one parent was "paid a salary by the American Friends Service Committee' and another was "an official in the Women's International League for Peace and Freedom." *Ibid.*

[79] This reflexive assumption was, as noted earlier, see text at notes 22–25, the conservative majority's position in *Wyman v. James*, where Justice Black joined with the Court majority. See Burt, *Developing Constitutional Rights of, in, and for Children*, 39 Law & Contemp. Prob. 118, 123 (1975).

[80] 99 S. Ct. at 2519.

tioning deference, the liberals see legitimacy only for authority that can justify itself by giving reasons, prodded by adversarial questioning. Both conservative and liberal Justices apply their distinctive legitimizing techniques to authority generally without discrimination between parental and other sources. Notwithstanding an occasional rhetorical flourish from spokesmen for both blocs, principled legitimacy for parental authority as such in preference to other sources of social power commands no adherents yet among liberal or conservative Justices of this generation.[81]

The conservative Justices have refused to give special deference to family authority as such because they were more centrally concerned with protecting social order and they correctly saw that deference to family authority would only occasionally serve that

---

[81] Recent Supreme Court cases regarding the rights of unwed fathers and of children in foster care might appear at first glance to contradict this generalization. But notwithstanding the Court's encomia in these cases for family feeling and the special immunity of family units from state custodial interventions, the Court has refused to give protection to family status as such. Regarding unwed father's claims the Court has seen constitutional significance only in two circumstances:

(1) Where the father has lived with his children for some substantial time and can thus justify his interest to a judicial officer on affectional instrumental rather than on a priori family status grounds, Stanley v. Illinois, 405 U.S. 645 (1971); where these special facts cannot be proven, the Court has unanimously held that the state remains free to terminate the father's rights without particularized judicial inquiry, Quilloin v. Wollcott, 434 U.S. 246 (1978).

(2) Where state law provides special protection to an unwed mother in resisting state adoptive placement of her child but withholds such protection from an unwed father, the Court has found a constitutionally invalid gender discrimination, Caban v. Mohammed, 99 S. Ct. 1760 (1979); the Court, in this case at least, required only parity between father and mother and not special protection to parental status as such.

Regarding foster care, a unanimous Court in Smith v. O.F.F.E.R., 431 U.S. 816 (1977), refused to invalidate state laws withholding procedural protections from children whose parents had placed them in foster care and then sought to regain custody; the Court justified this refusal in part by referring to the traditionally hallowed authority of parents over children. But the case did not present, and the Court did not address, state claims to override parental wishes to retake custody. State and parent were united here as in *Parham* in ignoring a child's plausible claim that his parents' wishes, supported by state authority, disserved his interests. For the psychological basis for the child's argument to this effect, see GOLDSTEIN, FREUD & SOLNIT, BEYOND THE BEST INTERESTS OF THE CHILD (1973). There is no more consistency in these cases, regarding the constitutional status of the family unit as such, than in the cases discussed thus far in the text. These cases are thus not inconsistent with my central argument thus far, that the Justices are concerned in the family cases with protecting something other than family status as such.

The Court's votes in these cases cut across conservative and liberal bloc lines, but this is also not inconsistent with my discussion of the characteristic differences between these blocs, for reasons discussed in the text *infra*, at note 123.

goal. The liberal Justices have rejected this deference because they want to establish reason as the legitimizing touchstone for authority. Thus they would require parents to give reasoned justification for decisions regarding children in common with any other authoritative source. The conservative vision has this vulnerability at its core: they have no answer to those who challenge the legitimacy of the social order either beyond pious exhortation or resort to nakedly unlegitimated force. The liberal vision has a comparable vulnerability: their reliance on reason itself tends to challenge the very idea of social order. The liberal Justices have difficulty in answering these critical questions within the terms of their legitimizing schema. On what basis is one person's reasoning better than another's? Where reason rules, who is the ruling reasoner? The liberal Justices' occasionally glib equation of rule by reason and rule by judges attempts to mask the profoundly individualistic, destabilizing, and even antisocial implications of their philosophic commitment to rationality.[82]

The critique of judicial activism that became widely current during the 1930s and in revised form again during the 1960s addressed the insufficiencies of judges as embodiments of right reason in solving social problems. Particularistic criticism of judicial capacities—pointing to the limited data provided by judicial process and the terse opaqueness of substantive standards independently available to judges through constitutional norms—rested against a more general vision of courts' antidemocratic character. Courts' manifest unrepresentativeness created special tensions for the liberal Justices' claim that they ruled, and were ruled, by reason. If they could not persuade most people that their reasons were correct, what standard of rationality did these Justices purport to rest their decisions upon? If these Justices claimed that the rationality of their decisions could be reliably demonstrated in some way other than their capacity to persuade others, the implicit model underlying this socially isolated, even disdainful, posture appears uncomfortably close to the very antithesis of rationality: the man who reasons by himself and whose reasons are persuasive or even intelligible to himself alone, the psychotic.[83]

---

[82] See Arrow, Social Choice and Individual Values (2d ed. 1963).

[83] The force of this imagery was not lost on Franklin Roosevelt when he attacked the Court as dominated by Justices, not who had lost touch with majoritarian

This problem may not be necessarily inherent in the liberal ideology that society should be ruled by reason. The liberal Justices, however, ostentatiously trap themselves in this problem because of their adherence to a further premise shared with their conservative brethren: that prolonged social conflict is in itself undesirable. I noted earlier the romantic visions of social harmony that Mr. Justice Powell invoked to describe the ideal teacher-student relation, that Mr. Justice Blackmun invoked for welfare workers and recipients, and that Chief Justice Burger invoked for general communal relations in his encomium to the Amish. The liberal Justices have an equally idealized attachment to social harmony which they implicitly believe attainable by appeal to reason.

The liberals' habitual willingness to give judges especially active roles in resolving social conflict does not necessarily come from their assumption that judges are more honest or intelligent than others but rather because they see the judicial methodology of dispute resolution as most nearly synonymous with reasoned deliberation. The judge's commitment to an umpireal stance—to impartiality, to hearing all sides before deciding—is an important aspect of this methodology. But this stance alone might appear to put a premium on conflict as such. The conservative Justices construe the liberal position in this way, accusing them, for examples, of provoking conflict between parent and child (as in *Parham*), or student and teacher (as in *Goss*, *Ingraham*, and *Tinker*). The liberals have, however, a deeper commitment to a vision of social harmony beneath this apparent celebration of conflict. That commitment is revealed in a further aspect of the judicial methodology that most starkly differentiates it from the posture of other governmental actors: the obligation to give reasons for decisions.

This obligation is not primarily directed toward the winning party, though it has its congratulatory aspects. The obligation is more fundamentally addressed to the loser. The judge is obliged to give reasons that in principle might persuade the loser that he should applaud, and not merely sullenly acquiesce in, his loss. In giving reasons, the judge attempts to show the loser how he should recon-

---

needs or wishes, but more fundamentally who were ailing, and by implication senile, "old men." By what route no one can say for sure, but a Court majority soon thereafter came to its senses. See BURNS, ROOSEVELT: THE LION AND THE FOX 291–315 (1956).

ceive his own position and abandon his initial claim of entitlement in the light of principles that dictate the decision for the winner—communal principles, that is, shared equally between loser and winner.

The underlying premise of the methodological insistence on reasoned judicial opinions is that the initial conflict between plaintiff and defendant is thereby transformed into a shared celebration that justice has triumphed. The methodology posits that both parties can be persuaded to see themselves sharing a victory in the judge's reassertion (or revelatory clarification) of the principles that bind plaintiff and defendant, that transcend their initial conflict and more fundamentally unite them in a harmonious community.

Judges do not own this premise; presidents and other elected officials often invoke it. But judges are constrained by it while other governmental actors are more free to justify their actions without reference to any principle beyond majority rule, resting on the force of numbers alone as an adequate reassertion of the communal identity that binds losers to acquiesce in their defeat in the controversy at hand. Invocation of the majoritarian principle by elected officials does not invariably obtain an acknowledgment of legitimacy from the losers, any more than every judge's reasoning persuades defeated litigants. But majoritarianism offers to the losers, on the face of its doctrine, a readily invoked technique for legitimated resistance—that is, to organize forces for the next election—that permits them to remain unreconciled to defeat for a long time before they are forced to define themselves as removed from the community, as rebels. The judicial principle of legitimacy does not necessarily buy time. The judicial methodology thus has a special problem in addressing stubbornly unreconciled combatants.

The contemporary Court has seen this problem at the core of its claim to legitimacy with special intensity in its approach to race relations, and particularly regarding school desegregation. The Court set out to buy time for itself in the "deliberate speed" formula of *Brown II*.[84] The Justices' evident goal here was to withhold definitive resolution of this apparently irreconcilable social conflict in order to create an orderly prolongation of the conflict that might itself at least soften its hard edges.

---

[84] Brown v. Board of Education, 349 U.S. 298 (1955).

This technique of dispute prolongation rather than resolution, paradigmatically expressed in *Brown II*, has occasionally been attacked as unworthy of judges, as antithetical to the commitment to principled adjudication on which judicial legitimacy rests.[85] These critics fail to see that judicial legitimacy fundamentally rests on judges' claims that losing litigants should acquiesce in their defeat on the ground that their loss was deserved. Judicial appeal to moral principle is an important aspect of the persuasive process that makes such claims most forcefully plausible. But such appeal is only part of this process. As with the majoritarian institutions, the central aspect of judicial legitimacy is the credibility of courts' claims that losing parties share a community of values and interests with the winners, that losers and winners are more fundamentally joined together than divided by their immediately opposed conceptions of the controversy at hand.

Majoritarian institutions, as noted, can plausibly make this claim without repeatedly explicit assertion because the recurring electoral process continuously offers losers the opportunity to reconstitute the community of winners. Judicial institutions, particularly in constitutional adjudication, must be more self-consciously attentive to techniques for attaining this same goal. The methodology of common-law case adjudication has implicitly served this goal by detailed, even obsessive attention to the peculiarities of individual litigants' circumstances, thus inviting others with apparently similar disputes to offer fine-grained distinctions for deciding future cases. At common law, no litigative victory thus ever appears secure except between the immediate named parties; for the rest, "winners" and "losers" appeared to remain potentially changeable categorizations for a long time. This methodology is not alien to constitutional adjudication.[86] But the heightened sense of public and self-importance that envelops the deliberations of the Supreme Court,

---

[85] See text *infra*, at note 107. See also Gunther, *The Subtle Vices of the "Passive Virtues"—a Comment on Principle and Expediency in Judicial Review*, 64 Colum. L. Rev. 1 (1964).

[86] Alexander Bickel's conception of the "passive virtues" made explicit what was only implicit in the common-law methodology as applied to constitutional adjudication. The specific dispute-avoidance techniques he addressed—denial of certiorari, ripeness and standing doctrines—should be seen as exemplifying but not exhausting judicial techniques for prolonging in preference to immediately resolving sharply divisive disputes. See Bickel, The Least Dangerous Branch: The Supreme Court at the Bar of Politics, 111–98 (1962).

and the airy grandeur of the substantive principles in the constitutional document, constantly tempt the Justices toward apocalyptic pronouncements intended to end dispute at once and for all.

Such pronouncements have been characteristic of the family cases that now crowd the Court's docket. In the microcosm of child-rearing conflicts, these cases present the same problem of the legitimacy of and rebellion toward constituted authority that has preoccupied the Court at least since *Brown I.*[87] In this context, the problem might appear more manageable for the Court than in the race cases. Entire cities are unlikely to explode in flames, armed troops are unlikely to be called to the barricades, if the Court miscalculates, for example, in *Parham.* But if the jurisprudential lesson of the race cases had been fully explicated and understood, the current Court should see these family cases as instances of irreconcilable, or at best persistently stubborn, disputes that pose a central challenge to the legitimacy of judicial adjudication. If the Court had developed an adequate jurisprudence, in the course of its dealings with the race cases, for addressing such deep-rooted conflict, neither conservative nor liberal Justices should fall with such ease into the fallacy that judges should set out to end such disputes, whether by commanding unquestioning deference to traditional authority or to the rule of reason as conceived by an authoritative reasoner.

Mr. Justice Brennan's dissenting opinion in *Parham* invokes a characteristically inflated vision of the commanding force of rationality and a conflated view of reason's judicial embodiment. Judicialized adversarial hearings for institutionalized children, he observes,[88]

> may prove therapeutic. Children who feel that they have received a fair hearing may be more likely to accept the legitimacy of their confinement, acknowledge their illness and cooperate with those attempting to give treatment. This, in turn, would remove a significant impediment to successful therapy.

What leads Mr. Justice Brennan to believe that a child who protests his parents' decision to hospitalize and who resists the psychiatrists' custody will regard as "fair" and "legitimate" a proceed-

---

[87] Brown v. Board of Education, 347 U.S. 483 (1954).

[88] 99 S. Ct. at 2521 n.22.

ing that ends with a judge's ratification of the other adults' disposition? The majority opinion in *Parham* implicitly attacks this assumption, citing studies of judicial civil commitment hearings for adult psychiatric confinements that reveal a mean hearing time ranging from 3.8 to 9.2 minutes. The Chief Justice concludes from these data that "the supposed protections of an adversary proceeding . . . [regarding mental hospitalization] may well be more illusory than real."[89]

It might nonetheless be argued that introduction of judicial hearings is worthwhile because it would not create, and may possibly remedy, either an arbitrary hospitalization decision or the appearance of arbitrariness from the child's perspective. This modest argument is at least plausible and the Brennan dissent can be read ultimately to assert no more than this. The modesty of this position has its pathos, however, because it is so likely to fail in practice and because its failure is symptomatic of the self-defeating limits of the current liberal ideological vision of the proper judicial role in legitimizing authority generally.

The liberal dissenters in *Parham* may be correct that parents, psychiatrists, and children alike should be obliged to give reasoned accounts of their decisions for or against psychiatric hospitalization. But certainly at the first moments, or even after a "limited period," of hospitalization, reasoned discourse is a scarce commodity between parents and child, the principal participants in the controversy. The notion that an extrafamilial authority can readily impose order on this controversy—whether that authority is psychiatrist or judge, whether the form of that imposition is shouted imprecation or cool reasonableness—is the fallacy that is shared by both liberal and conservative Justices. But in embracing this fallacy, the liberals—more than their conservative brethren—are untrue to the basic underlying premises of their ideology. Authoritative imposition is antithetical to reasoned discourse. But unless the liberal Justices can dissociate reasoned discourse from the idea of judge as the ultimate reasoner, whose conclusion warrants special respect apart from its persuasiveness, this liberal commitment to reason becomes a transparent mask for the conservative position that authority warrants deference simply as such.

---

[89] *Id.* at 2508 & n.17.

III. Toward a Jurisprudence of Legitimizing Dispute

A child facing psychiatric hospitalization may think of himself in two different ways: as permanently alienated from his parents and the adult community generally, so that he must premise all future relations on unremitting hostility and estrangement, or as profoundly aggrieved toward his parents and community because they will not acknowledge his claims to strength and dignity, but prepared for reconciliation when those claims are met. At the moment of hospitalization, both the child and his parents will most likely see him in the former mode. The goal of hospitalization is to bring both child and parents to see him in the latter mode, to assist them both in identifying and honoring his legitimate claims and abandoning those unworthy of mutual respect.[90]

Parents and child may never be reconciled on those terms. But unless the child can himself come to offer those terms, he will never in his own mind shake loose from his familial struggle, he will always demand what he knows they will never give. He will thereby be disabled from entering the adult community except on terms that offer no alternative in his mind between total victory or total defeat, to enslave others or be enslaved by them. To assist the child in becoming an adult capable of giving and obtaining reliable satisfaction regarding others, psychiatric hospitalization must not be seen by the child as the end of his struggle with family and community, as victory for one and defeat for the other. Hospitalization must be seen as acknowledging the existence and legitimacy of conflict but guiding that conflict toward terms that might promise some ultimate resolution.

A family that has come to consider psychiatric hospitalization for one of its members does not need an end to internal dispute on that specific issue or generally. It needs internal dispute to be prolonged, but transformed in that prolongation into an orderly process in which the disputants can progressively come to sort out their grievances and the possibilities of redress, whether from sources within or outside the family. Amid the cacophony of claims and counterclaims, the disputants need to be freed from the disabling bind that makes their conflict a life-death struggle for each, with the victory

---

[90] See, *e.g.*, Miller, Adolescence: Psychology, Psychopathology and Psychotherapy esp. pp. 370–74 (1974).

of one seen as inevitably equivalent to the destruction of the other. The disputants need to understand what gives legitimacy to any familial or social dispute: not necessarily that each party's grievance is equally justified but that neither party can claim the utter destruction or enslavement of the other, the forfeiture by either party of his sense of dignity and integrity, without thereby depriving the victor's claim of legitimacy.[91]

In all families, not merely in those ultimately driven to extrude one member into psychiatric hospitalization, struggles between parents and child typically implicate this issue of principle. Parents in such struggles appear to have clearly superior strength. When they come to see their own sense of integrity as deeply threatened by their children, their temptation to assert that strength can become intense and ultimately intensely destructive—even, where this dynamic expresses itself in physical child abuse, destructive of the child's very life.[92] When parents decide that their child must be psychiatrically hospitalized, that decision necessarily has extrusive, destructive implications for both parents and child. Those implications can be, and typically are, mixed with other meanings—to seek genuine help for the child in order to give him the freedom his parents had not succeeded in achieving for themselves.

The central therapeutic task for psychiatrists who accept custody of the child is to keep the destructive and constructive meanings of that custody in high visibility and in tension for both parents and child. This is a difficult task to achieve, and many forces in particular families and the broader society conspire against its success. It is seductively easy for the psychiatrists who preside over the institutions to ally themselves with the self-evident power of the adult (and the "mentally normal") world against the disruptive (or "mentally ill") child by legitimating his extrusion and isolation.[93]

The Court's reliance in *Parham* on studies demonstrating that hospitalized children virtually always have extensive prior records of psychological disturbance and disruptive conduct does not adequately answer the charge that such hospitals too readily become custodial "dumping grounds."[94] These studies do suggest, however,

---

[91] See Burt, Taking Care of Strangers: The Rule of Law in Doctor-Patient Relations 97–100 (1979).

[92] *Id.* at pp. 61–65.

[93] *Id.* at pp. 66–70.

[94] 99 S. Ct. at 2501 n.8, 2504.

that this concern cannot adequately be met by creating an individualized hearing mechanism that concentrates attention on the initial hospitalization decision, whether immediately or (as Mr. Justice Brennan proposes) after a "limited period" of hospital confinement. Some advantage might come from such a mechanism in screening out children whose prior disturbance is not adequately documented or for whom less drastic, less stigmatizing treatment alternatives have not been assayed. Such cases, however, are likely to appear infrequent. The persistent, intensive interpersonal struggles that inevitably mark any family whose child is presented for psychiatric hospitalization will inevitably distort the judgment of those performing initial screening functions. This conflict will magnify the appearance of the child's disruptiveness and psychopathy, no matter how "detached" or "neutral" this screening officer attempts to portray himself. This psychological reality lies beneath the speedy, apparently pro forma dispositions in adult civil commitment proceedings.[95]

This does not mean that no adult or child is likely to be inappropriately hospitalized or that a psychiatrist is likely to be more reliable in such screening than a law-trained officer. It means that a regularized, closely detailed review of the formal records of those persons institutionalized, focusing on objective elements such as prior outpatient psychiatric treatment provided and concurrence of different observers (psychiatrists, schoolteachers, neighbors, as well as family members) are more likely to offer significant protection[96] than a face-to-face adversarial proceeding where the hearing officer's inevitable interpersonal involvement (or felt need to detach himself from such involvement) will distort rather than aid judgment.

Even accepting all this, it might still be argued that a remedy such as regularized record reviews should be added to rather than substituted for adversarial proceedings. There is, however, one further and more fundamental objection to such proceedings: their likely impact on both the winning and losing parties. If the central therapeutic task in psychiatric hospitals is to prolong dispute, to ward off everyone's impulse toward forced, premature dispute termina-

---

[95] See ROCK, HOSPITALIZATION AND DISCHARGE OF THE MENTALLY ILL 151–57, 256–60 (1968).

[96] See STONE, MENTAL HEALTH AND LAW: A SYSTEM IN TRANSITION 65–79 (1975).

tion, an early adversarial proceeding is dramatically at odds with the goal.[97] For commitment of children, this proceeding necessarily ends with an apparent answer to such questions as: "Should the child be extruded from his family or forced back on them?" "Is the child the centrally disruptive and thus most blameworthy or most sick family member or is his disturbance only a mask for others' difficulties?" "Can the community of adults exert authoritative, effective force to silence this child or must his noisy provocation endlessly intrude on others?" The proper response—for therapist, judge, or any third party drawn into the parent-child dispute—is to refuse any answer to such questions and to redirect the disputants' attention to the central problem that divides and disturbs them: that is, why these questions—by which both parent and child seek to portray one as winner and the other as loser—have come to assume such divisive urgency between them.[98] The third-party intervenor's success in redirecting the disputants' attention to this underlying issue will be the measure of his capacity ultimately to help each party toward stable resolution of the dispute.

Structural aspects of typical psychiatric hospitals, however, clearly appear to answer every question in dispute between child and adults in a way that defeats and extrudes the child. These defeating and therapeutically self-defeating elements include the institution's physically isolated locations; their failure to insist on some form of continuing parental involvement rather than accepting wholesale delivery of the child's custody; failure to provide regular programmatic contact between hospitalized children and agencies serving other children such as afforded by public schools; excessive reliance on locked wards, barred windows, isolation rooms, and other accoutrements of prison life rather than acceptance of a significant risk of flight.[99] All these aspects of institutional life un-

---

[97] I have advanced the same proposition regarding the role of declaratory relief in disputes over life-threatening illness between doctors and patients, note 91 *supra*, at 17–21, 136–43.

[98] See, *e.g.*, BERMANN, SCAPEGOAT: THE IMPACT OF DEATH-FEAR ON AN AMERICAN FAMILY (1973).

[99] There are many opportunities in [an appropriate children's] psychiatric facility located within a community for contact by its residents with the world outside. Token confinement within physical facilities implicitly safeguards the adolescent's right to personal liberty. For most psychiatrically disturbed young people, the implicit opportunity to run away from a facility, without the pressure of an explicit commitment to stay, provides a reasonably accurate gauge of the patient's essential

derscore for the hospitalized child the proposition that he is "sick" and "dangerous" and must be isolated like a contagious leper from the ordinary world. Grafting adversarial hearings onto the entrance agenda of these institutions would not change this meaning for the large majority of children whose admissions would likely be approved; such proceedings would only reinforce this lesson. Even for those incrementally small numbers likely to be screened out in such hearings, the format of the hearing would conspire to define them as victors in their apocalyptic battle with family and other adults rather than assisting all of the disputants to redefine the terms of their conflict and see themselves as part of rather than as irreconcilably isolated from an inclusive community.

The Court majority in *Parham* argued that adversarial hearings would run counter to the institutions' therapeutic purposes. The majority was not necessarily wrong to conclude that those purposes and children's constitutionally sanctioned "liberty interests" could be adequately protected by the "independent judgment" of institution psychiatrists regarding commitment. The Court failed to consider, however, what the necessary components of that judgmental "independence" might be. The Court concluded that the Georgia statute was facially constitutional on the ground that no "single physician or other professional has the 'unbridled discretion' . . . to commit a child" but that "teams" of psychiatrists and other mental health professionals examine each child, his parents, and his medical and school records.[100] This conclusion is not convincing. The socially isolating institutional context that frames all aspects of the child's commitment makes the institution an inevitable ally in his parents' and other adults' wishes (however ambivalently held) to silence and extrude him. This context would rob an army of psychiatrists as readily as one of that independence by which they might protect the child's interests in securing "liberty" or "mental health."

But what if the Court had understood that the child's interests, however defined, could only be protected if the dispute between

---

evaluation of his or her placement. Implicit opportunities for elopement [also] avoid the therapeutic trap (set by individual court hearings) of forcing an explicit acquiescence or protest in response to hospitalization." MILLER & BURT, note 16 *supra*, at 155.

100 99 S. Ct. at 2510.

him and the adult world were prolonged in an orderly manner, rather than given the appearance of an abrupt conclusion? What could the Court do, what could any judicial reviewing agency properly do, to bring this result? The Court's opinion appears to see no judicial role here, which in part explains its slap-dash reasoning to support the facial finding that the statute assures adequate judgmental independence to commiting psychiatrists. Thus the Court begins its analysis of the due process independence requirement:[101]

> Since well-established medical procedures [for investigating the propriety of a child's hospitalization] already exist, we do not undertake to outline with specificity precisely what this investigation must involve. The mode and procedure of medical diagnostic procedures is not the business of judges. What is best for a child is an individual medical decision that must be left to the judgment of physicians in each case.

This prescription for judicial deference appears an implicit criticism of the actions of a substantial number of lower federal courts during the past decade attempting to vindicate constitutional "rights to treatment" in institutions for mentally ill or retarded children and adults.[102] In those cases, courts have directly grappled with aspects of institutional structure such as geographic locale and use of locked wards. The Supreme Court has thus far remained cautiously on the perimeter of those cases, apparently validating the theoretical underpinning of the constitutional right without addressing the remedial consequences of that right.[103] In cases involving other large-scale bureaucratic institutions, however, such as prisons and police departments, the Court has recently been led by its conservative bloc into retreat from extensively detailed judicial intervention.[104]

The Court's reiteration of this critique in *Parham* suggests the broader social and jurisprudential significance of the family dispute

---

[101] *Id.* at 2507.

[102] The leading case is Wyatt v. Stickney, 344 F. Supp. 387 (M.D. Ala. 1972) aff'd *sub nom.* Wyatt v. Aderholt, 503 F.2d 1305 (5th Cir. 1974); for citation to the extensive subsequent case law, see Plotkin, *Limiting the Therapeutic Orgy: Mental Patients' Right to Refuse Treatment*, 72 Nw. U. L. Rev. 461, 484 nn.147–48 (1977).

[103] See O'Connor v. Donaldson, 422 U.S. 563 (1975).

[104] Bell v. Wolfish, 99 S. Ct. 1861 (1979); Rizzo v. Goode, 423 U.S. 362 (1976).

in that case. The conflict between child and parent regarding psychiatric hospitalization mirrors and metaphorically represents general social conflict between fundamentally alienated disputants, and raises for the Court the question of its proper role in such disputes. This question has been of obsessive importance to the contemporary Court at least since its ruling in *Brown v. Board of Education.* In order to evaluate what the Court should have done in *Parham*, therefore, we must first understand and evaluate what the Court did in *Brown.*

The expansive interventionist assumptions of the lower federal courts in the mental hospital, prison, and police cases have been forged in the enforcement of *Brown* during the past twenty-five years.[105] That effort transformed almost beyond recognition the traditional conception of a lawsuit in which plaintiff and defendant confronted one another with clear-cut opposed claims, the judge decided the winner between them, and the controversy was thus ended. The conservative bloc on the Court is currently attempting to reassert the relevance of the traditional litigative framework as a limitation on judicial remedial power.[106] Even if that retrenchment could be justified in contemporary school desegregation cases, it is wrong to draw a general lesson from this—as the conservative bloc does—that the traditional conception should hold firm in litigation involving institutions such as prisons and mental hospitals. To put the matter in simplest terms, even if extensive judicial involvement in reshaping public school systems is less appropriate now than twenty-five years ago, it does not follow that such involvement is not appropriate for this newer litigative subject matter. The Court today, that is, fails to understand the temporal aspects of *Brown's* enforcement as a central part of the legitimacy of that judicial enterprise.

The "deliberate speed" formula of *Brown II* has gotten some bad press in recent years. Justice Black suggested in a 1968 television interview that the enforcement delay may have been a mistake, that a sudden, complete transformation of the segregated system would have been painful but—like yanking off an adhesive bandage—ultimately less painful and thus more effective than the long-drawn-out

[105] See Fiss, The Civil Rights Injunction 1–6 (1978).

[106] See Fiss, *The Forms of Justice*, 93 Harv. L. Rev. 1 (1979).

process.[107] This view makes most sense from a traditional conception of the litigative process and the judge's proper role. By this view, the plaintiffs correctly contended that racial segregation was wrong, and a judge should therefore declare them the winner and enforce their victory over the defendant. If the defendant proved recalcitrant, then he must simply be forced into compliance for he is as wrong to resist as he was wrong to maintain segregated schools.

There is, however, another way to conceptualize *Brown* and its enforcement that starts from the same premise that racial segregation was wrong. A more interesting jurisprudential lesson emerges from *Brown II* if we see that decision as limiting *Brown I* to a declaration that, because blacks' interests had been wrongly defeated in majoritarian institutions, the Court merely directed that the dispute between blacks and others be reopened. The Court from this perspective was not declaring either litigant to be the ultimate winner in that dispute. The Court may not have clearly seen its role in this light at the time.[108] Immediate popular reaction certainly did not give it that interpretation. The Southern proponents of massive resistance in particular saw the Court ruling as a stinging defeat that they would oppose forever, until they had reclaimed their victory over blacks.[109] The Court in *Brown II* apparently was trying to forestall this response by the defeated litigants. Their hope seemed to be that the defeated litigants could be persuaded to acquiesce in that defeat. In the terms that I have suggested earlier in this essay, the Court in effect hoped that Southern whites would redefine themselves in a more inclusive communal identity with

[107] *Black Believes Warren Phrase Slowed Integration*, N.Y. TIMES, Dec. 4, 1968, p. 1, col. 2.

[108] At the time of *Brown I*, it was not clear what victory for the plaintiffs would look like. Would wrongful segregation be adequately ended if state and local statutes were abolished so that all whites and blacks thus became "free to choose" their schools? What if all chose to remain segregated? Or would the wrong be corrected only when no public school was predominantly composed of one race of students or teachers? And so on. Thus it is possible to see the Court's hesitancy in *Brown II* as simply reflecting its uncertainty—and the litigants' uncertainty—about how to give victory to the wronged plaintiffs, in order to keep that decision within the traditional conceptual framework of litigation and judicial power.

[109] See MUSE, TEN YEARS OF PRELUDE 56–72 (1964). The Court responded to this challenge in equally contentious terms in Cooper v. Aaron, 358 U.S. 1 (1958). But the Court's ringing peroration in that case—that *Brown* was "unanimously reaffirmed," and that unquestioning "obedience of the States" is now "indispensable," 358 U.S. at 19–20, did not prompt the Court to abandon its tolerance for delay, expressed in *Brown II*, until ten years later. See text *infra* at n. 113.

black citizens on terms that would not be seen as a humiliating defeat for anyone.[110] This hope can be seen in the double-speak directive of *Brown II* that while constitutional principles must not "yield simply because of disagreement with them," desegregation decrees should nonetheless be "characterized by a practical flexibility . . . for adjusting and reconciling public and private needs."[111]

The Court in the school desegregation cases saw itself as confronting two opposed parties who appeared so deeply at odds that it was not clear they could remain members of the same community. Because blacks were shut out from majoritarian institutions, however, this dispute had no orderly, legitimate forum. In *Brown II*, the Supreme Court in effect declared that local federal courts would serve as that forum where the opposed parties might be led into clarifying what they truly wanted and needed from one another. In this way, some accommodation might ultimately be reached that would avert the apocalyptic, mutually destructive battle that otherwise appeared likely.

This may be an excessively optimistic and simplistic rendering of the Court's and the parties' visions in *Brown*. Many violent battles were fought in the wake of that decision; trial courts did not uniformly wish to reopen disputes that had been previously settled with unfair disadvantage to blacks,[112] and the Supreme Court itself ultimately abandoned the "deliberate speed" formula. But when the Court declared, in 1968, that "a school board today [must] come forward with a plan that . . . promises realistically to work *now*,"[113] the communal identities of blacks and whites had already been extraordinarily transformed by events in majoritarian institutions. Most notably, congressional enactment of the Civil Rights Acts of

---

[110] Gunnar Myrdal, in his influential and profound study, AN AMERICAN DILEMMA, pointed to misgivings among Southern whites regarding the degradation inflicted on Southern blacks that might have given the Court reason for this hope. See note 73 *supra*, at lxix–lxxvi, 997–1002. Nonetheless, the Court also had reason to fear, as Myrdal warned, a "critical" situation in the South and the prospect that "interracial tension in the South [will] get . . . out of hand and result . . . in bloody clashes." *Id.* at 1013, 1015.

[111] 349 U.S. at 300.

[112] See, *e.g.*, Hamilton, *Southern Judges and Negro Voting Rights: The Judicial Approach to the Solution of Controversial Social Problems*, 1965 WISC. L. REV. 74.

[113] Green v. New Kent County School Board, 391 U.S. 430, 439 (1968) (emphasis in original).

1964, 1965, and 1968 had required the unprecedented convening of an extraordinary majority of the Senate to break Southern filibusters. These efforts were prodded by lobbying enterprise in which black citizens did not stand alone but found allies in critical centers of political power throughout the country.

Furthermore, when it declared an end to the *Brown II* formula in 1968, the Court included a Justice who had been principal attorney for one party in *Brown I* and *II*. The alteration of Thurgood Marshall's status, from aggrieved petitioner to Supreme Court Justice,[114] symbolized that the national community had dramatically redefined itself and that the 1968 Court was not so much declaring a winner in the original controversy as ratifying that the terms of the controversy and the identity of the parties had been transformed in the process of the prolonged dispute which followed, and was purposefully provoked and directed by, the *Brown* decisions.

This vision of the Court's role in *Brown*—as dispute provoker rather than dispute resolver—finds some confirmation in the attitudes of Court members in 1954. At least two of the Justices in *Brown* explicitly asked themselves, in unpublished memoranda, whether the resistance of the losing parties would jeopardize the effective force of their decision and ultimately would draw the Court into such repressive action toward the rebels that the original litigants would appear—to themselves and to all others—simply to have reversed positions, the victimized oppressed now allied with judicial power to become the victimizing oppressor.[115] This is the dilemma that is presented, and not resolved, by the then (and still) dominant

---

[114] Marshall was appointed to the Court by President Johnson in 1967; he had been appointed to the Court of Appeals for the Second Circuit by President Kennedy in 1962 and resigned in 1965 to become Solicitor General at Johnson's appointment.

[115] Justice Jackson wrote, in an apparent draft of an undelivered concurring opinion, "[Whether the] real abolition of segregation will be accelerated or retarded by what many are likely to regard as a ruthless use of federal judicial power is a question that I cannot and need not answer." Justice Frankfurter stated the same concern in a similar draft format: "The legal problem confronting this Court is the extent to which [the] desirable and even necessary process of welding a nation out of . . . diverse elements can be imposed as a matter of law upon the States in disregard of the deeply rooted feeling, tradition and local laws, based upon local situations to the contrary." Kluger, Simple Justice: The History of *Brown v. Board of Education* and Black America's Struggle for Equality 688, 684–85 (1976).

conception of the Court's constitutional role in protecting minority rights expressed in *Carolene Products* footnote 4.[116] A judge may see—as was self-evident in *Brown* and more than plausible in *Parham*—that the blacks or children were unfairly disabled from protecting their interests against defeats in other forums. But if the judge attempted more than to reopen the dispute with the unfair disability removed, if the judge declared that the loser was now the winner, how can he answer the charge that adding his vote to make a new majority simply creates a new minority that deserves someone's protection?[117] The judge may, of course, answer that his vote is based on principles that transcend the parties' selfish conception of their interests, that he votes the truth while they vote their mere preferences. But what can the judge say if the litigative loser claims that the judge's truth is not his and that he will not remain a member of a community in which the judge's false assertion prevails?

Some judges may not be troubled by this rebellious stance and may confidently assert that their truth is the Truth.[118] But I believe that judges must hold back from forcing this issue. Underlying the practical limits on judicial power in overcoming such resistance, particularly if widespread, there is a more basic question of principle—whether an unconsented imposition loses legitimacy irrespective of its intrinsic merit, simply because the imposition lacks consent. A hallowed tradition lies behind this principle.[119] The American colonists argued that unconsented impositions made them "slaves" and justified their rebellion "to dissolve the political bands which have connected them with another, and to assume among the powers of the earth [a] separate & equal station."[120]

---

[116] United States v. Carolene Products Co., 304 U.S. 144, 152–53 n.4 (1938).

[117] See Fiss, note 106, *supra*, at 6–11.

[118] And some commentators appear to share this confidence. See *id* at 6–17, 30, 51.

[119] Thus George Washington, who himself had some firsthand knowledge of slave status, complained in 1774 that the English government was determined "by every piece of Art and despotism to fix the shackles of slavery upon us." MORGAN, THE MEANING OF INDEPENDENCE 37 (1976). This characterization was a recurrent part of the litany of the colonists' objection to the Stamp Act, see MORGAN & MORGAN, THE STAMP ACT CRISIS: PROLOGUE TO REVOLUTION 52, 55, 113–14, 118–19, 358, 362–64 (1962 rev. ed.), and then generally to British rule, see BAILYN, THE IDEOLOGICAL ORIGINS OF THE AMERICAN REVOLUTION 232–41 (1967).

[120] This famous language in the preamble to the Declaration of Independence is echoed, though in ironically revised form, in Louisiana's law segregating railway facilities, upheld in Plessy v. Ferguson, 163 U.S. 523 (1896).

The consensuality principle does not stand without contradiction in our history. It has been powerfully limited by the idea of inalienable minority rights with substantive content not simply cognizable through the workings of a consensual process. These two principles may not be irreconcilably opposed. But they are nonetheless difficult enough to resolve in particular contexts to warrant being seen at least as apparently irreconcilable.

The Court in *Brown* walked with considerable finesse between the poles of this apparent contradiction. The Court achieved this, though without self-conscious articulation, by unsettling the previously fixed positions of profoundly disaffected parties, by presiding over further dispute between them to give it order and coherence, and by refusing to declare an end to the dispute for a very long time. The *Brown* Court most likely would have preferred a speedy end to conflict and was led to this alternative jurisprudence because the intensity and visibility of racial conflict gave it no choice. But I believe that the experience of *Brown* demonstrates in retrospect that this jurisprudence was more than inevitable, that it was the jurisprudence of choice for responding to litigants who see themselves as fundamentally alienated from one another.

Litigants claiming violations of constitutional rights present the posture of basic alienation as a matter of course, simply because the litigants assert irreconcilably competing versions of fundamental principle. For much litigation, this stance is simply overheated rhetoric by which each party seeks marginal advantage over the other while each is readily prepared to accept defeat. But the stylization of fundamental alienation in constitutional adjudication has a deeper symbolism in it than the run-of-the-mill controversy suggests and that the grandeur and intensity of *Brown* reveals.

Majoritarian institutions systematically obscure this confrontation. Courts systematically highlight it. Anyone who feels aggrieved and who owns a pen can petition the legislature or file a lawsuit. But legislatures are structurally biased toward silence, toward sponge-like absorption of complaints. Court rules, in contrast, demand that the grieving party receive some response to his complaint; unless the target of the complaint, the named defendant, gives some response, he risks the penalty of default judgment.[121] Courts are thus more adept than majoritarian institutions at initiating and

[121] See Rule 55, F. R. CIV. P.

prolonging orderly conflict. Those who feel deeply alienated from and wounded by majoritarian institutions can at least always find some flesh to fight in court.

The very clarity of confrontation provided by litigation is not, however, an end in itself. The judge is charged to hear disputes, to find the just result, and to resolve disputes on that basis. Confrontation, through his office, is succeeded by resolution, by the reconciliation of opposites.[122] The triumph of Justice as the binding communal force has its special thrill because the forces opposed to community, the forces that threaten its destruction, are so palpably signified and even exaggerated in the stylized posture of adversarial litigation.

At least since *Brown*, the Supreme Court has been preoccupied with the staging of this drama. Through the Warren years, the Court was increasingly hospitable to litigation involving fundamentally alienated persons and bestowed "rights" on them as implicit offers of reconciliation: litigation involving blacks, criminal defendants and convicted criminals, Communists and atheists, aliens and illegitimate children, and even those whose alienation presented itself as a claim to be "left alone" which was elevated by the Court into a "right to privacy." The preoccupation with social alienation has led the contemporary Court into its concern with family relations. The crisis of authority that the current conservative bloc sees in the family cases has direct kinship with the crisis of community that the dominant liberal bloc of the Warren Court saw in their cases.

When vertical and horizontal bonds—the social linkages of authority and community—are seen as attenuated, conflict becomes more difficult to admit because fewer restraints appear to modulate the destructive implications of conflict, to confine its escalating potential. All the Justices in *Parham* failed to diagnose the problem as an absence of legitimated conflict and instead attempted to sup-

[122] Compare Mary Douglas's observation, from an anthropological perspective, regarding "men's common urge to make a unity of all their experiences and to overcome distinctions and separateness in acts of at-onement. The dramatic combination of opposites is a psychologically satisfying theme full of scope for interpretation. . . . [A]ny ritual which expresses the happy union of opposites is also an apt vehicle for essentially religious themes." DOUGLAS, PURITY AND DANGER: AN ANALYSIS OF CONCEPTS OF POLLUTION AND TABOO 169 (1966); see also BURT, note 91 *supra*, at 48–60.

press conflict. This failure is troubling not simply because, in that case, an opportunity to help children and families was missed. It is troubling because this failure speaks to an error evident throughout the Court's contemporary work. Rather than building on the *Brown* experience by refining judicial techniques to provoke and prolong dispute among litigants who see themselves as fundamentally alienated, the contemporary Court appears to have lost patience with conflict, and rushes instead to an imposed resolution.

This distaste for conflict and concomitant failure to see its prolongation as a proper judicial technique is particularly apparent in the most far-reaching family relations cases that the Court has decided during the past decade: the abortion and women's rights cases. Though the Court has not been unanimous in these cases, its divisions have cut across the conservative/liberal axes that characterized voting in the family cases discussed earlier. Perhaps this is because the abortion and women's rights cases do not directly raise questions regarding discipline of children and the Justices' attitudes about legitimizing authority are not so insistently called forward.[123] For whatever reasons, the contemporary liberal remnant has been joined by various conservative bloc Justices to invalidate state and federal laws restricting abortion and derogating women's status. No firm voting alliances have been established in these subject matters, and liberal and conservative Justices frequently disagree in reasoning even when their votes coincide. Beneath the variegated pattern of votes and reasoning in these cases, however, a unifying attitude appears. Both liberal and conservative Justices who vote to invalidate these state and federal laws ignore the existence of or potential for intense controversy in the majoritarian institutions and see themselves as properly ending this controversy by denominating a winning party.

Roe v. Wade[124] is a particularly striking instance of this shared liberal/conservative attitude. The Court's opinion, by Mr. Justice Blackmun, gives lengthy recitation of the history of social attitudes and conflict regarding abortion, from early Greek to modern times.[125] But this recitation is only a prelude for the Court's claim to identify the correct answer for our time. The opinion notes the

---

[123] See note 81 *supra*.

[124] 410 U.S. 113 (1973).

[125] *Id.* at 129–48.

dramatic recent shift in opinion, from a universal regime of highly restrictive to increasing availability of abortions. Legislatures in some one-third of the States had, since the late 1950s, significantly liberalized their abortion laws[126] and during 1970, four States—New York, Washington, Alaska, and Hawaii—wholly abolished restrictions.[127] Because New York's legalized procedures were not limited to state residents, the more restrictive regimes of the heavily populated neighboring States appeared undermined for practical purposes at least. Washington required ninety days' prior residence, and thus would most likely not have had a similar practical effect beyond its immediate borders.[128] In any event, these legislative changes clearly affected the popular debate on the principled issues, giving visibility and enhanced legitimacy to proponents of free abortion and signaling that campaigns to educate and mobilize popular force directed at majoritarian institutions were not clearly doomed to failure anywhere.

At the same time that this legislative ferment was increasing in intensity, proponents of free abortion turned to the federal courts. *Roe v. Wade* reached the Supreme Court in 1971. It was the Court's first case involving direct constitutional challenge to state abortion restrictions. The Court postponed decision and set the case for reargument in 1972.[129] In 1973 the Court awarded victory to the plaintiffs, with such completeness and detail that (I suspect) even they were surprised.

Roe has not ended controversy regarding abortion. It was indeed the impetus for new forces of opposition to identify themselves and to mobilize political effort which has had some considerable legislative success. The Court has reentered the dispute with some frequency, initially to defend its position in *Roe* but most recently to validate legislative restrictions aimed at poor women and minors.[130] Whatever their principled justifications,[131] the Court's rulings in net

---

[126] *Id.* at 140.

[127] See *id.* at 140 n.37.

[128] Wash. Rev. Code § 9.02.070. This abortion law revision had been submitted to, and approved by, popular election in November 1970. *Id.* at § 9.02.090.

[129] 402 U.S. 941 (1971); 408 U.S. 919 (1972).

[130] See Planned Parenthood v. Danforth, 428 U.S. 52 (1976); Beal v. Doe, 432 U.S. 438 (1977); Maher v. Roe, 432 U.S. 464 (1977); Poelker v. Doe, 423 U.S. 519 (1977); Bellotti v. Baird, 99 S. Ct. 3035 (1979). See generally ROTHMAN, note 69 *supra*, at 286–89.

[131] The justification for *Roe* has been sharply debated in academic as well as

result seem to have reproduced a rough facsimile of the wealth and race discriminations that held prior to *Roe*. Middle-class women can now obtain abortions in every State with greater convenience and easier consciences than was possible before *Roe*, at least for those women who were troubled at the prospect of traveling across state lines to avoid laws of their residence or of conspiring with a co-operative physician to exaggerate medical necessity or simply to flout state law. Other women are hampered in seeking abortions in the same ways that they were disadvantaged by the pre-*Roe* statutory restrictions.[132]

This apparently ironic result is an insufficient ground on which to argue that the Court was wrong in *Roe*. But the result raises a question nonetheless about what the Court expected to accomplish in its decision. If the Court meant to end dispute and to persuade most citizens of the moral propriety of freely available abortions, it has not accomplished that goal. If the Court meant to provoke a great national debate on this issue, to reopen the defeat of interests that had been unfairly disregarded in majoritarian institutions, its action was demonstrably unnecessary. The Court's action in *Roe* can be justified only if the principle at stake was so patently correct and important that its vindication could not depend on and would not be enhanced by the arduous effort of public persuasion and political organization that necessarily precedes legislative action. If there is no adequate public benefit from visible, prolonged, and legitimized conflict regarding the abortion issue, with its passionate psychological and moral significances, then the Court's swift proclamation in *Roe* was justified. But from these perspectives, there is no justification for *Roe*.

Feminists have had a second litigative goal—to persuade the Court that sex is as much a suspect legislative classification as race. The Court has, however, been less forthcoming here. Though sexual classifications have been invalidated in both federal and state laws with some frequency during the past decade, the Court has not ex-

political forums. See, *e.g.*, Ely, *The Wages of Crying Wolf: A Comment on Roe v. Wade*, 82 YALE L. J. 920 (1973); RAMSEY, ETHICS AT THE EDGES OF LIFE: MEDICAL AND LEGAL INTERSECTIONS (1978); Tribe, *Toward a Model of Roles in the Due Process of Life and Law*, 87 HARV. L. REV. 1 (1973); Thompson, *A Defense of Abortion*, 1 PHIL. & PUB. AFFAIRS 47 (1971).

[132] See ROTHMAN, note 69 *supra*, at 289.

plained its actions as an application of the suspect classification formula. In the confusing welter of opinions, accompanied by shifting voting coalitions among the Justices from case to case, it appears that the Court has not explained its actions at all but simply moves on an ad hoc basis mostly to invalidate, but occasionally to affirm, legislative sex categorizations.[133] In this cacophony, the Court has managed to prolong dispute but not in a constructive format; the effect of this prolongation is continually to invite litigation for the chance (apparently random) that a majority of Justices will be found to strike down some particular law. The result of this confusion is that the Justices remain at center stage claiming authority to issue final pronouncements rather than both systematically directing the parties' attention to other institutions and prodding those institutions into greater receptivity to the issues at controversy.[134]

In 1973 the liberal bloc of the Court—Justices Brennan, Douglas, and Marshall, joined for the occasion by Justice White—was prepared to settle the question by declaring sex a constitutionally suspect classification. In *Frontiero v. Richardson*[135] the Court (with only Mr. Justice Rehnquist dissenting) invalidated a congressional act providing that a married serviceman could claim special housing and medical allowances without any particularized demonstration that his spouse was financially dependent on him while a servicewoman was eligible for such allowances only by showing that her spouse in fact received more than half his support from her. Mr. Justice Powell explained his unwillingness to adopt the suspect classification theory on the ground that "[t]he Equal Rights Amendment, which if adopted will resolve the substance of this precise question, has been approved by the Congress and submitted for ratification by the States [and] democratic institutions are weak-

[133] Mr. Justice Powell stated the matter succinctly: "As is evident from our opinions, the Court has had difficulty in agreeing upon a standard of equal protection analysis that can be applied consistently to the wide variety of legislative [gender] classifications." Craig v. Boren, 429 U.S. 190, 210n. (1976) (concurring opinion.

[134] Excessive reliance on judicialized forums for case-by-case dispute resolution is a central problem with Laurence Tribe's suggestion that courts should invalidate legislative generalizations on matters of "rapidly changing norms" in order to "compel . . . a more individualized determination . . . not bound by any preexisting rule of thumb." Tribe, *Childhood, Suspect Classifications, and Conclusive Presumptions: Three Linked Riddles*, 39 LAW & CONTEMP. PROB. 8, 25 (1975).

[135] 411 U.S. 677 (1973).

ened, and confidence in the restraint of the Court is impaired, when we appear unnecessarily to decide sensitive issues of broad social and political importance at the very time they are under consideration within the prescribed constitutional processes."[136] The basis on which Mr. Justice Powell and his concurring colleagues voted to invalidate the act was, however, left utterly obscure. They thus gave no less an appearance that the Court was deciding this "sensitive issue" except for their apparent disingenuousness.

Mr. Justice Brennan's opinion in *Frontiero* was forthright in explaining his theory of invalidation. But his justification for finding sexual discriminations constitutionally suspect carried considerable, though unintended, irony. He found partial support for his conclusion from various congressional actions during the preceding decade: enactment of the Equal Pay Act of 1963 and Title VII of the 1964 Civil Rights Act proscribing sex discriminations by employers and by congressional passage of the Equal Rights Amendment in 1972. From these acts, Mr. Justice Brennan found: "Thus, Congress itself has concluded that classifications based upon sex are inherently invidious, and this conclusion of a coequal branch of Government is not without significance to the question presently under consideration."[137] But Congress had also enacted the statute under review in *Frontiero*, an enactment that was also the "conclusion of a coequal branch" presumably "not without significance." The 1963 and 1964 Acts cited by Mr. Justice Brennan did not apply to the United States Government as an employer.[138] More generous housing and medical allowances for men than women enlistees appeared to reflect Congress's view that men were more valuable and/or more difficult to recruit for the armed services than women. It may be that the Equal Rights Amendment, if ultimately ratified by the requisite number of States, would forbid Congress from saving public funds on this basis. In passing the ERA and the other antidiscrimination acts, Congress may have expressed contradictory policies, but the existence of this contradiction did not in itself justify or require Court resolution one way or the other.

---

[136] *Id.* at 692.

[137] *Id.* at 687–88.

[138] The Equal Pay Act of 1963 was an amendment to the Fair Labor Standards Act which generally excludes United States employees from its coverage, 29 U.S.C. § 203; Title VII of the 1964 Civil Rights Act contains the same exclusion, 42 U.S.C. § 2000 (e) (b).

This is more than simply an objection to the logic of the Brennan reasoning. He correctly sees the contradiction among these various congressional actions, but he does not see how his resolution of it, as a Supreme Court Justice, would perpetuate rather than resolve the deeper contradictory attitudes toward women's status that pervade our society. Mr. Justice Brennan's principal argument did not rest on his bowdlerization of congressional views but rather his perception of the nation's "long and unfortunate history of sex discrimination." He describes one aspect of this history thus:[139]

> Traditionally, such discrimination was rationalized by an attitude of "romantic paternalism" which, in practical effect, put women, not on a pedestal, but in a cage. Indeed, this paternalistic attitude became so firmly rooted in our national consciousness that, 100 years ago, a distinguished Member of this Court was able to proclaim:
>
>> Man is, or should be, woman's protector and defender. The natural and proper timidity and delicacy which belongs to the female sex evidently unfits it for many of the occupations of civil life.

It may be true that "romantic paternalism" had disguised the galling constraints and humiliations inflicted on women during the past century, and that this paternalism must itself be shattered so that women can be seen and see themselves appropriately. But this kind of national consciousness raising will not be helped by five or nine distinguished men viewing themselves as "woman's protector and defender" and consequently declaring that sex discrimination violates constitutional norms.

The Supreme Court is not our only governmental institution dominated by men. As Mr. Justice Brennan observed, "underrepresentation is present throughout all levels of our State and Federal Government."[140] But women have potential power over men in these other institutions that neither they nor anyone has regarding federal judges. Women, in common with all litigants, can appeal to judges' consciences, can assert the justice of their cause and thus provoke guilt unless their just demands are met. But appeal to guilt-ridden conscience is the bedrock psychology of Victorian paternalistic attitudes toward women.[141] In other institutions, women are

---

[139] 411 U.S. at 684.

[140] *Id.* at 686 n.17.

[141] See Smith-Rosenberg, *Sex as Symbol in Victorian Purity: An Ethnohistorical Analysis of Jacksonian America*, in DEMOS & BOOCOCK, note 17 *supra*, at 242–43.

not constrained to rely on appeals to conscience and good will; their voting strength can speak for itself. As voters they are less constrained by the supplicant posture that litigant status more intensively denotes and that litigative victory—even in the name of "equality"—cannot undo.

Women in this society have not yet used their full potential in numerical voting strength to secure equal representation or treatment in governmental institutions. This reluctance may be a result of the psychological constraints imposed by the past history of discrimination. Feminist advocates have argued that this past history has barred women from the self-conceptions on which men have based their social and political dominance: as self-determining individuals who share basic communal interests with others of their sex.[142] If this diagnosis is correct, and if the prescription follows from it that women should reconceive themselves toward self-determination and sisterhood, litigation is emphatically the wrong format for the realization of this prescription.

Even disregarding the inconsistency with the self-determination norm of litigant/supplicant status, the litigative process does not foster and readily interferes with the development of communal identity. Individual litigants may claim to represent others, and may even claim party status for others through class action pleadings. Notification requirements in class actions and generous attitudes toward *amicus* participation can be used to oppose the atomistic impetus in litigation.[143] But these devices are weak counterweights, particularly as compared to the greater potential sensitivity and fluidity of coalition formation in majoritarian institutions, the process by which communal forces both obtain recognition and recognize themselves.

Many important interests and groups can of course be shut out from this coalition formation process because the interests are so diffuse that no specific group sees itself as special protector of them or because the specific self-interested group lacks resources (numbers, funds, respect) that can be used to amplify its voice. *Carolene Products* footnote 4 finds its justification for judicial intervention

---

[142] See, *e.g.*, Heilbrun, Reinventing Womanhood 95, 105, 140 (1979); Rothman, note 69 *supra*, at 231–42.

[143] See Eisen v. Carlisle & Jacquelin, 417 U.S. 156 (1974); Fiss, note 106 *supra*, at 26–27.

in majoritarian institutions in this premise. And this premise can plausibly support an argument that the Court should override the failure of majoritarian institutions to ratify the Equal Rights Amendment, as Mr. Justice Brennan in effect argued in *Frontiero*. The ERA has apparently encountered difficulty both because women's rights issues are too diffuse to find electorally potent representatives —that is, though women are a numerical majority, a significant proportion identify themselves in ways inconsistent with the feminist agenda, more, say, as "wives" and "mothers" than as "women"— and because prejudice has itself led women to embrace this antifeminist vision of themselves.

This argument misconceives, however, the legitimate justification for the Court antimajoritarian role. If we start with the proposition that all legitimate governance rests with the consent of the governed, then legitimacy is in some doubt whenever unanimity is lacking— even by one vote among a million—for any particular measure. The apparent contradiction in our system between process consensuality and protection of minority rights can only be resolved through the unanimity principle. Unanimity is, after all, the only principle of social organization that gives full respect to the integrity and equality of all individuals. The idea of majority rule is a tolerable proxy for unanimous consent only because recurrent elections give the defeated dissenters opportunities to reopen questions until unanimity is reached or the dissenters, by choosing not to reopen questions at the polls, acquiesce in their defeat, thus giving effective *post hoc* unanimity in those matters.

If the premise of political legitimacy is unanimity, and not majority rule as such, then the Court can tell as well as anyone whether the legitimacy of any particular measure has been cast into doubt. The fact that a single litigant is sufficiently aggrieved to bring suit itself casts doubt on the legitimacy of the challenged measure. But if the absence of unanimity is the underlying justification for judicial intervention, the unanimity principle necessarily constrains the Court from imposing the litigant's will, or its will, on dissenters. From this perspective, the Court can forcibly reopen previously settled disputes but only in order to assist the pursuit of unanimity in the ultimate resolution of those disputes.[144]

---

[144] Unanimity should not be seen as a decisional rule that binds every governmental institution for every act or omission. Such a rule in practice would create logical contradictions by which the institution would be required both to act and

In practical political life, unanimity is rarely and perhaps never achieved. This fact does not mean that practical politicians ever abandon the pursuit of unanimity, but only that they typically fail to reach the prize. This pursuit does, however, present one critical practical and principled problem: where the claims of one person or group necessarily exclude the claims of another, unanimity is by definition not possible and even its pursuit must be read as defeat for all. This circumstance creates severe strains, especially where the mutually exclusive goals are intensely and persistently held.

I have suggested that this kind of conflict characterized those families that are driven to extrude one member into psychiatric hospitalization: this conflict equally characterizes those societies driven into revolution (or rebellion, depending on one's perspective). Any family or society that expects to survive such conflict with its members still bonded by mutual allegiance must find ways to redefine its members' goals. This, I suggested, was the central task that a psychiatric therapist must pursue for families. The same task in American society best characterizes the proper role of courts in constitutional adjudication. While every instance of constitutional litigation in principle presents this kind of conflict, the courts must be genuinely troubled and engaged only where the particular aggrieved litigant speaks to questions of wide social concern—questions where disagreement seems so widespread or, even if localized, so intense that acts or omissions by majoritarian institutions do not appear adequate to sustain the mutual allegiances that give the society its legitimate status as a communal body.[145]

---

to withhold action at the same time. See Rae, *The Limits of Consensual Decision*, 69 Am. Pol. Sci. Rev. 1270 (1975); Fishkin, Tyranny and Legitimacy: A Critique of Political Theories 65–72 (1979). The unanimity principle instead provides a moral touchstone signifying that any individual's objection in itself undermines the legitimacy of any communal arrangement, whether supported by governmental act or omission. The full implications of this demanding, implicitly anarchic theory of social legitimacy must be developed at greater length than is possible here. For present purposes, it is enough to see how the unanimity principle provides both a justification for the institution of judicial review and an agenda for judicial interventions.

[145] Robert Dahl referred to such circumstances in his persuasive argument that "it would be helpful for the development of democratic theory if we could assume that some means exist for comparing intensities of preference." A Preface to Democractic Theory 99 (1956). He concluded that neither Madison's structural solution in Federalist No. 10, nor the actual structure of American governmental institutions were adequate means for this purpose. In discussing the Supreme Court, *id.* at pp. 109–12, however, he did not sufficiently consider the possibility that it might self-consciously attempt this role.

Racial, ethnic, and religious questions have been at the heart of such fundamentally divisive disputes throughout our history, and courts have persistently attempted to remove such questions from the realm of dispute. The specific subject matters of the Bill of Rights were drawn from the colonial reading of the basic causes for alienation from Great Britain, and courts have also sought to treat these matters as beyond dispute. When the Supreme Court attempted to formulate its modern role in *Carolene Products* footnote 4, it began with these two kinds of questions but then clearly moved beyond, ostensibly to assure that majoritarian institutions remained open to dispute through judicial protection of electoral participation and to assure that "discrete and insular minorities" obtained special judicial solicitude. It is misleading, however, to see these judicial goals as ends in themselves. They are means by which the courts attempt to preserve the legitimacy of the bonds of authority and community in the society by leading its fundamentally alienated members to abandon their mutually exclusive goals and embrace the pursuit of unanimity. The techniques identified in *Carolene Products* had been, to that time, the most significant and apparently successful means employed by the Court to that general end.[146] But the subsequent experience with *Brown* has added a considerable gloss to the legitimizing techniques at courts' disposal.

One technique in particular has great promise for bringing opposed parties to redefine their disputes: that is, to show the parties that they were simply mistaken in believing their goals to be mutually inconsistent. This was the essence of the Court's purpose in overturning the Oklahoma statute setting different ages for males and females as concerns the legality of beer purchases[147] and in overturning the federal act providing welfare payments to unemployed fathers but not unemployed mothers.[148] Beneath the froth of equal protection doctrinal analysis in the opinions, the Court in both cases appeared decisively influenced by the view that the sex-based discriminations were not intended to accomplish any purpose at all, that they appeared in the statutes without any particular thought

---

[146] See Cover, *The Origins of Judicial Activism in the Protection of Minorities*, in Moore, ed., The Role of the Judiciary in America (to be published in 1980).

[147] Craig v. Boren, 429 U.S. 190 (1976).

[148] Califano v. Westcott, 99 S. Ct. 2655 (1979).

and therefore were a wholly gratuitous insult to feminist sensibilities.[149]

In these two cases, however, the Court invited the state legislature or Congress to reconsider the matter and to determine explicitly whether a gender discrimination was needed to accomplish any purpose at all. The Court's opinions in these cases might appear to suggest that if the only purpose of the gender discriminations was a loud legislative assertion that men and women were fundamentally unequal, then this would be an unconstitutionally invidious discrimination. Such a position would seem tantamount to the Court's independent ratification of the Equal Rights Amendment. But the Court's description of the history and likely purposes of both statutes conveys a wholly different sense, that the gender discrimination was simply thoughtless unintended rudeness rather than calculated insult.

In other women's rights cases, the Court has seen purposeful discrimination and it has responded differently. In *Geduldig v. Aiello*,[150] for example, the Court upheld the constitutional validity of a California state employee disability insurance program excluding pregnancy from coverage. While acknowledging that only women can become pregnant, the Court majority struggled nonetheless to argue that this was not a "sex-based classification."[151] If the Court could offer nothing beyond this verbal gyration, its result would be utterly incoherent. The result does make sense, however, on several grounds. The sex discrimination was an explicit and important part of the state program, because pregnancy coverage would markedly alter the expense of the program. Women anticipating pregnancy could obtain insurance coverage elsewhere; they must bear additional expense, to be sure, but their argument that all California employees must bear some additional (though indi-

---

[149] Thus Mr. Justice Stevens, concurring in the Oklahoma decision, stated: "There is, of course, no way of knowing what actually motivated this discrimination, but I would not be surprised if it represented nothing more than the perpetuation of a stereotyped attitude about . . . the two sexes." 429 U.S. at 213 n.5. Similarly in the federal case, Mr. Justice Blackmun wrote this for the Court: "From all that appears, Congress, with an image of the 'traditional family' in mind, simply assumed that the father would be the family breadwinner, and that the mother's employment role, if any, would be secondary. . . . We conclude that the gender classification . . . is not substantially related to the attainment of any important and valid statutory goals. It is rather, part of the 'baggage of sexual stereotypes.' " 99 S. Ct. at 2662–63.

[150] 417 U.S. 484 (1974).

[151] *Id.* at 496–97.

vidually lesser) expense in order to subsidize their pregnancies would only be convincing if the society had a clear prior commitment to avoid sex discrimination at all costs. The burden of subsidization would, moreover, fall on women who did not intend to become pregnant as well as men who have no choice in the matter. Thus the plaintiffs' claim in *Geduldig* presumes an as-yet-undemonstrated communal interest among women as such, as well as presuming a similarly uncertain social commitment to the principle of the Equal Rights Amendment.

The Court's ruling on the validity of pregnancy exclusion in disability insurance in *Geduldig* was not, however, the last word on the matter. The federal Equal Employment Opportunity Commission had, at the time of the *Geduldig* litigation, ruled that such exclusion was wrongful employment discrimination in violation of the Civil Rights Act of 1964.[152] Two years after its *Geduldig* decision, the Supreme Court overturned this statutory ruling regarding pregnancy exclusions on the premise that the words "sex discrimination" have a single meaning and the Court had fixed that meaning in its constitutional interpretation.[153] This literalism was short-lived. In another two years, the Court upheld the EEOC finding of wrongful sex discrimination in pension plans differentiating between men and women on the irrefutable statistical premise that women as a class live longer.[154] Dissenting Justices in this case plausibly argued that the pension plans discriminate on grounds of life expectancy and not sex, in the same way that pregnancy exclusions were not sex discriminations though only women could became pregnant.[155] Finding an intelligible pattern through the Court's different uses of the words "sex discrimination" was not made easier by tracing the varying compositions of the Court majority and dissents in these cases.[156]

---

[152] Mr. Justice Brennan, joined in dissent by Justices Douglas and Marshall, characteristically and wrongly relied on the EEOC statutory reading to support a judicial proclamation that the Constitution itself prohibited this sex discrimination. *Id.* at 501–02.

[153] General Electric Co. v. Gilbert, 429 U.S. 125 (1976).

[154] City of Los Angeles Dep't of Water & Power v. Manhart, 435 U.S. 702 (1978).

[155] *Id.* at 727–28 (Burger, C.J., dissenting).

[156] Thus Mr. Justice Blackmun noted: "Mr. Justice Stewart wrote the opinion for the Court in *Geduldig* . . . and joined the Court's opinion in *General Electric Co.* . . . Mr. Justice White and Mr. Justice Powell joined both *Geduldig* and

If, however, the Court had seen itself as leading the opposed parties to refine and particularize the issues that divided them, so that grounds for mutual accommodation might come into view, it would have seized the opportunity offered by the statutory interpretation cases that had been denied to the Court in the constitutional context of *Geduldig*. If the Court had upheld the EEOC statutory reading in both cases, it would have clearly signaled that the words "sex discrimination" had no fixed meaning at this moment in our history, and that questions of differential social impact and financial cost allocations buried in those words should be argued in other institutional forums. By refusing to differentiate between constitutional and statutory interpretation in the two pregnancy exclusion cases, the Court failed to offer the losing litigant in either case a realistic hope and incentive for turning to another forum for recouping the loss.

The Court's pension plan decision introduces some confusion which may serve this purpose, but it should have offered more than this. It should have embraced in sex-discrimination cases the traditional judicial preference for statutory rather than constitutional resolution of disputed questions, as another technique toward achieving orderly prolongation of conflict among disputants in preference to an at-once-and-for-all victory of one side over the other.[157]

Similarly, if the Court saw its role in the women's rights cases as I would have it, the *Frontiero* case would have been decided differently. While the gender discrimination in the armed services de-

---

General Electric. Mr. Justice Stevens, who writes the opinion for the Court in the present case, dissented in *General Electric*. . . . Mr. Justice Marshall, who joins the Court's opinion in large part here, joined the dissent in both *Geduldig* and *General Electric*. My own discomfort with the latter case was apparent, I believe, from my separate concurrence there.

"These 'lineups' surely are not without significance. The participation of my Brothers Stewart, White and Powell in today's majority opinion *should* be a sign that the decision in this case is not in tension with *Geduldig* and *General Electric* and, indeed, is wholly consistent with them. I am not at all sure that this is so; the votes of Mr. Justice Marshall and Mr. Justice Stevens would indicate quite the contrary." *Id.* at 723–24 (concurring opinion).

[157] This same helpful purpose would be advanced by Guido Calabresi's exploration of ways to import common-law judicial techniques into review of current statutes, in preference to exclusive judicial reliance on constitutional adjudication. Calabresi, "The Common Law Function in the Age of Statutes," Holmes Memorial Lectures, Harvard Law School, delivered March 8–10, 1977 (Cambridge, Mass.: Harvard Univ. Press, in press, 1980). See also Sandalow, *Judicial Protection of Minorities*, 75 Mich. L. Rev. 1162, 1183–95 (1977).

pendency allowance clearly rested on sexual stereotyping, this posture did not appear a thoughtless, reflexive action by the Congress. Ten years or so before the Court's decision, it might have been plausible to see the statutory discrimination in this light because there was no evidence in the statute's history that anyone had given serious consideration to this particular aspect of the dependency allowance.[158] But this view of the statute was no longer adequately plausible by 1973. As Mr. Justice Brennan observed in *Frontiero*, "Congress in recent years has amended various statutory schemes similar to those presently under consideration so as to eliminate the differential treatment of men and women"[159]—specifically, redefining "preference eligible veterans" in 1971,[160] extending veterans' spousal benefits in 1972,[161] and regarding federal employees generally, extending retirement benefits in 1971,[162] and prohibiting marital-status discriminations in 1966.[163]

It is possible that, notwithstanding this spate of particularized legislative action regarding sex discrimination in armed services and federal employment benefit programs, no one noticed the specific sex discrimination challenged in *Frontiero* but the litigants themselves, and they chose to seek a remedy from a court rather than Congress. Mr. Justice Brennan may be correct in implying that Congress's past actions in revising "various [similar] statutory schemes" indicated that Congress would revise the scheme in question. But, contrary to his argument, that likelihood does not justify the Court assuming the revisory task for itself. If indeed Congress had already shown itself quite sensitively aware of the sex discrimination under challenge, that is the central reason to direct the litigants' attention to the congressional forum for continuation of their dispute.

This speculation may be wrong. The *Frontiero* plaintiffs may already have been rebuffed in Congress or, if the Court had upheld the statute, they may fail to find a remedy there. But in either of these cases, the plaintiffs' defeat in Congress would have been a clear-cut indication that other interests saw quite specific advantages

[158] See Mr. Justice Brennan's depiction of the statutory history, 411 U.S. at 681 n.6.

[159] *Id.* at 687 n.21.

[160] 5 U.S.C. § 2108.

[161] 38 U.S.C. § 102(b).

[162] 5 U.S.C. § 8341.

[163] 5 U.S.C. § 7152.

to them in that defeat. It might be argued that the Court should remedy the plaintiffs' loss because they had been unfairly disadvantaged in Congress. But how then could one explain the legislative victories for others similarly situated to the plaintiffs? Mr. Justice Brennan was, of course, prepared to conclude that all gender discriminations were constitutionally invalid. But the concurring Justices who constituted the majority in the case were not so prepared, and their votes for invalidation are thus wholly incoherent.

I have suggested that Mr. Justice Brennan was wrong to pretermit the popular ratification process for the Equal Rights Amendment. How then can I justify overturning the congressional discrimination in the welfare case while leaving the *Frontiero* discrimination intact? If one views the Congress as a monolithic agency, there is no adequate justification for this differential result. But if one penetrates beneath this simplistic screen, it becomes clear that different groups inside and different constituency groups outside the Congress have addressed or failed to address the gender discriminations in question. The recent statutory revisions cited by Mr. Justice Brennan suggest that the congressional committees and lobbying groups with the most direct interests in the *Frontiero* subject matter are already engaged in active dispute regarding the proper role of sex discriminations in government employment generally and armed forces programs specifically. In this dispute, by 1973 at least, neither the forces opposed to nor favoring retention of sex discriminations had achieved clear-cut victory or suffered clear-cut defeat. The battle was in progress, and each side could see some concrete, significant victories. But simply because the battle over sex discrimination was being waged with clarity and vigor among one subset of the participants within the Congress does not show that these issues were being fought everywhere that they might in that institution. The federal welfare statutes are under different committee jurisdiction and the welfare recipient groups and their allies are constituted quite differently from those who lobby for benefits for government employees, veterans, or members of the armed services. And there is no record of any particularized debate on the sex-discrimination aspect of the welfare statutes, either in committee deliberations or general floor proceedings.[164]

---

[164] See Califano v. Westcott, 99 S. Ct. at 2663 n.7.

The Court could reasonably conclude that statutory sex discrimination raised questions of sufficient importance in principle and sufficiently undermined belief in the legitimacy of our social institutions among aggrieved individuals that the battle over their propriety should be waged in high visibility on every institutional front. From this conclusion, it could follow that conflict should be initiated regarding sex discrimination in the federal welfare statutes and that the Court could accomplish this—as it in fact did—by ruling that the legislative record failed to show how the gender classification was "substantially related to the attainment of any important and valid statutory goals," thereby inviting a more particularized record and creating a forum for newly legitimized dispute.

This judicial methodology for penetrating behind the monolithic appearance of other governmental institutions should equally have guided the Court in *Parham*. I suggested earlier that the institutional structure of psychiatric hospitals served to smother dispute both between patients and staff and between patients and the outside, extruding community. A court can, however, address specific programs and policies in the institution in order to disaggregate its monolithic structure and to stimulate disputatious conversation within the institution and with the external community. This disaggregating role requires intense involvement by the court in the detailed workings of the institution in order to identify places and means by which conflict can be introduced. Such involvement is justifiably characteristic of lower federal courts' remedial actions in recent cases regarding various large-scale bureaucracies such as mental hospitals, prisons, and police departments.[165]

From this perspective, the Court was correct in *Parham* to rule that judicialized adversarial hearings were not constitutionally required and that children's "liberty interests" might be adequately protected by hospital staff who were "independent" of both parents and child. But the Court should have understood that staff could not maintain adequately protective independence unless they persistently refused to take sides in the mutually destructive battle between parents and child. Hospital staff, that is, must do more than appear "neutrally detached" from parents or child at the first moments of admission screening procedure before abandoning neu-

---

[165] See Fiss, note 106 *supra*, at 31–35, 53–57.

trality to decide which of these disputants was correct in their conflicting wishes regarding hospitalization. The Court should not have found adequate institutional independence on the face of the state statutes. It should have identified the structural aspects of the institutions that could undermine such independence and remanded the question for inquiry and remedy in the same format that lower courts had been pursuing to protect constitutionally derived "rights to treatment."[166]

The purpose of these judicial interventions, whether into the workings of children's psychiatric hospitals or of Congress, is not to provoke dispute for its own sake. The purpose is to provoke dispute that is likely to lead the contending parties toward mutual accommodation, toward abandoning the diametrically inconsistent goals that had led each party to seek the other's total defeat. The impenetrable authoritarian face of the psychiatric institution is the hallmark of such defeat for its patients; the absence of any visible legislative conflict notwithstanding that some citizens feel intensely aggrieved, deeply abused, by legislative action or inaction is equally the hallmark of totalitarian defeat.

Both the liberal and conservative blocs on the Court fail to see their proper institutional role in leading fundamentally alienated combatants toward the pursuit of mutual accommodation. The Justices' failure—their willingness to demand unanimity as unquestioning deference either generally to traditional authorities or specifically to judges as the supposed embodiment of right reason—is the central error of the Court's contemporary jurisprudence. The Court occasionally finds its way back to the implicit jurisprudence of *Brown*, particularly in race relations questions where the social context provides guidance that compensates the Court for its failure to understand and articulate the lessons of the *Brown* experience.[167]

[166] See note 102 *supra*. The Court in *Parham* did envision that the adequacy of staff independence might be questioned on remand regarding state wards hospitalized without parental involvement and generally in later habeas corpus proceedings on a case-by-case basis. See 99 S. Ct. at 2511–12. But the Court's facial finding of constitutionality was clearly and wrongly inhospitable to the more searching general inquiry that is necessary to give effective meaning to the "independence" idea.

[167] See Mr. Justice Brennan's opinion in *Bakke* giving explicit attention to the state and federal institutions that had been or realistically might be directly engaged in the dispute regarding minority preferential admissions in higher education, and in which the losing litigant might pursue his claim. Univ. of Calif. Regents v. Bakke, 438 U.S. 265, 341–50, 372–73 (1978).

But in those matters during the past decade where the Court has staked out new territory for itself, its authoritarian posturing and reflexive impulse to shut off dispute have been unjustifiably indulged.

The family relations cases of the past decade epitomize this. *Roe v. Wade* is perhaps the most egregious instance with the most far-reaching social consequences. But *Roe* does not stand alone. The Court's recent decision in *Moore v. City of East Cleveland, Ohio*,[168] exemplifies the same indulgence. The Court majority here cut across the liberal and conservative blocs to invalidate a city housing ordinance that essentially limited residence to nuclear families composed of parents and their children.[169] Mrs. Moore, the plaintiff, violated the ordinance by living with her two adult sons and their sons, in a so-called matrifocal extended family that is disproportionately characteristic of black lower-income households.[170] Mr. Justice Powell, writing for the Court plurality, noted that the city ordinance was "unusual" and inconsistent with "the accumulated wisdom of civilization . . . that supports a larger conception of the family."[171] Mr. Justice Brennan, in a concurring opinion joined by Mr. Justice Marshall, found the ordinance "senseless and arbitrary . . . eccentric . . . [reflecting] cultural myopia . . . in the light of the tradition of the American home that has been a feature of our society since our beginning as a Nation;"[172] he concluded that "this ordinance displays a depressing insensitivity toward the economic and emotional needs of a very large part of our society."[173]

At first glance, the East Cleveland ordinance might appear anti-black and constitutionally suspect on that ground. But Mr. Justice Brennan observed that "the record . . . would not support [an] implication [of racially discriminatory purpose]."[174] Mr. Justice Stewart, in a footnote to his dissenting opinion, explains why: "In point of

---

168 431 U.S. 494 (1977).

169 *Id.* at 496. Justices Powell, Brennan, Marshall, Blackmun, and Stevens voted to invalidate the ordinance, though for differing reasons; Chief Justice Burger and Justices Stewart, White, and Rehnquist dissented, though for differing reasons.

170 Thus Mr. Justice Brennan noted: "In black households whose head is an elderly woman, as in this case, the contrast is . . . striking: 48% of such black households, compared with 10% of counterpart white households, include related minor children not offspring of the head of the household." *Id.* at 510 (concurring opinion).

171 *Id.* at 496, 505.

172 *Id.* at 507.

173 *Id.* at 507–08.

174 *Id.* at 510.

fact, East Cleveland is a predominantly Negro community, with a Negro City Manager and City Commission."[175] Although this fact was critical to a sympathetic understanding of the ordinance's purpose, the Court made nothing of it. The plurality viewed the ordinance as directed against "overcrowding, minimizing traffic and parking congestion, and avoiding an undue financial burden on [the] school system"[176] and observed that these "legitimate goals" could be pursued by other means and were served "marginally, at best" by the ordinance itself.[177] The plurality did not consider that the purpose of the ordinance was quite straightforward: to exclude from a middle-class, predominantly black community, that saw itself as socially and economically upwardly mobile, other black families most characteristic of lower-class ghetto life.

Perhaps the Court did not see this purpose or, if it did, considered this an "illegitimate goal," though in other cases the Court had been exceedingly solicitous of white middle-class communities' attempts to preserve a common social identity—"zones," as the Court had put the matter three years earlier—"where family values, youth values, and the blessings of the quiet seclusion and clean air make the area a sanctuary for people."[178] Mr. Justice Brennan dissented in the earlier cases and cannot be charged with inconsistency. But even so, I find in his characterization of the East Cleveland ordinance, as "senseless" and "eccentric," precisely what he alleges in it: "a depressing insensitivity toward the economic and emotional needs" of the current majority of residents in East Cleveland.[179]

---

[175] *Id.* at 537 n.7.

[176] *Id.* at 499–500.

[177] *Id.* at 500.

[178] Village of Belle Terre v. Boraas, 416 U.S. 1, 9 (1974). See also James v. Valtierra, 402 U.S. 137 (1971).

[179] Compare Christopher Lasch's observation: "[B]lacks themselves regard the male-centered household as the most desirable form of the family. . . . The defenders of the matrifocal family, posing as critics of cultural parochialism, have unthinkingly absorbed the rising middle-class dissatisfaction with the isolated 'privatized' suburban family, a dissatisfaction that has become especially pervasive in the very suburbs in which the 'sentimental model of the family' is said to originate. Claiming to have liberated themselves from the assumptions of their own class, these writers share the fashionable concern with 'alternatives to the nuclear family' and project the search for alternate life-styles onto the ghetto. They idealize the matrifocal family, exaggerate the degree to which it is embedded in a rich network of kinship relations, and ignore evidence which plainly shows that blacks themselves prefer a family in which the male earns the money and the mother rears the young." LASCH, HAVEN IN A HEARTLESS WORLD 162–63 (1978).

There is a conflict between the current city majority, who purport to uphold middle-class nuclear family values, and other black families who prize extended family households. As this conflict was presented to the Court, there appeared to be diametric opposition between these two groups—the city alleging that it could not maintain its cherished associations among like-minded people if it were forced to accept Mrs. Moore's family and Mrs. Moore equally alleging that she could not live with those she cherished if she complied with the city ordinance. But the city had a response to her complaint that she could not offer to theirs. The city, that is, could reasonably assert that she could preserve her preferred associations by moving to other communities in the metropolitan Cleveland area. She could not offer a similar accommodation to them. If Mrs. Moore and her family were forced to move, they would no doubt be considerably inconvenienced. But if Mrs. Moore succeeded in her argument that the city ordinance was unconstitutional, the nuclear families that had come together in East Cleveland could find nowhere to remain together as a self-consciously contained community.

The Court plurality saw Mrs. Moore as embodying the traditional American values of extended families—"uncles, aunts, cousins, and especially grandparents sharing a household along with parents and children."[180] There is an alternative, and probably historically more prevalent, American tradition of nuclear family households that see themselves bonded in an extended communal group linked by shared social identity that includes but is not limited to blood ties.[181] The city of East Cleveland apparently sought to constitute itself as such an "extended kinship" network, perhaps to differentiate itself with particular clarity from the ghetto life-style that had greater salience and threat for them than for middle-class predominantly white communities which could more comfortably absorb multigenerational families without disturbing the nuclear families' sense of social solidarity.

---

[180] 413 U.S. at 504.

[181] See Demos, note 69 *supra*, at 425: "Scholars have long thought that premodern society was organized into 'extended households'—large kin-groups, including several conjugal pairs, and spanning three or four generations. A corollary assumption has connected our own 'nuclear' pattern with the coming of the Industrial Revolution little more than a century ago. But recent demographic research has shown these notions to be quite unfounded. It is now clear that nuclear households have been the norm in America since the time of the first settlements, and in England for as far back as evidence survives. The fundamental unit, then as now, was husband, wife, and their natural children."

From this perspective, victory for Mrs. Moore was total defeat for the other residents of East Cleveland, while victory for them was not total defeat for her, except insofar as she wished to remain in their community while transforming its membership to her taste. If Mrs. Moore were shut out from many different communities that were readily accessible to the other residents of East Cleveland—if, that is, the city ordinance was not "unusual" or even "eccentric" but was common through the Cleveland area and even the country—then the Court might properly have seen some role for itself in protecting her interests, in fomenting dispute on her behalf against the prevalent social forces that scorned and shut her out.[182] But the very oddity of the East Cleveland ordinance suggests that Mrs. Moore is not alone in her opposition to it, that the city residents are more the vulnerable, isolated dissenters than she in the broader society, that they more than she deserve special judicial solicitude as a "discrete and insular minority." The Court in *Moore* myopically saw the case as a dispute between "a family" and "the state" rather than as a dispute among citizens about the meaning of "family."

Mrs. Moore did not rest her argument solely on a claimed constitutional right to family integrity but further alleged that the city ordinance violated her right to privacy in the choice of associates.[183] This conjunction in her argument points to the general kinship in the Court's doctrine between the privacy and family integrity claims. At the first moment that the privacy notion achieved explicit constitutional stature, in *Griswold v. Connecticut*,[184] it was used to protect a married couple's sexual relations from state regulation. This use of privacy was as myopic as the invocation of the family idea in *Moore*. *Griswold* was a dispute about the proper meaning of privacy in communal life, not a clear-cut confrontation between private morality and public power.

The specific occasion for the *Griswold* decision was not a criminal

[182] Compare, by contrast, the application of local zoning laws that, in excluding small group homes for mentally ill or retarded persons, perpetuate the pervasive state and local policies that have shut these people away in remote institutions. See, *e.g.*, Penna. Ass'n for Retarded Children v. Pennsylvania, 343 F. Supp. 279 (E.D. Pa. 1972); Burt, *Helping Suspect Groups to Disappear*, in BERMANT, NEMETH & VIDMAR, EDS., PSYCHOLOGY AND THE LAW 33 (1976); Burt, *Beyond the Right to Habilitation*, in KINDRED, ED., THE MENTALLY RETARDED CITIZEN AND THE LAW 417 (1976).

[183] Mr. Justice Stevens, whose vote for invalidation made the Court majority, embraced a version of the privacy claim which he portrayed as Mrs. Moore's "right to use her own property as she sees fit." 431 U.S. at 513.

[184] 381 U.S. 479 (1965).

prosecution against a married couple for using contraception; it was a prosecution to close a public clinic that offered, and widely advertised its offer of, contraceptive devices to married couples. The local officials knew that individual physicians regularly prescribed contraception and that devices were freely available for over-the-counter purchase in drug stores, though both physicians and druggists engaged in a discrete deception that contraception was for "disease control" and not "birth control."[185] The clinic proponents refused to participate in this morality play and demanded that the underlying principled conflict be identified and, at the same time, clearly resolved in their favor. These proponents first brought a declaratory action to invalidate the statutory ban both on the use of contraception and on "aiding and abetting" that use. The Supreme Court maintained that this was a sham conflict since the statutory ban had not been enforced against anyone for at least twenty years, and it dismissed the suit.[186] Immediately following this ruling, the unsuccessful litigants opened a public clinic where, they clearly announced, assistance for birth control as such was provided. Thus confronted, the local officials arrested the clinic's chief physician, Dr. Buxton, and its director, Ms. Griswold, who was also the Executive Director of the Planned Parenthood League of Connecticut.[187] The Supreme Court then ruled that these two had standing to raise the privacy claims of marital couples whom they might counsel, and thus reached and resolved the question of principle underlying the statutory ban.[188]

The local officials' action in closing the clinic appeared to reflect two beliefs: that some members of their community intensely believed birth control as such was immoral and that the clinic proponents' refusal to accept the previous tacit accommodation on the conflicting moral positions was an intolerably public flaunting of their private morality. The clinic proponents believed that, by accepting the prevailing regime of enforced hypocrisy, they were disabled from reaching many people who were either ignorant or ashamed of contraception. They did not seek to attract this potential clientele by placing on the public streets billboard signs of copulating couples. But for some members of their community, at least,

---

[185] See Poe v. Ullman, 367 U.S. 497, 502 (1961).

[186] *Id.* at 501–02.

[187] 381 U.S. at 480.

[188] *Id.* at 481.

the publicly visible identification of the Planned Parenthood birth control clinic was equivalent to these more patently lewd billboards, as offensive to them as the public flashing of private parts would be to others' sense of social decorum.[189] The identification of the "private" and "public" parties in this dispute was not clear-cut. The controversy was in fact about the definition and ownership of public space in the community.

The Connecticut statute did not clearly identify the dispute in these terms. The *Griswold* decision can be justified as a requirement that because this question so deeply touched contemporary conflicting moral sensibilities, the statute must now more explicitly be directed at the "public" flaunting of "private" acts than its total ban on any contraceptive use suggested. But the Court's opinion, by Justice Douglas, did not direct future communal debate toward this kind of mutual accommodation. Justices Goldberg and Harlan, in their concurring opinions, similarly failed to frame the issue in this way, and their explicit observations on the constitutional validity of statutes forbidding adultery or fornication[190] suggested that the privacy principle was nothing more than a vehicle for the Justices to serve as final moral arbiters for everyone.

This use of the privacy idea reached its apotheosis in the abortion cases. The Court's privacy doctrine in those cases reflects the same misunderstanding of their legitimate judicial role as their failure to see the significance of the ongoing debate about abortion in other institutions. The substance of the Court's actions must be guided by the same principle as its form: to provoke and to redefine disputes that might lead contending parties toward mutual accommodation, toward pursuit of the unanimity principle. For this purpose, the Court's expansive, simplistic invocation of the privacy concept in the abortion dispute is fundamentally misleading.

Perhaps it is plausible to argue that the fetus is so clearly nonhuman that others generally cannot claim communal identification

---

[189] Compare Sheila Rothman's observation that the statutory contraceptive bans, first enacted in the late nineteenth century, reflected a widespread social attitude equating contraception with obscenity apparently on the ground that contraceptive use permitted "the male to indulge all his lusts" while free of child-rearing responsibility and thus made the woman into a "slave to her husband's desires" and a "prostitute." ROTHMAN, note 69 *supra*, at 82–83.

[190] 381 U.S. at 498 (Goldberg, J., concurring); Justice Harlan had reached the merits in *Poe*, 367 U.S. at 553, and referred to his opinion there as the basis for his concurrence in *Griswold*, 381 U.S. at 500.

with it where its mother claims otherwise. But the Court's explicit assumption that the father of the fetus is as much a stranger to it as any other community member is not plausible.[191] The Court's apparent position that the mother always has the superior claim and interest, no matter how much the father might show that her burden in childbearing would be less than his burden in losing his child, appears to me an invidious sex discrimination.[192] Whether or not the Court should forbid all other institutions from engaging in such discrimination, it should not indulge in its own.

The Court's decision in the 1978 Term to invalidate even a requirement of notification to parents when their child proposes an abortion is also flawed.[193] The Court would permit a judge to decide whether parents should be notified,[194] thus rejecting the lower court's position that the child's privacy right mandates that her parents never be notified over her objections.[195] But both positions reflect and even reinforce the stark alienation of parent and child in this deeply contentious dispute. There is no easy way that any accommodation can be reached in this family conflict. But the Justices too readily assume that a judge should supersede parents in these matters—either in making a case-by-case judgment for a particular child or making a general judgment on the basis of constitutional doctrine for all children and parents.

This assumption reflects the same distaste for direct, prolonged

---

[191] The Court reasoned, "[T]he State cannot 'delegate to a spouse a veto power which the state itself is absolutely and totally prohibited from exercising.'" Planned Parenthood v. Danforth, 428 U.S. 52, 69 (1976). See Ramsey, note 131 *supra*, at 9–18.

[192] The discrimination is stated with particular boldness as part of a feminist agenda by Carolyn G. Heilbrun: "Childbirth must be seen as the commitment of two people, and, especially because of past history, as the commitment of the *father*, who must devote himself equally with the mother to the infant he calls into being. From such a commitment will arise . . . the initiation of men into intimacy and nurturance of which they have been long deprived, and which follows from the care of wanted children. . . . Women must retain control of their bodies, including the decision of whether or not to carry a child within them. At the same time, men must acquire control of their fatherhood—and choose acts of procreation only when they intend to endow the resulting child with time and attention." Note 142 *supra*, at 195–96.

[193] Bellotti v. Baird, 99 S. Ct. 3035 (1979).

[194] *Id.* at 3049–51.

[195] Baird v. Bellotti, 450 F. Supp. 997, 1001–02 (D. Mass. 1978). Mr. Justice Stevens, whose dissent was joined by Justices Brennan, Marshall, and Blackmun did not address the parental notification issue on the ground that it was not ripe for adjudication on the case record. 99 S. Ct. at 3055 n.4.

conflict and the same failure to appreciate the importance of such conflict in forging communal bonds that marks the contemporary Court's general jurisprudence. There is no easy way to overcome the social alienation that afflicts many people in this society, and that undermines the sense of mutual allegiance which alone can legitimate bonds of authority and community. The Court has an important, proper role to pursue in assuring these bonds, in continually renewing the constitution of our family feeling. But the Court's current authoritarian conception of itself is at war with that purpose.

INDEX--inside front cover
and preceding page